Con

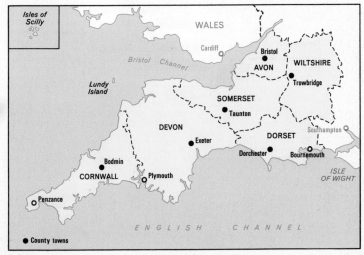

PRINCIPAL SIGHTS

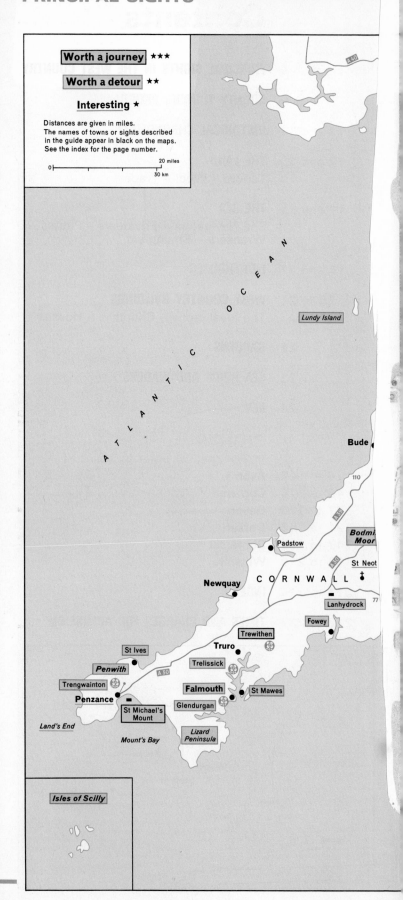

Worth a journey ★★★

Worth a detour ★★

Interesting ★

Distances are given in miles.
The names of towns or sights described
in the guide appear in black on the maps.
See the index for the page number.

0   20 miles
0   30 km

A T L A N T I C   O C E A N

Lundy Island

Bude

110

Bodmin Moor

Padstow

St Neot

Newquay

C O R N W A L L

Lanhydrock

77

Fowey

Trewithen

Truro

St Ives

Trelissick

Penwith

Trengwainton

Falmouth

Penzance

St Mawes

St Michael's Mount

Glendurgan

Land's End

Lizard Peninsula

Mount's Bay

Isles of Scilly

See index for detailed
description page numbers

with ★★

Overnight stop

0   30 km

          20 miles

A T L A N T I C   O C E A N

Morwe.

★★ Clit_

★ Boscastle

Tintagel   B 3263

B 3314

★ Padstow

B 3276   A 389

Newquay

A 30

C O R N W A L L

★★ St Agnes Beacon

A 3075

B 3269

A 390

B 3275   ★ Fowey

★★ St Ives

B 3306   B 3301   ★★ Trelissick

Mevagissey ★★

Penwith ★★

Penryn   Veryan ★

★ Penzance

A 394   ★★ St Mawes ★★

St Michael's
Mount ★★★

Falmouth ★★

B 3293

Lizard Peninsula ★★

BIRMINGHAM

Gloucester

R. Severn   80   M 5

THAMES

RIVER

Malmesbury

Swindon

Badminton House   M 4

Avon

7

RISTOL   A 4

7

The Ridgeway
Path   115

Corsham
Court

Bath

A V O N

W I L T S H I R E

Avebury   Marlborough

Kennet

LONDON

LONDON

Bradford   Devizes

Cheddar
Gorge

Wookey Hole   42   A 36

Steeple Ashton

Stonehenge

A 303

94

Wells

Longleat

Avon

Stourhead

Wilton

Somerton   A 303

83

Salisbury

41   M 3

elney

A 36

Montacute

M 27   74

65

eovil   Sherborne

SOUTHAMPTON

BRIGHTON

Blandford Forum

Wimborne
Minster

D O R S E T

arnham
House

A 31

Dorchester   A 35

107

BOURNEMOUTH

ISLE
OF WIGHT

tsbury

Maiden Castle

Corfe
Castle

Compton Acres

Swanage

Portland

A N N E L

Common gull *(After Nardin – Jacana photo)*

6

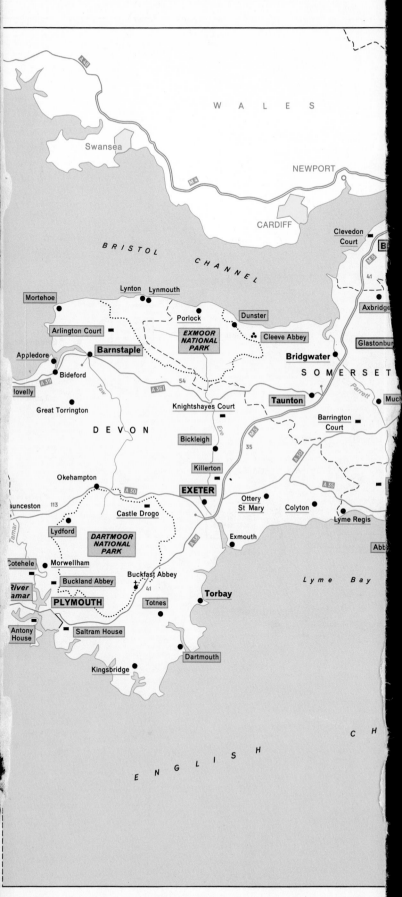

WALES

Swansea

NEWPORT

M4

CARDIFF

Clevedon
Court

B

M5

41

Axbridge

BRISTOL

CHANNEL

Mortehoe

Lynton Lynmouth

Porlock

Dunster

EXMOOR
NATIONAL
PARK

Cleeve Abbey

Glastonbur

Arlington Court

Appledore

ovelly

A 39

Bideford

Great Torrington

Barnstaple

Taw

A 361

54

Knightshayes Court

Bickleigh

Exe

Killerton

Bridgwater

SOMERSET

Parrett

Taunton

M5

35

Barrington
Court

A 30

Much

DEVON

Okehampton

A 30

Castle Drogo

EXETER

Ottery
St Mary

Colyton

aunceston

113

A 38

Lyme Regis

A 35

Lydford

DARTMOOR
NATIONAL
PARK

Exmouth

Abb

Tamar

Cotehele

Morwellham

Buckfast Abbey

Lyme Bay

River
amar

Buckland Abbey

41

Torbay

PLYMOUTH

Totnes

Antony
House

Saltram House

Dartmouth

Kingsbridge

ENGLISH

C H

Lyme Bay

5

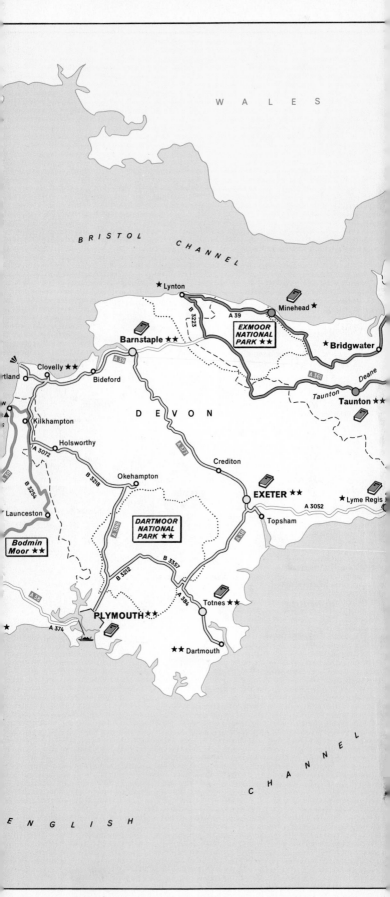

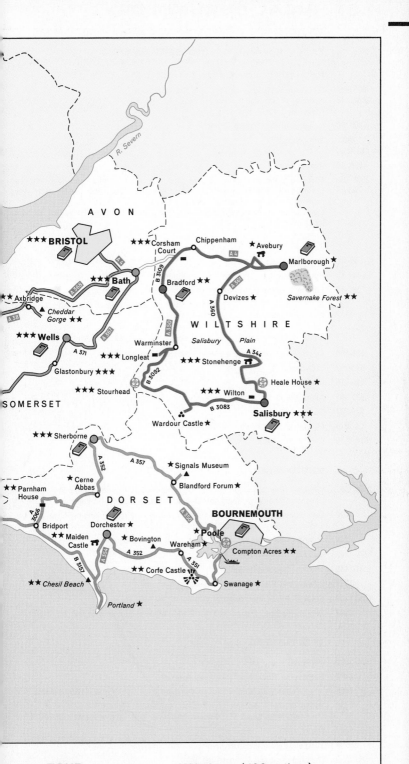

AVON

★★★ **BRISTOL**

★★★ Corsham Court

Chippenham

★ Avebury

Marlborough ★

★★★ **Bath**

Bradford ★★

A 4

A 361

Savernake Forest ★★

★★ Axbridge

Devizes ★

▲ *Cheddar Gorge* ★★

A 38

WILTSHIRE

A 360

★★★ **Wells**

A 371

Warminster

Salisbury Plain

★★★ Longleat

Glastonbury ★★★

B 3092

★★★ Stonehenge

A 344

Heale House ★

★★★ Stourhead

SOMERSET

B 3083

★★★ Wilton

Wardour Castle ★

Salisbury ★★★

★★★ Sherborne

A 357

★ Signals Museum

A 352

★ Cerne Abbas

Blandford Forum ★

★★ Parnham House

DORSET

A 350

BOURNEMOUTH

A 3066

Bridport

Dorchester ★

★ **Poole**

★★ Maiden Castle

★ Bovington

Wareham ★

Compton Acres ★★

A 352

A 351

B 3157

★★ Corfe Castle

★★ *Chesil Beach*

Portland ★

Swanage ★

R. Severn

TOUR	———	: Wiltshire (100 miles)
TOUR	———	: Somerset (200 miles)
TOUR	———	: Devon (250 miles)
TOUR	———	: Cornwall (300 miles)
TOUR	———	: Dorset (150 miles)

HISTORICAL CHRONOLOGY

EARLY INVASIONS AND SETTLEMENTS

Prehistoric and Celtic periods

600 000- 10 000 BC	Stone Age invasions on foot from the Continent Opening of the Irish Channel Ridgeway Path in being
6000 BC	Opening of the English Channel
2800- 1550 BC	Stonehenge
1800 BC	Avebury
2500 BC- 43 AD	First sea-faring invasions; Bronze and Iron Ages; Iberian and Mediterranean sea trading; Iberian invasions, early Celtic invasions, 600-33 BC; each wave pushing predecessors further west Cornwall and Devon settled by Dumnonii tribe; Dorset by Durotriges; Wiltshire by Belgae

The Romans

55 BC	Caesar invades Britain
43-407 AD	Roman conquest, occupation and withdrawal
300 AD	Saxons begin and increase coastal raids
432	St Patrick (c389-461), a Romano-Briton, undertakes conversion of Ireland; Irish missionary monks journey to Cornwall

The Anglo-Saxon Kingdoms; the Danish Kings

500-600	Kingdoms of Northumbria, Mercia and Wessex established
639-709	St Aldhelm
688-726	Ine, King of Wessex
871-901	Alfred the Great, King, wars against the Danes
924-988	St Dunstan
979	Murder of King Edward at Corfe Castle
1016-1035	Canute the Dane, King

THE NORMANS AND PLANTAGENETS

1066-1087	William I, the Conqueror (Conquest completed 1072 with submission of Exeter). Saxon land-holdings given to Norman barons, William's brothers and the church
1086	Domesday Book – national survey for taxation purposes of land-holdings, buildings and population (total: 1 000 000 of who approximately 8000 were Norman)
1215	Magna Carta signed between King John and the barons
1220-1266	Building of Salisbury Cathedral
1327-1485	The Hundred Years War
1337	Edward the Black Prince, lst Duke of Cornwall
1348-1350	Black Death – decimation of population by half
1362	English replaced French as the official language in courts of law (cf 1549)

THE TUDORS

1485-1509	Henry VII
1492	Christopher Columbus discovered America
1496	John Cabot sails from Bristol to discover Nova Scotia and Newfoundland
1498	Perkin Warbeck, accepted by Yorkists as the real Richard IV, brother of the murdered Edward V, advances on Exeter and Taunton (executed 1499).
1509-1547	Henry VIII
1535	Thomas Cromwell makes inventory of all monastic property
1536-1539	Dissolution of the Monasteries Construction of forts along the south coast
1547-1553	Edward VI: the "reign" of Edward Seymour, Protector Somerset (executed 1552)
1549	Cranmer's Book of Common Prayer published in English; Prayer Book Revolt in Cornwall
1558-1603	Elizabeth I The Age of the Navigators: Sir John Hawkins (1532-1595), Sir Humphrey Gilbert (1537-1583), Sir Francis Drake (c1540-1596), Sir Walter Raleigh (1552-1618)
1577-1580	Circumnavigation of the Globe by Drake in the *Golden Hinde*
1588	The Armada
1601	Foundation of the East India Company (monopoly ended 1813)

THE STUARTS AND THE COMMONWEALTH

1603-1625	James I
1611	Authorised Version of the Bible
1620	Pilgrim Fathers sail for America
1625-1649	Charles I
1642-1645	Civil War. Following Cromwell's victory at Naseby (1645), the future Charles II escapes through the West Country to the Isles of Scilly and eventually to the Continent
1649-1660	The Commonwealth; the Puritans
1651	Following defeat at the Battle of Worcester, Charles II escapes again via the West Country to France
1660-1685	Charles II
1673	Test Act (repealed 1828)
1685-1688	James II
1685	Monmouth Rebellion: Battle of Sedgemoor; Bloody Assizes
1688	Landing of William of Orange (future William III, 1689-1702) at Brixham

(National Trust / John Bethell)

Charles I at his trial

THE HOUSES OF HANOVER AND WINDSOR

	Wars in Europe (Austrian Succession; Seven Years) at sea, in N America and India
1769	Captain Cook makes first voyage to Australia
1773	"Boston Tea Party"
1775-1783	War of American Independence
1793-1815	French Revolutionary and Napoleonic Wars. Blockades at sea of France, England and America by England and France
1805	Battle of Trafalgar
1807	Slave trade abolished in British possessions (effectively ends 1833)
1810	Kennet and Avon Canal constructed: lst Transport Revolution
1812-1814	Anglo-American War (US revolt against sea-blockade)
1832	Reform Act (final act 1928)
1833	Isambard Kingdom Brunel appointed engineer to the Great Western Railway; 2nd Transport Revolution
1834	Grand National Consolidated Trades Union launched by Robert Owen; Tolpuddle Martyrs
19C	The Industrial Revolution Migration of industry to the coal rich areas of the North and Midlands; decline of wool and fishing industries and of tin-mining in the West Country
20C	The advent of the internal combustion engine: coaches and cars; 3rd Transport Revolution. Growth of tourism
1974	Realigning of county boundaries throughout Great Britain (Local Government Act, 1972)

In earlier times, when the monarch was personally responsible for the nation's finances, sources of revenue included the sale of royal forests; rents from the royal estates; customs dues; fees, fines, forfeits from the administration of justice; monies extracted on the basis of a vassal's duty to his overlord; and finally the system of licences, patents and charters, all of which had to be granted and purchased from the king or his appointed officer.

Licensing in the Middle Ages became a science : permits, often costly, were required to graze hogs and cattle in the royal forests; to fish, to hunt even the smallest game; to gather fallen branches for fuel; to cut coppice wood; crenellate a house, to keep a dog or hound; to transfer property; charters were needed to hold fairs and markets...

Tax-farmers or collectors took their tithe. Others purchased or were granted – usually in return for a gift! – export or import licences as was Sir Walter Raleigh (p 60) for commodities such as wool and woollen cloth.
Even the Elizabethan navigators had to obtain a licence (p 14) or had to present as tribute a proportion of their often hard-won treasure.

THE LAND

TENURE

Henry VIII Dissolved the monasteries – more than 800 of them – between 1536-9 thereby enriching his own coffers with their treasure and bringing about a major redistribution of land throughout the realm. Land held in mortmain or in perpetuity as a possession of the church, returned to the hazards of private ownership, of division, exchange, sale and, for many centuries, royal attainder.

Prosperous Tudor merchants, venturers, the newly ennobled, second sons, were able to purchase tracts of land; those with estates extended them or purchased property in other parts of the country. So much was available – one third of the total acreage of the kingdom, it has been estimated – that prices were not exorbitant. Commissioners were appointed for each area and sales continued into the latter part of Elizabeth's reign.

A condition of sale was that if the abbey church was not required by the parish (as at Sherborne or Stogursey) it should be razed (as at Glastonbury and Abbotsbury); if the church remained, monastic buildings must be obliterated. Whatsoever the alternative, the new owner, therefore, frequently found himself the possessor not only of his land but of a quantity of ready dressed stone. With this he built a house to rival those already in existence which went back Domesday and the Conquest. Together, 16C and mediaeval, they make up, in greater part, England's unique heritage of historic houses.

(A F Kersting)

Wilton House, Wiltshire

Earlier Centuries. – Dating from the time when kingdoms were considered to be the personal property of a king or chieftain, grants of land were the rewards made to favourites both secular and episcopal. When Edward the Confessor came to the throne in 1042, however, he decreed that all royal lands that had been assigned by his forerunners to the Saxon nobility should be returned to the crown.

William I, therefore, took over extensive crown lands. He retained very considerable territories, notably the royal chases or forests; he gave great swathes, particularly on the borders of the kingdom, to his half-brothers including Robert of Mortain, first Earl of Cornwall, and his barons including the de Redvers, appointed sheriffs and subsequently created the first Earls of Devon. The barons built motte and bailey castles to defend their, and the Conqueror's, land against the Celts and continental invaders.

William I also gave extensive property to the church for the foundation of new monasteries which by their preaching and care of the poor, would further the pacification of the kingdom and by their clearance of scrubland, draining of marshlands, farming and animal husbandry would increase its wealth. Many of the monasteries and convents founded by the king and by his barons were dependent houses of existing communities in France. By 14C, however, Edward III considered that the church should be restrained and passed a statute of mortmain. The Hundred Years War had begun (1327-1453) and although Henry IV rejected a parliamentary petition to disendow the church he fined monasteries with overseas connections; his heir, Henry V, under the Alienation Act forced all religious houses to sever overseas connections.

The church, which had reached a peak of learning and husbandry in 13-14C, was in decline; the number of religious, reduced by between one half and a third like the population as a whole by the Black Death in 1348-50, never regained its size or its energy; establishments were run by an abbot or prior, a handful of religious and numerous lay servants. The land remained in the church's possession but fell into neglect.

The 16C. – Henry VIII, urged on by Wolsey in the early years of his reign, began by dis-establishing the monastic houses with less than five religious... Thomas Cromwell made his inventory; the ambitious and the land hungry urged the king on to further action and Henry, who was by this time in dispute with the pope, demanded that all churchmen take the Oath of Supremacy; finally he decreed the Dissolution.

Post 16C Landholders. – The character of the houses erected after the Dissolution varied in different parts of the country, reflecting confidence in a peaceful future or the probability of border wars. In the West Country the houses were built as residences without fortifications – even where towers, crenellations and gatehouses were included there were also large Perpendicular-style windows!

Estates were let to tenant farmers who constructed the manor houses still to be seen in Wiltshire, north Dorset and Somerset.

Four areas only in the region were "different": the estates of the Duchy of Cornwall where, by definition, there are no "big" houses although there are many farmhouses, Bodmin Moor, and Dartmoor and Exmoor National Parks.

WOOL

"The history of the change from mediaval to modern England", G.M. Trevelyan wrote, "might well be written in the form of a social history of the cloth trade". The starting point of that trade was the Black Death.

There had been sheep in Britain since prehistoric times and Stone and Iron Age men had woven wool into cloth. The Normans improved the breeds and while wool was spun and woven for the home market, trade was almost entirely in raw wool.

In 1350s, after the plague had so decimated the population that there was insufficient manpower to till the fields, harvest the crops and tend cattle and those freemen who survived had put a premium on their labour and villeins demanded their freedom, the farmers turned to the labour-saving practice of sheep-farming. Soon every village in the West Country, especially in Wiltshire, Dorset and Somerset, appeared to have its regular sheep market and annual wool fair when the fleeces would be sold. Among the early successful farmers were the Cistercian monks of Norton-St-Philip priory, which, like many others, developed long-term trade arrangements for the export of fleeces to sister houses on the Continent.

Although by comparison with today's breeds, the sheep were small and many died or were killed for want of winter feed, flocks numbered many hundreds and the national total many million. The fleeces, more abundant but coarser on the larger, valley stock were lighter and finer on the upland sheep; they probably weighed between 3-6lbs as against today's 8-20 even 40lbs.

English native cloth remained coarse woven until 14C when Edward III brought in Flemish Huguenot weavers, fullers and dyers who gave a new impetus to the industry. Every cottage came to have its spinning wheal, most also had hand-looms – evidence of the weavers remains in the wide windows in their former cottages. Fulling mills became common wherever there was water, village greens and fields became quartered with the hooked tenter frames on which cloth was stretched and dried.

By the end of 14C 5000 pieces of cloth were being exported annually from England to the Continent in addition to raw wool; by the late 16C the number was 100 000 pieces. Wool had replaced corn as the most important crop in farming; raw wool was prohibited from export in order to maintain supplies for home weavers – a prohibition that gave rise to smuggling on a vast scale and was only repealed in 1824; the government alone could negotiate the sale of wool abroad as in the Methuen Treaty of 1703 with Portugal. As a further protection of the industry in 17C, parliament passed acts to lessen the import of linen and decreed that "no material (in other words, a shroud) unless made entirely of sheep's wool be allowed to be put in a coffin" under penalty of £5 fine.

The wool industry by 15-16C had grown to such an extent that new merchant guilds were formed to control the raw wool and cloth-weaving traders – the staplers and clothiers. Proof of this long period of considerable prosperity in the West Country appears in the great and small houses, and in Somerset especially in the parish churches with their exterior and interior decoration and, most individually, in their rival west towers. The industry that Daniel Defoe in 18C constantly refers to in his *Tour through the Whole Island of Great Britain* and describes as "the richest and most valuable manufacture in the world" continued as the mainstay of the West Country until textile fashions changed and processes were altered by the coming of the Industrial Revolution in 19C.

TRADE

Trade through itinerant merchants walking the Ridgeway Path, the Phœnicians and Mediterranean peoples shipping tin and copper from Cornwall, the Romans transporting lead from the Mendips to Pompeii, was transformed in 16-17C by the discoveries of the navigators, the spirit of commercial adventure: "our chiefe desire", Richard Hakluyt the geographer (1552?-1616) declared, is "to find out ample vent of our wollen cloth, the naturall comoditie of this our Realme". He went on to propose the opening of new markets in Japan, north China and Tartary.

In the early days boats were small and had only a shallow draft enabling coasters and cross-Channel craft to go far upriver to Exeter, Topsham, Bridgwater; as ships increased in size estuary harbours came into their own and finally the deepwater harbours of Plymouth and Fowey and Bristol where a constant water level was ensured by the construction of the Floating Harbour in 19C.

Bristol became the second city in England after London but even so only handled 10% of the national trade (the figure for London until the second half of 20C was always over 50%). Hampered by the smallness of the local population and the lack of local communications – transport was by pack-horse and cart – the West Country sought to improve facilities by the construction of canals.

These were almost immediately overtaken by the steam railway, but meanwhile the woollen cloth industry had been first mechanised and then removed to the Midlands and North, for which the local port was Liverpool.

With the road transport revolution, the construction of motorways, the Severn Bridge to South Wales, the continuing railways, trade prospects other than as provision for the local population are once more a potential reality.

THE SEA

THE NAVIGATORS

Britain "shifted" from being on the outer, western edge of navigational charts to being at the centre in 16C. The Venetian Empire and the Mediterranean powers, until then the hub of the universe, in 14-15C found the caravan routes to the Orient, open since Marco Polo's time in 13C, suddenly closed. Navigators, notably Portuguese encouraged and guided by Prince Henry the Navigator, and Genoese mariners financed by Venice and Spain, set out to sail round Africa and journey east. The prize was untold treasure, gold, jewels, silks and above all, fabulously priced spices – much used to give flavour to poorly preserved or even rotten meat.

Ports on the **Atlantic seaboard.** Lisbon especially, and later Bristol and Plymouth, assumed importance; Madeira and the Azores were discovered; the Portuguese, Bartolemea Dias rounded the cape of Good Hope (1488) and Vasco de Gama reached Calicut in southern India (1498); in 1492 Christopher Columbus, a Genoese under the patronage of Ferdinand and Isabella of Castile, set out westwards and discovered **America.**

The following year in 1493, under the Treaty of Tordesillas, the pope divided the discovered and the yet to be discovered world between Spain and Portugal along a meridian which, in the event, cuts through eastern Brazil. John Cabot, a Genoese settled in Bristol, set out westward with his sons in 1497 under letters patent from Henry VII – all voyages were licensed by the monarch. Cabot sailed in search of the Northwest Passage and discovered Nova Scotia and Newfoundland.

The next century, Magellan threaded the strait which bears his name (1520) and his ship – he died on the voyage – circumnavigated the world. In the same age, rivalry between the European nations and England and Spain in particular, grew and exploded. The great exploring, trading, warring **English mariners** were mostly Devon men: John Hawkins, Martin Frobisher (c1535-94), Humphrey Gilbert, Francis Drake, Richard Grenville (1541?-1591), Walter Raleigh. Two centu-

(Beken of Cowes)

The Golden Hinde

ries later came the Yorkshireman, James Cook, circumnavigator, surveyor and Pacific cartographer (1728-79).

Funds to support the quest of the unknown, the driving force of every navigator, were obtained by patronage and trade – the first often based on the promise of the latter. Christopher Columbus sought financial support for years before he was able to set sail; Queen Elizabeth was far from open-handed in support of Drake's ventures; Raleigh was executed for not finding El Dorado.

Already by 17C the **East India Company** (chartered in 1600), the earlier **Muscovy** and **Turkey** or **Levant Companies** (mid-16C) were in being, and the **Merchant Venturers of Bristol** incorporated (1552). (The Hudson's Bay Company was chartered by Charles II in 1670.) We exported first raw wool, then cloth; we imported hides, tallow, linen from Ireland, salt from Brittany, wine and brandy from Gascony, also wax, wood, iron and honey, and from Spain and Portugal, olive oil, figs, iron and wine.

After the discovery of the New World, Africa and the Orient, sugar, tobacco, fish, cotton, cocoa (for drinking chocolate), tea and coffee, revolutionised trade. Trading posts were established in distant lands – the maxim being "trade follows the flag".

PRIVATEERS AND LETTERS OF MARQUE

A code of practice dating back to 13C, operated on broadly similar lines by England, France, Spain, Portugal and Holland and with each country supreme in turn, licensed privately owned merchant ships under **letters of marque** to "annony" the sovereign's enemies of a named nationality in time of war. If war had not been officially declared, ships attacked in recompense for or on the pretext of previously suffered injury and loss under **letters of reprisal.**

Letters in England were originally issued by the monarch, later they were sold to ships' owners by the lord high admiral. Under this system Queen Elizabeth, without acknowledgment or expense, was able to ensure almost perpetual harassment of Spanish shipping. The rules of this licensed piracy were strict and £3000 bond had to be left as surety that they would be obeyed. The Admiralty, which judged the value, took 10% of every prize; customs duty (5%) was paid on all cargo captured which, in theory, had to be brought in as captured; two thirds of the remainder was then divided among the ship's promoters and the final third amongst the crew who relied on this "purchase" or booty together with "pillage" of the valuables not forming part of the cargo, as their pay.

The Spanish galleons were tall and clumsy; the British merchant ships or barques were at first of between 50 and 100 tons with crews of 40 to furnish boarding parties and men to sail prizes home. By an Order in Council of 1695 the ships were required to be of not less than 200 tons and 20 guns; half the crew had to be "landmen" so as not to attract sailors, often then impressed, from the navy.

Many owners, masters who sailed the ships, captains who controlled the crews including the lawless boarders, lost all, even their lives in this adventuring; others made sufficient; many turned to cut-throat piracy, for which the penalty, if caught, was death. Drake and several of his contemporaries made fortunes on the Spanish Main and off the shores of Spain capturing the treasure ships which returned home each summer from South America, laden with the treasure of the Incas, gold, silver, precious stones and rich cargoes. Queen Elizabeth's coffers were filled.

Prizes still to be seen in the region from those times include Tregothnan House, built with prize money in 18C overlooking the River Fal, the rose-silk damask furnishings in the drawing room at Pencarrow, the head of Christ in Golant Church, the pillars in the manor house at Bickleigh Castle in Devon, Sharpham House overlooking the River Dart... On a more modest scale are the half-timbered merchants' houses on the quayside in the Barbican in Plymouth – the Elizabethan House and its neighbour – and the quarter to the rear, erected by speculative builders of the time for returned sea-captains.

PIRATES AND PIRACY

Pirates, 15-18C highway robbers of the sea, owed allegiance to no one. All men's hands were against them and they were against all men.

The crewmen would sign on and, in lieu of wages, receive a specified share of any prize captured. Hard and brutal, each was in it for the adventure and the loot. They plundered any ship they could overcome in home waters and, when these were too well patrolled, they sailed to the waters around the West Indies and off the North American coast.

Booty was sold to Spanish, French and English colonists, who, in theory, were obliged to trade only with their countries of origin; countless island and mainland creeks became pirates' lairs.

The 15-16C **Fowey Gallants,** with their raids on the coasts of France and Spain, although sometimes referred to as pirates, were of an altogether different vintage as were the men of Devon who set out to avenge the Plymouth raid by Bretons in 1403, the Cornishmen who sought vengeance on the Spaniards who had burned Marazion – all were landbased groups, pirates for a day or a week only!

WRECKERS AND WRECKING

Wrecking, as every Cornishman, Devonian and coastal dweller, will tell you hotly has nothing to do with decoy lights and leading ships to their doom on the saw-toothed coastal rocks – nature alone has always seen to that. As many as 250 ships over the centuries, it has been estimated, have been wrecked along each mile of cliff and cove of the British Isles: Lyme Bay was known as the Bay of 1000 Wrecks; not for nothing are the Manacles so called...

What would happen, and happens even now, is that a ship, seeking shelter from gale winds, comes too close in and gets caught on underwater rocks or in a race or current and breaks up.

Warned by the watch, the villagers of old would gather in wait, all too often not to rescue the crew, but to sieze the ship and her cargo, to loot everything and finally break up the hull until not a spar was left. The cargo of treasure and coin, timber, coal, satins and finery, the provisions, china and glass, the anchors, cordage and sails were regarded by all as a legitimate harvest of the sea, a bumper beach-combing.

SMUGGLERS AND SMUGGLING

In 1784 the Younger Pitt calculated that 13 million lbs of tea were consumed in Britain annually, 7½ million lbs of which were smuggled!

The "trade", as smuggling was known along the length of England's south coast, began when customs dues were first levied in the early Middle Ages on incoming and outgoing goods; it flourished from 16 to the mid-19C, particularly in times of war, and ended when ships of the Royal Navy, freed from the centuries of intermittent war and coastal blockades against France, Spain and America, could patrol the coast in support of the coastguard cutters and small boats of the revenue or "preventive" men. Although everyone, particularly in Cornwall, was against the revenue men, it has been estimated that they succeeded in sieizing the contraband of one in three venturers. Where the boat was cáptured and the captain convicted – rarely in Devon or Cornwall – the hull would be sawn in three and sold for firewood together with her equipment and cargo.

The early "free traders" slipped across the Channel in 10-ton fishing smacks to take out raw wool and "bring in" brandy, wine, spices, fine silk and lace for local consumption; by 19C 300-ton armed cutters were making 7 or 8 voyages a year carrying as much as 11 tons of tea and some 3000 half-ankers of spirits a time (an anker or keg = 9½ gallon cask; the spirits were usually over proof and diluted on shore by the smugglers' wives). Goods were bespoke and handling and distribution by pack-horse from the landing place in cove or harbour was conducted by a waiting team. Where necessary kegs would be weighted and dumped overboard to be collected when the coast was clear if not previously discovered by the preventive men. Contraband also came in through cargo ships, including the great tea-clippers. When a trading ship was sighted, pilot gigs manned by 8 oarsmen would race to her, the leading boat gaining the right to pilot her into harbour and handle her cargo, not all of which would pass through the custom house.

With the abolition of many duties and the lowering of many more – a policy instigated by the Younger Pitt as the best means of knocking the bottom out of the illicit trade – with the revolution in official, retail distribution, the different style of living, smuggling – apart from drugs – is now on a small scale: tobacco, if brought it, is not by the ton but in cartons, whiskey is trans-shipped in bottles, wine and brandy comes in perhaps by the case but no longer by the cask!

LIGHTHOUSES

THEIR HISTORY AND CONSTRUCTION

There are nearly 100 lighthouses around the coast of England and Wales, 33 of them in the West Country. Since 1836, by Act of Parliament, lighthouses have been under the jurisdiction of **Trinity House,** a guild of shipmen or mariners incorporated in 1514 as the regulating authority for pilots in British waters.

In 1594 the Corporation acquired the rights of beaconage under which it marked navigational channels and erected daymarks; lighthouses, however, were constructed by individual venturers under patents granted by the crown. The licensee, who was also required to pay rent to the crown, recouped his expenditure at the custom house by levying tolls on passing shipping. **Flat Holm,** built for £900 in 18C with a nominal annual rent of £5 – £10, charged 1½d per ton to all Bristol ships; 3d to all foreign ships; 1d to coasters to or from Ireland; 1s to vessels from St David's Head or Land's End (market and fishing boats excepted). Shipping increased so colossally in 18 and 19C that when Trinity House bought out the owners under 19C Act, the lighthouse had become so profitable that the remaining 12-year lease cost the corporation £15838 18s 10d.

While the necessity, in some cases, for a light and, therefore, toll rates were hotly contested by Merchant Venturers, shipmasters and Trinity House, delaying the granting of a building patent for years, other lights came into existence modestly and personally: the first **Burnham** light is said to have been a candle set in her window by a fisherman's wife; the sexton eventually took over with a light in St Andrew's church tower and in 19C, the curate, when dues were fixed at 5s for British vessels, 10s for foreign and 3s for coasters. The short remainder lease was purchased in 1829 for £16 000.

Vested interests also delayed construction – to many the winter gales with ships driven on the rocks afforded rich plunder. There was a 50-year delay due to local opposition before the first lighthouse was built on the **Lizard** in 1619. Its existence was brief: shipmasters refused it tolls, declaring it to be a wreckers' decoy. In 1752 a new lighthouse was constructed with 4 towers each burning a coal fire; in 1812 the building was modified to its present outline and first an oil lamp then an electric light installed.

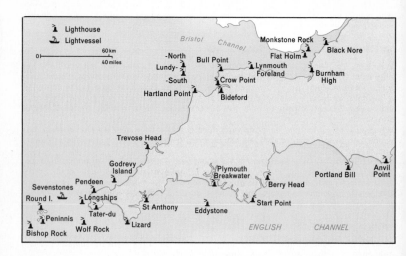

The patent for the **Portland Bill** lighthouse overlooking the Portland Race, the meeting of tides between the Bill and the Shambles sandbank, was delayed nearly 50 years before finally, in 1720, two lighthouses with enclosed coal fire lanterns were constructed. In 1789 a new building was erected which nine years later was fortified against possible Napoleonic invasion by the installation of two 18lb cannon. The lighthouse has since been twice replaced, the present 133ft tower dating from 1906.

Lighthouses were, at first, built upon clifftops and headlands until it was appreciated that although the height made the beam carry further in fine weather, the summit might well be hidden in sea fog just when a bearing was most urgent: the **Lundy** light was at first on Chapel Hill.

Eddystone, the Wolf, Longships and the Bishop, standing out to sea, pinned to rocks surrounded by the Atlantic swell, each signal a triumph of engineering construction. The many gales resulted in the first **Bishop Rock** tower being washed away incomplete after two years' work and the second tower taking seven years to construct inside a coffer dam. The feat was accomplished finally by dressing, dovetailing and numbering each of the 1 – 2 ton blocks of granite before transporting it to the site; the foundations were re-secured, the base re-cased and the light raised to its present position of nearly 160ft above the waves in 1881.

It was within a short distance of Bishop Rock that the British squadron returning from the Mediterranean under Admiral Sir Cloudesley Shovel in the *Association,* was wrecked with the loss of 1800 men on 22 October 1707. (The admiral, washed ashore alive, was murdered for his gold ring; *p 76*).

Construction of the **Wolf Rock** began in 1791 with the erection of 20ft wrought iron mast held by six stays and topped by a metal model of a wolf. It was immediately swept away. In 1835-39 an iron beacon was erected – on average only 60 hours work could be accomplished in any year; finally in 1861-70 the present 116ft granite tower with walls 7ft 9in thick at the base was constructed and the light shown.

Eddystone, lies 14m off Plymouth. It originated as a wooden structure put up by Henry Winstanley, showman and shipowner, who had lost a vessel on the rocks. Problems with the site, the elements, labour, were capped when, the date being 1697, a French privateer kidnapped Winstanley himself and took him across the Channel to Versailles. Louis XIV, however, ordered Winstanley's immediate return to Eddystone, with the words "France is at war with England, not humanity".

In November 1698 the Eddystone light was lit for the first time and survived, with improvements, until the worst gale ever recorded in Britain swept away the tower and its designer in November 1703.

By 1709 a new wooden tower with a lead roof and massive candelabrum was in operation. It endured for 46 years before it caught fire and burned for 5 days.

The third builder was **John Smeaton,** a Yorkshireman, who constructed a tower of dressed granite blocks, dovetailed on all four sides and secured by quick drying cement; the tower stood for 120 years before cracks appeared and it was replaced in 1882 by the present stalwart 167 ft lighthouse. (The Smeaton Tower was subsequently re-erected by public subscription on Plymouth Hoe.)

Many lighthouses, including the Eddystone, have now been automated.

The Trinity House Lighthouse Service is funded, as were the individual lighthouses originally, from dues levied on shipping arriving and departing at United Kingdom ports.

At the discretion of the principal keeper, whose jurisdiction is final, a few lighthouses are open to the public.
The times of opening are usually, in summer only, Monday-Saturday, 1pm to one hour before sunset. Enquire locally.

NAME	FIRST CONSTRUCTED	LIGHT CHARACTER
ANVIL PT	1881	1 wh flash : 10 secs
BERRY HD	1906	2 wh gp flashes : 15 secs
BIDEFORD (Instow Front and Rear)	1820	occulting wh lights, 5 + 8 in 10 secs
BISHOP ROCK	1858	2 wh gp flashes : 15 secs
BLACK NORE	1894	2 wh gp flashes : 10 secs
BULL PT	1879	3 wh gp flashes : 10 secs
BURNHAM HIGH	1832	1 wh flash : 7.5 secs
CROW PT	1954	1 red flash : 5 secs
EDDYSTONE	1698	2 wh gp flashes : 10 secs
FLAT HOLM	1737	Wh + red gp flashes × 3 : 10 secs
GODREVY ISLAND	1859	1 wh + 1 red flash : 10 secs
HARTLAND PT	1874	6 wh gp flashes : 15 secs
LIZARD	1751	1 wh flash : 3 secs
LONGSHIPS	1795	1 equal wh & red : 10 secs
LUNDY	1897	South : 1 wh fl : 5 secs North : 2 wh gp fl : 20 secs
LYNMOUTH FORELAND	1900	4 wh gp flashes : 15 secs
MONKSTONE ROCK	1903	1 wh flash : 5 secs
NAB	1920	2 wh gp flashes : 10 secs
PENDEEN	1900	4 wh gp flashes : 15 secs
PENINNIS	1911	1 wh flash : 15 secs
PLYMOUTH BREAKWATER	1844	1 wh & red flash : 10 secs
PORTLAND BILL	1720	4 wh gp flashes : 20 secs
ROUND ISLAND	1887	1 red flash : 10 secs
ST ANTHONY	1835	wh & red light for 11.25 secs : 15 secs
START PT	1836	3 wh gp flashes : 10 secs
TATER DU	1965	3 wh gp flashes : 15 secs
TREVOSE HD	1847	1 red flash : 5 secs
WOLF ROCK	1870	1 wh, 1 red flash : 30 secs

GALE FORCE WINDS

Wind strength is described according to a scale devised by the admiral and hydrographer, Sir Francis Beaufort (1774-1857).

Scale	Description	m.p.h.	(knots)
0	Calm	1	(– 1)
3	Breeze	12	(7-10)
6	Strong breeze	31	(22-27)
8	Gale	46	(34-40)
10	Storm	63	(48-55)
12	Hurricane	74	(64)

WEST COUNTRY BUILDINGS

THE LOCAL STONE

The rocks and strata of stone below ground in each region are to be seen everywhere above ground in the local buildings. While special types of stone were hauled hundreds of miles for great cathedrals and public buildings – Preseli mountain stone from South Wales for Stonehenge, Portland from Dorset for St Paul's, London – houses, tithe barns and parish churches were built of local materials from moor or outcrop stone, wood and cob, flint, limestone, slate and granite.

The transport of stone and other materials from earliest times was by water and, where there was no water course, by packhorse; only in 19C with the construction of canals and, soon after, the railway, did bulk transport over long distances become feasible: bricks manufactured as far away as East Anglia penetrated the West Country blurring the local idiom...

Dorset

Dorset is the source of **Portland** and **Purbeck** stone, some of the hardest fine-grained, building stone in the country; both Portland and Purbeck are limestones of the Jurassic period of some 150 million years ago.

On Portland Bill everything from the prison, to keepers' cottages and garden walls, is built of the stone dug out of the quarries which pock-mark the island; in Purbeck houses large and small and the churches have dressed stone walls and the churches inside, polished stone or marble pillars and fonts.

Wiltshire

Wiltshire has used local stone since the time of Stonehenge and Avebury when **sarsen stones** were brought to the Marlborough Downs. By 13C the silver-grey limestone to be found at **Chilmark** was being quarried, dressed and transported down the Avon to build the new cathedral at Salisbury.

Throughout the county delightful houses in the villages and small manor houses are built of the local stone which varies in hue from light to dark grey. The roofs are of stone or terracotta tiles and a few still of thatch.

The Ham Hill quarries of Somerset exceptionally provided the stone for Longleat; sandstone, cob and brick furnished more modest houses.

Somerset and Avon

Dundry stone, a pink conglomerate or puddingstone from the hills on the far side of the Avon Gorge is Bristol's native stone which can still be seen in the little old houses and church northwest of Broadmead. Much of the other stone used in building the old city was, of course, brought in by water.

Today the new buildings are of poured concrete or, newest of all, dark red brick.

The north Somerset landscape is dominated by the lines of the Mendips, which are of porous limestone as is demonstrated by the caves at Cheddar and Wookey Hole.

The Quantocks, the Brendon and the Blackdown Hills are formations of very hard, **Old Sandstone**, the stone of the Quantocks being true in its pink to dark red colour to the generic name of **Old Red Sandstone.**

A sedimentary rock formed by the cementing together of grains of quartz or detritus resulting from the denudation of granite, it dates from the Devonian period, 350-400 million years ago and proved to be the perfect building material for the area, notably in Taunton Deane, where it appears rough hewn for cottage and church walls, dressed for trimming house and church windows and tractable for the decoration and carving of the west towers.

In the southern part of the county the **Ham Hill** quarry provided a superb golden-ochre limestone from Roman and Norman times until recently. Whole villages were built of the second quality stone while the first grade was reserved for the construction of the parish church towers with their unique Somerset tracery in the bell lights or was despatched to build the several great houses in the locality.

Bath, with its own named stone, is a short story on its own *(p 28)*.

(National Trust / John Bethell)

Lytes Cary, Somerset

Devon

With Devon there begin in Dartmoor the **granite** bosses, the bone structure and bulwark against the peninsula's being washed away by the sea.

South of the granite tors of Dartmoor lie **Old Devonian Sandstones;** to the north ancient sedimentary stone known as metamorphic rocks which, under intense heat and pressure 5-600 million years ago, became transformed into **shale, slate** and **schist.**

The dense woods, maintained **half timber** construction longer than in many areas; when the wood became exhausted timber frames were retained and dense **cob walls** on moorstone foundations became widespread; finally in the mid-19C **bricks** were brought in by water and by rail. Plymouth, Exeter and Taunton all have fine large Elizabethan half-timbered houses. Where stone is used, as at Tiverton, it is for the most part rough hewn into blocks of approximately the same small size and laid in courses with quoins at the angles. In Exeter and Crediton, particularly, note the use of red sandstone and pink tufa.

Cornwall

The **granite** which forms the peninsula's backbone, appears in the tors on Bodmin Moor, in outcrops north of St Austell Bay, northwest of, Falmouth and throughout Penwith. In all these areas, small worker's cottages, solitary inns like Jamaica Inn, isolated farm-houses and outbuildings, and the churches are built of granite with slate roofs.

To the north, around **Delabole** where the slate came from not only for Cornwall but for the whole of the south of England, the houses, boundary walls and everything is built of **slate schist,** a laterally grained rust-grey stone.

Granite proverbially so hard, is sometimes carved; slate can be clean-cut and incised – note the beautifully lettered street name plates.

Mineral bearing rock lies below the surface in north and west Cornwall, as witness the ancient minehouses and chimneys.

The Lizard is unique with its **serpentine rock.** Cottages and churches alike were built of the blackish rock which when dressed begins to show its colour and when polished reveals the veining and tones which have given it its name.

CHURCHES

Stonehenge, Salisbury Cathedral and the Roman Catholic Cathedral of St Peter and St Paul in Bristol, each all of a piece or in a single architectural style, are the rare exceptions to what is almost the rule in England, namely that our churches, of whatever size, evolve in the building. Most churches stand, therefore, as examples of two or even three styles: walls, windows, pillars and arcades, chancel arches, towers and tower bases, were incorporated in rebuildings; until 19-20C and the Gothic revival, remodellings and additions were made proudly in the contemporary style.

Celtic and Saxon: 5-11C

Incredibly the sites of most of the 10000 and more cathedrals and parish churches in England were hallowed before the Conquest. Churches originated often as regular preaching stands which, in time, would be marked by a cross, an oratory and eventually a small church built of wood or stone. The most obvious relics of these early times are, in the case of the Celts, the up-standing Celtic Crosses with their individual shape, sculptured figures of Christ and carved interlacing. They stand in the churchyards in Cornwall *(usually E of S door)* and by the wayside *(p 216).*

Of Saxon work, there remain St Lawrence Church in Bradford-on-Avon, the altered St Martin at Wareham, typical "long and and short" stonework at the base of several towers and inside St James Church, Avebury, an area of solid wall with tapering windows. Except in a very few cases, both Celtic and Saxon churches, and those built later on their foundations, have always been oriented due east, unlike elsewhere in Europe.

Norman or Romanesque: mid-11 – mid-12C

Romanesque or Norman architecture came to England before William, Duke of Normandy, travel and close ties in the Church having already made it familiar.

The style, characterised by weight and mass, has great, thick, flat walls pierced by small **round headed windows** and **doors,** these last decorated with carved zig-zag, dog-tooth or beaked surrounds; filling the upper doorway might be a carved stone tympanum.

Inside, **cylindrical columns,** topped by plain cushion capitals were superseded, in time, by clustered columns surrounding cruciform pillars and carved capitals.

The **arcade arches** were circular as was the **roof vault** which was built of heavy masonry. Where two lengths of barrel (wagon or tunnel) vaulting crossed, diagonal ribs were formed at the intersection. Complications arose where communicating arcades of different height had to be roofed over; to get the inter-pillar arches to the same height the pointed arch, which allows any degree of sharp or wide curve, was invented. It came into general use at the end of 12C when it virtually solved all vaulting problems.

Gothic: mid-11 – late 16C

The period divides into three parts: **Early English** (EE) from 1150-1290, **Decorated** from 1290-1350 and **Perpendicular** from 1350-1550.

During these centuries church builders took advantage of the pointed arch and the new knowledge that weight could be channelled through supporting ribs to fixed points which could be buttressed or supported by flying buttresses, a further evolution. Windows were enlarged and elaborated. Churches were built ever higher and were more finely decorated with pinnacles, castellations, pierced stonework, niches and figures.

In EE times the **lancet windows,** which were sometimes stepped to form an east window, were eventually widened, the dividing mullion splitting at the top to leave a diamond; the apex diamond was then pierced by circles which contained **quatrefoil tracery.**

In the Decorated age the taller, **transomed windows** with ever more pointed apexes contained an increasingly **flowing tracery**. Ornament everywhere was elaborated.

In the Perpendicular period the window peaks flattened to produce a wider apex over vast areas of glass; above 5, 7, 9 lights the infilling was simplified to a **geometrical tracery**. Attention became focussed on the vaulting which reached its climax in the **fan vaulting** to be seen in Sherborne Abbey and the chapter house of Wells Cathedral.

The country was prosperous on wool and weaving in the Perpendicular period; faith was strong and the church, in mind of Henry VIII's constant need of treasure, invested in non-removable buildings. **Parish churches** soared on the old sites: techniques were taken over from the cathedrals and larger churches; towers moved to the west end, spires ceased to be built; Somerset led the way in beautiful towers *(p 147)*.

While vaulting ribs were spun in fine webs to support cathedral roofs, most west country parish **church roofs** continued to be made of wood. The barrel frames were boarded in or ceiled; the beams were carved and chamfered; tie-beam roofs developed centre king-posts or lateral queen posts, with braces and brackets, all able to be decorated with carving, cresting and tracery. Joints were hidden beneath small leaf mouchettes, foliate and flowered blocks, heraldic devices and bosses, carved with the patron's head; against the wall were carved **wall plates** and **corbels** – in both Dorset and Somerset figures often took the form of flying angels: in Dorset is the unique roof of Bere Regis with the apostles "oyled" and over-hanging in the manner of a hammer-beam roof, at Martock in Somerset there is a angel roof.

Many of the roofs are coloured, some are gilded, every one is different.

The Georgian Period: 1710-1810

In 18C a small number of late mediaeval churches were rebuilt in the new Classical style with pillars and often a portico, pedimented doors and windows in which the tracery had been replaced by glazing bars.

Inside, tall, single pillars divided the nave from the aisles, frequently supporting wide tribunes or galleries extending along the north, south and west walls.

Furnishings

Fonts. – Saxon fonts, small, circular and plain, are rare but Celtic fonts are still to be found in many churches in Cornwall. Huge, square blocks of granite, they stand often on five pillars (the five wounds of Christ), carved with bearded heads at the angles and foliate designs on the sides. They would have been coloured. They date from the end of the Celtic-early Norman period.

Tombstones and memorials. – The *Harrowing of Hell* in Bristol Cathedral, carved in *c*1050, is a rare example of Saxon carving. The stone was a coffin lid.

The representation of a person either by engraving or with an effigy, became general in the Middle Ages. There are stone recumbents of knights in full armour, sometimes accompanied by their wives, of bishops, robed and as cadavers. Many had the monuments which were to adorn their tombs, carved in their own lifetime. Others, more modest, are commemorated in fine brasses.

The Renaissance taste of the Elizabethans and Jacobeans is mirrored in their tombs: the earlier, dignified stone effigies were replaced as the century wore on by ruffed and robed figures presented with their spouses and their children aligned as weepers on the chest below; above were canopies or screens decorated with scrolls and strapwork, eulogies, heraldic devices, achievements, helms and obelisks. Brilliant colours heightened the effect. One of the finest examples is to be seen in Lacock church *(p 193)*.

The Classical influence of the late 17-18C introduced tombs with figures carved by the fashionable and famous sculptors of the day including Rysbrack and Nost.

Woodwork. – Lively **bench-ends** in Cornwall, **rood screens** in Devon dating from 15 – 16C for the most part, embellish many parish churches; in the cathedrals are **misericords, bishops' thrones**, and canopied stalls.

Following Archbishop Laud's (1573-1645) injunction to keep animals away from the altar and to prevent the theft of holy water, splendid **font covers** and **altar rails** were carved in the Jacobean period, also pulpit stair bannisters.

Chandeliers. – Cathedrals and parish churches alike in the region are often lit by beautiful brass chandeliers suspended, in a few cases, on wrought iron hangers. With the exception of two 16C Flemish lamps, all are 18C.

HOUSES

Houses, as they pass from owner to owner by inheritance or sale, as fortunes ebb and flow and fashions alter and because we live in them, are in a constant state of change. It must also be remembered that the cob, bricks and timber and thatched roofs used for the smaller houses, were not substantial and, if neglected, soon fell into decay; that labour for building was readily available and, therefore, when occupants died or streets were re-aligned, houses would be knocked down and re-built elsewhere; many were also destroyed by the repeated fires of bygone times. Few of the general run of houses to be seen in towns and villages, therefore, are more than 350-400 years old. Many appear older, local builders preferring tried ways of construction to new styles and choosing to follow fashion more in superficial decoration than in structure.

The rich merchants and landowners who bought the former monastic properties at the Dissolution were the trend-setters in house building. They commissioned architect-surveyors and craftsmen who travelled from property to property; they were also often in the sovereign's employ and would have travelled on the continent, seeing the Renaissance style in Italy and France. These new owners returned with a fund of ideas which they wished to see executed so that they could display the result to all, notably the monarch in the days of Elizabethan and Stuart royal progresses, and their relations and neighbours at all periods!

Tudor, Jacobean Periods, 15-17C

The houses have timber frames with exposed and cruck beams; the timbers, closer together in early work, have plaster or brick infilling. Oversailing upper floors were discontinued in Jacobean times as they were considered a fire-hazard. Great pointed **gables** characterise the roofs.

Chimney stacks appear for the newly introduced fireplaces; in Elizabethan times grouped, set symmetrically, often of brick and fancifully decorated.

The **windows** are small, sometimes single casements, but on occasion extend right across a front; the frames have flat arched heads beneath a hood.

Windows in the big houses, illuminating great halls and often the **long galleries** characteristic of the Elizabethan age, followed Perpendicular church architecture in comprising great expanses of glass.

Inside, the walls (except where clad with tapestries) were **oak panelled.**

Plasterwork came into its own with ceilings decorated with formal and imaginative patterning and great pendants; friezes and overmantels were full of interest, incorporating the favourite Jacobean strapwork and the display of arms.

The **stairs**, whether of monolithic blocks of stone or single timbers, mounted as spirals in the Elizabethan and as splendid wide staircases, cantilevered and turning in straight flights around open, square wells in the Jacobean period; the **bannisters**, of wood inches thick, were often deeply carved, the **newels** heraldic.

The Classical Period, 17 and 18C

The achievement of 17C was the **Queen Anne house** or the attuning of palatial, classical proportions and style to the measure of smaller country and town houses.

The precepts, as laid down by Palladio and imparted by Inigo Jones (1573-1652), were advanced by Sir Christopher Wren (1632-1732) and others.

House **fronts** became plain with centre **doorways** and symmetrically placed **sash windows,** the latter introduced in the early 18C. As the period progressed, window frames and glazing bars, at first thick and cumbersome, became ever more slender.

The houses stood four-square beneath **hipped roofs** (roofs sloping up on all four sides to a flat top). Where more rooms (and windows) were required than there was space for within the classical limits governing the height according to the frontage, those rooms would be built into the roof and lit by means of **dormer windows.**

The eaves were given a plain cornice-style decoration, the angles were often quoined with dressed stone – but the secret of their charm was the apparent simplicity of perfect proportion.

The **doorways** were almost invariably crested with pediments and broken pediments, shell canopies and other light fantasies supported on brackets or, more elaborately, on pilasters. Where the owners were wealthy, the **fireplaces** inside would be decorated after the manner of the front doors with framing pillars and a pediment; **ceilings** were ornamented with garlands of fruit and flowers carved realistically and almost in the round.

The **Georgian period** developed as a refinement of the Queen Anne style and marked its adaptation to the new requirements of crowded urban living.

The 18C prided itself on being "the age of reason"; precepts in architecture were formulated and adhered to: the Palladian-classical origin became more evident as doorways, for example, were less exuberantly decorated. Windows, proportioned and set as before, were pedimented, wrought ironwork was used to decorate balconies, railings and front gates.

In the middle of this stylised world there appeared the **Georgian terrace.** Following the obligatory rules of proportion, it could rise through several floors because the extent of the terrace gave it width, and each house, as a section of the whole, could, therefore, be provided with sufficient rooms. **Squares** and terraces, designed as single facades, became 18C versions of classical palaces, complete with central pediments, columns, porticos and arcades. Some were planned as single fashionable streets ending in a focal point such as St Mary Magdalene, Taunton, some, such as the squares, crescents and the **Circus** at Bath, were designed as elements in the most dignified city plan ever devised in England. Inside, houses were greatly influenced by the **Classical style decoration** of Robert Adam (1728-92) which can be seen much as he designed it at Saltram.

The 19C

The **Regency architecture** of the early part of the century continued the Georgian tradition, adding touches such as the prominent bow window, and in town, a great use of stucco. All too soon Regency gave way to the **Victorian style** and the long rows of bay windowed, steeply roofed, solidly built houses appeared, still to be seen in many seaside towns. In the late 18C Horace Walpole announced that he was going "to build a little Gothic structure at Strawberry Hill", Twickenham. Walpole's house was a pastiche, a mixture of the genuine, which he bought at sales in England and on the Continent, and what he had built and decorated in an increasingly extreme manner, so developing what came to be known as the **Gothick style.** Decoration, ornament, furniture and furnishings in the style became fashionable and were to be seen at one time in many houses.

At the same time many architects concerned with designing churches (or restoring them) and public buildings punctiliously followed traditional Gothic precepts.

Two 19C "big houses" in the West Country of particular interest, are Lanhydrock which, because of the fire which nearly destroyed it, was rebuilt within its 16C granite walls by 19C craftsmen to late 19C standards of taste and comfort (central heating) and Knightshayes which was constructed for a cotton-lace magnate by two temperamental architects and could only be of its time.

GARDENS

No holiday in the West Country would be complete without a visit to one or more of the great gardens where spring begins earlier, autumn continues longer than in many regions. A bonus is that several of the gardens are sited amidst beautiful valleyed parkland, overlooking river estuaries or the sea.

GARDEN DESIGN

Although there were forerunners, the English genius in garden design dates from 18C. The earliest gardens were the formal Elizabethan **Knot gardens,** with little beds containing herbs or small flowered plants outlined by miniature, clipped box hedges – the whole an intricate pattern of almost unrelieved evergreen. A later variation, still almost entirely green in aspect, was the Jacobean **Mount garden.**

THE 17C

As Renaissance ideas spread from Europe, the garden forms of Italy and France were adapted to England. Design remained geometrical but on a large scale : gardens were divided into separate "rooms" each surrounded by a tall hedge; flower-beds, symmetrically arranged and still edged with clipped box, were made larger and were brilliantly, if identically, planted as carpets or parterres; openings in the hedges afforded vistas, often onto water stylised into a circular basin and fountain or a "canal".

THE 18C

The Romantic Movement swept into garden design as a search to find "the genius of the place" which being interpreted meant enhancing the natural beauty of the site – **Lancelot Brown** (1715-1783) described the task as improving the "capability" of a site. Formal patterning and bedding were abandoned; enclosed spaces were opened out – **William Kent** (1684-1748) invented the ha-ha, an open ditch which enabled the garden to merge visually with the adjoining parkland landscape, at the same time keeping deer and cattle at a distance. Canals became serpentine ponds and lakes; hillsides were planted with trees selected for their leaf colours, their size and shape as clumps or as specimens; cedars of Lebanon, introduced to England in 1676, oaks, ashes and beeches – were sited to focus a view, counterpoint a house front.
Poetry and painting were almost literally translated in some cases: landscapes were transformed, lakes excavated, temples, grottoes, follies constructed and situated after the manner of pictures as may be seen at Stourhead.
Humphry Repton (1752-1818), the next in the line of designers, followed the landscaping precepts of Capability Brown, his famous Red Books giving his clients a detailed idea of how his plans would materialise. His avdance on Brown was to re-introduce flowers in beds and on terraces in close proximity to his clients' houses.

THE 19C

Plant hunting, inaugurated in 16-17C by the **Tradescants,** father and son, was undertaken on an ever-increasing scale in 19 – early 20C. Expeditions were financed by several members of a family or owners in a county; specimens would be parcelled out and enthusiasts set about improving and hybridising the plants before seeking registration with the Royal Horticultural Society.
To accommodate the new ranges of plants, garden design changed again to a labour intensive formula with flowers overwintered or raised in greenhouses and conservatories and bedded out each summer; herbaceous borders were crowded with plants; dense shrubberies were allowed to grow; collections of trees were planted as pinetums and arboretums: terraces were draped and decorated with climbers and plants in pots.

THE 20C

Reaction produced a less crowded appearance, and, with **Gertrude Jekyll** (1832-1932) and eventually **Vita Sackville-West** (1892-1962), a discrimination appeared that gives value to each plant for its flowers, its foliage and as a whole, to produce the plantsmen's and plantswomen's gardens of today.
Another "innovation", of 20C is the return to gardens divided into "rooms", sometimes by colour, more often by season. Listed below are 35 gardens described in this guide.

AVON	DEVON	SOMERSET
Claverton Manor	Bicton	Barrington Court
Clevedon Court	Cadhay	Clapton Court
	Killerton	East Lambrook Manor
CORNWALL	Knightshayes Court	Forde Abbey
	Mount Edgcumbe	Gaulden Manor
Cotehele	Sharpitor	Tintinhull House
Glendurgan	Tapeley Park	
Lanhydrock		**WILTSHIRE**
Pencarrow	**DORSET**	
Trelissick		Bowood
Trengwainton	Abbotsbury	Heale House
Trerice	Athelhampton	Longleat
Tresco	Compton Acres	Stourhead
Trewithen	Cranborne Manor	Wilton House
	Parnham House	
	Smedmore	

SEA BIRDS AND WADERS

Oystercatcher (1)

Grey heron (2)

Razorbill (3)

Gannet (4)

Shag (6)

Common sandpiper (5)

Guillemot (7)

Avocet (8)

Crested coot (10)

Curlew (9)

Common tern (11)

After Jacana photos : 1 Ferrero / 2 Davenne / 3, 4 Boët / 5 Saïller / 6, 9 Ermie / 7 Nardin / 8 Antony / 10 CVV / 11 Mallet.

KEY

Sights

*** **Worth a journey**
** **Worth a detour**
* **Interesting**

Sightseeing route	
with departure point	
■ Castles, historic house	
∴ Ruins	
⌐ Lighthouse	
± Wayside cross	
☀ ♈ Panorama – View	
⊤ Viewing table	
◡ ⋉ Dam – Windmill	

Ⓘ ⅰ	Ecclesiastical building
▭	Building
☆	Fort
●—■▪—	Ramparts – Tower – Gate
⊚ ▪	Fountain – Statue
	Gardens, parks, woods
▲	Miscellaneous sights
A Z B	Letters giving the location of a place on the town plan

---

Motorway	
◆▶ ❶ Complete interchange	
▶ ❷ Limited interchange	
Major through road	
┉┉--- Stepped street – Footpath	
├─────┤ Pedestrian street	
x======x Unsuitable for traffic	
●—•—•—• Tramway	
4ᵐ2 Headroom (given when less than 4.30m)	
35 Load limit of a bridge	
△ Swing bridge	
🚆 🚌 Station – Coach station	
✈ Airport	
Ferry services :	
Ⓑ } Passengers and cars	
⟱	
🚢 Passengers only	

✉	Main post office (with poste restante)
🅸	Tourist information centre
℗	Car park
⊞	Hospital
⬯	Covered market
🛒	Shopping centre
⚔	Barracks
✡	Synagogue
⸬	Cemetery
⬭ 🏃	Stadium – Racecourse
🏊 🏊	Outdoor or indoor swimming pool
⚓	Pleasure boat harbour
⛸ ⛳	Skating rink – Golf course
🏛 ⚙	Water tower – Factory or power station
⊤	Telecommunications tower or mast

MICHELIN maps and town plans are north orientated.

Main shopping streets are printed in a different colour in the list of streets.

---

c	County Council Offices	M	Museum	POL	Police
H	Town Hall	T	Theatre	U	University, colleges

tc Times and charges for admission: for further details see the green pages.

Additional Signs

⌶	Megalithic monument	⊛	Home park, garden
◇	Safari park, zoo, seabird colony	♦	Chalk hill figure

SIGHTS

in alphabetical order
by counties

(Vloo / J Alan Cash)

A West Country Garden – Stourhead

AVON

Area 520 sq m Population 915 176

The county, created under the Local Government Act of 1972, comprises the city of Bristol, which had been granted county status in its own right as far back as 1373 by Edward III, and an area of north Somerset including the city of Bath – but not Wells.
The Bristol Channel, or Severn Estuary, forms the county's northwesterly shoreline from which the view extends across the water to the hills of South Wales.

The two cities. – Bristol and Bath afford infinite variety to the visitor through their contrasting backgrounds, their current atmosphere: the one a former port made prosperous through the sea and merchant trading, the venturers closely allied and always generous to their city, the other, a city built for recreation and leisure in the Roman age, rebuilt and fashionable in Stuart times and rebuilt again as the supreme example in England of urban planning in 18C.

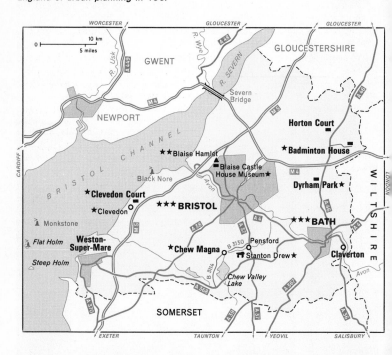

Each city has its "great man": Bath in 18C was transformed by **Beau Nash**; Bristol will always bear the imprint of **Isembard Kingdom Brunel** (1806-59).
In 1830 his design for the Clifton Suspension Bridge was accepted; in 1833 his plans for improvement of the city docks were agreed; in the same year he was appointed Engineer to the newly formed Great Western Railway with the specific task of opening the line between London and Bristol. As a result he supervised the laying of 118 miles of track (Stephenson's 11m Stockton-Darlington line: 1826) and the excavation of the nearly 2 miles long Box Tunnel; he designed Temple Meads Station and collaborated with the architects of Paddington Station. By 1841 he was engaged on what he saw as an "extension" to the London-Bristol railway, namely ships to provide a regular trans-Atlantic service: the Great Western, a paddlesteamer launched out of Bristol in 1837, the SS Great Britain and finally, the building of the colossal SS Great Eastern.

The countryside. – Country houses lie concealed in the undulating, wooded countryside, notably Badminton and Dyrham Park. In contrast, Horton Court offers just a doorway, an ambulatory and 12C hall; Claverton Manor meanwhile, has been transformed into The American Museum in Britain.

★ BADMINTON HOUSE

Michelin map **403** fold 27 – N29

tc Badminton is a palatial mansion in biscuit coloured stone, set in a park landscaped by **Capability Brown** on the edge of the Cotswolds; Badminton is where the original court dimensions and rules of the **game** of that name were devised from the size of the hall when bad weather compelled the younger members of the house to play battledore and shuttlecock indoors; where the **Three Day Event Horse Trials** are held each April; where the **Beaufort hounds** are kennelled; where signed photographs of members of the House of Windsor and royal houses of Europe make reminiscent viewing.

The house was built in 1670s and 1740s. There was already a "fair stone house" on the estate but in the eyes of its young owner it proved inadequate to entertaining Charles II when he came on a visit in 1663. By 1682, therefore, when the king created the man reputed to be his richest subject the first Duke of Beaufort, the house had been rebuilt and taken on much of its present appearance. The second phase came after the third duke had returned from the Grand Tour with a great enthusiasm for the Palladian style and commissioned **William Kent** to enlarge the house accordingly.

TOUR *1 hour*

If the earlier house had been designed as a potentially regal setting and furnished with bulk purchases as well as chosen portraits and pieces – to cover the oak staircase walls the first duke bought thirty pictures complete with frames for £250 which, he wrote to his wife, were "indifferent good in the judgment of those who understand these things" – 18C refashioning was intended to make it the showplace for the third duke's Grand Tour treasures of which there were 96 packing cases full.

Entrance Hall. – The five sporting pictures including *Staghunting at Badminton* with a view of the north face of the house, were painted by **John Wootton** in *c*1730; the map table is by **Chippendale**. Note also the Renaissance-style clock.

Octagon Waiting Hall. – The small hall is outstanding for its **plasterwork**; the vast blue and white bowl is a Spode **christening bowl**.

Oak Room. – Note the panelling and oak keeping cupboard from Raglan Castle.

Dining Room. – The wood carving by **Grinling Gibbons** is especially notable for the frame which embodies the ducal coronet of 1682, the Garter surrounding a cypher around the name Beaufort and cornucopias overflowing with fruit and flowers.

Red Room. – The room, so-called after 19C flock wallpaper, is historic with **Charles I memorabilia**: a Van Dyck portrait, royal shirt and handkerchief, half of the gold Louis the king divided with Queen Henrietta Maria when they parted in 1644, a letter...

The Library. – The library, in the oldest part of the house but with a Regency ceiling above the early cornice, is hung with family portraits, among them John of Gaunt *(above the fireplace)*.

East Room. – The many mementoes include a carpet worked by the ladies of Richmond for the Duchess of Teck on her marriage and which served later as her funeral pall and in a glass case, the wax figure of 18C Polish dwarf, Bébé.

Great Drawing Room. – The room, which is the principal show place for the Grand Tour treasures, is marked by a statuesque **chimneypiece** from Rome. Against the green damask covered walls hang **pictures** by Lawrence and Reynolds, and by Canaletto who in 1748-50 painted the north front of the house and the view from the roof looking towards Worcester Lodge.

The Beaufort kennels are about 500yds from the house.

EXCURSION

Horton Court. – *5m W; 1m W of A46. P 42.*

★★ BATH   Pop 80 771

Michelin map **403** fold 27 – M29

Bath uniquely combines the grace and beauty of 18C urban planning and domestic architecture with a centuries old past, a modern present, flowers, gardens...

Legend and history. – Britain's only hot springs probably broke through the earth's crust in the time of Neanderthal Man *c*100,000 years ago. In 500 BC, according to legend, **Prince Bladud** who, when afflicted with leprosy had become a wandering swineherd, noticing that his swine, after plunging in the mud, appeared healed of their skin ailments, plunged in himself – and emerged cured. He returned to court, succeeded to the crown, fathered the future King Lear and established his seat at Bath. True or apocryphal, by 1C AD, when the Romans had advanced west and were mining lead in the Mendip Hills, the village of Bath was known for its warm springs. The **Romans** transformed Bath into England's first spa resort, naming it after a native Celtic goddess, **Aquae Sulis**. They built baths, a temple, possibly a gymnasium or theatre – it was purely a pleasure centre, there were no military interests.

When the Romans left in 5C, the city declined; in 6C, Bath was taken by the **Saxons** who built a town within the Roman walls and an abbey not far from the Roman temple site; in 9C Alfred is said to have made Bath into a fortress; in 973 **Edgar**, the first King of all England, was re-crowned in the Saxon abbey.

The squabbles of pillaging Norman barons so reduced the city that **John de Villula** of Tours, Bishop of Somerset and Physician, was able to purchase it for £500. He began the creation of a vast Benedictine cathedral priory – the church today occupies only the site of the nave – built a palace, a guesthouse, a new suite of baths, founded a school of science and mathematics and encouraged the treatment of the sick (the Hospital of St John was founded in his name in 12C). His cathedral was never completed. Only in 1499 did building of the present minster begin. Bath was by then a prosperous wool town.

At the Dissolution the monks lost their jurisdiction over the baths and sold off lead from the minster's roof, the bells, glass and ironwork. Queen Elizabeth in 1574 ordered that a fund be set up to restore the abbey and St John's Hospital and ensure that "an unsavoury town... become a most sweet town".

By 1668 Pepys, on a visit, considered it had "many good streets and very fair stone houses". Although he "stayed above two hours in the water" he had reservations about the baths: "Methinks it cannot be clean to go so many bodies together in the same water". Others were less fastidious: where royalty went – Charles II and Catherine of Braganza, Queen Mary of Modena, Queen Anne – crowds followed, until by the early 18C Bath was becoming a place to attend not only for a cure but to be in the fashion. From the visitor's point of view, however, the city was dull and unorganised.

Beau Nash. – "The Beau" arrived in 1704 (d 1762); he was 31 and came to Bath in the wake of the fashionable fraternity. He had a flair for organisation and on his appointment as MC, laid down a programme for the highflyers to follow from early morning bathing to evening assemblies; he ordered that the streets be lit and made safe to walk in; that swords be not worn in the town and sedan chairmen charge the authorised tariff... Within a year he opened the first Pump Room where people might take the waters and meet in civilised society; he organised concerts, balls, cards, the gambling; he laid down eleven rules, which for fear of ostracism and public ridicule were implicitly obeyed. The town prospered, charities benefitted, he grew rich – Bath became the most fashionable city in England.

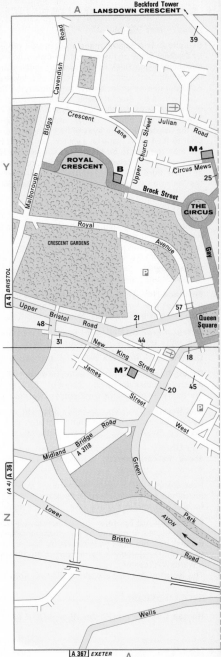

Gay Street	ABY		Bennett Street	BY	11
Green Street	BY	32	Bridge Street	BYZ	13
Milsom Street	BY		Broad Quay	BZ	14
New Bond Street	BY	46	Broad Street	BY	16
			Chapel Row	AYZ	18
Abbey Church Yard	BZ	2	Charles Street	AZ	20
Alfred Street	BY	3	Charlotte Street	AZ	21
Ambury	BZ	4	Cheap Street	BZ	23
Argyle Street	BY	6	Churchill Bridge	BZ	24
Bath Street	BZ	7	Circus Place	AY	25
Beckford Road	CY	9	Cleveland Place	CY	26
Belvedere	BY	10	Corn Street	BZ	27

Ralph Allen and John Wood. – While Nash refashioned Bath society, Ralph Allen and John Wood undertook the transformation of the city's architecture and whole urban plan.

Allen (1694-1764), a Cornish postmaster, came to Bath in 1710 where he offered the government £2000 a year for a seven year concession to make the region's highly unreliable postal service both efficient and profitable; it became a model and with the fortune he made out of it, Allen bought stone quarries at Claverton (p 39) and on Combe Down with the idea of building a new city with the honey coloured stone. John Wood (1700-54) was a Yorkshireman who, by 1728, had settled in the city. A Classicist inspired by Bath's Roman past, he sought to build principally in the Palladian style using the stone from Combe Down, now known as **Bath Stone.**

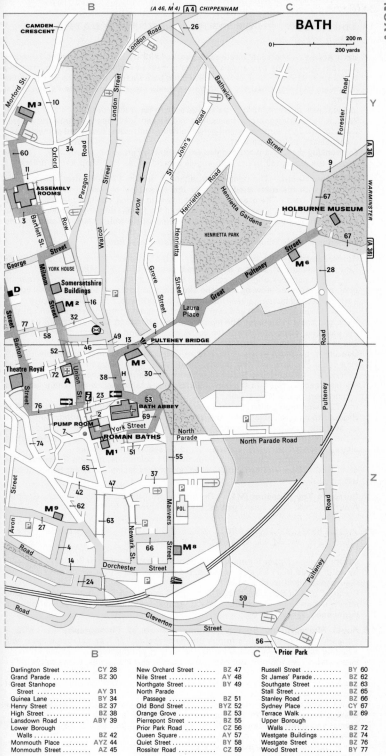

AVON

(A 46, M 4) **A 4** CHIPPENHAM

BATH

0 _____ 200 m
0 _____ 200 yards

CAMDEN CRESCENT

Morford St.

London Road

Bathwick Street

Forester Road

Y

A 36 WARMINSTER

M³ 10

34

60

Oxford Street

Paragon

London Street

St. John's Road

Walcot Street

AVON

Henrietta Road

Henrietta Gardens

HENRIETTA PARK

9

67

HOLBURNE MUSEUM

67

A 36 WARMINSTER

11

ASSEMBLY ROOMS

Bartlett St.

George Street

3

Row

York Street

M⁶

28

Milsom Street

YORK HOUSE

Somersetshire Buildings

M² 16

Grove Street

Henrietta Street

Laura Place

Great Pulteney Street

D

Barton Street

77

32

58

49

13

46

52

6

PULTENEY BRIDGE

Theatre Royal

72

A

H

M⁵

30

38

U

Union St.

23

76

2

53

69

BATH ABBEY

PUMP ROOM

7

York Street

ROMAN BATHS

North Parade

Road

Pulteney

North Parade Road

M¹

51

55

Z

65

37

47

42

Manvers Street

POL.

Avon Street

M⁹

62

27

63

Newark St.

66

M⁸

4

14

Dorchester Street

24

59

Road

Claverton Street

56

Prior Park

B   C

SIGHTSEEING IN BATH

The city, because of its architectural design, is best seen on foot; the three walks suggested, starting from the Abbey, each requires approximately ½ day.

If time is short see: the **Abbey**★ (exterior), go into the **Pump Room**★ (view the King's Bath – a full visit to the Roman Baths takes an hour), walk up Milsom and Gay Sts to the **Circus**★★★; bear right to the **Assembly Rooms**★ and **Costume Museum**★★★ or left to see the **Royal Crescent**★★★. Return down Gay St.

Watch out everywhere for **street vistas**, closed by a perfectly sited house, often pedimented; for the individual touches in a long range to lift it from uniformity; for the dressing of a crescent or square with iron railings, lamps, forecourt grass...

BATH★★★

★★ The ABBEY, PUMP ROOM and ROMAN BATHS (BZ)
time: ½ day

★ **Bath Abbey.** – The sanctuary was begun in 1499 by Bishop Oliver King following a dream in which he saw angels climbing to heaven and heard voices commanding that a king, which he took to be himself from his surname, restore the church. From the pillars of the Norman church there eventually arose the pure, late Perpendicular abbey.

Inside, nave, chancel, narrow transepts, soar to **fan vaulting** designed by Robert and William Vertue (designers of the vaulting in the Henry VII Chapel, Westminster Abbey). Outside, five-light windows stand between flying buttresses, crocketed pinnacles and a castellated, pierced parapet.

Overlooking the Churchyard, the **west end** presents a Perpendicular window, 17C door and, in the stone, tall **ladders** with angels ascending, as in Bishop King's dream.

★ **The Pump Room.** – The pump room, although built in 1789-99 after Nash's death, *tc* remains, with his **statue** presiding over the assembled company, redolent of "this omnipotent Lord". There are fluted pilasters with gilded capitals beneath a coved ceiling, apsed ends, a rounded bay containing the former drinking fountain and from which there is a view of the King's Bath, Chippendale style chairs, a Tompion long case clock, a trio, a glass chandelier... altogether the perfect meeting place for Catherine and Mr Tilney in Jane Austen's *Northanger Abbey*.

★★ **Roman Baths.** – The baths are fed by a spring which pours out approximately *tc* 280 000 gallons of water a day at a temperature of 116 °F (46.5 °C).

The Roman complex originally consisted of the Great Bath, a large, warm, swimming pool, once covered now open to the sky, and two baths of decreasing heat to the east; the second building phase installed on the west side, *a frigidarium,* or cold room, with windows at the north end overlooking the sacred spring or reservoir and further west, two heated chambers (the *tepidarium* and *caldarium*). Later alterations enlarged the east end, elaborated the baths at the west end and transformed the *frigidarium* into a cold plunge Circular Bath.

Due north, beyond the reservoir, was an altar and west of that the temple.

When the Romans left, the drains, unattended, soon clogged and mud invaded everywhere so that today Stall St lies above the temple site, the Pump Room above the altar and its court. In the early Middle Ages a tank lined with Mendip lead was constructed as the King's Bath.

In 1727, workmen building a sewer along Stall St, found the gilded bronze head of **Minerva**, known to have been the presiding goddess of the spring. Since then excavations, which still proceed, have revealed the repeated remodelling undertaken in the bath complex, carvings – including a **gorgon's head** *(p 42)* from the temple façade, altars, a lead curse, coins, vessels... all to be seen in the museum.

Return to the Abbey Churchyard, through 1791 colonnade, passing the uneven line of 17-18C houses and delightful 18-19C shopfronts facing the Pump Room, or bear left.

tc **Burrow's Toy Museum** (M1). – On display are 19-20C English, French, German, American toys: dolls, board games, theatres, improving books...

★★ ASSEMBLY ROOMS, MUSEUM OF COSTUME, The CIRCUS, ROYAL CRESCENT *time: ½ day*

Before crossing Upper Borough Walls, note the **Royal Mineral Water Hospital** (BZ A), built by John Wood in 1738 and, opposite, the **mediaeval wall** – over which cadavers from the hospital used to be thrown!

Continue up Old Bond St (1760-70) (BYZ 52) into **Milsom St** (BZ), the wide shopping street begun by John Wood, which epitomises the carriage, bonnetted and beribboned age of 1770s.

★★ **Royal Photographic Society National Centre of Photography** (BY M2). – *tc* Beneath 18C chandelier in a former private chapel of 1767, an octagonal room with a gallery supported on Ionic columns, the story of photography is displayed through every stage from trapping the light, waxed paper and wet plates, to the single reflex lens; elsewhere are a large collection of Leicas and, in three separate galleries, changing exhibitions of contemporary artistic, scientific and experimental photography.

In Milsom St once more, note above the Octagon, the grand, curved 18C **Somersetshire Buildings** (now a bank). At the top, **George St**, contains a range of houses along an upraised pavement to close the Milsom St vista and *(right)* an old, 18C posting inn, York House.

Cross George St to Bartlett and Bennet Sts.

★ **Assembly Rooms** (BY). – The rooms, built in 1769-71, were declared in the 1772 *tc* Bath Guide to be "the most noble and elegant of any in the Kingdom".

18C assemblies were evening entertainments at which dancing to gossip and scandalmongering by the spectators, card-playing and tea-drinking, occurred simultaneously.

The Ball Room. – The room, which is 100ft 6in long, 43ft 6in wide, and 43ft 6in high, was so designed that the dancers in their finery provided the colour below, while the decoration was concentrated above in columns, entablature and a deep Naples yellow coved ceiling from which are suspended five magnificent crystal **chandeliers**.

The Octagon. – The small room was intended as the card room.

The Tea Room. – Wood planned a rich and dignified 18C interior for the room where gossip would be rife! At one end is a screen of superimposed pillars which continue round the sides to support the coved ceiling, compartmented by enriched flat ribs.

★★★ **Museum of Costume.** – *In the Assembly Rooms building.* What our ancestors and *tc* we wore, in band-box condition, is displayed phase by phase from the Stuarts to the present, to fascinate in colour, texture, embroidery and revelation of living styles. Uncluttered, single figures, pairs and small groups, complemented by a single chair or beautiful small worktable of the period, show the changes in cut of sleeve, bodice, yoke and shoulder, of skirt and breeches, in stuff and silk. Presentations of underwear and accessories complete the picture in this most elegant of costume museums.

Go up Russel St and bear right into Julian Rd.

★ **Camden Works Museum** (BY M3). – One goes through the shop, small, dark, *tc* Victorian, of J B Bowler, a **brass founder** of the turn of the century, to look at his stock-in-trade which, since he was an engineer-craftsman, businessman and cordial manufacturer and never threw anything away, means tools, machines, ledgers...

Return to Bennet St and turn right into Circus Mews.

★ **Bath Carriage Museum** (AY M4). – Forty carriages are on view : a Black Maria, a hearse, *tc* a Royal Mail Coach, a Sociable (1876), Victorias, buggies and the Duke of Somerset's 19C state coach with the coachmen's gold velvet liveries and tricorne hats.

Return to Bennet St.

★★★ **The Circus** (AY). – The Circus, originally the King's Circus, was only built in 1754 although it was one of John Wood's earliest concepts. It comprises a tight circle of identical houses pierced by three access roads, equidistant and so each opposite a range. The houses of pale Bath stone, decorated with coupled columns, rise through three floors to a frieze and acorn topped balustrade. It is a design of Classical proportions and control.

Brock St (AY). – The street between the Circus and the Crescent, built by John Wood II in 1767 with houses of differing design, only reveals its dramatic surprise at the very end when suddenly you see the full sweep of the Royal Crescent.

(Unichrome, Bath)

The Royal Crescent

★★★ **Royal Crescent** (AY). – The great arc of 30 terrace houses in which the horizontal lines are counterbalanced by 114 giant Ionic columns rising from the first floor to the pierced parapet, was the great achievement of John Wood II in 1767-74.

★★ **No 1 Royal Crescent (B).** – The Georgian house has been authentically restored even *tc* to the small pane windows. Inside the wall coverings and furnishings based on contemporary printing blocks and drawings, provide the setting for Chippendale, Sheraton and Hepplewhite **furniture**, porcelain and 18C **glassware.**

Return to the centre by way of the Circus and Gay St.

Gay St (ABY). – The long street was the work from 1734-60 of the two Woods, father and son. No 41, on the corner of Old King St, was designed by the father and lived in by the son and is the Baroque exception to the Classical style of the street; note the semi-circular, recessed bow window on the corner and next to it a small, Delft tiled **powder-cabinet** with a shell niche, where gentlemen could powder their wigs before entering the reception rooms – this was the period of the *School for Scandal*. (In 1772 Richard Sheridan eloped with Elizabeth Linley from no 11 Royal Crescent.)

Queen Square (ABY). – The square was Wood's first example of urban planning. Note the **north side** with its pedimented centre and advanced ends: Wood himself lived at no 24, **Dr William Oliver**, inventor of the Bath Oliver biscuit, at nos 16-18.

Continue by Barton St to Beaford Square.

Theatre Royal (BZ). – The square of modest 18C houses, has been dominated since the early 19C by the Theatre Royal, resplendent inside in an appropriate finery of dark red Regency stripe, and in the horse-shoe shaped auditorium, of gilding and plum coloured plush. Adjoining are two houses once occupied by **Beau Nash.**

★ ORANGE GROVE, PULTENEY BRIDGE, HOLBURNE MUSEUM *time: ½ day*

Cross Orange Grove with its 18C houses, Terrace Walk which contains Bath's oldest **shopfront** (Messrs Eldridge Pope), and York St. Take the first turning on the right *(W)* into North Parade Passage, the former Lilliput Alley, where **no 3,** Sally Lunn's teashop, is a mediaeval house and **no 2,** next door, was Ralph Allen's town house. It was while living here that Allen had the folly, **Sham Castle,** built to complete the landscape on Combe Down.

Return to Orange Grove and continue N by way of the High St; turn right into Bridge St.

tc **Victoria Art Gallery** (BZ M5). – The gallery shows selected exhibitions of fine art.

★ **Pulteney Bridge** (BCY). – The bridge, with a central Venetian window, domed end pavilions and small shops, was designed in 1769-74 by **Robert Adam** for his friend Sir William Pulteney who hoped to develop a new city area beyond the Avon. (**River boat moorings:** *above and below the weir*).

Great Pulteney St (CY). – The city's longest vista, framed by the classically proportioned terrace houses, extends some 600yds from the end of the bridge. The eye travels along Argyle St, across the diagonally set Laura Place, and down the length of Great Pulteney St, to rest finally, on the Holburne Museum.

tc **Bath Postal Museum (M6).** – Small museum on the postal service in the Royal Mail coach period.

★★ **Holburne of Menstrie Museum** (CY). – The museum with considerable additions,
tc represents the collection and still bears the stamp of **Sir Thomas William Holburne** (d 1874), who served at the age of 12 in the *Orion* at Trafalgar. One of his proudest purchases was when he paid £60 3*s* 9*d* for a silver-gilt, **rosewater** dish of 1616.
Of especial note are: *(staircase)* the big early **Gainsborough** of Holburne's physician in a tricorne hat and blue frock coat – the artist lived at no 17 The Circus, from 1759-74; *(first floor)* the fine **furniture, silver** and **silver-gilt plate,** particularly Georgian, the apostle spoons, table silver and snuff boxes; the porcelain and 16C small Italian bronzes; *(staircase)* **18C Wedgwood,** and Roman and *art nouveau* glass; *(second floor)* the Italian Majolica, Flemish, Dutch and English 16 and 17C paintings.

ADDITIONAL CITY MUSEUMS

tc **Herschel House Museum** (AZ M7). – The House of Sir William Herschel (1738-1822), King's Astronomer, discoverer of the planet Uranus and "breaker of the barrier of the heavens".

tc **Museum of Bookbinding** (CZ M8). – History of the craft, 16-20C and examples of beautiful old and new bindings.

tc **Railway Display** (BZ M9). – Railway relics, including old timetables, signs and lamps.

CITY OUTSKIRTS

Go N up Broad St – Landsdown Rd to a 5 road fork; bear centre right.

★ **Camden Crescent** (BY). – The modest crescent, with its wide **view,** was built by John Eveleigh in 1786-92. It was never completed due to subsidence at the east end, so that the pedimented centre above five giant columns is, therefore, off-centre!

Return to the fork, and continue N; Landsdown Place East and the Crescent are 150yds up on the left.

★★ **Lansdown Crescent.** – The serpentine crescent and the continuing, more ornamented, **Somerset Place** ★ were built on this site superbly overlooking the abbey and the city centre in 1789-93. The crescent of three storeys with a rusticated ground floor and pierced balustrade, is accented at the centre with pilasters and pediment and at either end by bow windows and the whole subtly completed by area railings and graceful **lampholders.** Note the **bridge** between no 20 the Crescent and no 1 Lansdown Place West, built by William Beckford.

Return to Lansdown Rd and continue N to the tower, on the left.

tc **Beckford Tower and Museum.** – William Beckford, born in 1760 (d 1844), millionaire inheritor with a true 18C collector's taste in books, pictures and art objects, Grand Tour traveller, diarist and MP, was the builder of the fantastic **Fonthill Abbey** (no longer in existence). In 1882 he left Wiltshire for Bath where he purchased Lansdown Hill and two houses in the cresent. On the hill he erected this 154ft, Italianate tower in local stone, crowned by a lantern of eight cast iron columns and a cupola roof, all gilded. The tower, intended as a library retreat, contains the museum and, at the top, a belvedere which affords a **prospect** ★ of Bath, the Severn Estuary and Wales, the Cotswolds, Wiltshire...

tc **Prior Park.** – *Cross the Avon at North Parade Bridge; turn right into Pulteney Rd, left at the major junction into Prior Park Rd (A 3062). The house is a R C college.*
In 1730s, when Bath had become fashionable and crowded, **Ralph Allen** decided to build himself a seat away from all the bustle. The superbly sited mansion, which he had designed by John Wood in the Palladian style with giant columns supporting a pedimented portico, he believed would also serve to demonstrate to disbelieving architects in London that Bath stone from his quarries was supreme for fine construction.
Allen kept open house at Prior Park and among his visitors were Alexander Pope, Henry Fielding and Samuel Johnson, Gainsborough, David Garrick and Samuel Richardson.

Bristol is a trading city. It originated in 10C as a settlement by the bridge across the Avon at the western limit of the Saxon invasion. By the Middle Ages, as a flourishing port, it had grown to become England's second city after London. Prosperity increased until the Industrial Revolution drew interests north; with BAC, high technology industry and as a communications centre, it is once more in ascendance.

Architecturally this means that Bristol is a city which was increasingly prosperous from Domesday to 18C, or from the Norman, through the Gothic – particularly the Perpendicular – to the Jacobean and Palladian periods. For the most part it was spared 19C restoration to its mediaeval churches, while profiting from the engineering architecture of Brunel. In 20C, following heavy bombing in 1940-2, it was replanned and rebuilt.

"Shipshape and Bristol fashion". – Bristol's port has undergone three major transformations in its progress from riparian sailship harbour to tanker and container terminal: in 1240-8, the **Frome Trench** was dug to redirect the course of the River Frome, improve landing facilities and the water depth; in 1804-9, the **Floating Harbour,** 2 ½ miles in extent, was created to provide a constant water level and an immense quayside in the heart of the city; in 1877-9 the **Avonmouth** and **Portishead Docks,** and in 1977, the **Royal Portbury Docks,** were opened on the Severn Estuary.

The Floating Harbour, has become a pleasure boat harbour with floating restaurants and quaysides and warehouses converted into an exhibition site, clubs and museums. A ship in the Floating Harbour was liable to touch bottom at low tide: cargo had to be well stowed or "shipshape and Bristol fashion".

Trade and Venturing. – Bristol trade was concerned in 10C with Ireland; by 17C it had expanded to the Canaries, the Spanish American colonies, North America, Africa, the West Indies. In 18-19C new industries developed locally: iron, brass, copper, tin, porcelain and glass, chocolate, tobacco.

The merchants, several of them Quakers, incorporated in 1522 as the **Society of Merchant Venturers** were the city princes: they built and endowed churches – **William Canynges** even paid for the entire rebuilding of the most magnificent, St Mary Redcliffe *(p 37)* – they bought land freed by the Dissolution and erected great houses, they enabled the corporation to buy the Mayoral Chapel *(p 34)*, presented the city with schools and hospitals. By 18C many were moving out of the city centre to Queen Sq *(p 37)* Brandon Hill and Clifton *(p 38)* where they built great houses, some now University halls of residence.

★ CATHEDRAL QUARTER *time: 2 hours*

★ **Bristol Cathedral** (AZ). – The cathedral is a 14-15C Perpendicular Gothic church with a crenellated and pinnacled central tower, twin west towers and tall pointed windows, framed by finialled buttresses and pinnacled parapets. Although the foundation is ancient the church was only completed in 19C when the nave and west towers were built. It was an Augustinian abbey and already 400 years old when Dissolved by Henry VIII in 1539; three years later it was reconstituted as the Cathedral Church.

Interior. – *Walk directly up the nave.* From the crossing look through the screen and carved and canopied choirstalls (lively **15C misericords**) at the high altar before the 19C reconstructed reredos, then up and obliquely to either side to appreciate the fascination of the **roof.**

The sight is unique in English cathedrals, a feat of early 14C construction: the east end is a **hall church** with chancel and chancel aisles rising to an equal 50ft. Over the choir, the ribbed vaulting sweeps up directly from the pillars to form cusp lined kites at the crest; above the aisles it has been optically lowered for proportion's sake, by taking the arching to a cross–beam which serves also to spring the roof ribs. Vaults and spandrels are pierced to add a rare perspective.

Lady Chapels. – There are two chapels: the **Elder Lady Chapel** *(off N transept)* of 1210-20 with vaulting of 1270, is notable for its sobriety, its foliated capitals on slender Purbeck columns and small carved figures – St Michael and the dragon, a fox and goose, a lizard, monkeys; the **East Lady Chapel,** 100ft extension added when the Norman chancel was rebuilt in 1298-1330, is memorable for its riot of mediaeval colour highlighting stone carved into cusped arches, gabled niches, friezes, fleurons, heads, crests... In this chapel is one of the cathedral's special features: 14C **stellate tomb recess,** an interplay of curving lines and gilded ornament, surrounding 15C gabled tomb chest.

Sacristy. – *Off S chancel aisle.* The minute chamber is covered by a vault of flying ribs and arches beneath a flat stone roof; the ribs are bossaged, corbels foliated.

Berkeley Chapel. – *Down the steps.* There hangs in the chapel, transferred from the Temple Church *(p 37)*, a small, Flemish, brass **candelabrum** of 1460 at the heart of which stand St George and the Virgin and Child, above a flutter of golden squares *(p 70)*.

Harrowing of Hell. – *S transept.* The remarkable carving is 1000 year-old Saxon stone.

Go through the door on the far side of transept to the cloisters; bear left.

Chapter House. – A Norman columned vestibule leads to the chapter house of 1150-70 where the golden brown stone walls are patterned all over with interlacing and the roof is intersected by great, zig-zag ornamented ribs *(times witch)*.

Norman Arch (AZ). – The abbey precincts, when rebuilt at the end of 15C, retained the original, robust Norman gateway arch, framed by a collar of zig-zag decoration.

Council House (AZ C). – The curved, modern building, the city administration office, is distinguished by high stepping, golden unicorns, supporters of the city arms.

BRISTOL

★ **Lord Mayor's Chapel** (AZ).–
tc The chapel, part of the mediaeval Hospital of the Gaunts, was purchased at the Dissolution for £1 000 by the City Corporation.

A bird's-eye view from inside the door (orientation N-S) reveals a narrow 13C nave, to the right, a Perpendicular chapel with **15-17C tombs**, a large window of English and early Renaissance **glass** and 16C flat, black wooden roof highlighted in gold. Note the mayors' hatchments, a fine gilded swordrest, wrought, like the **iron gates** *(S aisle chapel)*, by William Edney in 1702 and formerly in the Temple Church *(p 37)*.

Hatchet Inn (AY). – The old gabled, farmhouse was first licensed in 1606.

tc **Harvey's Wine Museum** (AY). – The museum is in mediaeval cellars owned since the late 18C by Harveys of Bristol. Highlights of the visit are the collection of 500 silver decanter labels or **bottle tickets**, old **corkscrews**, 17C wine bottles, **18C glasses** and decanters and a pair of silver-gilt **coaster waggons**.

★★ **CABOT TOWER AREA** (AY) *time: ½ day*

★★★ **The Georgian House.** – No 7
tc was built for John Pinney, a sugar planter, on his return from St Kitts to Bristol where, as a merchant, he made a second, even larger, fortune. The Bristol architects, **Thomas** and **William Paty**, produced for him a typical late 18C design in Bath stone with a pedimented front door and rooms with Adam style decoration, while Pinney himself attended to every detail: "I desire you send me by the waggon a sufficient quantity of Glass for 4 Chinese doors for Book cases... Let it be the best glass as it is intended for handsome Cases".

Office and Hall. – The "handsome cases" in the office are a most satisfactory match with Pinney's original rich mahogany **bureau-bookcase** of 1750 and a complete contrast to the plain mahogany **standing desk** with brass ledger rails and candle brackets which he brought back from the West Indies to stand opposite in the hall.

Dining Room. – Mahogany is everywhere: in the table, sideboard, chairs, Stilton cheese rocker, dumb waiter and knife urn.

Upstairs. – Note especially the bleached mahogany **double secretaire bookcase,** the very small washstand with bowl and ewer, the **girandoles.**

Basement. – The house was well-run and comfortable: go down to look at the kitchen, laundry and the snug housekeeper's room.

tc **Cabot Tower.** – The slim red tower with a square balcony (**view**) and a white cap, was built high upon the hill in 1897 to celebrate 400th anniversary of the sailing, financed by Bristol merchants, of the navigator, **John Cabot across the Atlantic** *(p 14)*.

Berkeley Sq. – The square is framed by late 18C terrace houses in ochre coloured stone. John Loudon **McAdam,** Surveyor to the Bristol Turnpike Trust, was living at no 23, when he devised his new method of road surfacing in 1816. The **Cross** at the corner of the green is 19C replica of the upper section of the former Civic High Cross *(p 206)*.

★ **City Museum and Art Gallery.** – Glass is naturally the special subject of interest:
tc Bristol, Nailsea, Roman, pre-Roman and Chinese and 18C English drinking glasses. The earliest Bristol Clear of 1650, used for decanters and glasses, was followed by Bristol White – made to resemble porcelain and sometimes painted – the famous **Bristol Blue**, 1760-1820, Bristol Green with its gold decoration, and amethyst – two decanters of 1789, 1790. **Nailsea** is distinguished by trailed or splashed white on blue and green.

AVON

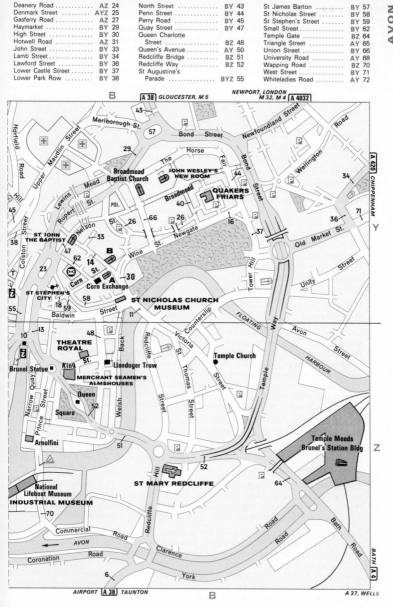

Other galleries display **porcelain** – hard and soft paste – and tin glazed earthenware, all once produced locally – paintings, including *Sunset at Sea after a Storm* by **Francis Danby** (1793-1861), who lived for many years in the city, watches and clocks and a notable selection of period Georgian to *art nouveau* **silver**.

Bristol University (U). – The University **tower** on the hill, a biscuit coloured, stone octagon ending in a circlet of low pinnacles, has been a city landmark since its completion in 1925. The University numbers 7 000 students.

★ Red Lodge. – The lodge is thought to have got its name when it was built in 16C with red painted beams.

Inside, the glory is **16C woodwork**, notably in the **Great Oak Room**, where the panelling is richly carved, one doorway is covered by a shell hood, the other decorated with caryatids. The furniture is massive 16-17C, except in the 18C **Drawing Room**.

★ The OLD CITY *time: 2½ hours*

Bridgehead (BZ). – The lead statue of Neptune dates from 1723.

Cross Broad Quay – Colston Av to Clare St.

★ St Stephen's City (BY). – The city parish church has a **west tower** which rises 130ft by stages of ogee arched bays to a distinctive crown and two-tier pierced balustrade linking 20ft corner turrets which culminate in fountains of close standing pinnacles. The tower *(illustration p 147)* was funded entirely by John Shipward, merchant, mayor and MP, and dates from 1470s when the church was rebuilt on 13C site.

In the irregularly shaped interior, supported on shafted piers with gilded demi-angel capitals, are memorials to **Edmund Blanket** (N aisle), a wealthy cloth weaver (d 1371) and **Martin Pring** (1580-1627), merchant venturer and general of the East India

Company, who discovered Cape Cod in 1603, explored Guiana in 1604, the Virginia coast in 1606 and surveyed the Bristol Channel for a fee of £11 1s in 1610 – the oval plaque was startlingly embellished in 18C with symbolic figures including the mermaid and merman. Note also 17C wrought iron **gates** (*N aisle*) and **swordrest** (*S chancel pillar*), both by William Edney *(p 34)*, and the mediaeval **eagle lectern**.

★ **Corn St** (BY). – The phrase "to pay on the nail" derives from these four **brass nails** on which Bristol corn merchants struck deals and paid in cash. The first nail was cast in 1594.

Corn Exchange. – The giant pilastered and pedimented exchange, before which the nails stand, was built by John Wood the Elder of Bath in the mid-18C.

Lloyds Bank. – The bank designed in Venetian Cinquecente style with columns, coats of arms and exuberant figures along the frieze and in every spandrel, dates from 1854.

Old Council House. – The sober Greek style building is early 19C.

Coffee House. – The house with a hanging sign on an iron bracket is 18C.

All Saints and Christchurch (BY). – Churches have overlooked this crossroads since Saxon times.

All Saints (A). – Although the tower is 18C, parts of the church, as can be seen immediately inside from two great circular pillars supporting single stepped arches, are Norman, and others, such as the slim shafted piers with foliated capitals beneath the open timberwork roofs, early 15C. Note the **memorial** carved by Rysbrack to the considerable local philanthropist, **Edward Colston** (d 1721; *S aisle*).

Christchurch (B). – The Georgian church of 1791, is known popularly for its painted wood **quarter-jacks**, helmeted, moustachioed, kilted and armed with axes.

Broad St (AY 14). – The wide street, which leads to the old city wall, is lined by 17C timber-framed houses and shops.

★ **St John the Baptist** (BY). – The church, including a battlemented tower with a spire, stands over a triple arch, one of the six mediaeval gateways in the city walls. It was founded in 14C by William Frampton (tomb in the canopied recess, *N chancel wall*), three times mayor, on the foundations of an earlier chapel, the site determining the narrowness of the nave and chancel.
The woodwork and furnishings are nearly all early 17C: the wooden lectern, **communion table**, the big **hour-glass** intended to curtail sermons. Much earlier is the **brass** *(chancel)* of Thomas Rowley, merchant and burgess (d 1478) and his wife.

The Conduit. – *Through the arch, in Nelson St.* The conduit which brought water from Brandon Hill to the old priory and the city in 14C, is on the right, still flowing.

High St (BY 30). – The street crosses an area of alleys, lanes and small courts. To its west lies the market with, at its centre, **The Rummer**, an inn of 1743 and holder of no 1 public house licence in Bristol.

★★ **St Nicholas Church Museum** (BY). – St Nicholas is a proud Georgian church which
tc was gutted by fire in 1941 and rebuilt with a soaring white stone spire.
Inside, in the unique setting, are the vast **Hogarth triptych** *(p 37)*, rare church **plate** and vestments and archaeological finds. 14C crypt is now a brass-rubbing centre.

★ **King St** (BZ). – The cobbled street has a unique character with the Floating Harbour at one end, 18 and 19C warehouses, the theatre, pubs and 17C almshouses.
Of the inns, the **Llandoger Trow**, named after the flat bottomed barges which unloaded coal on the adjoining Welsh Back quayside and the original Old Anchor Inn in *Treasure Island,* was built as three stout, half-timbered, merchants' houses in 1663; The Old Duke is an aged inn renamed after Duke Ellington; the Bunch of Grapes, Jolly Cobblers, Admiral Benbow, Naval Volunteer, were all originally private houses.

★★ **Theatre Royal.** – The oldest playhouse in the country still in use, opened to a prologue composed by **David Garrick** in 1766 and was granted a royal licence by George III in 1778.
Outside, the rusticated golden stone ground floor, is superimposed by giant Corinthian columns, a cornice and pediment bearing the George III royal arms. Inside, the wide foyers and staircase beneath a decorated ceiling are modern, the small, horseshoe **auditorium** on three levels with boxes on either side of the proscenium stage, 18C; the colour is dull green and gold with deep pink lining the walls.

★ **Merchant Seamen's Almshouses.** – *NW end.* The almshouses bear the coloured arms of the **Merchant Venturers** on the outside wall, and on the pink washed former quadrangle wall, a board relating how the houses were first built in 1544 and enlarged with funds from **Edward Colston** *(see above)* in 1696. The life story of one of the almsmen on the Spanish Main was used by Edgar Allen Poe as the basis for *The Golden Bug.*

Brunel statue. – At the top of the street, surrounded by new, well designed commercial buildings, stands a more than lifesize, top-hatted bronze of Isambard Kingdom Brunel.

BROADMEAD (BY) *time: 1 hour*

Within the vast new shopping precinct are three buildings of contrasting periods.

Broadmead Baptist Church. – The church of 1967-9 has a subtle simplicity.

★ **John Wesley's New Room.** – The chapel, which has large bronze statues outside
tc each of its two entrances of John Wesley on his horse and Charles Wesley preaching, dates from 1739 and is the oldest especially built place of Methodist worship.
Note the two decker **pulpit**, the **parliament clock**, mahogany communion table, box pews, and gracefully bannistered **gallery**.
It was at 1771 Bristol Conference, held here, that Francis Asbury was chosen to go to America where he became the first Methodist bishop.

★★ **Quakers Friars.** – The use by the Society of Friends from 17 - mid-20C of buildings
tc erected in 13C and occupied until the Dissolution by Dominican or Black Friars is
how Quakers Friars got its name. **Baker's Hall,** inside, with its amazingly ordered **roof**
of 14C oak beams, displays a modern **Historical Tapestry** (1973–5) illustrating Bristol's
1 000 years as a "place by the bridge", merchant venturers' port and modern city.

★★ ST MARY REDCLIFFE and SS GREAT BRITAIN *time: ½ day*

★★ **St Mary Redcliffe** (BZ). – The church is known, in the words of Queen Elizabeth as
the "fairest, goodliest and most famous parish church in England"; Thomas Chatterton,
the young poet born in Redcliffe Way in 1752, named it, more simply "the pride of
Bristowe". It represents the Perpendicular style at its most perfect.
Construction in the pale Dundry stone on an older site began in 1280.

Exterior. – The **spire** rises 292ft; crocketed pinnacles mark the west end, transepts,
porches, the angles of the tower; finialled buttresses separate the wide, pointed
windows of the nave and chancel, before flying to support the immense clerestory
windows.
The **north porch** highlights 270ft front's perfect regularity being hexagonal and set,
like a jewel, off-centre. It stands with two tiers of decorated gables, saintly figures
and a door with a triple, stellate surround, as the antechamber to the shrine of Our
Lady, situated in an inner, more modest porch.
The **iron grids** once protected relics.

Interior. – Slender shafted pillars sweep up to break into **lierne vaulting** in which every
one of the 1 200 and more intersections is masked by a different **boss**, all, except
those beneath the tower, covered in gold leaf. Such variety and richness – the bosses
were gilded in 1740 – is reflected everywhere in the monuments and furnishings.

American or St John the Baptist Chapel. – *NW end.* Abutting the pillars is a contemporary,
painted wooden effigy of **Queen Elizabeth I**, probably a ship's figurehead. On the nave
side of the pillar hangs the full armour of **Admiral Sir William Penn** (d 1670; *tombstone
at entrance to S transept*), father of the founder of Pennsylvania.

South Aisle. – Note the mediaeval octagonal **font** with an angel on the pillar and a gilded
dove; the richly coloured **arms** of Charles II *(over the porch)*; the **stellate tomb recesses.**

South Transept. – The transept serves in part as a chapel to **William Canynges** (1400-74),
shipbuilder, merchant prince, mayor, MP and benefactor, who paid for much of the
rebuilding of the church; in one tomb he lies beside his wife in full colour, in the second
in the vestments of the holy order he joined on his wife's death.

Ambulatory. – The ambulatory passes before the Lady Chapel, for 100 years a school
screened from the chancel by a triptych by Hogarth *(p 36)*. Note 18C brass **candelabra**.
At the crossing and in the chancel are the **lectern**, a really fierce 17C eagle, given
by James Wathen, "pin Maker" and **brasses** commemorating two churchwardens: John
Jay (d 1480), merchant, and John Brook (d 1512), servant-at-law to Henry VIII.

★★ **SS Great Britain** (AZ). – She must have been a wonderful sight at her launching in
tc 1843, and will be so again – one day. Meanwhile this first iron built, propeller driven
Atlantic liner lies in her original dry dock, a vast carcass 322ft long, 51ft across, with
forecastle dock renewed, 43ft bowsprit, reproduction figurehead and gilded
trailboards in place, her keel plates exposed inside, her masts shipped once more...
Museum and guide describe the innovations of **Brunel's** design, the saga of her history
until her return in 1970. Also shown are mementoes of all kinds from both *Great
Britain* and *Great Western* and Bristols' maritime history.

★★ **Industrial Museum** (BZ). – Industry, in the context of this museum in a 1950s
tc warehouse overlooking the Floating Harbour, comprises local manufacturing processes from brick moulding to pin-making, transport from penny-farthing bicycles to
the world's first purpose-built, horse-drawn caravan (1880), a 1948 Bristol car and
historic gauge 1 working railway models.
There is also the definitive collection of Rolls Royce aero engines, made in Bristol,
from the Lucifer of 1918 to jet engines in current production.
The museum steams its engine *Henbury* (1937) regularly and is restoring the steam
tug *Mayflower* (1861).

tc **National Lifeboat Museum** (BZ). – Four "retired" lifeboats from the RNLI service make
wondrous exhibits – one can be climbed into. Also displayed are the new inflatable
boats, battle honours, old photographs of storms, wrecks and launchings – including
the epic dragging of a boat over Porlock Hill *(p 172)* when the slip was stormbound.

ADDITIONAL CITY SIGHTS

Queen Square (BZ). – The square, dating from the time of Queen Anne, was
where merchants built their houses when leaving the ever more noisome city centre
and dockside area; it is graced by a large bronze equestrian **statue of William III** by
Rysbrack.

tc **Arnolfini** (BZ). – This centre of the visual arts, music, cinema and dance is on two
floors of a skillfully converted 1830s tea warehouse, overlooking the Floating Harbour.

Temple Church (BZ). – Bristol's "leaning tower", a monumental stone belfry dating
back to 1300, stands squarely, despite bombing and fire, as a reminder of the
mediaeval Knights Templar. The 144ft structure began to lean at an early stage in
its construction and is 5ft out of true (Pisa: 180ft with 15ft "lean"). *(See pp 33, 34)*.

Temple Meads: Brunel's Station Building (BZ). – Bristol's original GWR station of
1841 has been restored with the intention of transforming it into an exhibition centre
of civil engineering present and past, including notably Isambard Kingdom Brunel
(1806-59), whose unique imprint has become part of the city fabric.

Make for the Hotwell Rd which follows the river course through the Avon Gorge and affords the best view of the bridge.

★★★ **Clifton Suspension Bridge.** — The 702ft long bridge is amazing, as like a spider's thread, it spans the Avon Gorge 245ft above high water. It won Brunel *(p 26)* the designer's prize in open competition in 1829-31 when he was in his early twenties. (Signed drawings submitted by Brunel for the bridge competition, though not that of the actual bridge as built, may be seen at the GWR Museum in Swindon, *p 207*).

His "first child", "his darling", as he called it, despite "going on glorious" in 1836, suffered long delays and was only completed in 1864, five years after his death. Of countless bridge stories, Sarah Ann Henley's is the happiest: a lover's quarrel induced a lover's leap but Sarah Ann's petticoats opened and she parachuted gently down to the mud below – the year was 1885, she married and lived to be 85 !

Continue beside the gorge, under the bridge; bear right up Bridge Valley Rd.

(G Paxton / Aspect / Cosmos)

Clifton Suspension Bridge

Clifton Down. – The down was populated by sheep farmers until prosperous merchants came to build substantial residences overlooking the gorge, speculative builders to construct Georgian crescents, Regency squares and terraces and Victorian streets. In 18C the area became known through the short-lived Hotwells Spa; in 19C it acquired fame with the opening of the Suspension Bridge.

★★ **Bristol Zoological Gardens.**
tc – The famous zoo, opened in 1836, is delighted in by some for the brilliance of its flower-beds, the architecture of its newly built houses – the Reptile and Ape Houses especially – and by all for its elephants, pink flamingos, gorillas, rare okapi and unique white tigers...

★★ **Clifton R C Cathedral of SS Peter and Paul.** – After three years abuilding, the cathedral was consecrated on 29 June 1973 (in place of 19C pro-cathedral).

A white, 165ft, three plane steeple mark the new church: trees, gardens, a moat, blend the scene to receive with total naturalness the harsh sounding materials: white concrete, pink granite agglomerate, black fibre-glass, lead and glass.

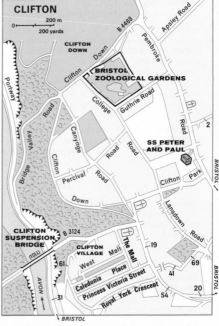

Interior. – The design motif is the hexagon – elongated to afford a direct view from all sides of the white marble high altar, regular in the flooring, the lanterns, the lights on high, the outline of the organ bay, reduced to a chevron for the flowing stream at the foot of the carved Portland and Purbeck stone font...

Warm colour comes from brown ochre furnishings and wood, limpid blue, greens, greys and jewel reds and yellows from the long, symbolic **windows** of massive glass.

★ **Clifton Village.** – The **Mall, Caledonia Place, Princess Victoria St, Royal York Crescent** and several other streets, with their late 18 – early 19C terrace houses and small shops, make a delightful village apart from the city bustle.

EXCURSION

★ **Blaise Castle House Museum.** – *5m NNW up A4018* **(AY)** *and B4055.*

tc The museum in 18C house at the centre of undulating parkland illustrates English domestic life in town and country between 1750-1900 by way of embroidered waistcoats and Victoriana, dolls, quilted bedcovers, children's and adults' games, bronze wool weights with George I's cypher, "dissected" or jig-saw puzzles, a case of Bristol watchmakers' timepieces...

★★ **Blaise Hamlet.** – *N side of B4057, Weston Rd.* The group of ten, originally thatched, all different, cottages were designed by John Nash in 1812 to stand round a green with no front door facing any other to stop gossip about visitors! The hamlet is a unique and highly successful example, suitably bedecked with bright flowers in the pocket handkerchief sized gardens, of chocolate-box or the cottage orné style of architecture.

★ CHEW MAGNA   Pop 1 411

Michelin map **403** fold 27 – M29

Chew Magna, well established by Domesday, was described in 1546 by John Leland, antiquary to Henry VIII, as "a praty clowthing towne". The wool market has shifted but the town remains, straggling along the main street and opening out by the church and the square. This last, triangular in shape, is overlooked by the Georgian, pink stone **Harford House**, a small town house again Georgian, and a range of cottages, some white rendered others of random pink stone.

The 13-16C church stands back from the road, its pinnacled and fiercely gargoyled west tower a proud 99½ft tall. Inside, note the **arcades**, of which the southern, with hexagonal columns, is 13C EE and the northern, 15C Perpendicular. The fluted Norman **font**, the restored mediaeval **rood screen**, 15 and 16C recumbents on the tomb chests and, in a niche, 14C highly coloured wooden effigy of a knight, smiling benignly as he plants one foot on a surprised, sitting lion. (The inscription is Victorian and inaccurate.) At the gate is **Church House**, a long, early 16C building.

EXCURSIONS

★ **Stanton Drew Stone Circles.** – *3m E; S of B3130. Just before the village bear left* *tc down a lane and left again for Court Farm.*

Walk through to the field, peaceful with chestnut trees, cows and the age-old stones. The scattered, Bronze Age site consists of **three circles:** the Great Circle, with a diameter of 370ft has 27 stones in place, 3 standing upright and the Northeast Circle, 100ft in diameter, 8 stones, 4 upright. The Southwest Circle is on private ground.

Return to the village and bear left, past the church to the Druid's Arms.

Behind the inn, a group of stones one fallen and two upright is known as the **Cove.**

The local legend. – Legends connected with the stones abound, the most popular being that "it's a company that assisted at a nuptial ceremony thus petrify'd": the Cove is the parson, the bride and groom, the circles are the company who danced through Saturday and from midnight, to the tune of a stranger who played ever faster until at dawn the hypnotised dancers turned to stone. The fiddler, the devil in disguise, said he would play again one day release them, but the dancers wait and wait...

Chew Valley Lake. – *4m S by B3114.*

The 1 200 acre (4 500 million gallons) reservoir lake lies in a beautiful, drowned valley.

CLAVERTON   Pop 109

Michelin map **403** fold 26 – N29

The village extends in name from the River Avon and the Kennet and Avon Canal, up a steep hill to the traditional manor house and beyond, on the down, to the new buildings of Bath University.

SIGHTS

★★ **American Museum.** – Room by room, with floors, ceilings, panelling re-installed from *tc* 18-19C houses in different states, the museum puts into context and fills out the gaps in impressions gained from films, westerns, songs, jazz, novels...

Keeping Room. – A late 17C room from **Massachusets** opens the sequence, illustrating with its stout beams, massive fireplace, wide planked floor and solid turned and highly polished furniture, life in the substantially built houses so different from the dwellings of the first settlers.

Four 18C Rooms. – The rooms present regional differences and changing fashions: the Lee Room from **New Hampshire**, is sheathed in blue-green wall boarding, the Perley and Deming Parlors from **Massachusets** and **Connecticut**, have pine panelling and painted walls, curving early Queen Anne and later Chippendale-style furniture; the Deer Park Parlor, from **Maryland**, shows the influence of Hepplewhite and Sheraton.

Greek Revival Room. – The early 19C room from New York displays an imaginative use of Classical themes.

Two Bedrooms. – The rooms are in complete contrast: the first from 1830 **Connecticut** house exhibits painted and stencilled decoration, the second, from **New Orleans** on the eve of the Civil War, large scale furniture adapted from the Louis XV style.

Spicing the exhibition are displays of **textiles**, including hooked rugs, patchwork and quilts, silver, pewter and glass. There are dioramas and set pieces on opening up the west, cowboys, Indians; rooms on the Spanish-influenced New Mexico, the Pennsylvania-Germans, the **Shakers**... Finally, there are 18C tavern, where gingerbread is baked and 19C country store.

The gardens. – In the gardens overlooking the wooded valley of the River Avon, are a covered Conestoga Wagon, a copy of a Northern Cheyenne Indian tepee, 19C milliner's shop with a delightful collection of band-boxes, George Washington's Mount Vernon garden and a folk art gallery with a collection ranging from naive portraits to weathervanes, cigar store to carousel figures, an Indian brave figurehead, tin marriage gifts...

★ **Claverton Pump.** – *On far side of A36. Take Ferry Lane across the canal; cross the*
tc *railway line.*

The pump of 1813 has been restored to raise water from the River Avon into the canal which from 1810 linked the River Kennet (navigable Reading – Newbury) and the Avon (Bath – Bristol) *(p 199)*.

The pair of elm paddelled, breast shot wheels, each 12ft wide and 17½ft in diameter, driven by the headrace, turn the pitwheel, flywheel, crankshaft, working beams and finally, the pumps, which, with a sighing, watery whoosh, lift 50 gallons a stroke or 87 000 gallons an hour.

★ **CLEVEDON COURT**

Michelin map **403** fold 35 – L29

tc The mellow stone house, begun in 14C, had achieved its present appearance by 1570; the interior, which displays every period, has all the attraction and comfort of an Edwardian country house.

TOUR *¾ hour*

Great Hall. – The 14C hall with Tudor windows and fireplace is hung with family portraits among who is **Abraham Elton**, purchaser of the house in 1709, Master of the Bristol Merchant Venturers, mayor and and MP. The chairs are Stuart, the **drawer table** late 16C, the Dutch **chandelier**, 17C.

State Bedroom. – The bedroom, 14C solar with an inserted Elizabethan window, reflects the family taste through ten generations. Among the contents are: a portrait of the merchant, Nicholas Elton, a Hepplewhite **tester bed**, Queen Anne **spoonback chairs**, Cromwellian chairs and chests, late Georgian and Regency pieces and small 18-19C **children's chairs**.

Hanging Chapel. – The chapel has unique reticulated **window tracery**. The prayer desks are 17C, the Biblical carvings, 15 and 16C, the glass, 19C.

Note in the smaller bedrooms portraits of and drawings by **Thackeray** including Jane Octavia Brookfield, model for Lady Castlewood in *Henry Esmond* and of Arthur Hallam, nephew of the then owner of Clevedon Court, in whose memory **Tennyson** wrote *In Memoriam*.

Justice Room. – The small room and walls of an adjoining staircase display a fascinating collection of the local **Nailsea glass** made between 1788 and 1873. There are bottles and jars and "friggers" or craftsmen's spare time mouldings including green glass hats, trailed, blotched and colour striped perfume bellows, rolling pins and a unique set of brilliantly coloured walking sticks.

Old Kitchen. – The kitchen contains a rare collection of **Eltonware**, the remarkable experimental pottery of Sir Edmund Elton, man of many parts, designer of Clevedon Clock Tower (*see below*), who essayed new shapes, decoration on coloured slips and metal lustrework.

The Garden. – The outlook is over Clevedon Moor to the Bristol Channel and Wales; immediately behind, the hillside rises steeply, covered in dense woods. Between is a long, steeply terraced garden on three levels comprising wide borders blooming at the feet of precipitous stone walls.

EXCURSION

★ **Clevedon.** – Pop 18 115. *1½m.*

The Victorian resort which grew out of a fishing village, retains its wide 19C roads bordered by substantial villas, Tuscan, Gothic or Italianate in style, rows of cottages built in local stone, unhurried shops and, along the promenade, gardens with closely mown lawns, flowers and trees, particularly pines all the more picturesque for being windbent. Characteristic of the time also are the **bandstand** (Green Beach Gardens), the **Clock Tower** and the pagoda roofed **pier** (1869).

From the park benches the **view**★★ extends across the channel to the Welsh hills.

tc **The building of the house.** – Dyrham Park presents a rare contrast in its two 17-18C fronts: the one is an example of formality and symmetry; the other, equally classical but lightened by touches of Baroque ornament... Both were built within ten years for the same man, William Blathwayt (1649-1717), an efficient administrator and diplomat in the service of the Stuart Kings and William III. His taste had been formed by his uncle, Thomas Povey of Lincoln's Inn, connoisseur, man of fashion, *bon vivant* and friend of Samuel Pepys and John Evelyn. Although he married an heiress – he inherited Dyrham through his marriage – and became rich by his appointments, he maintained that he "never pretended to any fortune".

Blathwayt's first architect took back the existing Tudor house to the Great Hall and built instead a formal, perfectly regular entrance front of local stone. In 1698 the second building phase began. Blathwayt chose as architect this time "the ingenious **Mr. Talman**", Comptroller of the Royal Works, second to Sir Christopher Wren, a travelled squire, collector and maverick architect. This front, 130ft long in Cotswold stone, with two storeys and an attic, the same balustrade and urns as on the other side, is mellowed by such touches as rustication of the ground floor, quoins, alternate pediments and carved panels above the first floor windows, Tuscan pillars framing the door... An additional "dressing" is the round windowed orangery added in 1701.

The garden and park. – To complete the house, Talman and the garden designer, George Wise, laid out formal gardens of parterres, fountains and waterworks including a stepped cascade.

By the turn of 18-19C garden design had changed *(p 22)*; the Bath – Gloucester road had been improved exactly reversing the best approach to the house. The fronts were accordingly inverted, and **Humphrey Repton** was called upon to replan the park.

TOUR ¾ *hour*

East Entrance Hall. – The walls are hung with richly embossed **leather,** purchased at 3*s* a skin when Blathwayt was in the Hague, where he possibly also obtained the blue and white **delftware.**

Great Hall. – The hall is all that remains, and that only in name, of the Tudor house; the sash windows – though the sills have been raised – the **book presses**, to the design of Samuel Pepys, were there in Blathwayt's time, also the pictures of the monarchs he served and **portraits** by Michael Dahl of himself and Mary Wynter, his wife. The fine set of Dutch walnut "parade" chairs date from *c*1700.

West Hall. – Note the **delft tile pictures** of exotic scenes and fruits by the fireplace, 17C **muskets** and Blathwayt's own "under and over" holster **pistols**, the fireside companion "pareing of an apple", the **Cromwellian chairs** re-covered in Dutch leather in *c*1700.

White Stair. – By the staircase are **licences** of 1511 and 1620 to enclose 500 acres as parkland, a **Kyp engraving** of 1712 and a drawing of the grounds after the Repton replanting.

The virtuosity of the *Great Perspective* painting at the top of the stairs was much admired by 17C London society, notably Pepys, when it hung in Thomas Povey's rooms.

Other rooms. – Among the furniture and furnishings note especially the period **blackamoor torchères** and delft flowerpot still standing in the chimney as recorded in 1710 (Balcony Room); the early 18C **Flemish tapestries**, bed and its hangings and **tortoise-shell chest** (Tapestry Room); the two **Rococo mirrors** by John Linnell, gilded side-table, Murillo's *Peasant Woman and Boy* and the most un-Spanish copy by the young Gainsborough (Drawing Room).

The **Cedar Staircase** is cantilevered.

The gilt **Leather Closet** was especially designed to increase still further the perspective in the illusionist *View down a Corridor* painted in 1662 by Hoogstraeten.

The **Mortlake tapestries** belonged to Povey who was a director of the factory (Diogenes Room); the **state bed** was ordered for a proposed state visit by Queen Anne in 1704 when the Carolean stools were recovered in the same material as the bed hangings.

ADDITIONAL SIGHTS

Dyrham Church. – *Access by road through the village or up from the garden.* The church with an embattled tower, a porch with quatrefoil parapets and Perpendicular windows, was rebuilt at different periods in 15C. The **Flemish triptych** is 15C.

Dyrham Village. – Pop 260. The village of 17-18C stone houses and cottages is named in the *Anglo-Saxon Chronicle*, as the site of the key battle of 577 after in which the West Saxons advanced to the Severn Estuary, dividing the Britons in Cornwall from those in Wales.

When visiting London use the **Green Guide "London"**

Detailed descriptions of places of interest

Useful local information

A section on the historic square mile of the City of London with a detailed fold out plan

The lesser known London boroughs – their people, places and sights

Plans of selected areas and important buildings.

HORTON COURT

Michelin map ▦ fold 27 – M29 – 3m NE of Chipping Sodbury

tc The small manor house, hall and church in Cotswold stone have stood as a group for centuries in this green valley: the hall is 12C, the church and court were rebuilt in 14-15C.

The Court. – At the centre of the gabled, stone manor house the modest **doorway** was exuberantly transformed in 16C by the then owner, William Knight, who was appointed prebendary of Horton, protonotary of the Holy See and, in 1527, Henri VIII's envoy in the unsuccessful divorce negotiations. Each of Knight's advances appears round the door: the **arms** granted on the prebendaryship, the **protonotary's hat** (resembling a cardinal's but with fewer tassels) and carved **Renaissance columns** for the return from Rome !

The Hall. – The building, a unique link between Saxon domestic halls and later mediaeval halls, dates from 1100-50. Despite strengthening, rebuilding, conversion to other uses – RC chapel in an inserted upper hall in 18C when the house belonged to a descendant of the letterwriting **Pastons**, and the introduction of a Tudor fireplace – there remain, unscathed, the **south doorway** and, opposite, the **north door** in a wall of early dressed stone.

The Ambulatory. – Walk round the house to see the valley, the garden with a giant **tulip tree** and the detached ambulatory, built by Knight after the manner of an Italian loggia.

The Church. – St James, built in 14C on the site of the Norman church contemporary with the hall, has been repeatedly altered and restored. It has a 14C arcade, wagon roofs, a re-cut Norman font with 17C cover, a Jacobean pulpit and several Paston memorial tablets.

WESTON-SUPER-MARE   Pop 58 194

Michelin map ▦ fold 26 – K29
See town plan in the current Michelin Red Guide Great Britain and Ireland

It's all there ! The dark gold sands extending as far as the eye can see, scoured twice daily by the tide, the donkeys, the arc of the bay fringed by hotels, restaurants, shops and stalls, the public gardens, model village, bowls tournaments, carnivals... and always the people: a population that has quadrupled since the turn of the century, ¼ million and more visitors each year and 1 ½ million who come on day-trips.

★★ **The view.** – Across the bay lie the islands of **Flat Holm** (light; *p 17*) and **Steep Holm** (bird sanctuary); to the south is the square towered **Uphill Church** (19C on 1 000 year old site), further over, the long finger of Bream Down Point (Somerset) and, on the horizon, the Welsh hills.

(After Unichrome photo)

The Gorgon's Head

CORNWALL

Area 1376 sq m Population 429 587

Cornwall is a county of "diversified pleasings" as Richard Carew phrased it (p 46); of wonderful coastal scenery, jagged headlands, sheer cliffs and offshore needles: of open moorland, rock outcrops and standing stones; of boats; of heron haunted river valleys with banks densely fringed with oak trees; of lone farms standing at the centre of high walled fields in the windswept, undulating countryside; of the Furry Dance and 'Obby 'Oss; of golden sand beaches and rock coves; of Celtic legend and the saints, of King Arthur and fairy tale giants. It is a land of heroic small churches; of the chimneys of derelict copper and tin mines pointing to the sky; of sunsets; of Cornish cream, fresh crab and fish direct from the sea; of slate, granite, red fuchsias, glorious gardens, views extending in the clear light to the always encircling sea... so many Cornwalls.

The land. – Farming has changed from the vast sheep flocks of the Middle Ages, 16 and 17C (p 13) to cattle and arable and, since the coming of the railway in 19C, to the production of early vegetables and in the far west and Isles of Scilly, to flowers.

Mining. – Diodorus Siculus, 1C BC Greek historian, wrote that the Cornish "work the tin into pieces the form of knuckle-bones and convey it to an island which lies off Britain and is called Ictis... the merchants purchase the tin of the natives and carry it from there across the Straits of Gaul" to Greece, Rome or Egypt.

An ingot of that period, shaped in an H form and weighing nearly 160 lbs, was found in the River Fal and is now in Truro Museum. The alluvial tin from which it was made was "clean" or nearly pure and could be smelted with charcoal obtained from the dense woods then covering much of the county; production was local and with tin so important, by the early Middle Ages the "streamers" or miners had acquired rights and privileges including special courts and a local parliament in four stannary or coinage towns chartered by King John – Truro, Helston, Liskeard and Lostwithiel (to which Penzance was added in 1663). There the courts sat, the ingots were assayed and stamped (see below) or "coined" with the Duchy seal – hence Coinage St in Helston.

Between 1770-1870 copper took precedence over tin: gun manufacture was changing; the Royal Navy became supreme; there were wars in Europe, the Napoleonic wars, in the Crimea; there were the American War of Independence and Civil War and always there was war at sea.

There were 340 mines in operation in Cornwall employing one in five of the population or 50 000 men, women and children – these last with the job of crushing the mined ore with stamping machines and picking it over; 30 million tons of ore were mined in the century, producing 1 ½ million tons (5%) of pure copper (smelted with coal in Wales); the peak price reached was £100 a ton. England in 19C became the greatest single copper producer in the world – to prevent parasites and barnacles attacking the hulls of British men o'war and increase their speed, they were "copper bottomed".

At the end of 19C, recession spread from America to Europe; new and more accessible deposits were discovered in every continent; prices fell; the mines closed; more than 30% of the miners and their families emigrated until it was said that at the bottom of every hole the world over you would find a Cornish miner. Today (1985) the search is again for tin; there are four working mines at Geevor (p 63), South Crofty, Wheal Jane and Tolgus and Poldark together which produce about ¼ of England's annual requirement or 4 000 tons. Relics of the old mines, in the form of disused engine houses and sentinel stacks (p 60), romantically mark the hills along the north coast and even Cape Cornwall.

China-clay mining around St Austell, by comparison, is a modern industry. Hugely profitable it has marked the local landscape with green-white slag pyramids, and is now Cornwall's economic mainstay.

The Duchy of Cornwall. – William of Normandy created his half-brother, Roger of Mortain, first Earl of Cornwall soon after the Conquest. Roger's lands extended far beyond the bounds of Cornwall into Devon, Somerset and even Gloucester.

In 1337 the Duchy of Cornwall was created by Edward III from the former earldom, for his son Edward, the Black Prince (1330-76). Since 1503 the monarch's eldest son as heir apparent has always succeeded to the title. The lands still extend beyond the confines of Cornwall into Devon (including much of Dartmoor) and Somerset today number 130 000 acres in the West Country alone.

The dukedom until 19C, gained its wealth from the "coinage" dues or stamp with the duchy seal which was required on every smelted block of tin before it could be sold, a duty performed in the Stannary Towns of both Cornwall and Devon. In 1838 the dues were abolished by parliament and compensation paid. Today the Duchy leases estates, farms and individual houses to tenants, farms land and manages great tracts of woodland on its own behalf. Work on the Duchy estates is displayed each year in exhibits at the Royal Cornwall Agricultural Show.

The Celtic Church. – Cornwall, the refuge beyond the Tamar of the pagan Celts, was evangelised by missionaries from Ireland and Wales, miraculous tales being told of how the saintly men sailed the sea in coracles, on millstones and on lillypads.

Patrick the future patron saint of Ireland, was born a Romano-Briton Christian in England,

43

Wales or Scotland in c389. When he was in his teens he was captured by pirates and taken to Ireland from where he escaped after six years to France. He travelled, possibly, throughout Brittany, then to Auxerre, where he was consecrated bishop, and finally to Rome. In c435 the pope sent him back to Ireland to convert the people which he largely succeeded in doing through tireless travelling, preaching, conversion of the chiefs and by his example. Whether he personally ever visited Cornwall or the southwest is not known; he died in c461 in Ireland.

As Ireland became converted, missionary monks set out for Rome along the route followed by traders since 6C BC when the Phoenicians would sail into southern Cornwall for local copper and tin and Irish gold; several of these Irish and, later, Welsh Celtic priests, deeply venerated while they were alive, were canonised by the early Church.

The evangelist monks preached in the open air; as sites became recognised places of assembly and worship they were marked by a cross and, later, by small chapels. The chapels were constructed of wood, except probably in west Cornwall where wood is scarce and stone cairns would have been built instead; the primitive chapels were gradually replaced by stone works as the Saxons began the subjugation of Cornwall in c830. In turn, the Saxon works were rebuilt in Norman-Romanesque style in 12-13C – there would have been a time-lag for the Norman style to reach the county.

The fervour of the people whose lives on the land had always been so poor, and at sea so perilous, the ardour of the church itself, brought about a new wave of rebuilding in 15-17C, in the Perpendicular style when there was a wave of prosperity among the tin-miners. Thereafter came a period, lasting 2-300 years, of almost total neglect, followed, in 19C, by vigorous restoration which, at least, saved the fabric. Work undertaken today has tended to bring out again the local character of the buildings.

What to look at generally in the churches. – Outside, the towers are all different, most noticeably those on the coast which served as important landmarks to mariners; slate, to be seen on the roofs, serves also as louvres in belfry openings, as biscuit thin tombstones in churchyards and memorial tablets against church walls outside and in and is often beautifully lettered and incised.

Inside, note the oak wagon roofs, sometimes with carved wall plates; the massive fonts, circular with bold geometric moulding, and, especially, the powerful, square-cut, granite vessels, with bearded heads, once coloured, at the angles. Finally, look out for 15-16C bench-ends, carved in oak with Biblical and local scenes and personalities.

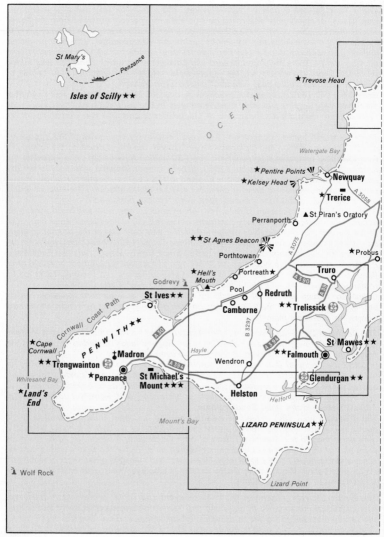

Celtic crosses. – There are some 300 crosses scattered in the county marking sacred sites (see above), in churchyards (usually E of S porch), by the wayside or in fields, indicating the route followed by pall bearers bringing a corpse for burial.

The crosses, incised on the shaft with typical Celtic-Irish interlacings and knots, are carved with signs of the Cross, the XP monogram, the figure of Christ, on occasion in a tunic (illustration p 216).

The See of Cornwall. – Historically the Cornish church remained independent of the Saxon Christian church established by St Augustine until 926 AD, when King Athelstan, having completed the political and religious conquest of Cornwall, created a Cornish See (p 46) on the Saxon model. The bishopric endured until 1043 when it was transferred first to Crediton then to Exeter. Only in 1876 did Cornwall once again become independent, a new cathedral being erected in Truro in celebration.

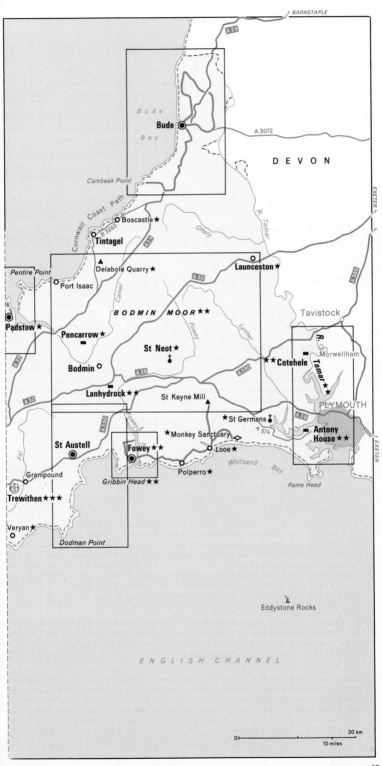

★★ ANTONY HOUSE

tc Visitors cross the park and turn into the forecourt. Before them stands a Classical grey stone house, extended through short colonnades to advanced wings built of red brick. It was completed in 1721; inside it is lively with portraits and mementoes.

TOUR *¾ hour*

The Halls. – The halls are dominated by one of the four unforgettable portraits painted by Edward Bower of **King Charles I** at his trial *(pp 11, 61)*. In addition there hang on the walls the likenesses of Sir William Carew, ardent Jacobite and builder of the house and **Richard Carew** *(by the staircase)* high sheriff, colonel of the troops guarding the estuary at the time of the Armada and author of the still fascinating *Survey of Cornwall* of 1602.

Staircase. – Note the three turned balusters to each tread and the original bubble lights.

Dining Room. – The **chairs** outside the door are covered by still bright 17-18C Soho tapestry, those inside are by Chippendale. Against the panelled walls hang early sporting paintings and between the windows a lovely Queen Anne pier-glass.

Saloon. – The room, again panelled, contains three **portraits** by Reynolds.
The Queen Anne **furniture** includes a pair of mirrors, each above a gesso table, made especially for the exact position in which they still stand.
The George I period chandelier is Waterford glass; the china includes Dr Wall (1752-76) Worcester vases, Chelsea vases and late 18C Staffordshire cockerels.

Tapestry Room. – The carved gilt wood, eight branch **chandelier** is William and Mary, the Diogenes tapestries are 18C Soho; the mirror in the chimneypiece was fitted when the house was built in 1721. The **tables** are William and Mary with seaweed marquetry, George I with satyr's masks and Queen Anne with carved Red Indians' heads. The **armchairs** are by Chippendale.

Library. – The library, which contains a copy of the *Survey of Cornwall,* is hung with Carew family **portraits** and a likeness of Sarah Jennings, Duchess of Marlborough.

Upstairs. – The sporting paintings on the west staircase walls are by Francis Sartorius (1734-1804); in the bedrooms, among the four posters note the rare 18C single beds.

EXCURSION

★ **St Germans.** – Pop 2 316. *9m WNW by A374 and a by-road.*
The old village, with neatly kept stone cottages set in gardens overflowing with roses and clematis, has at its centre the attractive and practically designed Sir William Moyle **Almshouses** of 1583 (restored 1967).

★ **St Germans Church.** – *1/2m E.* The church possesses a majestic **west front** in which dissimilar towers frame a Norman doorway, richly encircled by seven decorated orders carved in the local, dark blue-grey-green, Elvan stone.
The doorway was begun before 1185, the towers in *c*1200 but abondoned until 13 and 15C when the north tower was completed to an octagonal plan with EE lancet windows and the 72ft south tower in the Perpendicular style. Simultaneously work progressed on the attached monastery, for St Germans was a priory church of which Athelstan in 930, appointed the abbot Bishop of Cornwall. In 1403 the see passed to Crediton *(p 88)*.
Inside note the Lady Chapel window with glass by Burne-Jones, the Norman capitals, the battered Purbeck stone font and 15C porch with a groined moorstone roof.

BODMIN   Pop 12 269

Bodmin, named as Cornwall's only town in the Domesday Book, described as the "greatest Markett town in the Shere" with a population of 2 000 in Henry VIII's reign, was, for centuries, the centre of activity in the county. It was too active perhaps: in 1496 its citizens were among the leaders of a protest march on London against an excessive levy on tin – they were massacred; in 1497 they supported the unsuccessful Perkin Warbeck; in 1549, with Helston, Bodmin took part in the unsuccessful Cornish uprising against the imposition of the English Prayer Book. In 19C it replaced Launceston as the seat of the County, now the Crown Court... but in 1870s it refused access to the Great Western Railway and Bodmin Road Station was built 4 ½ miles away. It was thus spared commercialisation, but county offices, the library, museum, the cathedral and businesses established themselves in Truro.

★ **St Petroc.** – In 1469 the parishioners determined to rebuild their Norman church in the new Perpendicular style. It was completed in 1472, was 151ft long by 65ft wide and cost £196 7*s* 4*d* (half a million in today's money). Everyone contributed: the 40 guilds, the vicar, who presented a year's salary, while others gave materials and labour.

Interior. – Beneath the slim pillars with their small capitals are the free-standing tomb of Prior Thomas Vivian (d 1533) carved in grey marble and black Catacleuse stone *(p 48)*, 12C **font**, fantastically carved with winged heads (note the eyes: shut before, open after baptism) and deeply undercut foliage, trees of life and wierd beasts and 12C **ivory casket** *(S wall)*, richly decorated and once a reliquary containing the bones of St Petroc (d 564), a Welsh prince who became the master-builder of the Celtic Church in the west country. In the churchyard is the holy well of St Goron, Petroc's forerunner.

Bodmin with an elevation of 800–1 400ft and an area of less than 150 sq miles, is the smallest of the three West Country moors; it is gaunt and wild with rock outcrops, heather, high tors – a savage bleakness in winter, and a beauty all its own in summer.
Guarding the moor to east and west are two historic castles, Launceston and Restormel and encircling it, either just on the moor or in the deep wooded valleys which surround it, a number of small villages with attractive churches. The rivers, Inny, Lynher, Fowey, St Neot and De Lank, flow north – south; the only main road, A30, runs northeast – its staging post for the last 300 years the Jamaica Inn.

LANDMARKS, TOWNS, VILLAGES on the Moor

Altarnun. – Pop 2 173. The village, sheltered in a wooded valley high on the moor, gets its name from St Nona, the mother of St David, who came from Wales in *c*527 – the period of the **Celtic cross** in the churchyard.
The present **church ★** of weathered moorstone (outcrop granite) with 108ft, embattled and pinnacled tower is 15C. Of especial note are the superb Norman **font** with deeply carved rosettes between once coloured bearded faces at each angle, the monolithic pillars, capitals and bases, the wagon roofs, rood-screen, full width Jacobean **altar-rail** and the **bench-ends**, 79 in all, carved by Robert Daye (bench nearest the font) in 1510-30 with the Instruments of the Passion, St Michael, local worthies, a fiddler, bagpipe player, jester...

★ **Blisland.** – Pop 511. Church and village stand high on the moor, round a tree planted green. The 11C **church ★** has a tower which abuts the north transept and a staircase turret which overtops 15C pinnacles. Note 18C slate sundial, the faces among the **bosses** on 1420 south porch wagon roof and the fonts – one Norman, circular with herringbone moulding, one 15C, octagonal with shields in quatrefoils – the brass of 1410 *(chancel)* and **slate memorial** of 1624 with six kneeling figures.

Bolventor. – **Jamaica Inn,** at the centre of the moor, a staging post for those making the crossing in 16-19C was named after the West Indian island where a onetime owner had grown rich on his sugar plantations. Built of granite and roofed and hung with slate, the inn, is crowded in all its low beamed rooms all summer but out of season is worth a visit for its **views.** It is, of course, the setting for Daphne du Maurier's novel, *Jamaica Inn.*

Brown Willy. – At 1 375ft, Brown Willy is the highest tor on the moor.

★ **Camelford.** – Pop 1 880. The town, beside the River Camel, centres on a small square lined by 18-19C houses and the old town hall sporting a gilded camel as weathervane.
tc The **North Cornwall Museum of Rural Life,** in a onetime coach and wagon building, displays the full ranges of tools required by blacksmiths, wheelwrights, slate and granite quarriers, reapers, cobblers – there must be 100 pairs of lasts for feet of all sizes!

Cardinham. – Pop 438. The village, close to the wooded Glynn Valley, has a late 15C **church ★** with a three stage granite tower. Of earlier sanctuaries there remain 9-10C Celtic Crosses, a Norman font, inscribed stones *(by the sedilia)* and 14C **brass** *(beneath carpet, S of altar);* dating from 15C are the wagon roofs above the aisles and porch and 71 robustly carved bench-ends. Note also the plaster strapwork **royal arms** of 1661.

The Cheesewring. – The stone pile is a natural formation which, according to legend, was the dwelling of a druid who offered water to travellers from a cup of gold.

Dozmary Pool. – The pool, at 1 000ft above sea-level, is associated with Excalibur *(p 71)* and, by tradition, is bottomless, although it has been known to dry up!

The Hurlers. – The Hurlers, the only standing stones on the moor, comprises three circles numbering 9, 17 and 13 stones, in line but of unequal diameter.

Laneast. – Pop 134. From outside **St Sidwell's ★** one sees a tall Celtic cross, an embattled and pinnacled 14-15C granite tower and the church itself, an early 15C rebuilding of a Norman church. Inside are a robust Norman **font** with three corner heads, slate memorials, a rood-screen, early 16C pulpit and 38 **bench-ends** carved in 16C.

★ **Launceston.** – Pp 57-8.

Liskeard. – Pop 6 335. The town is on two facing hillsides with late Georgian (The Parade) and early Victorian houses and a portentous, Italianate town hall (1859). The **church ★,** high on the hill, was described by Leland as a "fair large thing". Repeatedly restored, there remain a Norman font bowl *(stoup in N porch),* a **chancel arch** – rare in Cornwall – 16C font, a Jacobean oak pulpit dated 1636, royal arms of George II, a notice about ladies' pattens, a sundial of 1779 *(S porch),* a number of consecration crosses *(N and S walls)* and, at the west end, a small **leper's window** of three equal lights divided by stone mullions (there was a leper hospital for 200 years at Maudlin, ½ mile away).
tc Modern glass is made in a mill in the main street (Merlin Glass).

Michaelstow. – Pop 225. The 15C **church ★,** with 9ft Celtic cross in the churchyard, is known for its furnishings: the wagon roofs rest on granite arcades, the benches are 15-16C, the octagonal font 15C; the beautifully lettered **slate memorial plates** are embellished with running line engravings of winged heads of cherubim, of young girls or even full length figures in costume – Jane Merifield 1663.

★ **Restormel Castle.** – 1½ m N of Lostwithiel.
tc The 12-13C shell keep of local slate shale rock, stands on a spur above the River Fowey. Walk through the gate-house and circle the walls to overlook the inner courtyard, the kitchen with its great fireplace, the hall and chapel and command the circular **panorama ★.**

Rough Tor. – The granite boss, pronounced "Rowtor", stands out at 1 311ft as the second highest point on the moor.

BODMIN MOOR★★

St Breward. – Pop 775. On the edge of the moor and at 600ft the highest **church**★ in Cornwall, St Breward stands on a site hallowed since Norman times – 5 fat round columns of uneven height with scalloped capitals remain as testimony inside the present 15C rebuilding. Note the copy of a watercolour by Rowlandson (c1800), the royal arms, the figured 17C **slate memorial plates** and, outside, the neat granite blocks of the **tower**. The sundial dates from 1792. Nearby is the stone-built, wind-buffeted, Old Inn, all beams and fireplaces inside.

St Endellion. – Pop 1148. The village is well-known as the setting in its Perpendicular **church**★★ for the major work of the sculptor, the **Master of St Endellion.** Anonymous in all other respects, he lives on through a tomb chest superbly carved in sleek, black Catacleuse stone with small columns and cusped arches. By the door is a stoup, again by the Master.

★ **St Kew.** – Pop 867. The **church**★ stands tall with a buttressed and battlemented west tower where the road turns between wooded hillsides. The only neighbours are the late Georgian vicarage, the Elizabethan St Kew Inn and the Craftsmen's Barn (studios, workshops).

St Kew is light inside with slender columned granite arcades beneath wagon roofs and wall plate angels. There are an Elizabethan **pulpit**, royal arms of 1661, **slate monuments** from 1601 – "All is vanity but vertue" – and 15C **stained glass** in clear colours depicting the Passion from the *Entry into Jerusalem* to the *Harrowing of Hell.*

St Mabyn. – Pop 471. The **church**★ is chiefly notable for its 15C **tower** of three stages, abutted partway by a stair turret and unusually decorated with carved figures.

★ **St Neot.** – *P 70.*

St Teath. – Pop 1 730. The 15C **church**★ is a rebuilding around a Norman foundation. Wagon roofs and font are complemented by a Jacobean **pulpit,** figure painted **almsbox** and a **slate memorial** of 1636 with carved figures *(W end, near porch door).*

★ **St Tudy.** – Pop 458. The attractive village has a 15C **church** on Saxon-Norman foundations with a tall, pinnacled tower. Perpendicular windows, granite **arcades** and **wagon roofs** with foliated wall plates, provide the setting for the square Norman font, an earlier carved head *(facing S door)* and 5-6C Celtic gravestone *(in porch).*

BUDE

Pop 5 662

Michelin map 408 fold 33 – G31

Bude, a haven in the cliffs standing tall against the incoming Atlantic, offers a pale gold sand beach, noisy with darting children, sheltered by the grass topped headlands and braided by a long line of beachhuts sprucely painted purple, mauve, blue, green...

★★ **The Breakwater.** – Walk out onto the breakwater beyond 19C Bude Canal at high tide for the view and a close feel of the sea.

Compass Point. – *Access by footpath (30mins Rtn) from the end of Breakwater Rd.* From the point, named after the octogonal daymark tower (with out-of-true bearings !) there are spectacular **views**★ along the line of 200-450ft cliffs, marked by offshore reefs. To the south one can see right round the white sanded, Widemouth Bay.

EXCURSIONS

In this corner of north Cornwall there are many villages with compact granite churches containing robustly carved mediaeval bench-ends, Norman fonts and brass and slate memorials. Two groups, one to the north, one to the south of Bude, are listed below.

1 **Round tour starting from Bude** *22m – local map p 50*
Leave Bude by A3072.

Stratton. – Pop 1288. The old market town **church**★ was built by stages: the north arcade of sea green-grey polyphant stone in 1348 was followed by the 90ft pinnacled **tower** – a landmark when Stratton was a harbour – and in the mid-15C by the granite south arcade. The chancel dates from 1 544. The font bowl is Norman, the pulpit Jacobean, the bench-ends are mediaeval, the **royal arms** restyled Stuart-Hanoverian; the east window is by **Burne-Jones.** In the porch is the old door to Stratton "clink".

Continue along A3072; bear left at the first turning.

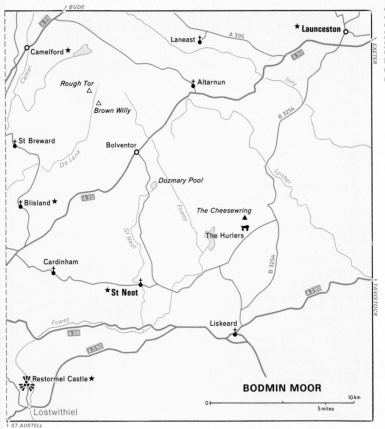

BODMIN MOOR

0   10 km

5 miles

BUDE

Launcells. – Pop 421. The 15C **church** ★ stands in a wooded valley, the tall pinnacles of its 54ft tower overtopping the trees. Inside, the arcades are of polyphant and granite, the **chancel** is paved with rare 15C Barnstaple encaustic tiles designed with fleurs-de-lys, Tudor roses, lions, pelicans and flowers. Note especially 15C **bench-ends,** 60 in all carved with the Crown of Thorns, nails and spice box, the *Harrowing of Hell,* the empty tomb...

Continue along the by-road to B3254.

Kilkhampton. – Pop 896. The **church** ★ with its 90ft embattled and pinnacled granite **tower,** was rebuilt on a Norman site in 1485. Note the Norman **south door** with three orders, zig-zag and beaked bird decoration and, inside, the 157 carved **bench-ends,** of 1567. The remarkable **monuments** sculpted in wood, stone and slate are by **Michael Chuke** (1679-1742), a Kilkhampton boy sent to London as a pupil to Grinling Gibbons.

By way of cross-country by-roads (Burridge, Woodford) make for the coast.

Morwenstow. – Pop 619. Morwenstow is known as the parish of **Parson Hawker,** who "lived a life made up of eccentricities", travelled this corner of his beloved Cornwall from 1834-75 in purple frock coat, white cravat, fisherman's jersey and boots, who was a poet and awesome preacher, rescued shipwrecked sailors and gave Christian burial to the drowned.

The **church** ★, which stands in a dell, the pinnacled and embattled tower a landmark to those at sea, was referred to as "ancient" in a document of 1296. It has a Norman **south door** with zig-zag moulding on small columns, two interior **arcades,** one with Norman and EE piers supporting an arch with chevron, ball and headed orders and at the base an antelope and other animal masks. Beneath the original bossaged wagon roofs are a Saxon **font** with cable moulding of *c*800 and mid-16C bench-ends. The **cliffs** ★★, 450ft high and reaching out to offshore rocks, are spectacular.

Take the by-road S to Coombe; turn inland to Stibb then right.

★ **Poughill** (pronounced Poffil). – St Olaf and Church House opposite, have been the kernel of Poughill village for centuries; Church House, dates from 1525.

The **church** ★★ on Norman foundations, has a 14C Perpendicular tower of granite, square and embattled with crocket pinnacles. Inside, two arcades, one 14C sandstone and tall, one of granite, 15C and short, march beneath late 15C wagon roofs with carved bosses. On the walls two mediaeval St Christopher frescoes were graphically repainted by Frank Salisbury in 1920s; the **royal arms,** incorrectly dated 1655, are of Charles II. Furnishing the church are splendid, deeply carved, oak **bench-ends** nearly all late 15C, polished each Epiphany to dark translucence with elbow grease, linseed oil and the melted down candle-ends from Christmas – note Jonah and the Whale, Biblical and local characters.

Continue S to Bude.

49

② Bude to Crackington Haven *12m – local map p 49*

Leave Bude by A3073 going S.

Marhamchurch. – Pop 435. Stone houses with slate or thatched roofs stand grouped round the small 14-15C **church**★ with its square tower abutted by a staircase turret. Of interest in the single arcade interior beneath the old wagon roofs, are the oak door with its **sanctuary knocker** *(p 175)*, the Jacobean **pulpit** with a sounding board, the **royal arms** by Michael Chuke *(p 49)* and, in the west wall, the window of 15C archorite's cell.

Return to A39 which you follow S.

★ **Poundstock.** – Pop 665. Church, lychgate and unique gildhouse form a secluded group in a wooded dell. One mile distant is the Atlantic, pounding the 400ft high cliffs from which the **view**★★ extends to Trevose Head, Pentire Pt, Sharpnose Pt, even Lundy.

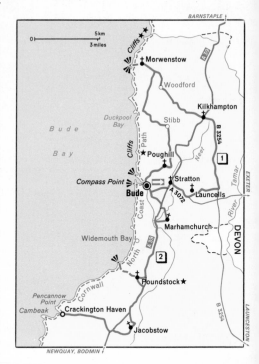

13-15C **church**★ with a square unbuttressed tower was restored in 19C. There remain a nail studded **south door**, a square granite **font** of 1300, the slate and brass Trebarfoote **wall monument** *(N aisle)* with a dapper little man in Stuart dress with centre parting and flowing moustaches, also finely lettered 17C **slate memorials**, wall paintings, an early 16C oak chest, Jacobean **communion table** *(back of nave)* and pulpit.

The **gildhouse**★, sturdily built in 14C, probably as quarters for the masons constructing the church, passed to the parish guilds as a place of meeting and festivity until such revelries were suppressed by the Puritans. It became a poorhouse, a school... Of cob and stone on two floors with buttresses, wooden mullions and a slate roof over stout timbers, the gildhouse stands as an example of once common, non-secular building.

Cross A39 to come out due S of Poundstock.

Jacobstow. – Pop 301. The 15C **church**★ stands in a hollow, its pinnacled granite tower emerging from the trees. A granite **porch** leads to the earlier nave and aisles, where stand 12C **font**, carved with faces at the angles. The pulpit was made from bench-ends.

Cross back over A39 to follow the by-road to the coast.

Crackington Haven. – A wide, lush valley leads down to the sea, each flank scored by a steep road making for the resort village and dark sand beach. On either side the headlands, Pencannow and Cambeak, rise sheer, hundreds of feet out of the sea.

CAMBORNE and REDRUTH   Pop 29 560

Michelin map **403** fold 32 – E33

The towns, with Pool between, form a continous line along the main road, A3047.

Redruth. – Redruth is and has the appearance of an industrial town, unique in Cornwall, with a main street punctuated by non-conformist chapels and granite clock tower.

Pool. – The between town is distinguished by past and present mining landmarks.

Camborne School of Mines. – The tall granite and glass buildings of the world famous school date from 1970s. Inside is a small **museum of minerals**, labelled and sparkling.

tc **Cornish Pumping Engines and East Pool Whim.** – The engines, one with a cylinder 7½ft in diameter were used for pumping water from mines 2000 and more feet deep and for bringing men and ore to the surface. The engines, one in motion (electricity driven), exemplify the use of high pressure steam, patented in 1802 by Richard Trevithick (1771-1883), engineer at the Ding Dong mine *(p 59)* and "father of the locomotive engine".

Just beyond, in Tuckingmill, is a **plaque** on a factory wall *(S side of the road)*, commemorating **William Beckford**, inventor in 1830, of the miners' safety fuse.

Camborne. – The town, the oldest of the three, and still aligned along the main road, is marked by 18-19C houses, a rambling half-timbered inn once a posting house, and 15C granite church with a distinctive west tower. In the churchyard are a 6C holy well and Celtic Cross and in the church, 10C Saxon stone altar slab, 18C marble altarpiece and chandeliers.

EXCURSIONS

★ **Tolgus Tin Streaming, Redruth.** – *1m N on B3300.*

tc Water-wheels, pumps, a stamping machine used to crush the ore, act as an introduction to the system used throughout Cornish tin mining in 19C, the streaming process. In this, cassiterite, a heavy oxide of tin, is separated from unwanted minerals by water. The tin particles, are dark grey-black, dead weight and smooth as silk to the touch.

To complete the picture, a museum displays tools, helmets, lamps, charges and fuses.

★ **Poldark Mine, Wendron.** – *7m S of Redruth on B3297. P 56.*

Carn Brea. – *1½m WSW of Redruth and 500yds S of Carnbrea or Brea village – last 150yds up a field track.*

Crowning the 740ft, boulder-strewn hilltop, is 90ft granite **monument**. A landmark for miles around, it affords a **view★★** over the length and breadth of Cornwall.

Gwennap Pit. – *1m S of Redruth, off A393.*

In the mid-18C, when Revivalism was strong in the West Country, the Pit, a natural amphitheatre formed by the subsidence of an old mine-shaft, was the setting for meetings numbering as many as 30 000 miners and their families on the 17 occasions when **John Wesley** *(p 36)* came to preach between 1762-86. In 1805-6 the amphitheatre was remodelled to its present 12 grass tiers; each summer it is the scene of a Wesleyan revival meeting *(see also p 63)*.

★★ COTEHELE

Michelin map **403** fold 33 – H32

tc The old fortified manor house stands overlooking the Tamar *(p 70)* from the crest of a wooded hillside. It is invisible from below although accessible up a steep zig-zag path through the woods from Calstock *(p 115; 1m)*.

Exterior, gardens and family history. – The house was built between 1485 and 1627 of grey granite, part rough rubble, part dressed blocks, which today are mellowed by camellias, roses, myrtles, wistarias and ceanothus. At the back are an **Upper Garden** of cut yew hedges, a golden ash and large tulip tree and, to the north, a 60ft high folly, the **Prospect Tower**, from which **views★★** extend far and wide.

Below the house, the walled **Valley Garden** encloses a mediaeval dovecote with a domed roof and a fish stewpond, spangled with red, white, yellow water lilies.

The manor descended through marriage to Richard Edgcumbe. He joined the unsuccessful revolt of 1483 against Richard III and some time later, finding himself pursed at Cotehele by the king's agents, tore off his cap, wrapped it round a stone and dropped it 70ft into the Tamar, whereupon the pursuers, in Richard Carew's words, "looking down after the noise, and seeing his cap swimming, supposed that he had drowned himself and gave over their hunting". Edgcumbe fled to Brittany; joined Henry VII and was richly rewarded after Bosworth Field. On his return to Cotehele he built the **Chapel in the Wood** to mark the spot from which he had thrown his cap into the river.

(After John Bethell / National Trust photo)
Cotehele – The Courtyard

TOUR ¾ *hour*

Gateway, tower and **great barn.** – The gateway, tower and great barn are late 15C.

Great Hall. – The hall, entered at the centre, was added in 16C by Richard's son who also built most of the major rooms on view. Note the hall's timbered **roof**, the massive Tudor **fireplace**, 18C campaign chairs and crested 18C pewter plates and mugs.

Old Dining Room. – The room, like all the residential rooms, is hung with tapestries less for aesthetic than practical reasons: the fabric reduced cold and drafts to a minimum – the hangings were ruthlessly cut to fit. (Nearly all those in Cotehele are 17-18C replacements.) The furniture, apart from the restored 16C centre table, is 17-18C; the long case, one handed **clock** (in a later case) is dated 1668.

Chapel. – The late 16C chapel with its original barrel **roof**, contains a rare **pre-pendulum clock** with verge escapement, no face but a bell to strike the hour. It is the oldest in England still in working order, an unaltered state and original position.

The painting of a tomb and the brass are of the Sir Richard, builder of this and the Chapel in the Wood, who died in Brittany in 1489; the Crucifixion panel is Flemish, the 1589 triptych is also Flemish.

Punch Room. – The room where the men retired after dining, is hung with gaily bacchic, **Soho tapestries** and is equipped with a closet fitted with small wine bins.

COTEHELE★★

Upper Floor. – The White Room, the Red, South, Queen Anne's and King Charles' Rooms are a haven of late 17C **four-posters,** each with its original hangings.

tc **Cotehele Mill.** – The estate workshops down by the river include a wheelwright's shop, a blacksmith's forge, sawpit, saddlery, cider house and mill.

Cotehele Quay. – Cottages, a small maritime museum of shipping on the Tamar and the *Shamrock,* a restored Tamar barge, give an idea of 18-19C activity on the river.

★★ FALMOUTH   Pop 18 553

Michelin map **403** fold 32 – E33
See town plan in the current Michelin Red Guide Great Britain and Ireland

A low crest, crowned, at its seaward point, by Pendennis Castle, runs back to divide the town in two: the hotel-residential area which faces south over Falmouth Bay, and the old town, with its waterfront looking north up the Fal Estuary, geologically a drowned river mouth and always known by its Cornish name of **Carrick Roads.**
The hotels and tourism began with the arrival of the railway in 1863; the harbour town, by contrast, evolved over centuries, the quay being built in 1670.
In 1688 Falmouth was appointed the most westerly **Mail Packet Station.** The designation brought prosperity: ships called making regular passage to the Mediterranean, the West Indies, North America; docks and boat-building yards were established; a mail coach service to London was instituted; ships required provisioning.
It was to Falmouth that HMS *Pickle* brought Collingwood's despatch on Trafalgar for it to be taken by mail coach to London *(see also pp 65-6).*
For 150 years Falmouth prospered, then ships turned to steam and the port died.

SIGHTS

The Waterfront. – The frontage which extends for over half a mile from Greenbank Quay to the pier is paralleled inland by the shop-lined **High St.** Note the porticoed, white **Custom House** of 1814. There is no continuous path along the waterfront; access to different quays and slips is through the alleys and **opes** descending from the main street.

Greenbank Quay. – The quay and 19C hotel stand on Penny-come-Quick or more properly Pen y Cwn Gwic meaning in Cornish, Headland in the Valley of the Creek.

Prince of Wales Pier. – *The embarkation point for river cruises.* The river, between Greenbank Quay and the pier, is overlooked by 18C houses and warehouses standing on 17C harbour wall. This is built after the Dutch fashion with large stone slabs set endways on to the sea and piled without mortar to allow slight play *(p 62).*

North and Custom House Quays. – The quays, which enclose the inner basin, date back to *c*1670. The strange, square brick chimney, at the landward end of the Custom House Quay, is known as the **King's Pipe** having been built to burn contraband tobacco!

★ **Pendennis Castle.** – In the face of "pretensed invasion" in 1539-43, Henry VIII began *tc* to fortify the coastline, erecting two forts at Falmouth and St Mawes *(p 68)* to safeguard the mile-wide entrance to the Carrick Roads. Crossfire overlapped and, as Carew *(p 46)* put it, "St Mawes lieth lower and better to annoy shipping, but Pendennis standeth higher and stronger to defend itself". Elizabeth increased the defences against surprise Spanish raids. The challenge finally came in the Civil War: St Mawes yielded without a shot being fired but Pendennis withstood 23 weeks' siege before starvation brought submission in August 1546.
Pendennis commands a superb **view★★.** Note over the entrance the royal arms with the Tudor lion and Welsh dragon supporters, also the splayed gun ports. In the keep are arms and an exhibition of coastal defence.

BOAT and FERRY TRIPS

★ **Cruises to Truro.** – The banks are densely wooded with oak trees down to the water's edge where there are herons, cormorants, and waders *(p 23)*. Villages with a church, an old pub, and half a dozen moored craft line the inlets: boathouses, slipways, laid-up ships of up to 30 000 tons and ships on the move, mark the course; above are open fields, more woods, a church or two, houses in their own parkland.

Landmarks include:

★ **Pendennis Castle.** – *See opposite.*

★ **St Mawes Castle.** – *P 68.*

St Anthony Lighthouse. – *P 17.*

Flushing. – The village was founded in 17C by Dutch settlers.

Penryn. – Pop 5 105. The ancient, still working quarry village, lies far up the creek.

Mylor. – Pop 5 267. The 16-17C church has a gable turret, detached bell tower and weather boarded upper storey. The village, now a yacht and pleasure craft centre, is a short distance further up the inlet which is straddled at its end by **Mylor Bridge**.

★★★ **St Just-in-Roseland.** – East bank: church and separate village. *P 73.*

Pandora Inn. – At the mouth of Restronguet Creek on the west bank, lies the 17C whitewashed and thatched inn, a former smugglers' hideaway no doubt.

Devoran. – On the same creek, Devoran was once a tin and copper port.

★★ **Trelissick House.** – The house stands on the promontory where the Fal turns east. *P 71.*

King Harry Ferry. – *P 74.*

Tregothnan. – The large 19C Georgian mansion with a forest of slim octagonal turrets and chimneys, can be seen on the point where the River Ruan joins the Fal *(p 15)*.

Malpas. – The town lies at the junction of the Fal, Truro and Tresillian Rivers.

Truro. – The town is two miles further upstream. *P 73.*

★ **Cruises up the Helford River.** – The scenery is, if anything, even more beautiful. There are no stops, few houses, two landmarks; Durgan hamlet *(p 55)* and Gweek Seal Sanctuary *(p 56)*.

★★ **St Mawes.** – *By ferry. P 68.*

EXCURSIONS

★★ **Glendurgan Garden.** – *4m SSW. P 55.*

tc **Military Vehicle Museum, Lamanva.** – *3m SW on B3291 from Penryn, by the crossroads before Treverva.*
The vehicles of World War II, British, American and German, range from a Mercedes staff car to Austin "Tilley" runabouts, Bren gun carriers, field ambulances.

★★ FOWEY   Pop 2 130

Michelin map **403** fold 33 – G32

Fowey is a town which grows on you as you explore it – the quay, the houses, the yards, the church, the museum. There are walks out towards Gribbin Head; there are boat trips to be enjoyed round the harbour and the coast where the cliffs rise dark and sheer from the water, or upriver below hillsides densely wooded with oak to the water's edge, past small creeks and the china-clay quays with long tails of loaded railway wagons. Most importantly of all there is the **river** to watch as ships of up to 10 000 tons – British, French, Belgian, Swedish, Danish, Norwegian, Spanish, Italian, German – come into load the clay; fishing boats go out in the evening; small yachts moored at Polruan, swing with the tide; launches and rowing boats go places; the pilot vessel comes and goes; the dredger keeps the channel clear; the ferries ply; and wicked rocks appear and disappear as the tide turns...

SIGHTS

Town Quay. – The square which marks the centre of the town and the waterfront, has as a backcloth an old inn, the **King of Prussia**, named after 18C smuggler *(p 66)*. The adjoining building was the fish or butter market with the counting house above.

Trafalgar Sq and Lostwithiel St. – The second square is overlooked by 18C granite ashlar **town hall** *(museum)*, built over 14C building, once the local "clink" – note the grilled window. **Toll Bar House** which dates back to 14, 15 and 18C, and the **Ship Inn** opposite, built by the Rashleighs *(see below)* as a town house in 15C, were linked by a bridge-room. Inside the inn are a carved ceiling and, above a fireplace, a marriage inscription: John Rashleigh – Ales Rashleigh 1570.

St Fimbarrus. – *South St.* The 14-15C church with a tall, pinnacled tower rising above the trees, a two storey Decorated **porch**, a long south aisle and clerestory, is the last in a line of churches on the site first occupied in 7C by a chapel to St Goran *(p 46)*. This was succeeded by a wooden chapel to St Finn Barr. A Norman church was destroyed by a pirate raid in 1150; a new church, rededicated in 1336, was set on fire by French seamen in 1456 in retaliation for raids by the **Fowey Gallants**, those "rich, proud and mischievous men", part traders, part privateers, part pure pirates – even today the carved pulpit, formerly a doubledecker, is Gallants' booty, being made from panelling from the captain's cabin of a Spanish galleon taken in 1601! Inside, beneath the 500 year old **wagon roof**, note the octagonal **piers** without capitals, the Norman **font** of dark catacleuse stone and, at the east end, the portrait **tombs**,

53

memorials and aged brasses and slates to the Rashleighs of Menabilly House (rebuilt 19C; setting for Daphne du Maurier's novels, *Rebecca* and *The King's General*) and the Treffrys of Place (19C house in the centre of the town behind high walls, distinguished by two, thin, dissimilar castellated towers).
In the tower is 18C **ringer's rhyme** *(p 138)*.

Fore St. – The narrow shopping street is lined by old houses with jettied gables or houses angled into corners as are 17C Lugger Inn and Globe Posting House.

tc **Noah's Ark.** – The half-timbered house with oversailing gables is Elizabethan.
It was built as a prosperous merchant's house with one or two larger and innumerable small rooms, closets and landings up twisting stairs. Today the rooms are filled with displays of the house's restoration or rather the removal of centuries' old accretions, old maps, engravings of the historic houses of Cornwall, Victoriana, Edwardiana and the writings of local authors (Quiller-Couch, the du Mauriers...).

Post Office. – The office in a handsome Georgian house facing down Fore St, is entered through a shell hooded doorway; adjoining is the Customs House of the same date.

Car Ferry. – Linking North and Passage Sts *(the continuation of Fore St)*, is the vehicle ferry to Bodinnick, known for the last 700 years as **The Passage.**
Lining the street are houses built by prosperous 17-19C townsmen overlooking their wharves and the river; the smaller houses, with windows and balconies overhanging the water, were built later on the former slips. At the ferry end, note **Captain's Row** of 1816, a modest range complete with Captain Bates' own brass knocker.

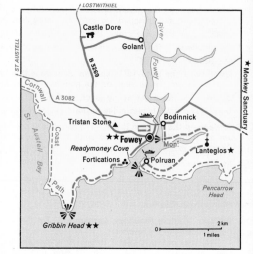

WALKS

★★ **Gribbin Head.** – *6m Rtn. Follow the Esplanade to its end (car park); then join the Cornwall South Coast Path.*

Fortifications at the water's edge. – 14C blockhouse and its pair opposite, were the anchor points for the harbour chain across the river mouth (note the marks on the rocks); **St Catherine's Castle**, now a ruin, was a Henry VIII fortification.

Readymoney Cove. – The small cove serves as the town beach (sand at low tide). The Coast Path comes out on the cliff top and makes a gradual climb to the headland.

★★ **Gribbin Head.** – The head, extending half a mile out to sea, 242ft high and topped by 82ft daymark, affords **views**★★ for miles in all directions.

★ **Lanteglos Church.** – *5m. Take The Passage or car ferry across the river.*

Bodinnick. – The ferry lands at the foot of the near vertical main street. To the right is a former boatbuilders' yard, long since converted into a private house and to the left, the mediaeval **Old Ferry Inn**; standing on each other's shoulders to climb the hill, are stone and slate houses with minute, flower filled gardens.

Take the path, Hall Walk, to the right, downstream and continue past the 1939-45 War Memorial to the monolith, the memorial to "Q" (Sir Arthur Quiller Couch).

There is a splendid **view**★★ across to Fowey. Further along the path is a shelter on which a **plaque** indicates that on this spot on 17 August 1644, **Charles I** narrowly escaped death from a sniper's bullet while surveying the Parliamentary forces occupying Fowey.

The path drops to the road bridge over the end of the creek at Pont; continue along S bank and where the road turns inland (beyond Carne), take the footpath (350yds) across the fields.

★ **Lanteglos Church.** – The very large 14-15C parish church stands isolated on a wooded valley slope. It is built with old masonry which includes a Norman doorway incorporating 7-8C **Chiro stone**, and mediaeval blocks of granite weighing as much as 8 tons. The interior, divided by unequally tall arcades of plain octagonal columns, is covered by the original carved **wagon roofs**. The carved **font** of Pentewan stone is early 13C.
At the east end are **tombs** of the Grenvilles and the Mohuns – Thomas Mohan supervised the building of his own tomb (in a canopied recess) but being still alive when the brass was finished, left the date of death incomplete!

The road leads west to Polruan.

Polruan. – Before the descent to the old town at the water's edge, bear left to the coastguard station from which there is a **view**★★ west to Gribbin Head, Dodman Point and the Lizard and east to Rame and Bolt Heads. Drop down to the harbour past the cliff and waterside houses, the pubs and boat-yards to the passenger ferry.

EXCURSIONS

★ **Polperro.** – *9m E by Bodinnick.*
Throughout the season visitors outnumber locals by some 10 to one – nevertheless this "fisher town" is attractive. The long road descends to the valley bottom, accompanied all the way by a running stream and cottages which get ever older as you reach the inner then the outer harbour, the haven and the open sea.
Twisting and stepped alleys are close-packed with cottages, millhouses, shops, forges and boathouses; from the headlands, **views** extend far out to sea.

★ **Monkey Sanctuary, Looe.** – *27m E by Bodinnick.*

★ **Looe.** – *Pop 4 509.* The town, renowned for its safe, fine sand beaches, lies in the open valley on either side of the river of the same name which divides almost immediately upstream into two tributaries. East and West Looe, are linked by 19C bridge.

> *Continue E by B3253.*

★ **Monkey Sanctuary.** – In an enclosure occupying much of the garden of 19C seaside villa
tc and in the villa itself, dozens of Amazon woolley monkeys live and breed, perform effortless acrobatics and, when inclined, come out to meet their visitors!

> *Bear W, A387, to Sandplace station then right by a by-road to St Keyne station.*

tc **Paul Corin Musical Collection, St Keyne Mill.** – The collection comprises a rare assemblage of automatic music instruments including pianolas, an orchestrion, street, fair, and cinema organs playing old favourites in the appropriate decorous or strident manner.

Golant. – *5m N. Leave Fowey by the Lostwithiel Rd, A3082.*

Tristan Stone. – *1¼ m from town centre, before Four Turnings, on right side of the road.* The stone, a relic of the Tristan legend *(p 71),* stands 8ft tall and was transferred from a nearby site where it was said to have been erected in 550 AD.

Castle Dore. – *3m by A3082 and B3269, 200yds N of Castledor crossroads, 15yds inside a field with a broken gate.* The second Tristan-Arthurian relic is an Iron Age lookout point, which in 6C AD is said to have been one of King Mark's wooden halls of residence *(now densely overgrown).*

> *Return to Castledor crossroads and take the left by-road (E) down to the river.*

Golant. – The riverside village has 15-16C, landmark **church** with a low, embattled tower. Inside, a single arcade divides the nave and aisle beneath original wagon and cradle roofs; **bosses** and wall plates are beautifully carved as are the **pulpit** and **stalls** made from mediaeval bench-ends (apostles, St Sampson, a jester). The **sculpture** of Christ's head in chestnut, is believed to be Spanish, possibly from an Armada vessel.

★★ GLENDURGAN GARDEN

Michelin map **403** fold 32 – E33 – ½ m SW of Mawnan Smith

tc Dropping down to Durgan hamlet on the Helford River, is a valley garden planted with English broad leav-
ed trees, conifers and ornamental foliage trees from all over the world. (Everything is unobtrus-ively labelled). In the spring and early summer all is brilliant with wild daffodils, bluebells and primulas followed soon after by rhododendrons, camellias, azaleas and magnolias. Later come hydrangeas and finally, a blaze of autumn tints. In the garden are also a **Giant's Stride** (maypole) and a famous **Maze** – all mazes, it is said have the same solution, even so allow one hour!

(Vloo / J Alan Cash)

Glendurgan Garden – The Maze

★ **Mawnan Parish Church.** – *½ m E.* The 15C granite church stands on a spur at the mouth of the Helford River – walk round to see the **view**★★. The church, incorporating part of an EE sanctuary and with massive granite piers, is outstanding for its **modern needlework** which gives colour and warmth to the interior.

HELSTON

Michelin map **403** fold 32 – E33

Helston is the home town of the famous Furry Dance. The other 364 days of the year it is the market town for the Lizard Peninsula. Its 600 years' tradition as a stannary or tin assay town is recalled in the name Coinagehall St *(p 43)*.

SIGHTS

Guildhall. – The Classical guildhall, surmounted by a striking clock, stands at the junction of the town's major thoroughfares, Coinagehall, Wendron and Meneage Sts.

tc **Folk Museum.** – *Church St.* In the old market halls at the foot of the wide granite steps by the Guildhall, the local museum of trades and domestic bygones, has extremely well laid out exhibits on fishing – note the flat "maglans" for scooping fish from the sea – agriculture, mining and housekeeping. Two Helston men given pride of place in the museum, are Bob Fitzsimmons the prize-fighter, 1863-1917 (born in 17C thatched cottage, 61 Wendron St) and Henry Trengrouse (1771-1854), inventor of the ships-to-shore rocket life-saving apparatus (tomb in churchyard).

St Michael's. – The 18C church with Furry Dance angels in the east window is lit by 24 branch 18C chandelier.

Cross St. – Characterising the street are the late Georgian **Great Office** with a columned porch, top floor bay window and iron balcony, 18C vicarage with an oriel window, and no 10 with its neat doorway and all over, small paned, **bow windows.** Leading off the street to the parallel Coinagehall St are a number of "opes".

Coinagehall St. – As you walk up the wide street, beware the rainwater "kennels" or gutters. Note above the shop fronts, the variety of old windows, the still thatched **Blue Anchor Inn** – pre-17C with 18C horizontal sash windows – **Chymder House,** early 19C, square and stuccoed, the **Angel Inn,** 16C with its own well, onetime Excise Office (see the string course above the porticoed entrance) and long a coaching inn.

★★ The FLORA DAY FURRY DANCE

Date: 8 May annually – or preceding Saturday if 8th falls on a Sunday or Monday. *The town is closed to traffic.*
Five **processional dances** are performed, at 7, 8.30, 10am, noon, and 5pm, all except the Hal-an-Tow at 8.30am, accompanied by the band. The 3-4mile route has minor variations but all dances begin and end at the Guildhall and go up Coinagehall St; all pass through houses, shops and banks and the doors and lower windows along the route are decorated with blue-bells and greenery.
The most spectacular dances are at **10am** when 800 **children,** aged 8-15 dressed all in white, set out and at **12 noon** when on the first stroke from the Guildhall clock 300 couples start circling in the **Invitation Dance** – the men in grey toppers and morning suits, the women in big hats and garden party dresses.

EXCURSIONS

★ **Cornwall Aero Park and Flambards Village, Culdrose.** – *3m SE off A3083.*
tc To the constant whirr of the helicopters of Royal Navy station, Culdrose, just a field away, one explores a Concorde flight deck, a gallery of World War II mementoes, worldwide satellite communications, a Westland Whirlwind and Widgeon...
In complete contrast is the lamplit, cobbled street of houses where one can look into crowded rooms, an inn and 19C shops with wooden counters and racks of jars, drawers, boxes and barrels: an apothecary's, a milliner's, a butcher's, a baker's...

★ **Poldark Mine, Wendron.** – *3m N on B3297.*
tc One mine among the 50 in production from 15-20C in the Wendron district, has been reopened to allow visitors to see the underground workings and 18-19C machinery in place.

Tour. – On the surface are steam locomotives, traction and beam engines...

Go to the mine entrance; put on a safety helmet. No smoking underground.

There are 12 marked **viewpoints** in the mine from which can be seen a bright blue chloride "lode" or seam in the roof, an access-ventilation shaft of 1730, a tunnel showing early working space, waterfalls, exposed tin lodes, an underground postbox, rock drills, a stamping machine and water-wheel, the latter in a chamber hollowed out in 1493. The wheel now generates the mine's emergency electricity supply. *(See also p 51).*

★ **Seal Sanctuary, Gweek.** – *5m E off A394.*
tc The sanctuary, in a beautiful **setting**★ overlooking the Helford River, cares for pups separated from their mothers or injured against rocks. Once recovered in the hospital, the young seals disport themselves in the pools before being restored to the ocean.

Times and charges for admission to sights described in the guide are listed on *the green pages at the end.*

The sights are listed alphabetically in this green section either under the place – town, village or area – in which they are situated or under their proper name.

Every sight for which there are special times and charges is flagged in the margin in the main part of the guide (pp 26-210) by the initials tc.

★ LAND'S END

Michelin map **403** fold 31 – C33

Land's End, which, inevitably, everyone visits at some time, remains magical as the Atlantic surges perpetually and beats relentlessly against the cliffs...

The Isles of Scilly are 27 miles away; the Longships Lighthouse at the centre of swirling currents and submerged reefs, 1½. Close inshore are the **Armed Knight** and the holed, **Enys Dodnan**. Local legend has it that the rocks and many others are the mountain peaks of the lost land of Lyonesse, that the race of water covers Atlantis...

For a solitary approach to Land's End, walk the Cornwall Coastal Path, taking in on the way possibly the finest **cliff scenery** ★★★ in the West Country; for a private view come early; for an unforgettable one, come at sunset and stay on to see the lights *(p 16)*.

(Gérard Sioen / CEDRI)

Land's End at sunset

★★ LANHYDROCK

Michelin map **403** fold 32 – F32 – 3m S of Bodmin

tc The fascination of Lanhydrock lies in the juxtaposition of the mid-17C exterior of granite, battlements and corner pinnacles and the Victorian-Edwardian interior.

In 1881 fire gutted all but one wing and the entrance. In four years it was rebuilt; externally exactly as it had been to match the unscathed north wing, but inside replanned to include all the latest in Victorian amenities including central heating, bathrooms and redesigned kitchens.

The gardens and grounds. – The house with three wings and a **formal garden** in place of the original forecourt, but still with its Renaissance style **gatehouse,** overlooks a **park** and rolling farmland. To the rear, are **terrace gardens**, planted with specimen and flowering trees, magnolias, azaleas, camellias, rhododendrons and hydrangeas.

TOUR *1 hour*

Grand Hall. – Inside the 17C porch, which was not consumed by the fire, the Grand Hall is Victorian-17C with family portraits on the walls and mementoes on the tables.

Inner Hall. – The **wallpaper** is a William Morris design.

Dining Room. – The stately 19C room with its 19C panelling, has a **table** set with fine china and glass and a **centrepiece** made in shining Cornish tin – the Robartes were tin mine-owners. Note on a side-table, the hand painted dessert plates.

Lady Robartes' Room. – The small room is cosy with family photos, books, a desk, a small piano, armchairs, a needlework box and a bobble chenil cloth on the table.

Corridor and Billiard Room. – The masculine area of the house is given character with game trophies on the walls, a fur-lined coat, hat and gloves ready for an outing...

Smoking Room. – The panelled room is furnished with a Turkey carpet, Eton and Oxford favours, a fish that did not get away and half a dozen easy-chairs, all different !

The Bedrooms. – The rooms reflect the owners' personalities with: cane furniture and innumerable photographs for the last Miss Robartes; practicality for Lord Robartes; and grace for Lady Robartes, from whose room there is a beautiful **view.**

Long Gallery. – The gallery, 116ft in length and occupying the north wing, is roofed with an outstanding 17C **plaster barrel vault**. The surface is divided into 24 sections each carved in deep relief with an Old Testament scene and separated from its neighbours by banding decorated with every conceivable and many surprising birds and beasts.

Servants' Quarters. – The rooms on the second floor give a vivid insight into the contrast in lifestyles enjoyed by those above and below stairs at the turn of the century.

★ LAUNCESTON

Pop 6 092

Michelin map **403** fold 33 – G32 – Local map p 50

Perched high on the Cornwall-Devon border, with a castle founded by William I's brother, Robert of Mortain, Earl of Cornwall *(p 12)*, a South Gate still standing from the time when it was a mediaeval walled town, narrow, turning streets, a market, shops with 18-19C fronts, galleries, a church and chapel of ease, houses of all ages from half-timbered Tudor to 18, 19C and post-war anonymous, Launceston is a place to explore. Until 1835 when the assize court moved to Bodmin, it was Cornwall's chief town.

EWC 4

LAUNCESTON★

SIGHTS

tc ★ **The Castle.** – Walk through the former bailey and up the motte steps to the shell keep; circle the wall before mounting 13C centre tower for the **view**★ of Dartmoor, Bodmin Moor (Brown Willy and Rough Tor) and the Tamar.

The castle's history is not adventurous: it was visited by the Black Prince, was siezed by the rebels in the Cornish Uprising of 1549 *(p 69)*, and changed hands twice during the Civil War. Until 1840 it served as an assize court and prison, being notorious for imprisoning or executing prisoners on the nod – **George Fox,** founder of the Society of Friends was incarcerated in it for several months in 1656.

★ **St Mary Magdalene.** – The Perpendicular church of 1511 gives the lie to the impossibility of carving **granite**: walls, buttresses, two storey porch, gables, are closely patterned with quatrefoils, coats of arms – Henry VII's on the east gable – fleurs-de-lys, roses, pomegranates and, below the east window, Mary Magdalene. The tower is 14C. The interior with slender piers, pointed arches and **wagon roofs,** contains a pre-Reformation painted **pulpit,** a brass on the south wall and the royal arms of George I.

tc ★ **South Gate.** – The last of the four mediaeval gateways, rises through two floors to a castellated parapet. Up the steps, in what has been a guardhouse and goal, there is now a gallery of luminous, hand-painted glass.

tc **Local History Museum.** – *Lawrence House, Castle St.* The museum presents a Pandora's box of bygones.

★★ LIZARD Peninsula

Michelin map **403** fold 32 – E33 and 34

The Lizard, England's most southerly point, the source of **serpentine rock,** the site of the windswept Goonhilly Downs (recognisable by its moonfaced telecommunications dishes), is a place to be visited for the coves and fishing villages strung like a necklace around its high cliffed shore.

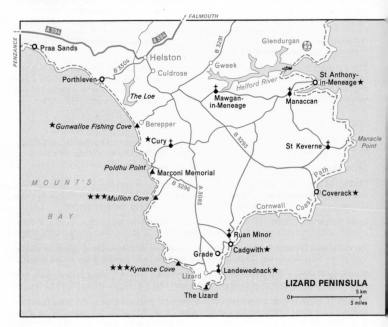

VILLAGES and COVES on the Lizard

Enjoy a few villages only at a time – a round tour of them all – 100m: 5½ hours – is possible but indigestible.

★ **Cadgwith.** – The delightful **fishing village** of thatched and slate roofed cottages with whitewashed walls, overlooks the shingle beach of a minute cove.

★ **Coverack.** – A 1: 6 descent brings you to the old **fishing village** of thatched and slate roofed cottages overlooking the harbour and wide cove. The village was famous for its smuggling – even the name means "hideaway" in Cornish! In 1840, the tale is told, officers seized some 125 casks of spirits from a band who then undertook a "second wrecking" or raid to recapture the kegs so as not to disappoint their customers – spirits were usually bespoken. The excisemen were left three casks as consolation prize!

★ **Cury.** – Pop 423. A 9ft tall **Celtic Cross,** a Norman **south door** framed by columns and a decorated tympanum, a rosette carved **font** and transept-chancel squint in which the cut away corner is replaced by an octogonal column, characterise 14C **church**★.

Grade. – Pop 894. The early 14C, two stage **tower** of square blocks of serpentine and granite with tall pinnacles is all, with the **font** and 16C brass, that remains of earlier churches so destroyed by wind and rain, that in 1862 a new building was erected.

★ **Gunwalloe Fishing Cove.** – The thatch roofs of Berepper mark the descent to the even smaller village of fishermen's cottages crowded behind the minute **cove**. Pieces of eight have been washed up on the beach from a galleon lost off the point.

★★ **Kynance Cove.** – The high cliffs, sand beach uncovered at low tide and pinnacle rocks emerging from the brilliant blue green sea on a clear day are unforgettable. Go out of hours though – 10 000 visitors have been counted on a fine summer's day!

★ **Landewednack.** – Pop 811. **Serpentine** is the hallmark of the pretty, old thatch roofed village where the **church** ★ and its tower are made of the glossy green and black-velvet stone, the Norman **door** in the battlemented porch is framed with black serpentine columns and zig-zag and circle decorated voussoirs and the pulpit and lectern entirely carved out of the stone. Today village craftsmen turn and polish it into ornaments.

The Lizard. – The lighthouse *(p 16)* is the only feature of interest on the point.

The Loe. – The freshwater **lagoon** known as The Loe (no bathing or fishing) is a drowned valley, dammed at its mouth by the shingle bar swept up by the Atlantic.

Along the foreshore the sand extends from Gunwalloe Cove to **Porthleven**, a resort, active fishing port and boat-building harbour, distinguished by 19C clock tower.

Manaccan. – Pop 313. The Norman church, altered in 13-15C and restored in 19C, is known locally for the fig-tree growing out of the 14C, slate tower wall. Note the Norman **door** with three orders of columns ribbed voussoirs, also the **squint** inside.

Mawgan-in-Meneage. – Pop 1 514. The village and granite **church** ★ with a proud, 15C, three-stage **tower** with ribbed pinnacles on angel corbels, stand in a creek off the Helford River. There are coats of arms by the door and inside, **angel capitals** in the tower arch, a transept-chancel **squint** and the **sword** and **helmet** of the Royalist, Sir Richard Vyvyan.

★★ **Mullion Cove.** – The cove, which lies back from the line of cliffs, is framed by a white sand beach, small harbour, a natural **rock arch,** pinnacles and an offshore island. Pick your way through Mullion village, which lies nearly a mile inland, to the 15-16C **church** ★ with its mixed granite and serpentine **tower,** polished lime ash floor and early 16C carved **bench-ends.** The **font,** with a serpent, is 13C, the royal arms are those of Charles II. The "dog door" in the nailed, south door allowed sheep-dogs attending service with their masters, to leave when nature called!

Poldhu Point. – The **Marconi Memorial,** a granite obelisk at the cliff edge, 200yds south of the point, marks the site of the radio station from which signals were first sent out by Marconi and successfully received in Newfoundland on 12 December 1901.

Praa Sands. – Praa Sands, just west of the Lizard, is known for its three mile beach.

Ruan Minor. – The **church** ★, once a Norman chapel, of the local dark green serpentine stone and granite, was enlarged in 14C when 25ft serpentine tower was added.

★ **St Anthony-in-Meneage.** – Pop 199. St Anthony and Gillan lie on either side of a small creek. The church, to which Gillan parishioners come by boat at high tide, is 12-15C.

St Keverne. – Pop 1 874. The church's original, octagonal, ribbed **spire** was at once replaced when struck by lightning in 1770 so invaluable had it become as a landmark to shipping steering clear of **The Manacles** underwater reefs. The **church** ★ itself is 15C except for the **arcade** in green-grey-white-rose stone, brought possibly from Brittany and erected in 13C. There appear to be three sets of **rood screen stairs**, in addition to carved **bench-ends**, 15C font, Jacobean pulpit and a faded St Christopher **wall-painting.**

MADRON   Pop 1 145

Michelin map 403 fold 31 – D33

★ **St Maddern.** – The third church on the site overlooking Mount's Bay, was completed over a period of 200 years beginning in the early 14C – the 250 **bosses** carved to 16 different patterns and the **cornice angels** (retained when the roof was renewed) are 15C. The furnishings and monuments are very various: an **inscribed stone** *(SW wall)*, believed to be 8C from a Celtic church; EE sedilia in the Lady Chapel, five pre-14C, animal **bench-ends**, 17C brass, 14C English **alabaster panel** of ten angels, probably from a reredos or shrine. Nearby is a wooden panel carved with the Tudor rose and the royal arms of Henry VII as an earnest of the vicar's and congregation's loyalty after a lapse in support of Perkin Warbeck! The **rood screen**, with faintly coloured original wainscot panels and crocketed gables, dates from 1450.

By the south door is the bell from the local Ding Dong Tin Mine, closed in 1878 and on the wall opposite, a panel of **tin marks**, in use locally from 1189. Also on the walls are several remarkably carved 17C slate memorials.

Nelson banner. – Against the north wall is the historic Nelson banner made in haste to be carried before the mayor and burgesses of Penzance processing to Madron for the first ever Trafalgar Service in 1805 *(pp 65-6)*. A Trafalgar service, when the banner is still processed, is held annually on the Sunday nearest 21 October.

NEWQUAY   Pop 16 050

Michelin map 403 fold 32 – E32
See town plan in the current Michelin Red Guide Great Britain and Ireland

Newquay is a resort of golden sand at the feet of cliffs which advance into headlands and points – East Pentire, Towan and Porth Island, all once settled by pre-historic man. By 1439 the villagers were building a "new quay"; by 18-19C Newquay was a pilchard port, exporting salted fish to Italy and Spain – the **Huar's House** from where the huar would summon the fishermen with his long horn when fish entered the bay, still stands on the clifftop. In 1870s, with the arrival of the railway, the town became a china-clay and mineral port and, finally, a resort.

EXCURSIONS

★ **Trerice.** - *3m SE by A392 and A3058. P 72.*

★ **The Pentire Points and Kelsey Head.** – From each of the headlands there is a **view** ★ ★ north to Towan and Trevose Head, south to Godrevy Lighthouse *(p 17)* and St Ives and, inland, from the St Austell china-clay pyramids to Camborne and Carn Brea.

> *The Coast Path turns away before the end of Pentire East but follows the cliff line of Pentire Point West and Kelsey Head. Roads lead out to both Pentire Points stopping short about ½m from the cliff edges.*

The Coast to Hell's Mouth. – *26m S.*

Perranporth. – Three miles of beach provided the setting, the coming of the railway the opportunity, for Perranporth to turn itself early this century into the resort which it has been ever since. The time also was ripe: the pilchard, after 100 years, had vanished, smuggling had ended and the mines were ceasing to be profitable.

St Piran's Oratory. – *2m on foot Rtn across the sand dunes.* St Piran's stood like a rock, appearing and disappearing in the tide of sand which surrounded it from its construction in 6-7C on the burial site of the saint who, according to legend, crossed the sea from Ireland on a millstone. In 1835 the sands, always shifting, blew away from 7C oratory, revealing a building 29½ft long, 16½ft wide and 19ft high, of granite, porphyry, slate, quartz and rubble. In 1980 the ruins were reburied *(site marked by a plaque).*

★★ **St Agnes Beacon.** – The beacon *(last 500yds up a field footpath)* at 628ft, between the village and the headland, affords a **panorama** ★★ from Trevose Head to St Michael's Mount. In the foreground, between 300ft high Cligga Head, where the granite begins, and the beacon, there extends the typical, north Cornwall landscape, short turfed, undulating, windswept, speared by old mine stacks.

(After BTA photo)

Old engine-house, North Cornwall

Porthtowan. – The attractive small cove is known for its surfing.

★ **Portreath.** – A 1 : 6 road descends the valley on either side to get down to the cove, the harbour with its stalwart breakwater, and the small village resort.

> *Follow the coast road, B3301.*

★ **Hell's Mouth.** – *Car park beside the road.* From the cliff edge, the sea, blue-green-black, breaks ceaselessly against the sheer, 200ft encircling **cliff-face;** the only sounds are the screaming of the sea-birds and the ceaseless wash of the waves.

For hotels and restaurants of every price
*Look in the **Michelin Red Guide Great Britain and Ireland.***

★ PADSTOW   Pop 2 806

Michelin map **403** fold 32 – F32

Padstow was for centuries a major port, being the only safe harbour on the north Cornwall coast, provided you could navigate the rocks, the cross winds and currents at the mouth of the Camel Estuary. In 6C, St Petroc, landing from Wales, founded a Celtic minster before journeying on to Bodmin; in 981 minster and town were destroyed by the Vikings. The town recovered, developing over the centuries into a fishing harbour and mineral and china-clay port and even a harbour from which trans-Atlantic emigrants set out in craft as small as 10 tons. As boats became bigger however, fewer could make port owing to the sand or **Doom Bar** at the estuary mouth, formed, according to legend, at the curse of a dying mermaid shot by a local man !

SIGHTS

Harbour. – The harbour, filled with fishing boats and launches *(see below)* is surrounded on three sides by quays each backed by old houses, boathouses and pubs.

South Quay. – Opposite the Harbour Master's Office is 16C, two-storey, granite group of houses with slate roofs, comprising the **Old Court House** with a shell hood over the door, **Raleigh Cottage,** where Sir Walter Raleigh *(p 140),* as Warden of Cornwall, collected dues, and the minute **Harbour Cottage.**

North Quay. – The 15C **Abbey House,** once a nunnery, has a nun's head carving dripstone.

A network of narrow streets runs back behind the quay, the alleys darkened by tall houses, many with exposed beams and oversailing upper floors above small shop-fronts.

St Petroc Major. – The church with its embattled west tower begun in 13C, contains an octagonal **font** of Catacleuse stone carved by the **Master of St Endellion** *(p 48).* The cross-shaft in the churchyard is Celtic, the wrought iron gates are 18C.

The PADSTOW 'OBBY 'OSS

The May Day celebrations, their origin lost in the mists of antiquity, begin at midnight in the square or Broad St with the singing of the Morning Song – "let us all unite for summer is acome unto day". In the morning there appear a children's horse, **a blue 'oss** and the original **red 'oss** which prance throughout the day to accordion and drum bands.

BOAT TRIPS

Despite what the boatmen say, to a landsman, it is frequently quite choppy. The cruises take you out beyond the estuary to see **Stepper Point**, **Pentire Point**, the **Rumps** and, in Portquin Bay, the spectacular **cliffs**, caves and rocks and quite likely a modern wreck, caught on the rocks, possibly with her back broken by the waves.

EXCURSIONS

★★ **Bedruthan Steps.** – *8m SW by B3276.*

Portcothan. – The tiny village lies at the back of a deep square cove.

★★ **Bedruthan Steps.** – Look *tc* over the cliff edge at the 1½ mile arc of sand spectacularly scattered with giant rocks, worn to the same angle by waves and wind *(illustration p 74)* – the stepping stones, legend has it, of the giant Bedruthan!

★ **Trevose Head.** – *6m W by B3276 and by-roads; the last ½m on foot.*
The 243ft head stands halfway between Hartland Point, 40 miles to the northeast and West Penwith – four lights are visible at night *(p 16)*. By day the **view**★★ is of bay following bay, offshore rock islands, small sandy coves palisaded to seaward by towering rocks.

Trevone. – *3m W by A3276.*
The village and chapel with a slate spire, stand in a small sandy cove, guarded by fierce offshore rocks. The spectacular approach to the village from Padstow is by way of the **Cornwall Coast Path**★★ *(5m on foot)* which circles 242ft **Stepper Point** with its white daymark and passes the natural rock arches of **Porthmeissen Bridge**.

St Issey. – *5m S by B3274. Turn left on to A389 to Little Petherick.*

Little Petherick. – The remodelled mediaeval church lies as the bottom of a steep sided valley, its tower just visible in the trees; from the hilltops on either side there are **views** far across the Camel River.

St Issey. – Pop 630. The mediaeval church tower collapsed in 19C necessitating a total rebuilding and meticulous repiecing of the catacleuse stone altarpiece by the Master of St Endellion *(p 48)*; a second carving is on the south altar.

★ PENCARROW

Michelin map **403** fold 32 – F32 – 4m NW of Bodmin

tc The Palladian style house with Delabole slate roofs and pediments at the roofline and above the first floor windows, has been in the same family since it was built in 1770s.

The Gardens. – Pencarrow is known for its trees, conifers especially, from all over the world, planted in 1830s and since diversified to include English broad-leaves. Superb specimens soar 75-100ft, line the mile long drive and continue beyond a sunken Italian garden to a lake and American Gardens. Spring bulbs, rhododendrons, camellias, azaleas, and the bluest hydrangeas, carpet the ground.

The House. – Inside the house, **Joshua Reynolds** family portraits, an **Arthur Devis** conversation piece with St Michael's Mount in the background *(anteroom)*, Continental, English and Oriental porcelain, Georgian wine glasses and several beautiful items of Georgian furniture, highlight the different rooms. Note a small Georgian **envelope table**, the giltwood **Adam furniture** *(Drawing Room)* upholstered in the same rose silk damask as the curtains – "treasure" from a Spanish ship captured by a relative off the Philippines in 1762. The portrait above the Louis XVI settee is of the "little Cornish baronet" *(p 69)*.
On the walls enclosing the cantilevered staircase which leads to the bedrooms with their William IV and George IV four-poster beds, are Samuel Scott paintings (1755) *The Tower* and *London Bridge* and one of the unforgettable portraits of Charles I *(p 46)* painted by Edward Bower from sketches he made in Westminster Hall at the trial.

61

** PENWITH

Michelin map **403** fold 31 – C and D33

Penwith, the western tip of Cornwall, the most westerly headland in England with Land's End unmistakably pointing the fact, has a bleak beauty all its own deriving from its granite foundation, the wind, the blueness of the ocean, the stalwart small granite churches with their individual, landmark towers, the Celtic wayside crosses. Spiking the undulating hillsides along the north coast are the chimneys and derelict engine-houses of old mines; even older are the prehistoric villages and ancient hill forts which crown the hill tops. It is an area of legend and wide open space. The area described below is that west of A30, Penzance-Hayle road.

SOUTH PENWITH
Penzance – Land's End

Lamorna and Lamorna Cove. – Half a mile separates the village from the cove below the Carndu headland which marks the boundary of Land's End granite.

★ **Land's End.** – *P 57.*

Logan Rock. – *Access on foot from the Coastal Path.* The "logan", a 70-ton boulder which moved at the touch of a finger, was displaced by a Royal Navy party as a prank last century; although repositioned it has never been as keenly balanced.

★ **The Merry Maidens and The Pipers Standing Stones.** – The Pipers, 15 in number and 13½ft tall, stand hauntingly, in the field just north of the road, the 19 Merry Maidens, 4ft high, squat and still, in a circle in the field to the south – the story being that the maidens were turned to stone for dancing on a Sunday to the pipers' tunes.

★ **Mousehole.** – Mousehole really is an attractive small village – which is, of course, why so many people go there ! The **harbour** is almost enclosed by a quay of Lamorna granite, and a **breakwater** dating back to 1393 *(p 52).* Lying just back from the fishermen's low granite cottages at the water's edge, is the half timbered Keigwin Arms, the only house left standing after 16C Spanish raid. Beyond the end of the harbour the beach leads past **Merlin**, an offshore rock, the Battery Rocks, site of a gun emplacement until 19C and The Mousehole, an old smuggler's cave.

Spaniards' Pt further on, is where the raiders landed in 1595 to pillage the countryside, burn **Paul Church** – the 15C pinnacled tower survived and remains a major seamark – and sack Mousehole, Newlyn and Penzance before eventually being driven off.

★ **Porthcurno.** – The road, which drops through the trees to the village, ends at the cove where the Atlantic laps the cream coloured shell sand beach, protected on either side by bluff headlands. *Shelving beach.*

Minack Theatre. – *Access by road from the beach car park also by a steep, uneven, path up from the beach (20mins Rtn).* The idea for the theatre with its ocean back-drop, came in 1929 when a local lady decided personally to terrace part of cliff as a future stage.

★★ **St Buryan.** – Pop 3 220. The village and surrounding landscape are dominated by 14C granite **church tower**★★, 92ft tall, square and pinnacled, from which it is claimed, the the towers of 16 other Cornish churches can be seen. King Athelstan built the first St Buryan Church in 931 AD, following his conquest of the Scilly Isles *(p 75).* The major features today, are the **porch**, amazingly worked in granite, 15C **font** with three angels and a Latin cross; 17C **slate tombstone** finely carved *(W wall; other beautifully lettered 18C stones outside);* 13C coffin shaped tombstone *(NW corner of the tower),* and 15C **rood screen**. Note the **Celtic Crosses** outside.

WEST PENWITH
Penzance – Land's End – Pendeen Watch

★ **Cape Cornwall.** – *1½m from St Just, last 400yds on foot – 30mins Rtn.*
The **view**★★ opens out as you begin to climb the path to the "summit", distinctively marked by a ruined mine chimney. As you walk, even on a fine day, all may be momentarily obscured as a wisp of cloud tangles with the 230ft hillock. From the vantage point by the stack you will see the **Brisons Rocks,** Whitesand Bay, **Land's End,** the **Longships Lighthouse,** possibly the Isles of Scilly.
A promontory to the northeast hides the ruined, now legendary, **Botallack Mine,** which had long shafts running out under the sea.

Carn Brea. – *E of B3306.* The ground rises to 200ft in a rounded hillock, known since **John Wesley** preached there as Carn Brea Chapel *(p 51).*

★ **Carn Euny.** – *5mins walk across the fields from Sancreed – St Just Rd.*
tc The outstanding feature of this Iron Age village, inhabited from 7C BC to mid-Roman times, is the **fougou** (Cornish for cave). This comprises a creep and 40ft long passage, dry stone walled and roofed with large granite slabs, which leads to the unique round chamber, some 10ft across, stone walled, corbel roofed and once domed.

★ **Geevor Tin Mine.** – Geevor *(off B3306 by Pendeen)* is one of Cornwall's four **working**
tc **mines.** Vertical shafts descend 250-350 fathoms; underground workings extend over 4sq miles including "drifts" or horizontal tunnels 250 fathoms below the ocean.
The **tour** is through the tin treatment plant to see the process by which tin, copper, iron and arsenic are separated from the bedrock. Also seen is the magnetic separator which produces the high (70 % tin) and medium (25 % tin) grade concentrates.
The **museum,** contrasts 19C and present day mining; it also exhibits candles and old lamps; helmets and hats; minerals; tin marks and a three-dimensional, scale model to illustrate the vertical system of Cornish tin mining and of Geevor in particular in 1960.

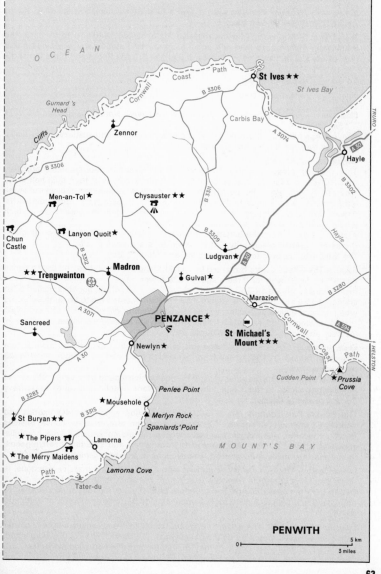

PENWITH

Land's End Aerodrome. – Short coastal flights.

Pendeen Lighthouse. – *P 17.*

★ **St Just-in-Penwith.** – The prosperity enjoyed in 19C by a tin mining town is reflected in the substantial buildings lining the triangular square.

The **church**★ just off the square, has 15C pinnacled **tower**, walls of dressed granite, and an elaborate 16C porch. Note two faded **paintings**, the most interesting for its illustration of 15C craftman's tools, a *Christ of the Trades*. From the mid-5C, when St Just himself was alive, is a gravestone with a Chi-Rho monogram, known from its inscription, as the **Selus Stone** *(before N door)*. In the churchyard are part of a wayside cross and a market cross bearing a Crucifixion.

Sancreed. – Pop 627. The **church**★★ is a rebuilding dating from 15C when the population of the village numbered less than 100 – it reached its maximum of 1398 in 1851 when the local tin mines were in peak production.

The two stage granite **tower** of alternate deep and shallow courses is crowned by battlements and corner pinnacles. Inside, the arcade of five bays on solid granite columns, transept arching, a traceried window *(W end, S aisle),* 14C Norman **font** with crowned angels at the bowl corners, remain from earlier sanctuaries. The **rood screen** shows typical mediaeval human and animal figures half-hidden in the foliage on the lower panels.

Outside in the churchyard are 5 **Celtic Crosses**★★ – two of 8-11C outstanding with carved shafts and Christ in a tunic with expanded sleeves on the heads.

Sennen. – Pop 722. St Sennen on the cliff-top, the most westerly **church** in England, its three stage, pinnacled, granite **tower** a marker for ships at sea, is an enlargement of 13C chapel of which the chancel, transept and north wall remain. The south aisle, granite arcade, and the tower were completed by 1430 when a petition was sent to the pope requesting a licence for a local burial ground since experience showed that attendance of funeral services at St Buryan three miles away left the village open to local pirate raids! By the tower is a 7ft, **wayside cross**★.

Go down to the cove.

If you walk *(20 mins Rtn)* you will pass, in a field, small, nameless standing stones – relic from the unknown past.

★ **Sennen Cove.** – The cove with the massive Pedn-men-du headland at its back, the breakwater, fishermen's hard and small harbour, RNLI station and slip, houses and pub, offers a wide **view**★ over Whitesand Bay, the Brisons Rocks and Cape Cornwall.

NORTH PENWITH
Penzance – Morvah – Hayle

Chun Castle. – *From the farm at the end of the road, walk ½m up the marked hill track – 45mins Rtn.*
The Iron Age hillfort, 100yds across, with gateway uprights and scattered stone walls, can only be seen before the bracken grows.

★★ **Chysauster.** – *100yds across a field.*
tc This, the best preserved, **prehistoric Cornish village,** never fortified, inhabited probably from 100BC to 250AD, consists of eight houses in two lines of four, built below the crest, across a hillside. The roughly circular houses are constructed of blocks of stone – the massive walls are up to 4ft high – with entrance passages to inner courtyards. At each house would have been a pole – post-holes evident in some cases – which would have supported a cone-shaped, thatched roof.
A stream flowed from the hilltop to the marsh below where thatching reeds grew. It was an agrarian community. Off to one side is a *fougou (p 63)*.
The **view** extends over towards Penzance and Mount's Bay.

★ **Gulval.** – The village centre is marked by a vivid triangular flowerbed and by the parish **church**★ of 1440 with its three stage granite tower.
Inside the church are 14-15C **font** with an angel on one corner, angel capitalled **pillars** stained where iron rings were attached by the Parliamentarians to tie up their horses when using the nave as stables, a **cross** *(S aisle window sill)* of mother of pearl inlaid in dark, ancient wood, said to be from a tree from the submerged Forest of Lyonesse, located, according to some, in Mounts' Bay.

Hayle. – Pop 6 179. Copper, tin and iron were smelted in the estuary town before it became famous in 19C for the foundries which produced the famous giant **Cornish beam engines** *(p 50).*
Today its great asset is the miles of sand beaches which extend from Carbis Bay across Porthkidney Sands to the 3 mile long, Hayle Towans Beach which ends at Godrevy Point – *towan* is Cornish for sand-dune.

tc The **Paradise Park** *(Foundry Hill, B3302)* bird collection which includes exotics and home-bred endangered species, fills the large garden of a Victorian house. Besides free-flying scarlet, blue and gold macaws, there are parrots, cockatoos, cranes, hornbills, snowy and great horned owls, eagles, blue crowned and bleeding heart pigeons, flamingoes, penguins and waterfowl and even the near extinct **Cornish chough** *(p 43).*

★ **Lanyon Quoit.** – The quoit of three upright stones supporting a massive capstone, is immediately recognisable from the road *(climb the style for a close view).*
Dating from the Neolithic Age and therefore *c*4000 years old, quoits (also known as cromlechs or dolmens) were burial chambers inside barrows or mounds of earth and stones.

★ **Ludgvan.** – Pop 4 856. The village, straggling along the road, opens out on a corner with a small green, bordered by the churchyard. The **church**★ is 14C, the three stage, buttressed, granite **tower**, rich in gargoyles, battlements and corbelled pinnacles, 15C. Christianity is said to have been brought to the area by Ludewon, 6C Irish missionary.

A contemporary **Celtic Cross shaft** has been built into the tower steps while inside is a small wedge shaped, **granite slab** with two incised crosses, believed to be 7C Christian grave marker *(on a window sill)*. The scalloped **font** is Norman.

Madron. – *P 59*.

★ **Men-an-Tol.** – *On the moor, to the right of the lane*. The stone, once known as the Devil's Eye, stands between two upright boulders, a 5ft disc with a large hole at the centre, through which, "to bracken" disease, one had to crawl nine times against the sun.

Morvah. – Pop 72. The village with a **church tower** which long served as a seamen's beacon, is a place from which to make for the **North Cornwall Coast Path** (200yds) for a spectacular **view**★★ of the 300ft granite cliffs which drop vertically into the Atlantic.

★★ **Trengwainton Garden.** – *P 72*.

tc **Zennor.** – Pop 213. The outdoor **museum** shows the evolution of implements from stone to iron: pounding and grinding stones to miners' iron picks, smiths' anvils, hammers, ox and horse shoes...

Half a mile inland, in a dip in the rock-strewn, windswept countryside, Zennor church tower rises high above the surrounding cottages and the old local pub.

Inside St Sennen, 12-13C granite **church**★ on 6C site, enlarged in 15C and restored in 19C, are a **tithe measure**, now serving as a holy water stoup, two **fonts** of Hayle limstone, and the legendary **mermaid** – a small seductress on a bench-end-chair, neatly carved in 16C with floating hair, a tiny waist and a long scaly tail !

Note outside the church, 1737 sundial and three Cornish Crosses.

★ PENZANCE

Pop 19 579

Michelin map **403** fold 31 – D33
See town plan in the current Michelin Red Guide Great Britain and Ireland

Penzance with its wonderful **outlook**★★★ on Mount's Bay and St Michael's Mount *(p 69)*, has been a holiday resort for 150 years. Progress in communications has brought about each successive stage in the town's development: from mineral and passenger port to spring vegetable and flower despatch point, fish market within easy reach by train of London and the Midlands and now holiday resort accessible by train, coach, car, helicopter and airplane.

The town extends for a couple of miles in each direction around the bay. Within the overall area it divides into three distinct quarters: Harbour-Quay, east of the Battery Rocks; the Western Promenade; Market Jew, Chapel and other streets, the first two, the principal shopping streets, meeting at right angles at the centre of the town.

The HARBOUR – QUAY QUARTER

The Harbour. – The MV *Scillonian*, the boat to the Isles of Scilly *(p 75)*, berths daily throughout the summer in the harbour, crowded with pleasure craft, small cargo vessels, fishing boats and the pilot's launch.

The Quay. – At the end of the quay, on the corner between the dock and the Battery Rocks, behind the typical massive Cornish sea wall, stands a mid-18C granite "cellar" or fish store, known as the **Barbican** and now a lively, working craft centre.

Behind the quay, a maze of alleys leads back to the main streets.

Penzance Heliport. – *1m E off A30*. The heliport at the east end of the town, is the jumping off point for BA helicopters to the Isles of Scilly *(p 75)*.

The WESTERN PROMENADE

The wide promenade and the Queen's Hotel built in 1861, epitomise the confidence Penzance so rightly had that it would become a prime resort. Half a mile long, and extended by the road to Newlyn *(p 66)*, it affords a **view**★★★ of St Michael's Mount and the headlands round to the Lizard.

Behind the wide road, inland at the town end, the network of short streets includes **Regent Terrace**, **Voundervour Lane** and **Regent Square**, lined by small, 18-19C town houses.

MARKET JEW and CHAPEL STREETS

The heart of the town is 18-19C, older buildings having perished in the Spanish raid of 1595.

Market Jew St. – The street rises from the station and harbour to a statue of **Humphry Davy**, (1778-1829), chemist, physicist, inventor of the miner's safety lamp.

Market House. – The granite building of 1837 is distinguished by a bright green copper dome.

tc **Local Museum.** – Penlee House *(W of the Market House)*. The museum is notable for its **tin mining exhibit** which includes a rare, early **ingot** recovered from the bed of the River Fal. Note by the house entrance 7ft, inscribed Celtic Cross.

★ **Chapel St.** – The street cuts down from the side of the Market Hall to a goose's foot of four lanes leading to the Battery Rocks, the Quay, the Dock, and the Promenade; it admits something of both the old harbour and the spacious 18-19C days in its distinctive character. Among other notable landmarks are:

Egyptian House. – The amazingly decorated house dates from *c*1835 and is the sole survivor of several designed in the style at the time.

Union Hotel. – The hotel, refronted in 1810, was built twenty years before as the Town Assembly Rooms and was where, from the minstrels' gallery in the ballroom (now the dining room), the news was first announced in England of the victory at Trafalgar and the death of Nelson *(p 59)*. The master of a Penzance fishing boat crossed the course of HMS *Pickle* as she was making for Falmouth with Collingwood's despatch on board, received the news and thus broke it to the mayor before their lordships received it in London!

No 44 and Abbey House. – *Abbey St.* The 17C group of buildings are said to have been associated with St Michael's Mount when it was a priory.

The Turk's Head. – The inn with a "new" front added after the Spanish raid of 1595 *(p 62)*, is 13C and is probably the oldest building in the town.

Admiral Benbow. – The 15-16C Benbow was a smugglers' meeting place and is even named after 18C band, the Benbow Brandy Men, whose second in command, during a raid, clambered on the roof and fired off his pistols to create a diversion. The revenue men rushed out and shot him down but the inn and the band were saved and he recovered, to be rafishly commemorated in the figure lying along the roof ridge! The inn has been restored with ships' timbers and decorated with vividly coloured coats of arms, figureheads and the gilded carving of a cherub's head from the *Colossus,* the man o'war from Nelson's fleet wrecked off the Scilly Islands when bringing back Sir William Hamilton's collection from Sicily in 1798.

★ **Museum of Nautical Art.** – *19 Chapel St.* The museum, smelling richly of rope and tar, *tc* displays shipwrights' tools, sailor-made models and half-models – the latter made, as are architectural models today, to see what a drawing or plan looked like in three dimensions and its wind and water resistance. There are hanging church ships, a model of a dockyard with two wooden walled battleships under construction, a full size section – through which one walks – of a four-decker, 95-gun, man o'war of *c*1750... There are cannon, an ancient handgun and telescope and thousands of everyday things found on the seabed: flintlock pistols, silver and pewter forks and spoons, keepsakes and medicine chests, treasure, and objects from Sir Cloudesley Shovell's flagship *Association* which, with three other men o'war, *Romney, Eagle* and *Firebrand,* foundered in October 1707 off the Isles of Scilly *(p 76)*.

EXCURSIONS

★★★ **St Michael's Mount.** – *5m E by A30, A394 and Marazion. P 69.*

★★ **St Ives.** – *7m NNE by B3311. P 68.*

★ **Prussia Cove.** – *9m SE by A394.*
The cove just inside Cudden Pt is renowned for its smugglers' tales. The most famous have as hero John Carter, known like his inn, as the **King of Prussia** *(pp 15, 56)*.

★ **Land's End.** – *10m W by A30. P 57.*

The Coast from Penzance to Mousehole. – *3m S.*

★ **Newlyn.** – Pop 2 090. Newlyn has always been and remains the major fishing harbour in Mount's Bay and the west: daily the deep sea fleet lands catches of mackerel and whitefish which are marketed for local canning or processing or are despatched to Billingsgate in London. Newlyn is also the centre for lobster and crab fishing.
The village, with cottages typically clustered round the harbour and on the hillside, retains its individuality – a characteristic which, with its beautiful light, attracted a group of painters, the **Newlyn School,** in 1880s **(Newlyn Art Gallery;** on the main road). In the harbour can be seen the new Penlee lifeboat, 52ft, *Mable Alice.*

> *Continue along the coast road.*

Penlee Point. – The old lifeboat house from which the *Solomon Browne* set out on a heroic rescue attempt and perished with all on board in December 1981, now shelters an auxiliary boat, RNLI memorabilia, and "honour boards" of boats manned by Mousehole men. Adjoining is a memorial garden to the men of the *Solomon Browne.*

★ **Mousehole.** – *P 62.*

(BTA)

Mevagissey

ST AUSTELL   Pop 36 639

Michelin map **403** fold 32 – F32

The old market town of St Austell rose to importance in the mid-18C with the discovery in the area by **William Cookworthy**, of china-clay which has been mined locally ever since. The residue, green-white slag pyramids, have become a distinctive local landmark. In the town, where the streets are steep and camellias bloom in the front gardens, are 17C **Market House**, the White Hart, once a posting inn and, on an island site, the parish church.

★★ **Holy Trinity.** – Outside, the church is remarkable for its tall, late 15C **tower**, embattled, corner pinnacled and profusely decorated on all four sides with masks, angels and niches containing statues and groups of the Annunciation, the risen Christ and the Trinity.

Inside, beneath the old wagon roofs and 15C arcade, note how the **nave** is out of line with the tower and the older, 13C chancel. The granite **font** of *c*1200, one of the most impressive in Cornwall, is carved with "gorgons, hydras and chimeras dire".

EXCURSIONS

★★ **Wheal Martyn Museum, Carthew.** – *2m N on A391.*

tc China-clay, or kaolin, used to manufacture porcelain, has seemingly become a constituent of nearly all manufactured products worldwide. The 26 pits worked by the English China Clays Group has the greatest **production** in the world at nearly 3 000 000 tons a year. Of this 15 % goes into fine china, earthenware, tiles and sanitary ware, 75 % into papermaking and the rest into plastics, rubber and synthetic rubber, paints, pharmaceuticals, cosmetics, fertilizers, textiles, leather goods... More than 70 %, or 2 100 000 tons is exported annually *(p 53)*.

A short film explains the old pumping and modern pressure jet extraction and the refining process which can then be followed outside through drags, settling tanks and a drying kiln, water-wheels, old engine houses, horse wagons, steam engines...

Roche Rock. – *6m N on A391, B3274.*

Out of the manmade landscape of calm fields and distant china-clay pyramids, there suddenly towers an elemental rock outcrop, an aeons old upthrust of grey-green-black schorl which, in the early 1400s, an anchorite crowned with a granite block chapel – it is of no importance, but it is memorable.

★★ **St Austell Bay.** – The wide bay circles from **Gribbin Head**★★ *(p 54)* to the long cliff-line, which terminates to the south in the 373ft **Dodman Point.**

Biscovey. – The **Mid-Cornwall Craft Galleries** present, in a former Victorian school building *(N side of A390 by Par crossroads)*, a brimming display of pottery, modern brasswork (fenders), textiles and knitting, painting and sculpture in wood and stone.

Charlestown. – On either side are beaches and small coves; at the centre, at the end of the long main street bordered by colour washed houses, is the town's historic mainstay, the **dock** from which the china-clay boats sail and an outer **harbour** from which emigrants once set out for America. Men and boys line the harbour wall fishing.

Gorran and Gorran Haven. – Gorran Haven, an old village, retains **houses** of those and earlier days in Church St, Fox Lane and the surprisingly named Rattle Alley. St Just, the minute **church** was first built as a seaman's chapel and lantern with a distinctive pentagonal **tower** in 15C.

★★ **Mevagissey.** – A fishing port with houses irregularly terraced up the hillsides, colour washed, half-timbered, or weather-boarded with oversailing upper floors; an inner harbour with 1770s pier, old quayside boathouses and sail lofts (now shops and restaurants); a maze of twisting back streets and steps; nets drying on walls; slate everywhere, on roofs, as front door steps and window sills; a fisherman's loft with nets of every variety of mesh size, weight and colour – such is Mevagissey. Of course all summer long it is crowded with visitors like yourself – but a few minutes' walk and you can get up on one of the headlands for a gulls' eye view.

67

ST AUSTELL

Par. – The onetime pilchard harbour and processing town, tin port and smelting works, is now powdered white from the clay loaded into ships in the dock.

Pentewan. – Stone for many of Cornwall's churches and large houses was quarried nearby for centuries and shipped from the harbour, which lies sheltered between the promontories.

★ **Polkerris.** – The small village with a sand beach, is sheltered to landward by steep cliffs, to seaward by a curving sea wall.

★★ ST IVES Pop 7 508

Michelin map **403** fold 31 – D33
See town plan in the current Michelin Red Guide Great Britain and Ireland

St Ives, a fishing harbour, home for several years of a group of famous artists and still a working artists' centre, is crowded all summer with visitors. Areas of interest include the small headland known as the **Island,** the network of stepped and winding alleys, hillside terraces, archways, "back doubles", all lined by colour-washed fisherman's houses, crowded shoulder to shoulder. The curving quayside and main street are known as **The Wharf** and **Fore St.**

SIGHTS

★ **St Ia.** – The church with its pinnacled, 85ft **tower** of Zennor granite, clearly visible from the harbour, dates, except for 20C baptistry, from 15C when it was built in a single phase. Note the **wagon roof, bench-ends** and carved **font.**
The **Lady Chapel** is unique for the tender *Mother and Child* by **Barbara Hepworth** (1953) who also designed the stainless steel, Christmas rose candlesticks.

★★ **Barbara Hepworth Museum.** – Bar-
tc bara Hepworth (1903-75) was in the line of artists who, beginning in 1880s with Whistler and Sickert, have lived in the town.
The house, filled with a lifetime's **sculpture,** the studio with unfinished blocks of stone, contrast with the small, white walled garden, dense with trees and vivid flowers, which, somehow, provides an uncrowded setting for some twenty sculptures in bronze and stone. Two Hepworths stand before the Guildhall and in Malakoff Gardens (bus station).

Penwith Gallery. – *Back Road West.* The gallery, in a converted pilchard factory, displays painting, sculpture and pottery in rotation by Penwith artists.

★ **Barnes Museum of Cinemato-**
tc **graphy.** – *Fore St.* Cameras and projectors, posters, books, broad-sheets, lamps and lighting appliances, evoke the development of the medium from shadow-play and magic lanterns to the movies.

(Hepworth Museum)

Barbara Hepworth garden sculpture

St Nicholas Chapel. – The chapel on the "Island" is the traditional seamen's chapel built as a beacon. It commands a wide **view**★★ including Godrevy Lighthouse *(p 17),* across the bay.

Smeaton Pier. – The pier was constructed in 1767-70 by the builder of the then Eddystone lighthouse *(p 17).* At its shore end is the small St Leonard's sailors' chapel.

tc **St Ives Museum.** – The local museum is filled with everything to do with historic St Ives.

Sloop Market. – The old market with studio workshops and enamellers, leather workers, a potter or a silversmith at work, can be an interesting port of call.

★★ ST MAWES

Michelin map **403** fold 32 – E33

The small low-lying stone houses, thatched, pink-washed or ivy covered – one dated 1760, another with a Sun Life insurance firemark – the hotels, pubs and small shops along the curving line of the waterfront, continue up the steep road and tributary alleys behind the square. Flowers everywhere confirm that St Mawes has the mildest, sunniest of climates.

★ **St Mawes Castle.** – The clover shaped castle, constructed as a pair to Pendennis
tc (p 52), commands a **view**★ up the Carrick Roads and across to Falmouth.
Unlike Pendennis which withstood many weeks of siege in 1646, St Mawes capitulated to the Parliamentarians; neither fort, in the event, defended the Roads, the purpose for which were originally constructed with their overlapping gunfire.

tc St Michael's Mount is the focal point of every **view**, of every glance, across the bay and itself commands views★★ towards the Lizard and Land's End.

The castle is approached up a steep zig-zag path through the trees *(25 mins Rtn)*.

Legend, foundation, Dissolution. – In 4C BC ships came from the Mediterranean to the **Island of Ictis**, as they named it, to trade in tin, copper and gold; in 495 AD, according to Cornish legend, fishermen saw St Michael standing on a westerly ledge of the granite rock which rises high out of the sea, whereupon the island became a place of pilgrimage. By 8C, it is said, a Celtic monastery had been founded upon the rock which endured until 11C.

At the same time, in 708 in France, St Michael appeared three times in a vision to Bishop Aubert of Avranches who then built an oratory to the saint on the island, from then known as Mont-St-Michel. By the time of the Battle of Hastings, the oratory in France had developed into an important Benedictine community to which St Michael's Mount passed as a dependency. The English house, always modest by comparison with the French monastery, was ultimately appropriated during the course of the Hundred Years War by Henry V as alien property and was finally Dissolved in 1535.

Strongpoint. – Even while it was a pilgrimage goal, the Mount was a the centre of French and Spanish raids on the coast. In the Middle Ages it became a strongpoint from which Perkin Warbeck set out in 1497 and the Cornish Rebels tried to resist the imposition by Edward IV in 1549 of the Book of Common Prayer in English which they claimed not to understand. In 1588 it was from the church on the summit that a beacon signalled the approach up the Channel of the 130 galleons of the Spanish Armada.

17C saw the Mount involved in the Civil War: the harbour became a port of entry for arms purchased with Cornish tin from the French in support of the Royalist cause; in April 1646 the island surrendered to the Parliamentary forces and a year later received its last military commander, Col John St Aubyn, who subsequently purchased the castle as a family residence. In times of war the island is still garrisoned.

The Mount's owners. – Col John St Aubyn, who died in 1684, according to tradition being swept off his horse by a mighty wave when riding along the causeway, began repairs to the fabric and positioned his arms over the entrance when he was still governor. His great grandson (d 1744), the third baronet became famous when in an age of corruption, Sir Robert Walpole, as Prime Minister, declared in the House, "All these men have their price except the **little Cornish Baronet**".

He rebuilt the harbour and the causeway (1727) and altered and embellished the castle interior in 18C style.

(D Bayes / Aspect / Cosmos)

St Michael's Mount

A third phase of alterations occured in 1873-8 when Piers St Aubyn, architect and cousin of the then Sir John St Aubyn, first Lord St Levan, added a Victorian domestic wing to the southeast which descends by as many as five storeys down the rock face to preserve the familiar mediaeval skyline.

Jack the Giant Killer. – Giants once abounded in Cornwall, according to an old map still in the house. They sat on the hilltops, dressed in a loose tunics and floppy hats. St Michael's Mount was even built by a giant, a black-beard named Cormoran who would wade ashore to capture sheep and cattle and then return to the rock to sleep. Jack, a local boy, decided to kill the giant. One night he rowed to the island and halfway up the path he dug a very deep pit; as dawn was breaking, Jack sounded his horn and woke Cormoran, who, with the sun in his eyes, came rushing down the path and fell into the pit and died – the **pit** into which the giant fell is halfway up the hill.

ST MICHAEL'S MOUNT★★★

TOUR *1½ hours*

Doorway. – The doorway is Tudor with the St Aubyn arms above it *(see above)*.

Entrance Hall. – The hall, guardroom and garrison room in the oldest part of the house, are 14C and still much as they were in the priory-fortress period.

Armoury. – The armoury, altered in 19C, displays, among the trophies, sporting weapons, coat of arms and silken banner, the **oak chest** of the first Col John St Aubyn and 1944 paratrooper **beret** of the World War II member of the family. Note the first of many **paintings** of the Mount throughout the centuries and in the rooms which follow the family **portraits** in oil, in silhouette and in miniature.

Library. – The library, in the oldest part of the castle, was transformed in 18C. Note the water-colours of Mont-St-Michel and views from the lancet windows.

Chevy Chase Room. – The former monks' refectory was given the lively plaster **frieze** of men and animals in the field in 17C. The main roof timbers date from 15C, the **royal arms** from 1660 (the 1641 date is a mystery). The dado and doors are 18C Gothick. The great **oak table** dates from 1620s, the **chairs** were made by the estate carpenter in 1800 after the pre-Dissolution Glastonbury model still in the room; the **triangular chair** is Elizabethan; the court cupboard, 17C.

The Church. – The church at the island summit, dedicated in 1125, was rebuilt in 14C following an earthquake. In 15C the windows were enlarged to include the two roses.
Note the banners, the **alabaster panels** in the altarpiece – the smaller ones are 16C Flemish, the larger, rare 15C work from Nottingham – also the late 15C Flemish gilt brass **chandelier** with figures of the Virgin and Child and St Michael killing the dragon *(p 33)*.
At the church entrance is a restored Gothic **Lantern Cross**, carved with the Crucifixion, the Virgin and Child and the heads of an unknown king and pilgrim.

Anteroom and Blue Drawing Rooms. – The creation of the three rooms was the idea of the "little Cornish Baronet" in 18C. Blue walls, deeper blue furnishings, **Chippendale chairs** and settee, a highly ornate Louis XVI **clock** on a marble topped commode, two alabaster and jasper **vases**, stand beneath delicious **Rococo plasterwork**. On the walls are choice family portraits by Gainsborough and Opie and 18C conversation piece by Arthur Devis with two Misses St Aubyn before a distant outline of the Mount *(p 61)*.
The **chairs** in the anteroom are Strawberry Hill Gothick *(p 21)*.

The Battery. – The battery *(below the entrance as you leave)* is armed with guns from a French frigate driven aground by fire from the Mount during the Napoleonic Wars.

The Dairy. – The octogonal walled dairy was built in 1870s when there were 9 cows on the island.

MARAZION Pop 1 415

Pilgrims, waiting for the ferry or for the tide to fall so that they could cross the sands to St Michael's Mount, gave Marazion an increased importance throughout the Middle Ages. Pillage by local raiders, the Dissolution of St Michael's Priory and finally the Spanish raid of 1595 *(p 62)* so reduced the town that it never recovered.

★ ST NEOT

Michelin map **403** fold 33 – G32

The approach to the moorland village of houses of tawny stone and a Perpendicular church of 1425, is up a wooded valley, enclosed by sweeping hillsides.

★★ **St Neot's.** – Outside, pinnacles and battlements line the aisle and west tower; inside, the building is the setting for 12 **windows** of rare, mediaeval English glass.

The Creation *(E window, S aisle)*. – The finest, the oldest, the least restored window, has God measuring out the universe and, at the end, Noah doffing his cap, having received orders to build the Ark.

The Flood *(1st window E, S aisle)*. – Noah builds the Ark which is a real sailing ship of the period, and the story continues with it surmounting perilous seas.

St George *(W window, N aisle)*, **St Neot** *(5th window E, N aisle)* and **Robert Tubbe**, the vicar from 1508-44 who was responsible for obtaining the glass, all appear, as do the donors, the young men and young wives of the village in the lower sections of the aisle windows.

★★ River TAMAR

Michelin map **403** fold 33 – G, H31 and 32 – Local map pp 114-5

The Tamar, is the river boundary between Cornwall and Devon, between Cornwall and the rest of the world, the outsider may sometimes feel – places are situated in conversation, as in the county or "beyond the Tamar". Although traders came to Cornwall by sea from the Mediterranean in the earliest times, the Roman legions never crossed the river – it remains, despite bridges and modern transport, a dividing line.

Boat trips. – Trips up the Tamar start from Plymouth *(p 110)*.

Michelin map 403 fold 32 – F32

Tintagel especially and the West Country in general have always been associated with the elusive legend of Arthur, "the once and future King". The tale has existed in the telling since 8C and in ms form since 12C; the story has been retold in the spirit of the time, with locations shifted, in 12C by William of Malmesbury (p 197), Geoffrey of Monmouth and the chronicler, Wace, who added the Round Table, Sir Thomas Malory, Spenser, Tennyson and Swinburne, T H White...

ARTHURIAN LEGEND in Cornwall and the southwest

Arthur, son of Uther Pendragon, was born or washed ashore at Tintagel, where he had his castle and lived with his queen, **Guinevere** (p 186), and the **Knights of the Round Table** among who was **Tristan** (p 55), nephew, or son, of **King Mark** whose fort was Castle Dore (p 55). **Merlin,** the magician, lived in a cave beneath Tintagel Castle, and on a rock off Mousehole (p 62); the sword, **Excalibur,** forged in Avalon, was withdrawn by Arthur from the stone and finally thrown into **Dozmary Pool** (p 47); **Camelot** is believed to be Cadbury Castle (p 182). The Battle of Mount Bladon in c520, when Arthur defeated the pagan Saxons, was possibly fought at Liddington Castle near Swindon or Badbury Rings, Dorset and the **Battle of Camlann,** the last struggle, against Mordred the king's usurping stepson, on the banks of the River Camel on Bodmin Moor. Finally after being mortally wounded, Arthur sailed into the sunset, to the Islands of the Blest, the Isles of Scilly, or to Avalon, held by some to be close by Glastonbury where his tomb was "discovered" with that of Guinevere in 12C (p 162).

SIGHTS

tc **Arthur's Castle.** – *Access by a steep road from the main street; 30 mins Rtn.*
The **site**★★★ overlooking the sea from precipitous rocks, is a greater feast to the eye than is the fragmentary **castle ruin.** There remain walls from 1145 chapel and great hall built on the site of 6C Celtic monastery and other walls dating from 13C – all, of course, centuries later than Arthur's time !

★ **Tintagel Church.** – Small and lowlying on the cliff, with its rough, early 15C granite **tower** standing four square against the wind, Tintagel church has long been a sailor's landmark. It was first built between 1080-1150, and retains 12C features including the south door, the north doorway with tiny side windows, crossing arches, the EE triple lancet window in the north transept... The **font** is Norman with rudely carved heads and serpents; a second smaller font has cable moulding. There are also 13C **memorial stone** with a carved foliated cross (crossing, S side), a mediaeval slate topped **stone bench,** a brass of 1430.

★ **Old Post Office.** – The small, rambling manor house, built with 3ft thick stone walls
tc and undulating slate roofs at the centre of the village, dates from 14C.
Inside are a small, two storey mediaeval hall, stone paved and with an ancient fireplace beneath exposed roof timbers, also the postmistress' office and, up the narrow wooden staircase, two bedrooms below a maze of beams and collar braces.

EXCURSIONS

★ **Boscastle.** – *3m NE off B3263.*
The village straggles downhill from the road to a long tongue of sea which pours in at high tide between 300ft headlands. The inlet is the only **natural harbour** between Hartland Point and Padstow. The inner jetty dates from 1584, the breakwater from 19C; the onetime coaching inn is 15C; the cottage gardens are bright with flowers.

★ **Delabole Quarry.** – *4m SE by B3263 and by-roads.*
tc Delabole, a name synonymous with slate in Cornwall and once much further afield, is the oldest continuously worked slate quarry in Europe – Beaker Folk on Bodmin Moor in 2 000 BC used slate as baking shelves. The quarry, one of the largest **manmade holes** in the world, has a perimeter of 1¾ m and is 500ft deep – *viewing terrace.*

Museum. – Demonstrations of slate splitting and a display of the old tools once used in quarrying. Roofing slates are sized down from queens and duchesses to mere ladies !
The village is made of slate – church, houses, walls, steps, sills, gates and posts...

★ **Camelford.** – *6m SE by B3263 and B3266. P 47.*

Port Isaac. – *9m SSW by B3263, B3314 and by-roads.*
The ancient fishing village with narrow streets and alleys and a small, protected harbour from which Delabole slate was once shipped, stands in a designated area of outstanding natural beauty: cliffs drop to the sea in an almost unbroken line, any break being occupied by minute hamlets such as **Port Gaverne,** and **Portquin.**

★★ TRELISSICK GARDEN

Michelin map 403 fold 32 – E33

tc The Classical style, giant porticoed, house of 1825 stands on a high promontory, superbly overlooking, and clearly visible from, the Carrick Roads (p 52). Walk round the house to where the **view**★★ extends towards Falmouth and the open sea.
There are three gardens at Trelissick: the woodland **Valley Garden,** which drops down towards the Fal (both sides of the road) with tall trees underplanted with foliage, exotics, bulbs, wood anemones and primulas, and the **East Lawn Garden,** where the beech tree trunks frame glimpses of the Roads and azaleas, rhododendrons, and hydrangeas bloom luxuriantly in season, and the **Flower Garden.**

★★ TRENGWAINTON GARDEN

tc The garden lies along the half mile drive to the house which is covered in wistaria and the New Zealand scarlet lobster claw plant. Beyond is a second garden of island beds of azaleas and rhododendrons, from which there is a **view★★** of Mount's Bay. An early owner, Sir Rose Price, who was a great tree planter, built the walled gardens to the right of the drive with beds banked up to face the sun, to produce early fruit and vegetables. Sir Edward Bolitho, in 20C, financed, with the owners of Trewithen *(p 73)* and Hidcote, Glos, Kingdon Ward's plant collection expeditions of 1927-8 to bring back specimens from Burma, Assam and China from which the rhododendron and azalea collections have since been built up and hybridised.

All the important plantings are fully labelled.

The GARDEN

(National Trust / Tymn Lintell)

The stream garden in spring

Rhododendrons greet you from the start: majenta, pale yellow and large pure white blooms and overtopping them, the first of many tree ferns from Australia.

Two paths branch off the drive: the left makes for a stream and glades of rhododendrons beneath the trees, which include a maidenhair and the beautiful white ladies' handkerchief or *Davidia involucrata*. The right hand path enters the series of five walled gardens, now particularly rich in tender magnolias, pink flushed, dark purple, narrow white, saucer large and fragrant, besides a host of other flowering trees such as a Tasmanian cider gum, the small white flowered New Zealand tea, the Canary bird, the scarlet lobster claw, the passion flower, acacias, rhododendrons, camellias, fuschias...

Beside the drive, the stream garden is a brilliant contrast with primulas, astilbes and wax-white arum lillies in front of a magnolia *stellata,* a tulip tree...

★ TRERICE

tc The small, silver-grey, stone manor house stands in a wooded valley, framed by the walls and yew hedges of its flower gardens.

The manor house was rebuilt in 1572-3 to an E shaped plan with, on the east front, highly decorative scrolled gables and a hall with a beautiful window, stone mullioned and transomed with twenty-four lights and 576 small panes of 16C glass.

TOUR *¾ hour*

The interior is particularly notable for 16C **plasterwork.**

Great Hall. – The fine **ceiling** which is ribbed and pendented, the scrolled **overmantel** and the miniature **arcade** which fronts the musicians' gallery demonstrate the plasterers' skill. Note also, from inside, the **great window** and among the furniture, 20ft table made from oak from the estate in 19C, the mid-16C chest, late 17C travelling desk and 18C oak travelling case beneath an Aubusson tapestry.

Library. – The library, with a faded green 19C Donegal carpet, is furnished with 18-19C mahogany and walnut pieces among which are a domed **coffer,** and chiming, longcase **clock.**

Drawing Room. – The room, the former solar, is again decorated with outstanding **plasterwork,** notably a barrel roof with the family arms high on the wall at one end, and a decorated overmantel on telamons, dated with hybridised numerals.

Musicians' Gallery. – As you cross the gallery glance down into the hall. Look up also for an unusually close view of the plasterwork ceiling.

Court Chamber. – Among 17-18C walnut furniture is a double dome **secretaire-bookcase.** Note also the longcase **clock** by Thomas Tompion (*c*1680).

North Chamber. – The Georgian **mahogany furniture** is highlighted by a four-poster with clustered columns and a painted cornice. The ebonised bracket clock is by Joseph Knibb (1650-1711).

Lobby. – The lobby contains a second Tompion longcase **clock.**

Mower Museum. – In the barn is a collection of mowers which traces their development since the early 19C.

★★★ TREWITHEN

Michelin map **403** fold 32 – F33

Trewithen is famous, above all, for its beautifully landscaped, 20 acre garden.

The GARDEN

tc Already in 1730 the ancestor of the present owners, was reported as having "much improved the seat, new built a great part of the house, made good gardens". His successor planted trees to such good effect that, by 1904, a descendant decided "it was necessary to take an axe and claim air and light from amongst the trees, first for the house and those that should live in it and then for the plants". In 1905 there arrived 100 hybrids of *rhododendron arboretum* – precursors of the present 50 or more different varieties of rhododendron, 30 of camellia, 40 of magnolia, which give the garden its especial beauty. Planted in great bays at the edge of a lawn to frame a **vista**, beneath the trees, in alleys and dips, contrasting with the dark red feathered leaves of *acer palmatum atropurpureum,* they present an ever changing billow of colour, a waxen stillness, a waving of white or pink handkerchiefs against the sky... Of specialist interest are the **house hybrids**: rhododendron Trewithen Orange, Alison Johnstone, Jack Skilton, Elizabeth, camellia Trewithen pink, Glenn's Orbit and Donation.

The HOUSE *time: ½ hour*

The 18C country house with all the classic features of proportion and panelling, includes amongst the period **furniture** several lovely smaller pieces and, in addition to portraits and paintings, Bristol glass, **Chinese small bronzes** and **porcelain,** notably blue and white ware, and a collection of **Japanese great plates.** There is also a collection of clocks.

TRURO Pop 16 348

Michelin map **403** fold 32 – E33

In 1859 Truro seized the opportunity, which Bodmin had rejected *(p 46)*, of bringing the railway into the centre of the town.
A onetime river port, mining centre and stannary town *(p 43)*, it had come to be considered by 18-19C, with its theatre and assembly rooms, county library (1792), horticultural society, Royal institution of Cornwall, and, since 1850, the cathedral, as the county "metropolis". It had also developed into the most notable Georgian town west of Bath with 18C houses in Boscawen, Lemon and other streets.

SIGHTS

Truro Cathedral. – Requests made throughout centuries for Cornwall once more to become an independent see *(p 46)* were finally acceded to and in 1850 the cathedral foundation stone was laid. Bishop Benson sought a church "exceeding magnifical", rural parishioners wanted "a proper job", the architect J.-L. Pearson, steeped in the last of Gothic Revivalism, a "house of prayer" in 13C EE style. The approved design, an admixture of Normandy Gothic with upswept vaulting, space and vistas through tall arcades and, outside, three steeple towers which give the cathedral its **characteristic outline,** was completed by 1910.

★ **Cornwall County Museum.** – *River St.* The museum is the learned and colourful
tc showplace of the Royal Institution of Cornwall (f1818) with displays of English ceramics complementing an exhibit on **William Cookworthy** *(p 110)*. There are also English pewter, a group of **silver spoons** made in Truro in 17C and works by **John Opie** (1761-1807), the "Cornish Wonder", the son of a St Agnes mine carpenter who found fame with his portraits.
The archaeological department displays early Bronze Age **gold collars** and other objects made of Cornish and Irish gold, a fragment of a bronze dagger probably imported from Greece *c*1200 BC and Roman gold coins found in south coast harbours.
The tin and copper mining tools' exhibit takes one from the streaming, or panning, done *c*2000 BC for alluvial deposits to the opencast mining of the Middle Ages and, finally, underground working. A 1C BC **tin ingot** shaped in a knuckle or H form and weighing nearly 160lbs found in the River Fal, is visible evidence of the age of the industry *(p 43)*.

EXCURSIONS

★★★ **Trewithen.** – *3m NE by A39, A390. See above.*

★★★ **St Just-in-Roseland Church.** – *23m S by A39, A3078.*
The church stands in the most perfect **setting** imaginable. The path leads down steeply from the lychgate through the churchyard garden of rhododendrons, brooms, fuschias, hydrangeas and a strawberry tree, to the church which stands so close to the creek that when the tide is in, its mirror image is reflected in the water. The sanctuary, on a 6C Celtic site, is partly 13C, largely 15C but suffered a fierce restoration in 19C.

  Continue S to St Mawes.

★★ **St Mawes.** – *P 68.*

St Anthony-in-Roseland. – The forked peninsula between the Carrick Roads and the open sea is known as Roseland, meaning promontory. The headland points are marked respectively by St Mawes Castle *(p 68)* and the lighthouse *(p 17)* on St Anthony Head from which the **view★★** extends up the Carrick Roads and, on a clear day northeast towards Dartmoor.

★★ **Trelissick.** – *8m S by A39 and B3298. Turn right at Four Turnings.*

Come to Good. – Come to Good, which appears from outside to be just a whitewashed, thatched cottage with linhey stables under the same roof, is a Quaker Meeting House. Built in 1710, it measures 27ft long by 20ft wide, cost £68 18*s* 3*d* to construct, and is still in use.

Feok. – Pop 3 252. The **church** ★, standing above the village which overlooks the Carrick Roads, is distinguished by having a separate, west **tower belfry** with a pyramid roof dating from 13C. The church is 15C restored in 19C. Note the carved Catacleuse **font**.

★★ **Trelissick.** – *P 71.*

King Harry Ferry. – How the ferry, which has 18ft tide rise and fall and is now a chain ferry, got its name and how long it has been running no one knows, though the **Ferry Boat Inn** on the bank is, obviously, several centuries old.

★★ **Veryan.** – Pop 880. *13m SE by A39 and A3078.*
Imagine living in a small white walled, **round house** with Gothick windows and a conical thatched roof surmounted by a cross – there are five such in Veryan.

★ **Probus.** – Pop 3 512. *9m NE by A39.*
The granite **church tower** ★, at 125ft 10in, is the tallest in Cornwall. Dating from 1523, it rises through three stages of niches, fenestration, carved string courses and gargoyles, to a castellated crest complete with pinnacles and sub pinnacles. In the lofty interior, note the **tower screen** with its alphabet from the time when the room was used as a school, the royal arms of 1685, the two figures **brass** of 1514 *(aisle, under the red carpet)*.

The **County Demonstration Garden** ★ is full of ideas and information for well established and new gardens. Within its 54 different sections it displays shrubs, flowers, plants for shady and exposed positions, ornamental trees, herbs, hydrangeas in acid and alkaline soils, garden design for small spaces, vegetable growing...

Follow A390 to Grampound.

Grampound. – With its 12ft high cross in the market place, Grampound, which in 1620 returned John Hampden as its MP, in 18-19C had become a by-word for parliamentary corruption: bribery had gone so for that the town was disenfranchised in 1821, eleven years before the Reform Act, by special act of parliament!

(BTA)

Bedruthan Steps

Michelin map **403** - inset
Access: See Penzance in the current Michelin Red Guide Great Britain and Ireland

The climate. – There is an almost constant wind from the Atlantic and clouds, bowling in low over the ocean, hit the rocks and drop their moisture in short, soaking showers – wind and waterproof clothing and shoes, therefore, are essential. On all the islands' leeward sides are long white sand beaches, coves, walks or flower filled gardens. The water, clear, safe (except over the sandbars) and tempting, is icy!

The Archipelago. – The islands are the mountain peaks of Atlantis? The lost land of Lyonesse? The uncertainly located Cassiterides or westerly tin islands of the Phoenicians? The Islands of the Blest where dead heroes were buried? Anything could be believed as from the sea or the air (500-2 000ft up, 120 knots) you get a **view★★★** of the archipelago of 5 inhabited, 40 uninhabited islands and 150 named rocks, set in a close group in the clear, blue-green ocean. Headlands, reefs and saw-toothed needles stand, ruffed in white spume, the larger islands lush and green.
What is certain is that the isles were Bronze and Iron Age settlements, the Roman outpost of Sylicancis, the Viking Syllanger; that from 400-1 000 AD there were Christian hermits on the isles, monks on Tresco; that Athelstan dispatched the Danes from the islands in 930 AD and that in 1114, Henry I granted Tresco to Tavistock Abbey to establish a Benedictine priory. In 1830s Squire **Augustus Smith** became Lord Proprietor; in 1920 the Duchy took over all the inhabited islands except Tresco.
With the arrival of the Lord Proprietor, the islands knew 40 years of prosperity: houses, churches, and schools were built, five shipbuilding yards were established on St Mary's, the **flower industry** was begun.

Gig racing. – On Friday evenings from May to September, the six-oared island gigs race in the St Mary's roadstead, starting usually off Samson and finishing at the Quay. The gigs of elm planking ¼in thick, 28-30ft long, with 5ft beam and less than 2ft draught, were built as rival pilot launches and smuggling craft – they were banned from having more than six oars not to have an advantage over the excise cutters!

ST MARY'S

St Mary's (pop 1 650) is the principal island and the largest – 3m across at its widest and with a coastline of 9m; it is the island where all but a few hundred Scillonians live; where visitors land by sea and air. At its Old Quay lie the excursion launches which are one of the main attractions of a holiday in Scilly.

Hugh Town. – The town, which runs the length of the sand bar between the main part of island and a hill to the west, the **Garrison,** overlooks the sea on two sides; south, across the silver **Porth Cressa Beach**, north, over the harbour, **St Mary's Pool.**

Museum. – Local life is illustrated from prehistoric times to today by specimen tools, coins, log-books, boats, posters, wrecks and treasure, including brooches found in HMS *Association* (p 76). There is also an excellent **bird section** (native and migrant).

★ **The Garrison Walk.** – *Preferably an evening stroll; 1 hour.* Go through the **Guard Gate,** built in mid-18C when the defence was fortified with 18 batteries. Star Castle, eight pointed on the brow of the hill (now a hotel), dates from the time of Queen Elizabeth's feud with Spain. Continue inside the rampart wall which circles the headland, scanning the **view★★** and naming the islands and rocks if you can! The range of houses, one with a crest, at the walk's end, are the **Duchy of Cornwall** offices (p 43).

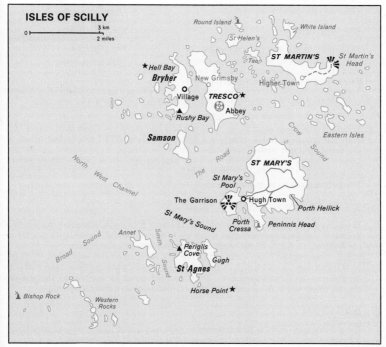

Old Town and the eastern end. – Roads and paths make it possible to follow the coastline, cut across in any direction or even start out on or, halfway round, pick up the bus which makes regular circular tours. Features of interest include:

Porth Mellon. – *W shore, just beyond the lifeboat.* The remains of a Henry VIII square fort are known as **Harry's Walls.**

Telegraph Tower. – At 158ft the island's highest point.

Bants Carn. – *15mins walk Rtn from the tower.* 3C BC burial chamber of stones and capstones and the walls of an Iron Age village.

Porth Hellick. – The large inlet is marked by a rough monument where Sir Cloudesley Shovell was washed ashore from the wreck of the *Association* in 1707. A gate close by opens the way to the top of the Down and 4 000 years-old passage grave.

Old Town Church. – The church, rebuilt in 19C on 12C foundations, is surmounted on its east gable by 10C stone cross; in the churchyard are the graves of seamen from many shores.

★ **Peninnis Head.** – The head is spectacular with eroded granite rocks of majestic size.

★ TRESCO

Smith built himself, in the island stone and using wrecked ships' timbers, a Victorian-mediaeval castle mansion. Below the house, in the sheltered hollow around the old abbey ruins, he created from seeds and plants brought back by Scillonian sailors and professional plant collectors, the soon famous, subtropical gardens.

★ **Abbey Gardens.** – The plants, despite the salt sea wind, burgeon and self-seed *tc* everywhere. The 12 acre garden, facing the sun, is divided by two long straight paths: the east-west, **Long Walk** and the north-south, **Lighthouse Way** with flights of steps rising to a bust of Neptune, from where there is a **view★★** across to other islands and over the Tresco garden itself with its hundred and more varieties of trees and brilliant flowers.

Valhalla. – Some fifty ships' figureheads, trailer and name boards, fiddles and carved ornaments from the thousand ships wrecked off the islands in the past two centuries, stand gilded and boldly coloured, facing into the wind.

The isle's two tower forts, **King Charles'** and **Cromwell's Castles,** date from 16 and 17C.

BRYHER

Visitors land on the east shore from where a road leads past 18C church to the **village** on Watch Hill (**view★**). The path divides, going south to the sheltered beach at **Rushy Bay,** north to Shipman Head and **Hell Bay★** *(white painted marker stones)* where the Atlantic plays out an often thundering and always splendid drama against rocks and cliffs. Incredibly from the minute fields on this and other islands, the islanders produce more than 1 000 tons of cut flowers a year – 12 daffodils weigh 5 oz...

(After Gérard Sioen / CEDRI photo)

Ship's figurehead

ST AGNES

St Agnes and the islet of **Gugh** *(accessible across a sandbar at low water)* are separated from the other main islands by **St Mary's Sound,** a deepwater channel followed by the *Scillonian* at low tide. The channel is said to have made the islanders the most independent, the men the finest pilots, the fiercest smugglers and wreckers.

Follow the road up to 17C lighthouse (private house).

The right hand path leads down to **Periglis Cove** and the small **church** built in mid-19C from the proceeds of the wreck of a foreign frigate of 1781 whose bell hangs in the turret. The **east window** dates from 1960s.

Continue south by the footpath *(marked),* past the miniature, pebble stone **maze** to the grandiose rock scenery of **Horse Point★.**

The path continues to the lighthouse.

ST MARTIN'S

The two mile long granite spine which is St Martin's, presents a rugged shore to the northeast and fine sand beaches on all other fronts. Minute flower fields shelter in the hollows; tumuli or burial mounds crown the more exposed sites.

A path from Higher Town leads to the red and white day mark erected in 1683 on St Martin's Head, a 160ft high **viewpoint★★** from which to see the **Sevenstones Reef** *(7m N),* grave of the *Torrey Canyon* in 1967, and, two miles further off, the **Lightship,** on station since 1841. On a clear day the mainland coast is clearly visible.

SAMSON

The uninhabited island is characterised by twin hills joined by a narrow sand isthmus – a desert isle with megalithic remains and the ruins of 19C cottages.

DEVON

Area 2 591sq m (3rd largest county in England after N Yorkshire and Cumbria) Pop 958 745

"Devon, glorious Devon" ran the song so popular in drawing rooms and music-halls at the turn of the century, and everyone agreed. The county had become accessible with the advent of the railway in the mid-19C and now is even more so with the construction of motorways and dual carriageways (M4, 5, 6, A30 and 38).

The scenery. – The landscape becomes more smiling as you journey south.

North Coast. – Except at Wesward Ho!, Croyde and Woolacombe, where the sand beaches stretch for miles, the coast comprises spectacular cliffs and headlands.

South Central Devon. – The granite boss which is Dartmoor, is tilted towards the south with the highest tors, the widest horizons to the north, the network of wooded lanes and villages to the south.

South Coast. – The long south coast (accessible at every point by the South Devon Coast Path) is so diverse as to suit every mood: coves, headlands and beautiful estuaries.

The American Connection. – The early history of the United States, it has been claimed, owes more to Devon than any other English county; more emigrant ships left Devon bound for North America, more expeditions sailed westward from Plymouth than from all other English ports put together. The most famous expedition, of course, was that of the Pilgrim Fathers who finally sailed from Plymouth in the Mayflower on 6 September 1620 and landed at New Plymouth, now Plymouth, Mass, on 21 December.

The 17-19C colonists. – Jamestown, Virginia, established on 14 May 1620, was the first permanent English settlement in the New World.
In the early 17C, the fishermen were not only coming ashore to dry their catches and re-supply their boats but had set up trading posts with the Indians for furs. Numbers increased: it has been estimated that between 1600 and 1770, 750 000 people crossed the Atlantic. The passage cost £10; the ships, some of only ten tons, were not adapted to passenger transport, returning home with timber and fish.
By 19C the traffic divided into bulk traffic through the larger ports for the poorer people – it is estimated that half a million emigrants sailed out of Plymouth alone – and individual passages on ships using the smaller ports such as Bideford and Torquay. The middle of the century saw a further transformation with the development of steam, the increase in the size of ships, the inauguration of regular trans-Atlantic services with ships such as the SS Great Western and SS Great Britain (p 37).

Place-names. – Although English immigrants were not the most numerous, a large number of place-names in the United States derive from the towns, villages and counties of England, 120-150 from Devon alone.

★ A LA RONDE

Michelin map **403** fold 35 – J31 – 2m N of Exmouth

tc The unique, 16-sided house, once thatched, was designed by Jane Parminter in 1795, a lady who could so easily have been a character in a Jane Austen novel.
Miss Parminter, the daughter of a Devon merchant, spent her early years in London where, under the influence of Mrs. Delany, she learnt many of the genteel arts of the period, using such mediums as shells, feathers, paper, paint and needlework to create decorative effects. In the 1780s, with companions, she set out on a Grand Tour which was to last 10 years. She incorporated many of the impressions gained into the design of her house and utilised the skills learnt in London to decorate its interior. The result is a delightful **period piece**.

(A La Ronde)

The 16-sided house

The **interior plan** comprises eight rooms, each of different shape, and interconnected via wedge-shaped ante-rooms, all radiating from a central octagon 45ft in height, surmounted by a shell gallery reached through Gothick grottoes. The drawing room is decorated with a feather frieze and examples of the ladies' needlework, cut paper and seeweed and sand pictures.

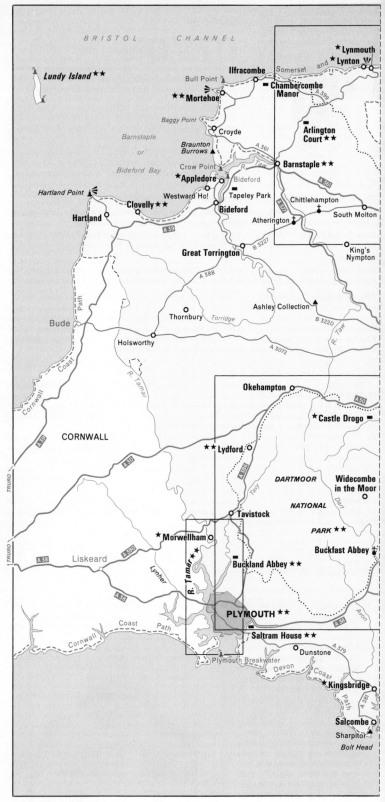

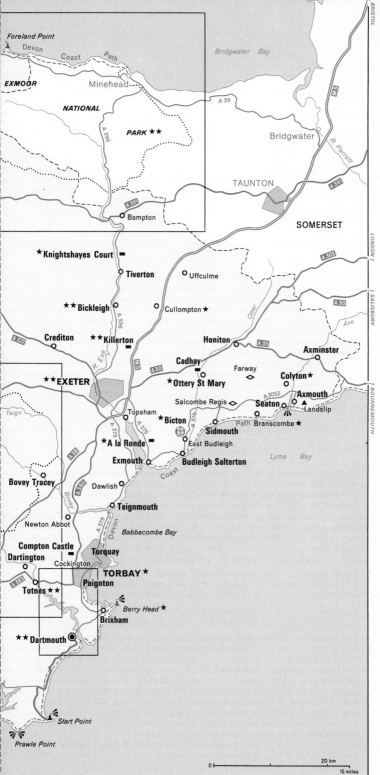

★ APPLEDORE   Pop 2 180

Michelin map 403 fold 24 - H30

Drake's *Golden Hinde* was built in replica in an Appledore yard in 1973. The same yard builds pleasure-craft and fishing vessels while at the other end of the scale, Europe's largest covered yard, Appledore Shipbuilders Bidna complex, produces container ships, sand-dredgers, coasters...

Over the centuries a network of narrow streets evolved. It was in 1845 that the quay, until then an irregular, tide covered strand, lined by a straggle of cottages, was first constructed (rebuilt 1941).

The Streets. – Follow the line of the point along the **Quay**, with its views across the Torridge to Instow *(irregular passenger ferry in season)* and north to the Braunton Burrows *(p 105)*; trickle back along the very long **Irsha St** with its older, vividly painted cottages (one named Smugglers' Run is dated 1664), centre gully and minute courts. In the narrow **Market St** note the white painted, bow windowed houses.

tc **North Devon Maritime Museum.** – *Odun House.* The house of 1834, named after a Saxon chieftain who defeated Hubba the Dane in 878 in a battle just outside Appledore, displays ship development from the building of wooden ships on open beaches to the construction of steel vessels by flow-line production. There are also girthing chains, traverse boards, gammon corners, fiddleheads and carpenter's tools.

★★ ARLINGTON COURT

Michelin map 403 fold 25 - H and I30 – 8m NE of Barnstaple

tc The model ships alone – 36 made by French Napoleonic prisoners of war, 10 Dunkirk Little Ships and some 70 others – would make the Court unique, but the ships comprise only one of the collections made by the house's former owner, Miss Rosalie Chichester. Miss Chichester was a Victorian-Edwardian lady who was born in 1865, the year her father enlarged the classically styled house, creating the grandiose staircase and hall as a background to his and his wife's glittering social life. Miss Chichester died in 1949, 16 years before her step-nephew, Sir Francis Chichester, made his epic voyage round the world in *Gipsy Moth* (1966-7).

When she was three and again at twelve, Rosalie Chichester went on long Mediterranean cruises with her father aboard his 276 ton yacht, and became imbued with a lifelong interest in ships; when she was 16, however, her father died, leaving the estate heavily mortgaged – it took 47 years but she cleared all the debts. Meanwhile, modestly at first, she began the collections which were to furnish and characterise her home.

The HOUSE *time: 1 hour*

Entrance Hall. – Among the photos is one of the young Miss Chichester in 1885 in a large straw hat.

The State Rooms. – The 70ft long south front gallery was designed with scagliola marble columns to form one long gallery or be divided into three rooms.

In the **Morning Room** are a typical 19C collection of shells, several ships and a Portuguese pottery bull; in the **Ante Room** a notable collection of silver, English and Irish glass, a Chinese rock crystal cat and small jade, soapstone and crystal animals and scent bottles, a Bristol glass ship of 1851 and the **William Blake** painting *Cycle of the Life of Man* (1821). The **White Drawing Room**, at the end, has a late 18C Donegal glass chandelier, a carpet with the Chichester herons in the corners, English, French and Chinese porcelain, precious snuff-boxes and a unique red amber elephant.

Small Boudoir. – The enriched plaster ceiling, faded rose and gold silk hangings, Chinese porcelain and 19C *papier maché* furniture, stand reflected in the obliquely set mirrors. A display case contains more small animals, snuff boxes and vinaigrettes.

Corridor. – The cabinets contain **commemorative mugs** of the years 1887-1937 and an important collection of English pewter from platters to spoons, dominoes and chessmen.

Staircase hall, gallery and lobby. – The fleet of ships can be seen assembled, including the Little Ships that went to Dunkirk and *Gipsy Moth*, made as a colophon to the collection.

The **Napoleonic prisoners' ships** date from 1814, in the main – 122 000 men were taken between 1794-1815. Almost immediately they were set to constructing prisons and public works – Princetown on Dartmoor, the Floating Harbour in Bristol... Among the men in the south of England were a number of Flemish ivory carvers who from making and selling small ornaments from beef and mutton bones, had graduated by 1814 to carving ships which they produced to scale in every detail and embellished with figureheads – the only inaccuracies are the British names and colours given to French vessels for reasons of salesmanship! The distinction of the Chichester collection is that it contains examples of almost every class of ship of the Napoleonic period, from three-deckers to sailing frigates.

The GROUNDS

Paths *(about 1¼ m)* lead down to the lake where an urn marks the place where Miss Chichester's ashes were buried; there is also a memorial in the church by **John Piper**.

★ The CARRIAGE COLLECTION

The handsome 19C stable block, crowned on the clock tower cupola by a Chichester heron, contains the National Trust collection of 19-early 20C horse-drawn carriages. They range from Queen Victoria's **pony bath chair** to a hooded buggy, a royal "canoe" landau, hansoms, gigs, phaetons, wagonettes, an omnibus.

AXMINSTER
Pop 4 954

Michelin map 403 fold 35 – L31

The carpet weaving which was to make the 2 000 years old town's name a household word, was introduced in 1755 when the Axminster clothier, Thomas Whitty returned from a visit to London where he had seen a very large (36 × 24ft) and beautiful Turkey carpet. He promptly erected an upright loom in his own factory which still stands in Silver St (now the Conservative Club), trained his five young daughters, charged his sister as overseer and on midsummer's day began weaving his first large carpet.

The Church. – By the Middle Ages Axminster was a community of sufficient prosperity to rebuild its Saxon Church in 12C Norman style, to add a tower in 13C (recased in 19C), to rebuild again in 14 and 15C in the Decorated and Perpendicular styles, to repair the tower after it was damaged in an affray against the Parliamentarians in 1644 and to enlarge and remodel it in 18-20C.

Note inside the cut down Jacobean **pulpit** and **reading desk**, the charity boards, the **royal arms** painted in 1767 at a cost of £9 14s and, in the chancel, the tomb with the lovely recumbent **effigy** with steepled hands of Lady Alicia de Mohun (d c1257).

The Streets and Squares. – The two squares, Trinity and Victoria Place, and the streets between, are marked by occasional Georgian houses, rounded shop-fronts and a coaching inn with a Venetian window above the wide yard entrance.

tc **Carpet Factory.** – *Off King Edward Rd, down by the station.* You see looms being threaded with hundreds of bobins of different coloured wool yarn; automatic weaving from jacquard cards; shearing and the inspection at every stage.

AXMOUTH
Pop 447

Michelin map 403 fold 35 – K31

If you come up-river from Seaton old harbour, watch the mud flats for waders *(p 23)*. Once a bustling riverport, the village is now a tranquil place with a winding main street overlooked by small houses, some still thatched, occasional 15-16C larger houses on the hillside and two old thatched pubs, one half-timbered and 800 years old.

The Church. – The church was rebuilt in c1140 on what may have been a Saxon site, and again in 1330, so that now it appears with Norman round columns marking the south aisle and a Norman north doorway, Decorated chantry chapel and a Perpendicular tower. Note the Italian-style mediaeval **paintings** on the Norman pillars of an unknown saint and a *Christ of Pity*, also the 1667 Charles II **hatchment**.

★★ BARNSTAPLE
Pop 19 178

Michelin map 403 fold 34 – H30

Butchers' Row and 17C cast iron and glass roofed **Pannier Market**, which come vividly to life each Friday when farmers' wives and smallholders pack in to sell dairy produce including Devon cream, vegetables, fruit and preserves, are a reminder of the town's 1 000 year history as the regional agricultural centre, trade and cattle market. Alfred recognised it as a burgh and gave it defences, the Saxons a charter in 930.

SIGHTS

★ **The Long Bridge.** – The bridge, 520ft in length and 10ft wide, was first constructed in stone in c1273. In 1539 the drawbridge connection, which until then had existed at the town end, was replaced by three arches making a total of 13; in 1796, the year a regular coaching service was inaugurated with Exeter, it was widened and again in 1834.

The Parish Church. – The church was rebuilt in 1318 adjoining, on its south side, the older tower which, in 1636 was overlapped with a lead covered, broach spire. Note especially inside, 17C **memorial monuments** *(S aisle)* and the large **mayoral pew** with a lion and unicorn.

Horwood and Paiges Almshouses and **Alice Paige School.** – The almshouses and school, which was endowed to take "20 poor children for ever", were all built in 17C in the quiet, cobbled and bollarded Church Lane *(courtyard through the arch)*.

tc **The Guildhall.** – *High St end of Butcher's Row.* The hall, 19C replacement, contains the **Dodderidge Parlour**, a room panelled in 17C oak from a wealthy merchant's house, in which is displayed the town's famous collection of **corporation plate**. There are three silver-gilt steeple cups of 1620 – a replica was presented to Barnstaple, Mass. in 1939 on the tercentenary of its foundation – maces, lidded tankards and a vast **punch-bowl** used at the proclamation of the annual fair. (Wednesday prior to 20 September).

Queen Anne's Walk. – *Downriver from the bridge.* The walk was built as the merchants' exchange in 1609, enlarged 20 years later and rebuilt in 1708 to comprise a single colonnade beneath a statue of Queen Anne. Note the **Tome stone** on which bargains were struck and wall tablets about the Armada.

tc **Craft Market.** – *Church Lane.* Original quality items by local workers.

tc **North Devon Athenaeum.** – *The Square.* The collection includes mediaeval tiles, pottery and pewter and a local history library of 400 000 volumes.

EXCURSIONS

★★ **Arlington Court.** – *8m NE on A39. P 80.*

★★ **Morthehoe.** – *25m NW by A3261, B3261 and by-roads. P 105.*

★★ BICKLEIGH Pop 210

Michelin map **403** fold 25 – J31

Bickleigh looks like all that a Devon dream village should: from the old stone bridge over the Exe there is a view across to thatched houses and cottages with whitened cob walls and gardens running down to the water's edge, against a backdrop of rising fields and trees.

SIGHTS

★★ **Bickleigh Mill Craft Centre and Farms.** – *S side of the bridge.* The mill stands
tc restored with a working water-wheel and machinery.
The 19C farm displays rare and traditional breeds, uses Shire horses and oxen for power and milks its cows and goats by hand. Old fashioned pigs, ornamental bantams and hens scratching in the farmyard, add to the atmosphere. A farming life museum depicts the everyday round at the turn of the century.
Craftsmen and women – potters, painters, spinners – can be seen at work in individual log cabins.
There is also a fish farm where trout and carp may be fed or fished.

★ **Bickleigh Castle.** – *Right (A 3072) before the bridge, then follow the signs.*
tc Pink and white water lilies and irises transform the moat, wistaria decks 14C tufa-stone gatehouse walls, thatched buildings form part of the whole which has approaches marked by 17C Italian and 18C English wrought iron gates.

Norman Chapel. – The chapel, which is thatched, was built between 1090 and 1110. The nave and chancel masonry, the doorway arch are original, also two windows the others being 15C when the chancel was barrel roofed.
Note the **sanctuary ring** *(p 175)*, EE font, mediaeval glass, 15C poppy-head **benches** and hour long sand-glass sermon **timer**.

The Castle. – Of the castle itself, only the gatehouse remains, Fairfax having ordered all to be slighted so that the Royalist Sir Henry Carew was compelled to construct an adjoining farmhouse of cob and thatch.
Go through the vaulted **Gatehouse,** on either side of which, are an Armoury and the former Guard Room which now contains Tudor furniture.
At the top of the early Tudor wooden staircase, the **Great Hall**, over 50ft in length and containing two stone fireplaces, extends across the full width of the gateway. The panelled minstrels' gallery is Tudor, the furniture Carolean-Queen Anne.
The rooms in the **Farmhouse Wing** are notable for their ingle-nook fireplaces: the first has 1588 fireplate and a bread oven to one side; the second a large vaulted oven and an aperture to control the smoke in the adjoining bacon-curing store; the third, in the Garden Chamber, 17C carved overmantel which depicts crowded, possibly historic scenes from the lives of 14-17C castle owners.
Note also the wooden Ionic pillars in the first room, believed to have furnished the stateroom of a Spanish man o' war and the very old French china in the Garden Room.

★ BICTON

Michelin map **403** fold 35 – K31

tc The grounds and gardens of Bicton House, which is now an Agricultural College, have been progressively designed and planted with specimen trees over the last 200 years.

★ The GARDENS

In 1730s, Baron Rolle, the first in a line of keen horticulturalists, rebuilt the house and had the formal **Italian Gardens** laid out after a design of 17C French landscape gardener, André Le Nôtre. To these gardens have been added conservatories, an **American Garden** (started in 1830s), a secluded **Hermitage Garden** with its small summerhouse and lake, heather and dwarf conifer plantations, a pinetum and acres of close mown lawns banked by rhododendrons, azaleas and magnolias.

Woodland Railway. – The 18in gauge railway, originally from the Royal Arsenal, Woolwich, takes you on a journey of more than 1¼ miles through the grounds, running close beside the lake and through the woodlands and plantations.

The MUSEUM

The James Countryside Collection. – The collection shows the tools and implements that were in use on the land almost unaltered for centuries and the revolution in the same equipment over the last 50 years: there are horse-drawn harrows and a blacksmith's forge, a regal gipsy caravan of 1902, a steam traction engine of 1894, 1917 Fordson tractor, a cider press of 1800...

BIDEFORD Pop 12 296

Michelin map **403** fold 33 – H30

Bideford gets its name from its site at the foot of a hillside "by the ford" across the River Torridge. It achieved fame as a port in 16-18C and is always recalled as the town with one of the most "beautiful and stately" **bridges** in the kingdom.
As a port it gained early prosperity from having been given by William Rufus to the **Grenvilles** who held it until 1744 by which time they had obtained borough, market and fair charters for it. Through Sir Richard Grenville's colonisation of Virginia and Carolina, Bideford developed a trans-Atlantic trade by 16C which was greatly

increased in the mid-17C by Newfoundland codfishing and at the turn of the century, by tobacco imports from Maryland and Virginia. In addition there developed a trade in wool from Spain for the local textile industry and a general commerce with Mediterranean – the mile long quay was built by the town corporation in 1663.

Prosperity declined, except for coastal shipping, until the arrival of the railway in 19C brought the town into the tourist network.

(Vloo / J Alan Cash)

The Bridge

** The BRIDGE

The first bridge was built of **oak** in the last quarter of 13C. In c1460 a **stone bridge** was constructed, using the timber as scaffolding and following its line exactly even to the width of the arches which had varied according to the length of the original timbers! It is 557ft long, numbers 24 arches which are between 12 and 25ft wide and spring from piers of correspondingly different size – it has been repaired and widened many times, but remains as individual as ever.

ADDITIONAL SIGHT

★ **Burton Art Gallery.** – The modern gallery stands in the extensive and brilliantly
tc flowered Victoria Park at the end of the quay beyond the statue of **Charles Kingsley** who wrote a great part of *Westward Ho!* while staying in the town in 1855.
On display are fine **English pewter** of 17-18C – chargers, platters, jugs and tankards – Bideford and Fremington pottery, notably great, late 18C slipware **harvest jugs**, English domestic silverware, English 17-19C porcelain including small figurines and paintings. The museum's speciality derives from a rare bequest of 800 **card-cases** – English, French, Oriental in origin and made of ivory, silver, tooled leather, silk, wood marquetry, lacquer, Scottish silk tartan, *papier mâché,* needlework, mother-of-pearl, tortoise-shell... About 100 cases are on display at any one time.

EXCURSIONS

★★ **Clovelly.** – *11m W by A39 and B3237 N. P 86.*

★ **Appledore.** – *3m N on A386. P 80.*

tc **Tapeley Park, Instow.** – *2m N on A39, right turn beyond Westleigh.*
The house, at the end of the long drive banked high with trees and rhododendrons, stands in a spectacular **setting** overlooking the Taw and Torridge estuary and a beautiful terraced, Italian garden.
Built of brick with stone dressings, the mansion is 17C, much altered and enlarged but still retaining 18C plasterwork ceilings. Interest inside ranges from 18-19C service memorabilia to fine porcelain and glass and William Morris furniture.

Westward Ho! – Pop 1 315. *3m W by A386 and by-road.*
The golden sands extend for three miles; the Atlantic rollers bring the surf-riders thunderously towards the shallows then subside harmlessly to wash around the ankles of paddling, squatting toddlers – Westward Ho! is Devon's safest beach.
Backing the sands is a ridge of pebbles and behind these the grass covered **Northam Burrows;** at the opposite, west end of the beach, the pebbles end in rocks and pools. Above rise the **Kipling Tors** from which there are views towards Hartland Pt *(p 99).*

BOVEY TRACEY   Pop 4 226

Michelin map **403** fold 34 – I32 – Local map p 91

The small town is a gateway to Dartmoor *(p 89).* Many of the cottages are built of moor granite but in typical Devon fashion are mellowed by thatched roofs.

★ **St Peter, St Paul and St Thomas of Canterbury.** – The church was founded, it is said, in repentance for his part in St Thomas Becket's murder in 1770, by Sir William de Tracey *(p 105)* whose family had long been owners of the village. The slender tower is 14C, the church, with Beer stone arcades with well carved capitals, is 15C and considerably restored. Of especial interest are the **Jacobean tombs,** 15C brass **eagle lectern** with three small lions at the base, the pre-Reformation stone **pulpit,** carved with ten still perfect figures all coloured and gilt and, above all, a remarkably carved 15C **rood-screen** of 11 bays with figures of the saints in the lower panels.

tc **Parke.** – *½m W on N side of B3344.*
At the heart of 200-acre woodland estate on the edge of Dartmoor, a rare breeds farm has been established in restored, traditional farm stone outbuildings. Among the breeds on view are Long Horned cattle, sheep, old fashioned pigs and brightly coloured poultry.

BUCKFAST ABBEY

Michelin map 403 fold 34 – I32 – Local map p 91

The present abbey church was consecrated in 1932, some 900 years after the original foundation made under King Canute. The new church and monastery, built by members of a community of French monks which had fled to England in 19C, followed in plan the rediscovered foundation of the Cistercian house Dissolved by Henry VIII in 1535.

TOUR ½ hour

The style is Norman in grey limestone relieved with yellow Ham Hill stone; at the centre is 158ft crossing tower.

Interior. – The church of pure white Bath stone rises above the arcades, triforium and clerestory to a plainly vaulted rib roof, 49ft above the nave floor. There is no pulpitum or screen and the eye is immediately drawn the 220ft length of the church to the **high altar**, rich in gold, enamelwork and jewels. Suspended above the altar is a 48-light, gilded **corona**.

Continue round behind the altar and east up the steps from the ambulatory.

Blessed Sacrament Chapel. – In contrast to the abbey, the chapel, dedicated in 1966, is in the present idiom with **walls of stained glass**. The chapel was designed by the monks who also built it and made and set the glass in all its shades of blue, purple, red and pale yellow.

★★ BUCKLAND ABBEY

Michelin map 403 fold 33 – H32

tc **Drake** purchased the house, for which he paid £3 400, through nominees in 1581. The seller was his lifelong rival, **Sir Richard Grenville**, who had inherited the manor from his grandfather, a property owner in N Devon who had bought 13C Cistercian abbey after the Dissolution in 1541. Sir Richard, cousin of Sir Walter Raleigh, naval commander and privateer, who was to die off the Azores aboard the *Revenge* in 1591, had completed the conversion of the abbey church into a house before he sold it. Drake in 1581 was forty; he had sailed to West Africa and the Spanish Main; in 1577-80 he had circumnavigated the globe. He was famous, newly knighted and he was rich: the house was intended to provide a suitable setting should he retire from the sea – but of course he didn't. In the next few years were to come expeditions to Vigo (1585) and Cadiz (1587), where he "singed the King of Spain's beard", the capture of a Spanish vessel off the Azores with cargo worth £114 000 and the Armada.

TOUR 1 hour

The abbey is arranged as three domestic rooms and a kitchen and three museum galleries, two rooms and one gallery being specifically devoted to Drake.

Great Banqueting Hall. – The great room with its pink and white paving, is panelled in oak decorated with fluted pilasters and a holly and boxwood inlay; above is a moulded ceiling with pendants and, on one side, an allegorical frieze.
Furnishing the hall are 16C oak table, chests, the patent with the royal seal for the Cadiz raid, a replica **medallion** engraved with the circumnavigation route and two original oil paintings – contemporary **portraits** of Drake by Marc Gheeraerts, and his second wife, Elizabeth Sydenham. At the centre, still and silent, is **Drake's Drum.**

The Chapel. – The simple chapel stands on the site of the abbey church high altar.

Traditional Devon Crafts Gallery. – Among the crafts and artefacts displayed are shipbuilding and sailmaking, lacemaking, Plymouth porcelain *(p 110)*, pewter, horse brasses, cider-jugs and village Friendly Society pole-heads.

Drake Gallery. – The gallery, on the first floor, has murals of the circumnavigation and displays the **Armada accounts** and silk banner made to dress the *Golden Hinde* when the queen knighted Drake at Deptford in 1581.

Drawing Room. – The oak panelled room is furnished with finely carved 16-17C pieces and hung on the walls with contemporary **portraits** of the queen and Drake's cousin, Sir John Hawkins (by Hieronymo Custodis).

Georgian Staircase, Georgian Room. – The staircase and Georgianised room were installed in 18C. The stairs rise 60ft in four flights from two impressive **dog gates.**

Naval Gallery. – The long gallery under the roof is filled with scale models of ships from ancient times to today's warships.

Tower Room. – Drake's coat of arms fills the overmantel; note 14C traceried window.

Tithe Barn. – The great barn in the grounds, buttressed, gabled and once thatched, dates back to 14C abbey.

BUDLEIGH SALTERTON   Pop 4 456

Michelin map 403 fold 35 – K32

The small town, to some degree, maintains the atmosphere of a mid-19C watering place. An old sea wall lines the short parade above the beach of steeply shelving shingle – Sir John Millais' was living in the town in 1860s and used both wall and shingle as the setting for his famous painting *The Boyhood of Raleigh.*
Salt pans in the marshes beside the River Otter gave Budleigh Salterton its name.

EXCURSIONS

East Budleigh. – Pop 859. *2m N on A376.*
The small, one time wool town, has a **church**★ which dates back to 12C and has a close connection with Raleigh whose father was a church warden. Note especially the carved and coloured **bosses** and 16C **bench-ends**, carved with a sailing ship, craftsmens' tools, dolphins and portrait heads – there are 60 in all.

Hayes Barton. – *2m by A376 then left (1m) through East Budleigh.*
The long, thatched farmhouse where Sir Walter Raleigh was born in 1552 can be seen from the road.

tc **Otterton Mill.** – *2½m by A376 and right at main crossroads beyond East Budleigh.*
The present mill is early 19C. Flour is stoneground on the premises which also house craftsmen and women making Honiton pillow-lace, potting, spinning and weaving, blowing glass, wood turning, cabinet-making and working leather. Note the stream running the length of the village street with individual **stone bridges** to the houses.

CADHAY

Michelin map **403** fold 35 – K31 – 1m NW of Ottery St Mary

tc "John Haydon esquire, sometime bencher of Lincoln's Inn, builded at Cadhay a fair new house and enlarged his demesne" – the period was probably in the early 1540s. Haydon was a successful Exeter lawyer, who had married Joan Cadhay in 1527 and had become rich as one of the local commissioners responsible for selling the Dissolved priories in and around Exeter.

Contruction. – The house, incorporating the earlier Great Hall, was built round three sides of an oblong courtyard.
John Haydon's heir, Robert Haydon, installed massive Tudor fireplaces with ornamental emblasoned tracery inside and, in a second building phase, enclosed the open side of the courtyard known as the **Sovereigns' Court.**
The 18C owner included among his alterations the horizontal division of the Great Hall and the "Georgianising" of several rooms.
The furniture includes 16C oak refectory table, 18C mahogany tables and chairs, chests, chests on stands, a secretaire.... each is a "working" piece for Cadhay is a house lived in by its owners; their taste is reflected everywhere, their interests in the collection in the Long Gallery and Roof Chamber, in the flowers which illumine every room and in the garden itself, enclosed by tall hedges and white clematis-draped walls, as it runs down to the old, 15C canons' fish-ponds.

TOUR ½ hour

The Court of Sovereigns. – The court, the house's unique feature, which was enclosed at the end of 16C, was further transformed by the **walls** being refaced with dark knapped flints and small sandstone blocks in an irregular chequer pattern and the setting of four elaborate Renaissance style **niches** above the doors at the centre of each range. In the niches, in full robes of state, stand Henry VIII, Edward VI, Mary Tudor and Queen Elizabeth – hence the court's name; it was completed in 1617.

Dining Hall. – The hall, part of the original Great Hall, has a high coved ceiling, an arcade, formerly open, at one end, and one of the giant Tudor fireplaces.

Drawing Room. – The room is one of those Georgianised in 18C.

Roof Chamber. – The chamber is the upper part of the Great Hall and although the timbers have been much cut about, many are the original 15C beams.

Long Gallery. – The gallery runs the length of the Court of Sovereigns.

★ CASTLE DROGO

Michelin map **403** fold 34 – I31 – 2m NE of Chagford – Local map pp 90-1

tc Castle Drogo is the romantic dream of a man, **Julius Drewe,** who was born in 1856. The son of a clergyman, Drewe was sent on leaving school, as a tea-buyer to China. On his return, he started the Home and Colonial Stores and within ten years had made a fortune. At 33 he retired from active business. He bought himself a country house in Kent, married and bought a larger house, Wadhurst Hall in Sussex, which he took over complete with its tapestries and Spanish furniture.
Julius' elder brother consulted a genealogist who "proved" that the family was descended from Dru or Drogo, a Norman noble who came over with the Conqueror; his descendant in 12C, Drogo de Teigne, had settled in Devon and given his name to the village of **Drewsteignton** *(p 90).* Julius Drewe, on discovering the family history, began to buy land and a quarry in the area as a first step towards materialising his dream. The second step was his introduction to an imaginative architect at the peak of his career, **Edwin Lutyens** (1869-1944).

Construction. – The foundation stone of Castle Drogo was laid on the bluff overlooking the Teign Gorge and vast horizons of Dartmoor in 1911 – the plans were still being evolved as they continued to be throughout the next 19 years of building. Constructed of rough hewn and dressed granite from Drewe's own quarry, it presents two, three-storey ranges each approximately 130ft long, on different levels, meeting in a wide angle of 160°. Towers, mark either end and the centre; windows, in the form of giant canted bays with stone mullions and transoms, the east and southeast fronts overlooking the moor.

CASTLE DROGO ★

TOUR *1 hour*

The characteristic **features** throughout are the interplay of heights and levels between the ranges, marked where there are changes in direction by saucer domes; the use of bare white **granite**; the beautiful **views** from the windows.

Walk through the front door.

The Hall. – *Ground floor*. The first of several tapestries brought from Wadhurst hangs in the hall. Also on view are 17C Spanish chest, 18C English dummy board figures by the hearth, 16C Limoges enamel roundels.

Library. – *Ground floor*. The lustre dishes above the Lutyens oak bookshelves are Spanish; the marquetry bureau is Dutch, the lacquer screens are Chinese.

Drawing Room. – *Ground floor*. The room is highlighted by the **views** to be seen through the windows lining three sides of the room. The chandeliers are Venetian. Among the exotic furniture and furnishings, note the lacquer cabinets and 18C *famille verte* vases from China, a French Empire clock of *c*1810.

Main Staircase. – On the walls are portraits of Mrs Drewe in her Sussex garden and Mr Drewe in full fishing regalia in Scotland – about which Lutyens commented that "At least he (the artist) could paint boots".

Dining Room. – *Lower ground floor*. The room serves as a family portrait gallery.

Service Corridor, Pantry, Kitchen, Scullery. – *Basement*. The dolls' house of 1906 in the vaulted corridor was made for one of Mr Drewe's daughters. In the kitchen and scullery, note the oak cupboards and round table designed by Lutyens.

North Staircase. – The stone staircase, which rises through five floors, is cantilevered out from the wall, while the oak balustrade is constructed independently round a cage. The **Green Corridor**, one of three similarly designed, overlooks the Teign Gorge.

The Chapel. – *Access from outside*. The chapel lies beneath the south range.

The Gunroom. – The adjoining, vaulted room is now used to display a number of Lutyens drawings and plans for this extraordinary house.

CHAMBERCOMBE MANOR

Michelin map **403** fold 24 – H30 – 1m SE of Ilfracombe

tc The 15-17C house, lowlying amidst farm buildings in a wooded dell, is white painted over stone and slate roofed where it was once thatched. Its owners have been many and various: relatives of Lady Jane Grey, tenant-farmers, wreckers.

TOUR *½ hour*

Downstairs. – Inside, the house presents exposed beams, open fireplaces, wide planked floors, 2-300 years-old polished **lime ash floors,** hard as granite, and said to be made of wood ash and scrumpy laid as would be cement. Note the court cupboard dated 1595, the oak dresser, 17C refectory table, 13C Peter's Pence **almschest.**

Upstairs. – The principal room is **barrel vaulted** and decorated with a Tudor plaster frieze and the arms of Lady Jane Grey in commemoration of a visit to the house. The room was formerly part of the Great Hall which was divided horizontally in 16C. Among the furniture, note the Elizabethan four-poster bed robustly carved from Spanish oak timbers, a Cromwellian oak **cradle** and Jacobean chest of drawers, a William and Mary **tallboy** in yew, and, in the Victorian room, the lace-edged bed-linen, *papier mâché* chairs inlaid with mother-of-pearl and the parasols.

The **garden,** is bright in summer with roses and fuchsias.

★★ CLOVELLY   Pop 419

Michelin map **403** fold 33 – G30 and 31

Clovelly lives up to its picture postcard image: the **High St** is incredibly steep, stepped and cobbled, a course for pedestrians and pack donkeys and known, according to which way you are facing, as **Down-a-long** or **Up-a-long;** fuchsias, geraniums, hydrangeas deck the small, whitewashed 19C houses which seem to stand on one anothers' shoulders all the way down. The minute harbour, or Quay Pool, at the bottom is often bright blue, dappled with fishing boats and pleasure-craft. Of course there are crowds, everyone like yourself, having come to the village to see it for themselves!

(B Gérard / Explorer)

Clovelly: Up-a-long

SIGHTS

Quay Pool. – Overlooking the harbour, which is protected from the open sea by a curving breakwater, are a typical old inn, stonebuilt fishermen's cottages and balconied houses, and boats drawn up on the shingle beach. The **view** extends from Lundy to Baggy Pt.

Clovelly Church. – The church, a Perpendicular rebuilding with its Norman font, Jacobean pulpit of 1634, and contemporary benches, is remarkable for its **monuments** which include a brass of 1540, 17C epitaphs and 18C sculptures.

Hobby Drive. – *3m from the car park to A39.*
The private road meanders 500ft above sea-level through the woods, affording sudden, open **views** of the coast and cliffs. It was built in 19C by the owner of Clovelly Court *(not open)* and so named because its construction became his hobby.

★ COLYTON   Pop 2 435

Michelin map **403** fold 35 – K31
Alternative recommended access by tram from Seaton, see p 113

Colyton is very venerable and very small; it has thatched and slate covered houses with stone or cob walls, an oblong square and, dominating every view, a church with a rare octagonal lantern with pinnacles, castellations and a pointed pyramid roof. The village is Saxon in origin. It came into the hands of the Courtenays, the Earls of Devon, and when Henry VIII executed the titleholder as a traitorous aspirant to the crown in 1538, into those of the king. Twenty townsmen, mostly merchants and yeomen farmers, raised £1000 and in 1546 purchased the hundred back from the crown.

★ **St Andrew's Church.** – The church closely mirrors the village's history. It was built on a Saxon site (reconstructed Saxon cross in S transept) with a stout crossing tower, when the Courtenays, who were of Norman origin, were lords of the manor; in the prosperous 14-18C, it was enlarged and embellished.

The lantern tower. – The pinnacled, octagonal lantern was superimposed on the tower in 15C, being paid for, it is said, by a rich wool merchant who saw it not only as a church enrichment but also as a beacon for his ships sailing up the then still navigable River Axe. The clock is early 18C.

Chancel. – The church's east end was enlarged in 14C; note the carved capitals.

Nave. – The nave, which was enlarged in 15C when the great Perpendicular west window was inserted, was heightened in 18C – note the classically plain capitals.

Transepts. – The **screens** are 16 and 17C – one Perpendicular with lacelike stone tracery surrounding a canopied tomb with recumbent figures, the other Jacobean with characteristic strapwork and surmounting obelisks.

COMPTON CASTLE

Michelin map **403** fold 34 – J32

tc The massively fortified manor house stands on land granted in 12C to the de Comptons who married into the Gilbert family who, except between 1800-1930, have held the manor ever since. Among the family were **Sir Humphrey Gilbert** (1539-83), navigator, founder of the colony of Newfoundland (1583), his brother **Adrian**, navigator, colonist and seeker after the NW Passage (both half-brothers of Sir Walter Raleigh) and **Raleigh Gilbert**, founder of Sagadahoc Colony in the State of Maine (1607).

The Castle. – The castle was constructed in three phases. In 1320s the **Great Hall** measuring 42 × 21 × 33ft high, was built running from west to east; in 1450 a west range, including the north-south oriented chapel, was rebuilt on a larger scale; in 1520 the same operation was undertaken on the east side and the **fortifications** were constructed – the curtain wall with its machicolated and portcullised gateway, the towers, which at one time numbered six, and the massive surrounding wall. These defences were designed as protection not against a national enemy but against the regular and often large-scale raids of French and, since the Armada, more especially Spanish marauders and pirates *(p 15)*.
A high wall at the back encloses a small garden.

CREDITON   Pop 6 198

Michelin map **403** fold 34 – J31

"When Exeter was a fuzzy town", the old rhyme goes, "Kirton (Crediton) was a market town" and such it remains with a long wide main street of mostly 18-19C houses with local shops at pavement level and in some of the taller, three storey houses, traces of weaving lofts from when the town was known for its woollen serges (1800-50). At the lower, east end of the main street stands the vast church built on the site of the earliest cathedral of the See of Devon.

St Boniface. – In *c*680 a boy, who was christened Winfrith, was born to newly arrived Anglo-Saxon invader-settlers in the town. He became a Benedictine and after missionary work in Frisia (NW Netherlands), went to Rome where Pope Gregory II gave him the name Boniface. He was sent first as a missionary then as primate to Germany where he remained until in his seventies, when he returned to Frisia only to be murdered (755).

★ **HOLY CROSS CHURCH**

In 739, Aethelheard, King of Wessex, founded a monastery in Crediton, which in 10C became the seat of the new bishopric of Devon and Cornwall *(p 46)*. In 1406 the see passed to Bishop Leofric who transferred it to Exeter *(p 94)* and the church at Crediton became a college of secular canons.

In 1539 when the college was Dissolved, the town raised £300 to "purchase" the former collegiate church and annexe the rich Exminster living. The transaction was confirmed in 1547 under a charter granted by Edward VI which incorporated 12 "governors" to supervise the church's temporal affairs including the collection of tithes, providing for the poor and establishing a Free Grammar School (in the Lady Chapel, 1572-1876).

Tour *½ hour*

The church is constructed in the local pink volcanic stone with creamy Beer stone used to highlight the Perpendicular window tracery and crossing tower pinnacles.

The Nave. – The pink tuffa stone interior of 1415, illuminated by clerestory windows – rare for Devon – and 19C tie-beam roof, is dominated by a "period" memorial of 1911 in an extraordinary assortment of marble and mosaic. Note, at a lower level, the stone benches, the Norman font bowl *(left of the porch)*, the modern wooden statue of St Boniface *(N aisle)*, 19C, also wooden, lively carving of the eagle lectern.

The Crossing. – At the crossing, built in *c*1150 and the earliest part of the church, among the capitals carved with snakes, scallops and zig-zag decoration, is a pair of solemnly perched birds with spread wings.

South Transept. – Note 15C human head corbels and 20C armorial window.

Former Chapter House and Governors' Room. – The three-storey, EE building dating from *c*1300, contains the former chapter house, now the vestry, a museum with a large model of the High St in 1743 and, in the Governor's Room on the second floor, 17C armour, a buffcoat, a musket and pair of boots from the Civil War, 15C **angel boss**, charity boards and an ingenious vote-casting **box**.

Chancel. – The chancel and aisles, contain a number of **monuments**: Sir John and Lady Sully (full length effigies), he a Knight of the Garter, warrior of Crécy and Poitiers, who is said to have died aged 105 in 1387; Sir William Perryam (d 1650), a judge at Mary, Queen of Scots' trial, leaning on one elbow in his judicial robes above his family of weepers; 17C, Elizabeth Tuckfield between her be-ruffed husband and father-in-law. In the St Boniface Chapel is 15C Flemish merchant's **chest**.

DARTINGTON

Michelin map **403** fold 31 – I32

Fifty years after its foundation Dartington flourishes, expanding further the concepts of the founders, the Elmhirsts, who believed in the encouragement of personal talent and responsibility through education and rural regeneration which, in practical terms, meant the establishment of a working community where people would find scope for their personal development and a sense of fulfilment while earning a living.

Within relatively few years of the Elmhirst's purchase of the long desolate, 14C house and 800 acre rump of its estate, the name Dartington had become a synonym for "advanced" co-education, summer schools, art courses, exhibitions and concerts... The school today numbers 300; the college of arts, 350; there continue to be summer schools, concerts, courses; the estate has been increased to 2 500 acres, and includes new hamlets and farms; there are a dozen local enterprises; there are Dartington Glass *(p 98)* and the Beaford Centre which takes programmes of music, theatre, dance and film to towns and villages in N Devon; there is Morwellham *(p 105)* on the Tamar. About 750 people are employed by the trust.

Dartington Hall and Gardens. – The **gardens** and courtyard are open to visitors and, when not in use, 14C Great Hall with its hammerbeam roof *(through arch beneath clock tower)*.

tc **Cider Press Centre.** – *Shinners Bridge.* The centre, converted out of an old cider house, affords a permanent exhibition and sales centre for work executed by craftsmen and women with studios in Dartington and the southwest and for the output of the trust's local enterprises including the Tweed Mill and Shop *(½m W on A385, Plymouth rd)*, Dartington Furniture, Staverton Joinery *(½m N off A384)* and Dartington Glass *(p 98)*.

Guard against all risk of fire.
Fasten all gates.
Keep dogs under proper control.
Keep to the paths across farmland.
Avoid damaging fences, hedges and walls.
Leave no litter.
Safeguard water supplies.
Protect wild life, wild plants and trees.
Go carefully on country roads.
Respect the life of the countryside.

★★ DARTMOOR National Park

Michelin map 403 fold 34 – I32

Dartmoor, 365 square miles in extent, and with a great sense of space, is the largest of the five granite masses which form the core of southwest England. The centre is an **open moorland** at a height of approximately 1 000ft; to the north and west, with a small additional group in the south, are the **tors,** the highest rising to 2 000ft; to the east and southeast lies a pattern of **wooded valleys,** with hanging oakwoods above cascading streams, fields, farms and small villages.

The moor is divided by two ancient **trackways,** now the east-west Ashburton-Tavistock road (B3357) and the northeast-southwest Moretonhampstead-Yelverton road (for Plymouth, B3212). The roads meet at Two Bridges *(p 92),* the most famous with Postbridge *(p 91),* of the clapper bridges on the moor.

(Vloo / J Alan Cash)

The clapper bridge at Postbridge

Dartmoor is a **National Park** which means that it belongs to the nation as a heritage and cannot be despoiled; it does not mean that the public have a right of access any and everywhere – on enclosed land, access is by public footpaths and bridleways; *it is an offence to drive or park more than 15yds off a road.*

The land is not common ground: much, about 70 000 acres, is owned by the Duchy of Cornwall *(p 43),* the rest by farmers and other landowners including Devon County Council, the Forestry Commission, the Water Authority and the Ministry of Defence. A **Commoner,** the occupier of land in a parish or manor which possesses Common Rights, may graze cattle, ponies and sheep, dig for peat, take heather for thatching and stone and sand to repair his house. All **livestock,** on the open moor is owned by farmers; animals are rounded up once a year, branded or tagged and culled with young stock being sold at the famous Widecombe *(p 120)* and other fairs.

The number of visitors annually to the moor has been calculated at 8 million; the number of people who live and work in the villages and towns on the moor's edge and the few small villages upon it, 30 000.

The ponies. – The ponies are probably descended from domesticated stock turned out to graze on the moor perhaps as early as the Iron Age. Do NOT feed them – it encourages them to approach cars and the roads where they get run down.

The sheep. – The Blackfaced Scotch, which were brought in in 1880s for their hardiness and agility, and the Cheviots with prick ears and a cumbersome dignity, are to be seen all over the moor in place of the original White Face.

The cattle. – Galloways and Belted Galloways, black, stocky and hornless, are most often seen, also occasional groups of shaggy, long horned Highland Cattle.

The birds. – Buzzards can be sighted high above the moor, and, more commonly, kestrels. There are also ravens and, beside streams, woodpeckers, wagtails, dippers...

LANDMARKS, TOWNS, VILLAGES on the Moor

Ashburton. – Pop 3 610. The former stannary town *(p 43)* stands on a tributary of the River Dart at the beginning of the old packhorse road across the moor to Tavistock (B3357). At the time the church with its tall Perpendicular granite tower was built in 15C, it was a wool town and thereafter, from 16-18C, a slate mining centre – hence the many slate-hung houses of the period.

Barrator Reservoir. – The reservoir, an artificial lake ringed by wooded banks and with a background of granite tors, was originally constructed to supply Plymouth with water in 1891. It now has a capacity of 1 026 million gallons.

Becka Falls. – The Becka Brook cascades down from the moor, circling boulders in its rush to descend some 70ft into a wooded glade. (Not in dry weather !).

Brent Tor. – The hill, which rises to 1130ft at the western edge of Dartmoor and is volcanic in origin, is distinctively crowned by **St Michael's**, a small stone church with a low stalwart tower. Climb up for the **views**★★.

Buckfast Abbey. – *P 84*.

Buckfastleigh. – Pop 2 894. The market town on the southeastern edge of the moor, once an important wool and cloth centre, is now best known as the terminus of *tc* **Dart Valley Railway,** the former GWR line, always known as one of the most picturesque in England.

A centre now includes engine sheds with locomotives and stock, 7¼ in gauge miniature steam railway, steam traction engines and a museum. The GWR standard gauge line has been re-opened over 7 miles, crossing the river at Staverton Bridge, where the station has been restored, and terminating at Totnes Riverside station *(no exit or access)*.

Buckland in the Moor. – Pop 93. The village epitomizes one's dream of a Devon village with thatched, stone cottages set in a wooded dell. The late-15, early-16C moorstone church on older foundations, is known for its clockface inscribed MY DEAR MOTHER in place of the usual numerals. Inside is 16C painted rood screen.

★ **Castle Drogo.** – *P 85*.

Chagford. – Pop 1 400. The market town, which in the Middle Ages was one of Devon's four stannary towns *(p 43)* and a wool and cloth centre, stands on high ground above the Teign Valley with good **views** of the high tors and of Castle Drogo. A farseeing vicar in 19C recognised the town's advantages as a "headquarters for excursions" and encouraged the local people to create the moor's first tourist centre.

Old inns, one built in 13-16C as the manor house, and substantial small houses of ashlar granite or whitewashed cob, surround the **market square** and its quaint market house known as the Pepperpot. Overlooking all is the tall, 15C, pinnacled **church tower.** Inside are monolithic granite pillars, carved roof bosses, the tomb of Judge Sir John Whyddon (d 1575).

Dartmeet. – The West and East Dart Rivers, descend from the open uplands to join forces and flow on through an almost gorge-like valley between wooded hillsides. Footpaths follow the course of the river for some distance.

The swift flowing streams and the fields and woods on either bank, are lively with birds including larks, dippers, green woodpeckers and the occasional heron.

Drewsteignton. – Pop 1 249. The village of thatched granite and white cob houses surrounding a central square, stands high above the **Fingle Gorge.** Overlooking the square are an early perpendicular granite **church** and the mid-16C **Church House,** which when built served the community as a village hall. *(See also p 85)*.

Fingle Bridge. – The three-arched granite bridge which spans the most picturesque reach of the Fingle Gorge, was built in 16C and has been a famous "beauty spot" since the early 19C. The hills rise up all round, the highest to the north at 700ft, being crowned by the ruins of an Iron Age hillfort (Prestonbury Castle). Riverside paths lead through the water meadows and hanging oakwoods beside the Teign.

Grey Wethers. – *6m NW on foot Rtn from Postbridge by way of Hartland Tor and White Ridge*.

The Wethers comprise two large circles of medium sized stones.

Haytor Rocks. – 1 490ft. *5m W of Bovey Tracey.* The by-road from Bovey to Widecombe runs close to the rocks. The **view**★ extends to the coast at Teignmouth and west towards Widecombe.

High Willhays. – 2 038ft. The highest of the tors stands within the military zone and is not often accessible. *Enquire at Okehampton.*

★★ **Lydford** and **Lydford Gorge.** – *P 104*.

Manaton. – Pop 447. The village is centred on the green which, in turn, is overlooked by a typical 15C moorland **church,** notable inside for its full width **rood screen** depicting the Twelve Apostles and other saints on the lower panels.

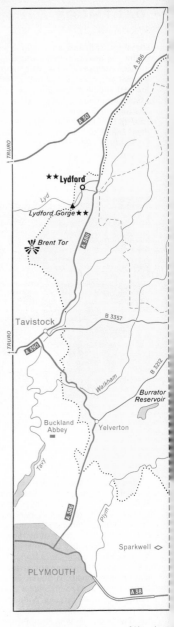

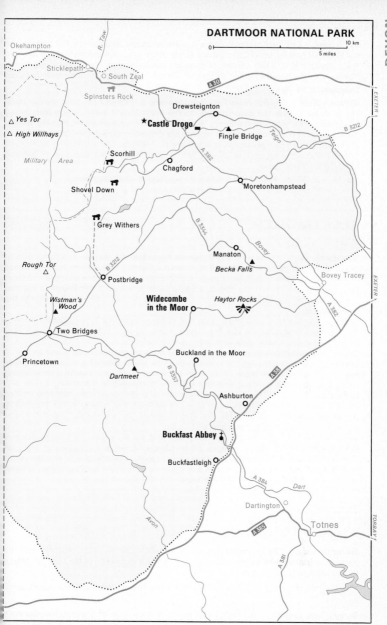

DARTMOOR NATIONAL PARK

Okehampton
R. Taw
Sticklepath
South Zeal
Spinsters Rock
Drewsteignton
★ Castle Drogo
Fingle Bridge
△ *Yes Tor*
△ *High Willhays*
Teign
B 3212
EXETER
Scorhill
Military Area
Chagford
B 3212
Shovel Down
Moretonhampstead
Grey Withers
B 3344
Manaton
Bovey
Becka Falls
Rough Tor △
Bovey Tracey
EXETER
Postbridge
Widecombe in the Moor
Haytor Rocks
Wistman's Wood
A 382
Two Bridges
Buckland in the Moor
Princetown
B 3357
Dartmeet
A 38
Ashburton
Buckfast Abbey
Buckfastleigh
A 384
Dart
Dartington
Avon
A 385
Totnes
A 381
TORBAY

Moretonhampstead. – Pop 1 420. The town, which is known locally as **Moreton** (Moor Town), was an old market town on the edge of the moor in 14-15C when its granite **church** was erected with a commanding **tower**. It also possesses a remarkable row of thatched and colonnaded, granite **almshouses** dating from 1637.
The early 19C **White Hart Inn** is a reminder of when Moreton was a coaching stage on the Exeter – Bodmin road.

Postbridge. – Pop 121. The **clapper bridge,** doubled by a road bridge in 1780s, is the largest and most upstanding on the moor, with granite slabs weighing up to 8 tons apiece set on tall piles above the waters of the East Dart River. It is believed to have been constructed when tin-mining and farming were being developed in the centre of the moor in 13C.

Princetown. – Pop 842. The town, which stands at 1 400ft and is the highest in England, is dominated by the prison built in 1806-8 to hold Napoleonic prisoners of war – in 1809 some 5 000 men were confined in the then much smaller buildings; by 1813 with the addition of some 2 000 American sailors who refused to join the British against their own countrymen, the number had increased to 9 000. After a period as a factory it was reopened as a convict prison in 1840s (when the practice of deportation ceased).

Rough Tor. – 1 791ft. The tor stands out to the north of Two Bridges and Wistman's Wood at the centre of the moor.

Scorhill Circle. – *4m ESE from Chagford along Teigncombe rd to Batworthy then 1m Rtn over Teign foot-bridge.* A rare stone circle on the moor.

Shovel Down. – *4m ESE from Chagford along Teigncombe rd to Batworthy then 1m S on foot Rtn.* A single stone and five stone files stand on the down from which there is a wide view.

Two Bridges. – The two bridges, one a mediaeval **clapper bridge**, mark the crossing of the West Dart River by the two tracks which since time immemorial have traversed the moor (p 89). A small cluster of cottages has grown up round the bridgehead. Nearby was the meeting place of the old Tinners' Parliament on Crochern Tor (NE).

Widecombe in the Moor. – P 120.

Wistman's Wood. – 3m Rtn from Two Bridges along a marked path from the car park. The path leads over the moor parallel to the West Dart, a swift stream frequented by dippers. The wood is low-lying, the oaks stunted, primaeval; their living trunks, growing out of the boulder-strewn slopes, are draped in grey-green lichen. The trees appear to be self-perpetuating yet there are no saplings, nor are there any animals or birds within the wood. It is all very reminiscent of an Arthur Rackham illustration for Grimm's Fairy Tales.

Yes Tor. – 2 030ft. Within the military zone. Enquire at Okehampton.

★★ DARTMOUTH   Pop 6 211

Michelin map **403** fold 34 – J32

Dartmouth, synonymous with the Britannia Royal Naval College – the long, turn of the century pink building on the hill (not open) – presents visitors not, in the parlance of guidebooks, with buildings of great architectural merit, but the diversion of short and winding streets, narrow slypes, steeply stepped alleys, a Butterwalk, a pannier market, bookshops, stores, antique shops and pubs (from the bogusly nautical to the centuries old).

There are ferries (one passenger, two car) to Kingswear, the Torbay Steam Railway (p 118), boat trips, and the **view**★ across the estuary in which Defoe declared, 500 ships of any size could "ride with the greatest safety".

Closely encircled by hills and surrounded by the sea, the town has never grown to unwieldy size. It originated half a mile inland on either side of a creek; as it grew, first the inlet then ever more of the river bank was reclaimed, the final undertaking being the extensive gardens and embankment completed in 1930.

A deepwater haven almost invisible from the sea, the town grew wealthy on sea trade – land communications even now are tenuous, the railway never reached it. It was an embarkation port for the Mediterranean; in the Middle Ages it traded particularly with Brittany, Gascony and Spain.

When venturing turned to the Spanish Main and the Americas, Dartmouth became the base from which the navigators, Sir Humphrey Gilbert (p 14) and John Davis set out and to which prize Spanish galleons were brought after capture on the high seas. In 17C trade concentrated in Bristol and London; Dartmouth became purely a naval port as the presence of the College testifies.

SIGHTS

Between the Embankment and the Church

Embankment. – The pontoon landing stage with Victorian cast ironwork, now the passenger **ferry embarkation point,** was built in hopeful anticipation of the railway coming to the town in 19C.

The Boatfloat. – The pool, until the building of the Embankment, was the town's inner harbour.

tc **Newcomen Engine.** – In the garden just upstream, one of Thomas Newcomen's (1663-1729) atmospheric steam engines, model for 75 years for pumping-engines in many mines, can be seen impressively at work.

The Quay. – The Quay, fronting the Boatfloat, was constructed in 1548 when it served as the centre of the town's activity. Merchants' houses were built in 17C along its length, four being combined and refronted in the early 19C to form the still standing coaching inn.

The Butterwalk. – Duke St. The Butterwalk has protected shoppers in Duke St at the end of the Quay, since 1630 when a terrace of four shops was built with oversailing upper floors supported on eleven granite pillars. Note the **woodwork** and carved corbels.

No 12, The Butterwalk (the chemist's). – Ask for permission to go upstairs to view the plaster Tree of Jesse **ceiling.**

tc **No 6, The Butterwalk: Local Museum.** – The panelling is 17C as is the **plaster overmantel** with the arms of Charles II. The exhibits comprise principally model ships.

Pannier Market. – Victoria St – continuation of Duke St. The market "shops" are now occupied by craftsmen – leatherworkers, silversmiths, copper enamellers... On Fridays fresh produce is brought in by growers and sold on the stones.

St Saviour's Church. – Anzac St. The tall, square pinnacled tower has been a landmark for those sailing upriver since it was constructed in 1372.

The **chancel** was built by John Hawley (d 1408; p 93) who may be seen in a brass between his two wives (chancel floor). MP and mayor, merchant venturer, buccaneer, property speculator in the town, churchgoer, he was typical of the leading citizens who in 15C brought prosperity to the town. His fellow townsmen continued to support the church so that it was largely rebuilt in 1630s.

Note especially the **south door** with its two ironwork lions and rooted tree of life, the mediaeval **altar** with legs carved like ships' figureheads, the pre-Reformation carved and coloured pulpit, 16C **rood screen.**

Downstream from the Embankment

Turn up one of the alleys just below the Ferry Pontoon and, after crossing the wide Newcomen St, bear left.

High St. – The street was the shambles or mainstreet of the mediaeval town and is still lined by houses of the period, some half-timbered, some refronted in 18 and 19C; most notable are the early 17C, four storey **Tudor House** (Dept of Social Security) and, on the corner, complete with its coloured and carved emblem, **The Cherub,** a late 14C, half-timbered merchant's house now an inn, with oversailing upper floors.

Continue along Higher St and, by Newcomen Rd, make your way into Lower St.

Agincourt House. – *Lower St.* The four-storey house around a spacious courtyard, was built, as the name suggests, in the early 15C for a rich merchant; it was restored in 17C and again this century when the courtyard was glassed over.

Continue down to the water's edge.

Bayard's Cove. – The "cove", a short cobbled quay is lined by 18C town houses, the most attractive being the pedimented **Old Custom House** of 1739 with a shell hooded porch.

Mayflower Stone. – The 180 ton *Mayflower,* accompanied by the *Speedwell,* put into Dartmouth for repairs to the *Speedwell,* which was finally abandoned, leaving the pilgrims to sail on in the *Mayflower* only *(p 110).*

Bearscove Castle. – The now ruined circular fort was constructed in 1537 to supplement the Castle *(see below)* as part of Henry VIII's coastal defences.

DARTMOUTH CASTLE

1m by Newcomen Rd, South Town and (left), Castle Rd.

tc The fort commands excellent **views★★★** out to sea, across and up the estuary. It was built in the late Middle Ages by the merchants of Darmouth who wanted to protect their homes, warehouses and their deepwater anchorage from foreign raiders. Their ships traded in the regular fashion but the custom of the day was also for all vessels on the high seas to turn privateer and plunder or capture any prize they might spy; in addition raids were organised on foreign coastal towns and other English ports, booty was siezed and buildings fired – the damage from such raids was often long-lasting, the pirates numbering sometimes a single ship's company, sometimes several thousand men – Dartmouth suffered two major retaliatory French raids in 1377 and 1400 and in 1404 was "invaded by 6 000 Bretons on the rampage *(p 15).*

In 1336 Edward III had ordered the estuary to be protected; in 1374 John Hawley *(see above)* and others were commanded "in consideration of the damage and reproach which might befal the town of Dartemouth through hostile invasion... to fortify the same, array the men of the town and do all other things that may be necessary". By the end of the century "a fortalice" or **small fortress** had been constructed which was re-inforced in 1462 by stretching a chain across the harbour mouth to a fort at Kingswear (visible on the far bank). Twenty years later, the townspeople still described as "warlike", began to build the fort standing today. Edward IV and Henry VII both contributed to the cost.

The most interesting architectural fact about the castle, begun in 1481 (altered and added to in 16 and 18C), is that it was the first in England to be designed to have **guns** as its **main armament.** Gunpowder had been in use in warfare since the mid-14C but gunports were generally inserted in old buildings and took the form of enlarged arrow slits; in Dartmouth the **ports** were splayed internally to allow a wide traverse without an enlarged opening. The guns were strapped to flat wooden beds – 50 years later, in Henry VIII's forts they would be mounted on wheeled carriages and mobile. Dartmouth was never attacked from the sea again once its castle was built.

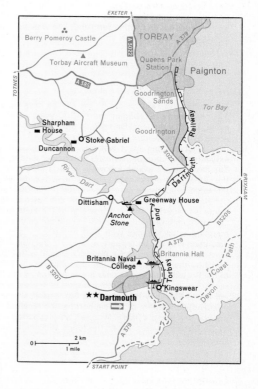

St Petrox. – The church in Gothic style almost abutting the castle, dates from 1642 when it was rebuilt on 12C site. It is believed that in its earliest days it bore a light to guide mariners navigating the narrow estuary entrance.

Of interest inside are two large and outstanding 17C **brasses** (E end), another small brass, the **pulpit** dated 1641, funeral **hatchments**, charity boards and Charles II's arms.

tc RIVER DART BOAT TRIPS

In addition to the landmarks, there are an exceptional number of **waterfowl** to be seen on the river banks (p 23). Note also how the salt water has cut back the lower branches of the trees.

West bank landmarks

Britannia Royal Naval College. – P 92.

Anchor Stone. – The spot is said to be where **Sir Walter Raleigh** occasionally came.

Dittisham Village. – Pop 470. The creek, Bow Creek, is the longest on the river.

Sharpham House. – The house was built on an older site in 1770 in a park designed by Capability Brown. The money for the house's building came from exploits such as the capture of the Spanish ship *Hermione* off Cadiz, worth £65 000 in prize money.

Home Reach. – The long and narrow reach brings you to Totnes (p 119).

East bank landmarks

Kingswear. – Pop 1 310. The town is distinguished by its old church which has 13C landmark tower.

tc **Torbay Railway.** – P 118. You may see the train puffing away and even entering the tunnel.

Greenway House. – The house, formely Greenway Court, was the birthplace of Sir Humphrey Gilbert (p 87), and for several years the home of Dame Agatha Christie.

Stoke Gabriel. – The pretty small village has 15C church.

Duncannon. – The village was once known for its red sandstone quarries (St Mary's, Totnes).

EXCURSION

Start Point. – 14m plus 1m on foot Rtn; S by B3205 and A379 to Torcross; W to Stokenham and S by-roads to Kellaton, Hollowcombe Head Start Farm and the track to the lighthouse car park.

The road follows the curve of the bay fringed by long fine sand beaches and at Slapton rides the low ridge separating the lagoon and the sea. The final few miles inland are typical wooded, undulating farmland. The walk to the point and lighthouse (p 17) is across open country with an ever increasing **view**★.

★★ EXETER   Pop 96 516

Michelin map **403** fold 34 – J31

The cathedral's twin towers on the skyline have signalled the city's presence since 12C. Its history had begun some 1300 years earlier when a settlement had been established by the local **Dunmoniorum** tribe on the westward sloping hillside at the limit of the navigable waters of the River Exe. In I C AD the Romans captured the settlement, built it up as their most westerly strongpoint and brought it out of isolation by extending the London-Silchester-Dorchester road to it.

The **Saxon** period, which followed, when a monastery was founded in what is now the cathedral precinct, was peaceful until, despite **King Alfred**, the **Danish invaders** began the raids which were to continue from 876-1003. After the final devastation, the people rebuilt their town once more and were rewarded in 1050 by Edward the Confessor authorising the translation of the metropolitan seat to Exeter (p 88).

The city's embroilments were not over: it defied the Conqueror until in 1068 William marched upon the city with 500 horsemen – after 18 days it was realised that discretion was the better part of valour; in the **Wars of the Roses** it changed sides more than once; it resisted **Perkin Warbeck's** assault with 600 men in 1497 and a siege in 1549 by the rebels against the imposition of the English prayer book (p 69). It fell to the Royalists and when later it was retaken by the Parliamentarians, whose troops ransacked it, it became a minor centre of royalist plots – toasts being drunk, at an inn in the Blackboy Rd – the **Black Boy** himself, Charles II, came in 1671 to the city in acknowledgement of the support he had received. James II, by contrast, was not popular and first the **Duke of Monmouth** was supported – 80 local men were condemned at the Bloody Assizes – then the future William III was welcomed by the citizens in the streets.

★★ The CATHEDRAL (Z) time: 1 hour

Edward the Confessor appointed Leofric as the first bishop in 1050 (d 1072). The builder of the cathedral's distinctive transept towers was Bishop William Warelast, nephew of the Conqueror (110-37); the builder of the cathedral church much as we know it today was **Bishop Walter Bronescombe** (1257-80), who while retaining the **transept towers**, remodelled the major part of 12C building. The work was finally completed a century later under **Bishop John Grandisson** (1327-69) who was buried in a chapel built within the thickness of the wall of the final achievement, the Decorated west front image screen. (See also p 107.)

Exterior. – Behind the seated figure in cap and gown, of **Richard Hooker,** priest and scholar (1553-1600), on the Green, the cathedral of grey-white Beer stone rises through buttresses and flying buttresses, windows of five lights and Decorated tracery, to crocketed pinnacles and castellated parapets. The long lines are massively interrupted by the twin but not identical towers which mount solidly through tiers of rounded blind arcading and intersecting arches to castellations and the angle turrets with pepperpot roofs, substituted in 15C for the traditional Norman pyramids *(p 107).*

(Vloo / J Alan Cash)

Exeter Cathedral

At the west end, one good idea was obviously superimposed upon another: the upper gable window is half-hidden by the main window which, in turn, is masked at the base by the pierced parapet edging the **image screen.**

The Nave. – The **vaulting** immediately strikes the eye as it extends 300ft from west to east in an uninterrupted line of meeting ribs with huge, gilded and coloured bosses studding the junctures. The ribs fan out from shafts which descend through the small triforium stage to important gilded and coloured **corbels** between the pointed arches of the arcade, in turn supported on **piers** of sixteen clustered columns with plain ring capitals.

Note also in the nave, the **minstrel's gallery** *(N side)* with 14 angels playing contemporary musical instruments – a bagpipe, recorder, viol, harp – the west **rose window** with its reticulated tracery (19C glass) and again the great **corbels,** each illustrating as many as three biblical themes.

Except at the crest, the view east is blocked by the pulpitum, a pierced stone screen of 1320, superimposed by a top-heavy organ.

The Chancel. – The high altar stands before the **Exeter pillar,** the prototype of all the pillars in the cathedral with sixteen shafts and ring capitals. Through the just pointed arches on either side can be seen the clustered pillars of the ambulatory and the Lady Chapel and above, the late 14C **east window** containing much original glass.

The 19C canopied choirstalls incorporate the oldest complete set of **misericords** in the country – 49 in number, carved in 1260-80.

The **bishop's throne** is of 1312, a fountain of Gothic wood carving in oak, entirely held by pegs – a fact which has enabled it to be twice dismantled in times of danger: during the Parliamentary period and in 1939-45.

The double canopied, Decorated **sedilia** are 13C.

The 13C effigy in black basalt, on a later gilded and canopied tomb, is **Bishop Bronescombe** *(see above).*

North Transept. – Note the Bishop Grandisson **15C clock** with the sun and moon revolving round the earth.

CATHEDRAL CLOSE

The close is diamond shaped with the cathedral at the centre almost abutted to the southeast by the gabled, red sandstone bishop's palace. Marking the limits are the old **city wall,** a small spired church, a school and some houses, and a curving line of tall 17-18-19C shops and houses ending in a white, Georgian four-storey hotel.

St Martin's Church (Y). – Pinched into the northern corner of the close is the minute, red sandstone church, dedicated in 1065 and rebuilt in 15C.

St Martin's Lane (Y 19). – The alley cuts through between the church and the hotel to the street. On one side is the **Ship Inn** (Y), half-timbered, heavily beamed, dark and brightly lit and as crowded as in the days when Drake, Hawkins and the queen's admirals used to meet inside.

Cathedral Close Walk (YZ 6). – The northeast side of the close begins at the black and white painted **Mol's Coffee House** (Y), a four-storey house of 1596 beneath an ornate gable with windows extending across its full width. It is also reputed to be one of Drake's onetime haunts.

Small shops with bay windows below, oriels above, merge into Tudor beamed houses with oversailing upper floors over possibly older red sandstone ground floors and beyond, neat, porched, 18C houses of brick with stone trims.

New Cut. – At the far end, New Cut leads out of the close beneath 19C cast **iron footbridge** complete with the donor's names.

Southernhay (YZ). – The double terrace of 18C three-storey houses in brick with stone trims, iron railings and tall, rounded ground floor windows and doorways, is completed in its appeal by a wide central garden of trees, lawns and vivid flower-borders.

★★ **MARITIME MUSEUM** (Z) *time: 1½ hours*

tc The museum is of ships – more than 100 – and ships only: afloat, when one can often go aboard, and in two 1835 warehouses and a fishmarket, where one can peer and touch and measure up against them.

Most of the boats are propelled by oar and sail and are frail looking craft which, nevertheless, have undertaken long voyages. High prowed, flat, circular, long and thin, made of hollowed out tree-trunks, planks, birch-bark, reeds, they include dhows from Arabia, lighters, ferries, seaweed gathering boats, painted fishing boats from Portugal, gondolas, guffas from Iraq, a gouffern from Shetland and a skiff from the Orkneys, curraghs and coracles, sampans from Burna, Bangladesh and Hong Kong, fishing luggas, the boats of four lone Atlantic oarsmen, a Fijian proa, a Danish steam tug, *St Canute,* once the Odense harbour ice-breaker and fire-fighter and Brunel's Drag Boat, *Bertha* built in 1844. On occasion in summer boats are steamed and some are sailed on the river.

The Quay. – The quayside, where the museum is situated, dates back to Exeter's earliest days when it was a tidal river port. The period of prosperity was brought to an abrupt end in 13C when a weir was built across the river three miles below the city port. 300 years of litigation followed and though the city won the suit the river was no longer navigable; to restore trade the corporation had the first **ship canal** in the country dug in 1563-6. *(See also Topsham, p 98.)*

EXETER

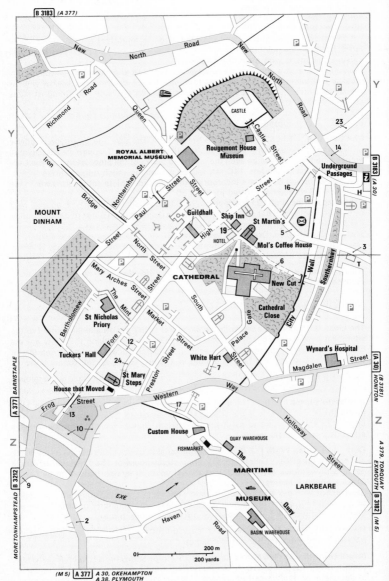

Custom House. – The trim 18C house, a symbol of the canal trade at the time, was one of the first buildings in the city to be constructed of **brick**, probably partly shipped as ballast from Holland.

Warehouses. – In 19C range of warehouses and a nearby shed *(on the far river bank)* are craftsmen's stalls and workshops, including a wrought ironsmith and a skilled potter.

ADDITIONAL SIGHTS

★ **Royal Albert Memorial Museum** (Y). – The Exeter-made **watches and clocks gallery**
tc and the unique gallery of 16-19C **West Country Silverware**, provide the high points of the general interest museum.
Exeter was for long an assay town with a large number of gold and silversmiths, jewellers and clockmakers working in the city. On display are communion cups, alms dishes, tankards and flagons, Apostle spoons, a baby's sucking bottle, Georgian coffee and chocolate pots, cream jugs and tea pots... The work was little influenced either by the Baroque style of the Huguenots, who did not journey so far, nor by the French Rococo favoured in George II's reign, but retained its purity of line almost until 19C. In a case apart is a quite beautiful bequest of 60 16-17C **West Country Spoons**.

tc **Guildhall** (Y). – The decorated Tudor portico was added in 1593 to, it is believed, the oldest municipal building in the country, erected in 1330 on a possibly Saxon site.
The Chamber. – The hall has a timber roof of 1468-70 and outstanding oak **panelling** with no two panels carved alike. Note the bear and ragged staff supporters of Warwick the Kingmaker and the Yorkist cause, the Carolean chairs, the mayoral regalia of several periods, the great 18C brass **chandelier** and the **portraits** of Princess Henrietta daughter of Charles I, born in the city, and of the Devonian, General Monck first Duke of Albemarle (1608-70), Parliamentary and later Restoration land and sea general.

tc **Rougemont House Museum.** (Y). – Just inside the great red sanstone gate built originally at the entrance to the long disappeared Norman castle, an attractive Georgian house has been converted into a history museum of Devon.

tc **St Nicholas Priory** (Z). – The sandstone building is the only remaining range, the former domestic and guest wing, of a small Benedictine priory founded in 1087 and Dissolved in 1536.
The **entrance hall, undercroft-crypt** with massive round columns supporting low, stone ribbed vaulting, the kitchen and, upstairs, the impressive sized, **guest hall** with an arch braced roof, also the adjoining solar and bedrooms, are furnished with 16-17C tables, chairs, chests, a painted **virginal** of 1697 and a tester bed and cradle.

tc **Tucker's Hall** (Z). – The hall of the Weavers, Fullers (Tuckers) and Shearmen, created in 1638 when 15C chapel was divided horizontally, is an example of Devon high craftsmanship in oak with its **barrel roof** and carved **panelling**. Note the **royal arms,** the **boards of benefactors,** also the items discovered when the false plaster ceiling was removed – halberds, pikes...

tc **Underground Passages** (Y). – The cut rock or stone built narrow passages, with an entrance in the modern shopping precinct, were part of the city's aqueduct system and may have also afforded escape routes in times of siege.

Stepcote Hill (Z 24). – The hill with shallow cobbled steps and a centre runnel is lined on either side by small, adjoined stone and half-timbered 16C houses.

St Mary Steps (Z). – The 16C church, built in red sandstone, at the bottom of the hill is known for its clock which has **striking jacks.**

House that Moved (Z). – The tall, Tudor merchant's house (now a shop) with oversailing upper floors was so named in 1964 when it was transported 75yds.

White Hart (Z). – The 14-15C inn which has massive beams, flagged floors, dark panelled rooms and a flowered courtyard, was the house of William Wynard, Recorder of Exeter.

Wynard's Hospital (Z). – The almshouses, an attractive group of cottages surrounding a cobbled courtyard containing a well, were founded for 12 poor and infirm citizens and a chaplain, by Wynard *(see above)* in 1435. *(Not open.)*

The University (Y). – *2m N of city centre up the continuation of Queen St, New North Rd.* The University, numbering 1 500 students, is mostly situated in new buildings including the Northcott Theatre, on an undulating 320-acre site marked by splendid trees...

EXCURSIONS

★★ **Killerton.** – *7 NE by B3181. P 101.*

★ **Cullompton.** – Pop 4 487. *14m NE by B3181.*
The market town comprises a long main street punctuated by shops, a Tudor manor house (now a hotel), the Walronds of the same date, small courts and alleys and the occasional Georgian house.
Over-riding all is 120ft red sandstone tower of **St Andrew's Church** ★, vast and Perpendicular throughout on a much older site. Inside are a richly painted and gilded **barrel roof,** an equally gorgeous **rood screen,** aisles with diamond patterned roofs and the 1528 Lane aisle with pendented fan vaulting. At the west end note the Jacobean oak gallery on wood Ionic columns and the mediaeval **Calvary** or Golgotha carved from a single oak trunk. Outside, carvings illustrate 16C cloth machinery.

Topsham. – Pop 4 573.4m S on A377.

The small port on the point of land between where the Rivers Exe and Clyst flow into the long Exe Estuary, reached the height of its importance in 13C, when Isabella, Countess of Devon, built a weir across the river and successfully diverted all trade from Exeter to Topsham *(see above)*. Boat-builders set up yards, craftsmen, dockers and sailors appeared on the waterfront and, in 17C, merchants built the Dutch gabled houses still to be seen along the Strand.

Today Topsham is a good place in which to wander, following the High St into Fore St and finally the **Strand;** to look at the old, half-timbered pubs, the **Shell House** with its hooded doorway, the sailing dinghies on the river, waders on the mud flats *(p 23).*

EXMOUTH
Pop 28 964

Michelin map **403** fold 35 – J32

The **beach** of fine sand is two miles long.

Exmouth was a port in pre-Roman times; in the Middle Ages it was subject to North African and other pirate raids and was supplying ships and men for English return ventures.

In 18C it went with the fashion and determined to become Devon's first watering place: Georgian terraces were built such as those in Bicton Place and on the **Beacon,** where among the early tenants were the sad wives of Lords Nelson (at no 6) and Byron (no 19).

Littleham Church. – *1m E along Maer Lane (Sandy Bay Rd).* The church, Exmouth parish church, was built on an older site between 1234-1528 when the north, or Drake's aisle was added. Note the **hammer beam roof,** rebuilt in 19C using the original 15C carved oak **bosses** and **angels;** the piers with unusually carved **capitals** of Beer stone; the lectern made from an old oak beam in 13C; the **rood screen** which is early 16C and the late 15C **glass** *(N aisle, 3rd window)* depicting Christ with a reed and crown of thorns. In the chantry chapel is a memorial to **Lady Nelson,** who is buried in the churchyard.

St John in the Wilderness. – *1 ½m NE; N off A376, Budleigh Salterton Rd.* The church with its unique **boss** has had a chequered history. After rebuilding in 15C it was first abandoned then demolished except for the tower and north aisle. In 1936, as restoration work was nearing completion, King George V died and, in anticipation of the coronation of the new king, a boss with the cypher **ER VIII,** the only one ever to be carved, was set in the chancel roof.

In the churchyard *(SE corner)* is the grave of the Romantic artist, **Francis Danby** *(p 35).*

★ **A la Ronde.** – *2m N by Exeter Rd, A376 and Summer Lane. P 77.*

The Travellers' Friends
Great Britain and Ireland:

Michelin Red Guide *for hotels and restaurants.*
Michelin Map **986** *14 miles to 1 inch.*
Michelin Maps **401** **402** **403** **404** *6.3 miles to 1 inch.*

GREAT TORRINGTON
Pop 4 130

Michelin map **403** fold 24 – H31

Great Torrington, or **Torrington** as it is known locally, was selected in 1966 by the Dartington Hall Trust *(p 88)* as the site for an entreprise which has since become known as Dartington Glass.

SIGHTS

★ **Dartington Glass.** – *Left down School Lane, off New St opposite the church.*
tc The factory now employs over 200 men and women, many of who one sees from gantry walks at work in small teams, gathering, blowing, shaping the glass, always keeping it turning to produce the well known pieces.

Parish Church. – "The church was blown up with powder Febre ye 16 ano 1645 and rebuilt in 1651" – a matter of the Royalists storing 80 powder barrels in the church which, when 200 were packed into the building as prisoners of the Parliamentarians, were inadvertently set off. How much of 14C church, built on an older site – the town dates back to pre-Saxon times – was destroyed is not known, but notice in the arcade how the east pillars have a detailed 14C decoration while those at the west are square, solid and more utilitarian as though erected at speed in 1651.

The oak **pulpit** and **sounding board,** carved with cherubs and wreaths, are 17C; the **white ensign** *(by the organ)* flew at the Normandy Landing in 1944. Note the inclusion in the lists of rectors and vicars, of Master, afterwards Cardinal, **Thomas Wolsey.**

High St. – The High St or market place, which forms an L round the Georgian-style **Town Hall** (museum of bygones) is highlighted at the south end by 1842 **Pannier Market** and on the west side by the twin gabled **Black Horse Inn** of 1681.

Castle Hill. – *250yds S.* The 12C castle disappeared long ago but the site affords a good **view** south across the River Torridge and beyond towards Dartmoor.

EXCURSIONS

★ **Devon Museum of Mechanical Music, Thornbury.** – *15m SW by B3227, A388*
tc *and by-roads E.*

Some 20 working pianolas, fairground organs, barrel organs, musical boxes, a polyphon and barrel piano surround you, playing music from discs, barrels, perforated paper rolls and folding down card-books. The collection has one or two examples of each type of instrument with bellows and precision parts exposed in most cases so that you can see "the works" and development from hand winding to "steam" and electrification. You will be serenaded by the polyphon and musical boxes, given a chorus, sentimental song or classical recital by the pianola, roused by to Sousa marches and be blasted by the huge Belgian fair organ, The Trumpeter.

Holsworthy. – Pop 2 421. *15m SW on B3227 and A388.*

The town, with a lively pannier market (Wednesday), centres on the **square** which is lined by colour-washed and half-timbered shops and pubs. Streets lead off at the corners to the church with a tall ashlar tower and downhill to an old mill.

tc **Ashley Countryside Collection.** – *8m SE along B3220 to Berner's Cross (before Winkleigh); bear left, then right.*

There are some 40 breeds of sheep, some rare, in the collection. Walk into the field, armed with photofit pictures and try, not to count the sheep, but to identify the breeds ! There are a Devon Longwool, a Clun Forest, an Exmoor Horn, a St Kilda, a Badger Face, a Lincoln Longwool, a Blue Faced Leicester...
In the old farm outbuildings have been accumulated "1001 bygones of the horse and open fireplace era"!

King's Nympton. – Pop 345. *17m E by B3227, A377 and left turn before the station.*

The hilltop village, which retains a few thatched houses, has a Perpendicular **church** with a green copper octagonal spire.
Inside, the **wagon roofs** with carved bosses have been enriched above the screen. Note the **box pews**, pilastered **reredos** and **communion rails** with alternating balusters, all of 18C, the royal arms over the south door, and, between the church interior and the porch, the sill which appears to be the shaft of a Celtic cross.

South Molton. – *15m NE on B3227.*

Atherington Church. –   The church, much restored in 1884 but with the original wagon roof, has a **rood screen** which at right angles becomes a **parclose screen** with a rare and beautifully decorated gallery.

Chittlehampton Church. – The church overlooking the village square, has a spectacular 115ft **tower** which rises by four stages, each underlined by a frieze and pinnacled buttresses, to a crest of pierced battlements, pinnacles and sub-pinnacles after the Somerset style *(p 147).*

South Molton. – Pop 3 611. The old wool town with colour-washed houses along its streets, bustles with life particularly on market day (Thursday).
The **guildhall**, on an island site in the main, Broad St, dates from 1743. Note also 19C **pannier market**, the **Medical Hall** with an iron balcony supported on columns, 15C **church** with 107ft pinnacled **tower.**

Quince Honey Farm. – *Off A361, Barnstaple Rd.* From a walk-through gallery behind glass,
tc one sees bees in the hive and the processing of honey from flower to table.

HARTLAND   Pop 1 421

Michelin map **403** fold 24 – G30

This most remote corner of Devon lies behind 750ft ridge which is the watershed for small, local streams which leap spectacularly from the cliffs into the sea, and for Devon's major westerly rivers the Torridge and the Tamar.
Beyond the ridge the wooded valleys give place to almost bare rock which rises as it approaches the sea and at Hartland Pt reaches 350ft before plunging vertically into the ocean. The **Devon Coast Path**, as it follows every indentation of the rugged cliffs, affords breathtaking **views**★★★ of the pointed offshore rocks as they rise out of the swell as far as the eye can see.

SIGHTS

Hartland Village. – Among the shops spaced along the street and square in the now small village, is one (North St) selling especially well made and utterly practical artefacts produced by local craftsmen in wood and pottery.

★ **Hartland Church.** – *2m W at Stoke.* The 14-15C church, the "Cathedral of North Devon", has a four-staged, buttressed and pinnacled **tower**, 128ft tall with a niche containing the figure of St Nectan. Like its predecessor, the tower serves as a landmark for ships at sea – the earlier tower, legend has it, was erected in 11C by Gytha as a thank-offering for the safe passage in a storm of her husband, Godwin, Earl of the West Saxons and father of King Harold.

Interior. – The nave, which is tall with wide arcades, is covered by ceiled, carved, painted and gilded **wagon roofs**. A 45ft carved **rood screen**, in typical Devon style, extends across the full width of the church, the nave arcades having had to be raised to accommodate its 13ft height and the 6ft wide gallery above the crested cornice and multi-ribbed coving.
Note also the square Norman **font** with zig-zag carving on the shaft, arcading on the bowl and faces at each angle, a small **brass** of 1610 and the late 14C carved tombchest in Cornish catacleuse stone which came from the Dissolved Hartland Abbey.

(P Tweedie / Colorific / Cosmos)

The coast at Hartland Quay

★ **Hartland Quay.** – *1m W of Stoke.*
In a rage of storms at the end of 19C, the Atlantic "removed" the centuries old quay which had been newly rebuilt. Today a row of cottages, a hotel and shipwreck museum mark the main street while the quay foundations afford a **viewpoint**★★ from which to look at the striated cliffs, inlets and offshore rocks which characterise the beautiful, wild, length of coast.

HONITON   Pop 6 627

Michelin map **403** fold 35 – K31

The **pottery** and **lace** which have for so long made Honiton a household name, are both still made in the town. A new jabot made in 1983 for the Speaker of the House of Commons took 500 hours to complete.
The town, despite its 17-18C Georgian appearance – the result of numerous fires which swept the wide main street from the Middle Ages to 18C – dates back to 12C when it was founded as a village settlement on either side of the London-Exeter road *(A30 – now by-passed)*. By 1257 a pannier market and the annual July fair were in being; by Tudor times fine glove-making was complementing, as a cottage industry, the important local sheep and wool industry and by the late-16, early-17C, pillow lacemaking, brought over by refugees from the continent, had also been established. In 18C Honiton became a staging town with coaching inns flanking the wide High St.

★ **All Hallows Museum.** – *High St, next to 19C parish church.* **Lace** is the high point
tc of the local museum where are displayed a fine wedding veil, a matronly overskirt with 40in waist, handkerchiefs, flounces and a lacemaker's sampler with prices.
Other exhibits include Honiton pottery, Victorian scent and **smelling bottles,** bead purses, card and table games, and 19C kitchen-laundry, complete with tub and washing on the line.

EXCURSIONS

★ **Ottery St Mary.** – *7m SW by A30 and B3177. P 107.*

tc **Farway Countryside Park.** – *6m S by A375 and B3174.*
The **views**★ from the 189-acre hilltop park extend over the fertile east Devon landscape of fields, woodland and the Col River valley. One walks past pens of rare breed sheep, a Brahman bull, Bagot and Pygmy goats, spotted pigs and small hogs bred back to resemble those of the Iron Age. In the paddocks are deer, ponies, and Long Horned cattle.

ILFRACOMBE   Pop 10 479

Michelin map **403** fold 24 – H30

The town, long the most popular resort on the North Devon coast, achieved success in 19C with the development of steamship day outings from South Wales and the arrival of the railway bringing visitors in their thousands from the Midlands and the North Country.

SIGHTS

★ **Capstone Hill.** – From the "summit" of 156ft high hill there is a good bird's-eye **view**★ of the town, the harbour mouth, the rock enclosed bays and beaches on either side.

Hillsborough. – The hill on the town's eastern edge, at the centre of the pleasure ground, rises to 447ft and affords an even more extensive **view**★★ along the coast.

tc **St Nicholas' Chapel.** – *Lantern Hill.* In 14C the beacon set as a marker on Lantern Hill was replaced by this mariners' chapel which though much altered, still shines a red bearing light at night to guide shipping in the Bristol Channel.

From the rock platform on which the chapel stands, there is good **view** ★ out to sea and of the almost land-locked harbour. A promenade *(starting from the quay)* half circles the headland a few feet above sea-level.

tc **Tunnels Beach.** – *Granville Rd.* The pools, which are still popular, were an early 19C enterprise by which the hill between the road and the sea was tunnelled by Welsh miners and the rock cove, on the far side, made accessible. The cove was then equipped with a sea wall to prevent the tide running out and so provide all day bathing. In 19C, water was pumped to the baths at the entrance and heated in winter.

★★ KILLERTON

Michelin map ▮▮▮ fold 37 – J31 – 7m N of Exeter

tc The house of 1778 stands at the foot of a wooded hillside in glorious parkland on a site purchased by the Aclands in 17C. After successive remodellings it now houses Acland portraits, contemporary 18-19C furniture including some pieces especially made for the house, and the National Trust's Collection of 18-20C Costume.

The HOUSE *time: ¾ hour*

The downstairs rooms are fully furnished with, in the drawing room, costumed figures completing the setting.

Music Room. – The **chamber organ** dates from 1807, the late 18C **square piano** was made by Clementi, the grand piano is of 1870. The 18C mahogany **china cabinet** is from Exeter. Note the portrait and figurine of **Hannah Moore** *(p 154)* who was supported in her work by, Sir Thomas Acland, the then owner of the house.

Drawing Room. – The mahogany **secretaire-bookcase** is late 18C, the giltwood **pier glasses** are after Chippendale.

Library and Dining Room. – The walnut **bookcases** were especially designed for the house; note the **dumb-waiter, pier glasses** and marble **folio cabinets,** also custom made.

Upstairs. – The rooms which serve as the setting for displays from the National Trust **Costume Collection,** are peopled with men, women and children in period tableaux: 1930s cocktail-party, a mid-18C musical or painting group, 1920s nursery, a Victorian mourning group complete with one of Queen Victoria's 45in waist dresses, jet, crèpe, and a child in funereal black, a line of 1900s bathing costumes... the displays, historic and sometimes amusing, change every year.

The GARDEN

The garden near the house is bright with flowers from early spring to late summer, with bulbs, early flowering shrubs, clouds of rhododendrons banked along the hillside, in island bed and interspersed with magnolias. Later the wide herbaceous borders on the terrace come into their own and, finally, the broad-leaved trees with their autumn tints against the silver grey, pale gold and dark green of the conifers.

★ KINGSBRIDGE   Pop 4 236

Michelin map ▮▮▮ fold 34 – I33

The old market town at the head of the estuary is the capital of the area known as **South Hams.** A very steep Fore St leads down to the quay and a weekly market, opened in 1217 and still going strong (Wednesday, Market Hall, Fore St).

SIGHTS

The Quay. – The Quay stands on land reclaimed from the once important harbour.

Circle the open square and, by way of the wonderfully named Squeezebelly Passage, turn right into Fore St.

Fore St. – The street is bordered by slate-hung houses dating from 15-19C, between which run narrow passages leading to small, mediaeval courtyards.

Town Hall. – The hall with a clock and arcaded front is 19C.

The Shambles. – The colonnaded walk *(p 173)* is fronted by eight Elizabethan granite pillars which support 18C upper floor.

St Edmund the Martyr. – The church with 13C tower and spire, was rebuilt in 15C when the town was prosperous, and restored in 19C. Note inside the variation in the **chancel arches,** the **two squints** and 13C **font.**

King's Arms Hotel. – The 17-18C inn near the top of the street *(on the right),* became a stage in 1775 for the Exeter-Plymouth coaches.

tc **Cookworthy Museum and Old Grammar School.** – The long stone building on two floors was erected by Thomas Crispin, a fuller, in 1670 as a grammar school.

The **panelled schoolroom** with a **master's seat** surmounted by the royal arms of Charles II, contains a display on **William Cookworthy** (1705-80), born nearby, Quaker apothecary and discover of kaolin (china-clay) and petunze (china-stone) near St Austell in 1756 *(pp 67, 110).* The one-time school kitchen which produced food for 60 boarders, a costume room and a farm gallery complete the local museum.

KINGSBRIDGE★

★★ BOAT TRIP to Salcombe

tc The sail down the estuary with the open downlands on either side, the six wooded creeks and additional inlets headed by small waterside villages, the tern and even buzzards overhead and, if the tide is falling, the waders including heron in the shallows, makes the sail very enjoyable. *(Salcombe p 111; birds p 23).*

★ KNIGHTSHAYES COURT

Michelin map **403** fold 34 – J31 – 2m N of Tiverton

tc The house, which is a fine example of Victorian Gothic architecture, is situated on the east bank of the Exe Valley facing south overlooking parkland and the town of Tiverton in the distance. It was here that **John Heathcoat,** a prosperous lace-mill owner, born in Derbyshire in 1793, built a new mill in 1816 after his Midlands works (where he had installed his own bobbin net (1808) and other machines), was wrecked by Luddites. Philanthropist and man of liberal ideas, as well as an inventor, Heathcoat represented Tiverton in parliament from 1832-59.

His grandson, **John Heathcoat-Amory** inherited the business, took over the parliamentary seat and, in the late 1860s, commissioned an architect to build him a new house out of town.

(Vloo / J Alan Cash)

The gardens

William Burges, was a skilled and inventive architect – there is a brilliantly balanced or compensating asymmetry about the house exterior which gives it life – but he was dilatory and so in 1874 Heathcoat-Amory sacked him, employing in his stead **J D Crace,** who was strongly influenced by the pre-Raphaelite movement. The final result is a country house, complete with conservatory, which is a true period piece.

The GARDENS

The gardens are not old – the transformation and expansion to the present 25 acres, began in 1950s when the then Sir John and Lady Amory began by transforming the elaborate scheme of regular, stepped parterres designed by Burges, into **terraced gardens**.

They next incorporated the yew hedges planted east of the house in 1880s, into Pool and Formal Gardens with a brilliant Alpine terrace below. Look out for the **topiary fox and hounds** of 1920s.

Finally extending the cultivated area yet once more they created the interesting **Garden in a Wood** and **Willow Garden**.

The HOUSE *time: ½ hour*

The furniture is 18 and 19C English with some 18C Dutch marquetry pieces.

The interest throughout the rooms is to note the contributions of each architect: and also where the decoration is a combination of the work of each.

In the **hall** the corbels of men and animals are by Burges, the other decoration by Crace; in the **bedroom corridor** the walls are covered by Crace's original stencilled designs.

In the **boudoir**, the teak panelling, chimneypiece and repainted ceiling are all by Crace.

Downstairs in the **dining room** the decoration is by both architects; the walnut chairs were made in Wales in the early 19C.

The ceiling in the **morning room** is by Crace; the brass chandelier is after Pugin's Gothic style. Note the collection of 17C Italian majolica.

Beneath Burges' elaborate ceiling in the **library sitting room** are a *Madonna and Child* by Matteo di Giovanni (1435-95), a Flemish **Annunciation** of *c*1400 and a Claude. The mahogany drum table is 18C; the bracket clock is French with an English movement. Finally in the **drawing room**, the ceiling and chimneypiece are by Burges; among the pictures are a Constable, *Field Flowers and Poppies,* a Bonington, a Turner and a Rembrandt, *Self-Portrait.*

Michelin map **403** *is the map to use for the West Country.*
Michelin map **404** *for South East England,*
      the Midlands and East Anglia.
Michelin map **402** *for Southern Scotland,*
      the lake District and Northern England.
Michelin map **401** *for Scotland.*

LUNDY ISLAND

Michelin map **403** folds 23 and 24 – F and G30
Access: see the current Michelin Red Guide Great Britain and Ireland

Staying on Lundy is a carefree adventure: there are no cars – except the estate landrover and farm tractor – no phones, no morning papers; there is a shop selling necessities and the island's own, puffin stamps, a tea-house, an inn and a farm with Galloway cattle, Welsh Mountain sheep and a free-running herd of handsome, dun-coloured Lundy Ponies (a New Forest-Welsh Mountain cross established in 1930s). The important, though completely non-urgent, thing is to explore the island.

GEOGRAPHY

The island is a triangular granite rock mass, three miles long, less than a mile wide, rising 400ft out of the Atlantic-Bristol Channel breakers. The west face mounts sheer from the sea, the cliffs advancing and retreating behind sharp offshore rocks and coves; as you stand looking north, the line of the cliffs appears to extend to the horizon. The east coast is less precipitous, descending in steps and by way of hanging valleys to wide bays and shingle beaches all covered by the sea at high tide.

The undulating tableland is clothed with turf, close-cropped at the island's south end by the farm stock and to the north by the wild goats, the dark Soay sheep brought over from St Kilda's in 1920 and now naturalised, and rabbits in whose burrows puffins sometimes nest in the spring. Gorse, bracken and peat bogs are to te found in the hanging valleys; sycamores in the sheltered hollow at the southeast end of the island. In the spring pink thrift covers the upland grass, rhododendron groves light the east cliff lower path.

HISTORY

The Mariscos, a Norman-Somerset family came to Lundy in 12C, a lawless, violent group who built a stronghold where Bronze and Iron Age man and Celts had previously settled; in 13C, a Marisco plotted against Henry III, who had him hanged, drawn and quartered before seizing the island, destroying his stronghold and appointing a royal constable who in 1243 completed the castle still confusingly known as Marisco's Castle.

The island's position in the Channel made it the perfect hideout for pirates throughout the centuries of Bristol's trade with Europe, America and the West Indies. In 1750 Thomas Benson, MP and High Sheriff of Devon, leased the island and became the biggest pirate of all, diverting prisoners he had undertaken to transport to America to work the quarries, preying on cargo ships and swindling insurance companies. The modern era dates from 19C when the quarries were worked industrially, the road built up from the beach and the church erected. The last private owners introduced the **Lundy ponies,** the rarely seen **Sika deer,** the **Soay sheep,** also the **puffin stamps.**

SIGHTS

A complete circuit of the island is 11 miles, a walk to NW Point about 6 miles there and back; add a couple of miles for diversions! Allow a day and take a picnic.

NW Point Walk. – The path, which runs along the island's spine, is lined by 2½ ton stones set by Trinity House as markers for the lighthousemen who had to find their way in fog and darkness to the northern light. There are constant changes of view and that straight ahead, because one is on a tableland and because of the space all around and the light, appears to go to infinity...

Old Light. – The original lighthouse of 1819 was erected on the island's highest point where, shining out at 567ft into the mist and clouds, it was invisible from the sea. To one side is the new, skeletal, winged aerogenerator which supplements the island's electricity supply.

Walled Enclosure. – The ground is an early Christian burial ground.

The Battery. – *W coast.* The battery was built by Trinity House as a fog signal station in 1863 *(path down just S of Quarter Wall),* blank rounds being fired in bad weather every 10 minutes from the George III cannon.

Quarter, Halfway and Threequarter Walls. – The cross walls date from 18C.

Quarries. – *E coast.* The quarries were worked in 18C by Benson *(see above)* and industrially in 19C – the Quarry Pool is inhabited by great orfe.

Pondsbury and Punchbowl Valley. – The large dewpond drains towards the west.

Tibbetts Point and Cottage. – *E coast.* The Admiralty look-out and granite building were constructed in 1909 on the second highest point on the island.

Devil's Slide. – The steep slip, which is far up the northeast coast, is a proving ground for rock climbers.

North Light. – The now automatic light was built, with its pair, in 1896 to replace The Old Light. The stones in the fields are from Bronze and Iron Age hut circles.

East Cliff Lower Path. – The path, noted for its rhododendrons, extends from just beyond the Battlements to below Quarter Wall.

Marisco Castle. – The castle stands witness to the island's rugged history.

Millcombe House. – The Classical style granite house was built in 1830s as the home of the island's then owners. It is now NT island hotel.

St Henena's. – The large, strangely urban looking church, was erected in 1896.

South Light. – Below the light *(p 17),* skin-divers explore offshore wrecks.

★★ LYDFORD Pop 1 880

Michelin map 📘 fold 33 – H32 – Local map p 90

The long village on the western edge of Dartmoor *(p 89)*, straggles down from the main road towards the River Lyd and the gorge, the buildings getting ever older until you come on a group of cottages and the rector's onetime house, built with stout oak timbers in 16C. Now an inn, it displays coins minted in the village between 978-1050, the time of Ethelred the Unready.

★★ LYDFORD GORGE *2 hours for the joint Upper and Lower Path walk*

First right over the road bridge or, for those not wishing to walk far, continue 1 ½m along the road to the Waterfall entrance.

tc The gorge is about 1 ½ miles long with rock walls in places 60ft high. The cleft narrows and widens by turns, the river swirling at the feet of tall beeches, sycamores and a dozen other varieties of tree. Among the birds to look out for are green spotted woodpeckers, dippers, possibly a heron.

The Paths. – There are three marked paths from the main entrance – two interconnect, near the Waterfall, enabling you to return by a different route.

Upper Path. – *1¼ m.* The path follows the NE-SW course of the gorge from above, affording bird's-eye **views** of the river and glimpses of Dartmoor.

Lower Path. – *1 ½m.* The path at the water's edge, skirts the northwest bank *(handrails in more difficult parts – liable to be wet and slippery after rain).*

Third Path. – *1m Rtn.* The path leads in the opposite direction from the Pixie Glen to the Bell Cavern by way of the thundering whirpool, known as the **Devil's Cauldron.**

White Lady Waterfall. – The fall, 100ft single strand of water, is at the south end of the gorge.

ADDITIONAL SIGHTS

(Vloo / J Alan Cash)

The Gorge in spring

Lydford Castle. – From 7-13C Lydford was of military importance as a Saxon outpost, first against the Celts and later against the Danes – Lydford was sacked in 997.
The present ruined **keep,** two storeys high on top of its mound, represents the remains of a stronghouse, erected in 1195 and rebuilt to hold prisoners and tinners awaiting trial before their own stannary court *(p 43)*. By 14C the court was notorious, "Lydford law" being such, it was said, that "in the morn they hang and draw and sit in judgement after". The castle continued as a prison until 17C and as a stannary court until 1800.

St Petroc's. – The church, one of 30 possibly founded personnally by St Petroc in 6C, was rebuilt and enlarged on Norman foundations in 13, 15 and 19C – the south aisle and tower are 15C, note how the latter was mis-joined onto the earlier nave. Inside, the plain **tub font** is Norman; the tower-nave arch is decorated with carved Gothic panelling; the **rood screen** in the traditional style, is modern as are the 69 **bench-ends** carved between 1923-6 by two men, one for the figures, one for the borders. Outside, by the south porch, is the **tomb** with the entertaining epitaph "Here lies in horizontal position, The outside case of George Routleigh, Watchmaker..."

★ LYNTON and LYNMOUTH Pop 2 075

Michelin map 📘 fold 25 – I30

Lynton and Lynmouth, complementary small towns in a hollow at the top and at the foot of 500ft North Devon-Exmoor cliffs, rejoice in glorious **views**★★ across the Bristol Channel to the distant Welsh coast, in sweeping moorland, cliff walks and wooded valley walks beside rushing torrents and waterfalls and, since 1890, in a **Cliff Railway.** The architecture in **Lynton** is predominantly Victorian-Edwardian, the larger houses in their own gardens now largely converted into hotels; **Lynmouth** remains a traditional fishing village with small stone cottages and houses, a few still thatched, to which have been added seaside villas and more recent buildings following the flood disaster of 1952 when the River Lyn burst its banks, broke bridges and swept through the village, bringing down mud and 40 000 tons of boulders and broken tree trunks in its storm waters.

tc **Cliff Railway.** – The railway is 900ft long and rises at a gradient of 1:75 to connect the two resorts. The two cars operate by gravity, the top car taking on water to hoist the lower one and discharging as it reaches the bottom.

EXCURSIONS

★ **Valley of the Rocks.** – *1m W along the Coastal Rd.*
The rocks, swathed in bracken, rise from the wide, grass covered, valley floor to crests of bare shale, spectacularly carved by the wind into fancifully named outlines...

★ **Watersmeet.** – *1½m E by A39, then 200yds along a footpath – local map p 159.*
The spot is where the waters of the East Lyn and Farley rivers meet in a deep, wooded valley, dappled with sunlight and green with ferns; the river bed is strewn with great boulders around which the water swirls and falls in an unending cascade. A fishing lodge of 1832 stands on the far bank, across a footbridge.

Lynmouth Foreland. – *4m E by A39 and a by-road.*
Foreland and its lighthouse *(p 17)* provide a **vantage point** from which to overlook the hogsback cliffs on either side. The Foreland itself, composed of ancient red and grey quartz grits and slate, most unusually for this coast, is bare of trees.

Heddon's Mouth. – *5m W by the Coastal Rd to Hunter's Inn then 3m Rtn on foot through the woods.*
The road skirst three bays from above before coming to the village of Martinhoe and, just beyond, Hunter's Inn. The rift followed by the Heddon is spectacular with rock walls rising 700ft in places before it opens out into a small, sheltered, pebble bay.

Combe Martin. – *Pop 2 310. 16m W by A39 and A399.*
The village between Exmoor and Ilfracombe, straggles the length of the combe, marked by 19C folly building, the **Pack of Cards Inn** and a pink sandstone **church** with a west tower 99ft tall, decorated with gargoyles. Lead and silver mines were worked locally from 13 to 19C.

tc **Combe Martin Motorcycle Collection.** – *Cross St.* The machines of early and late manufacture, include a Brough Superior said to be that on which T E Lawrence met his death *(p 144).*

Ilfracombe. – *21m W by A39 and A399. P 100.*

★★ MORTEHOE   Pop 1 552

Michelin map **403** fold 24 – H30

The point marks the end of the spectacular Somerset-North Devon coast.

Morte Point. – *½m Rtn on foot.* The interest of coming to Mortehoe is to walk out over the close-cropped turf on the gently rising headland, to survey the coast and other headlands from the 200ft **vantage point**★.

★ **Mortehoe Church.** – The late 12C Norman church, increased by the addition of the solid northwest tower, was enlarged in 13C by the building onto the south side by the then rector, Sir William Tracy, of a chantry to St Catherine. In the chapel he placed a **coffin chest** said to contain the bones of Sir William de Tracy, one of the three murderers of Thomas Becket in 1170, who subsequently fled to Devon. Note also in the church the mosaic on the early arch which was designed this century, the finely carved, 16C **bench-ends** and three contemporary **paintings** of *The Fall* and the *Crucifixion.*

EXCURSIONS

The excursions south to Devon's best known sand beaches provide a constrast to the rocks and cliffs which characterise the north coast.

Woolacombe. – *1m S by B3343.*
The holiday village overlooking Morte Bay is known for its miles of yellow sands.

Croyde. – *6m S by B3343 and B3231.*
The small village lies in a bay between Baggy Point and a lesser headland.

Braunton Burrows. – *10m S by B3343 and B3231.*
The burrows or dunes extend for some 300 acres, ending at the sea's edge in some of Devon's most beautiful golden beaches.

★ MORWELLHAM

Michelin map **403** fold 23 – H32 – 4m W of Tavistock

tc Morwellham's heyday was the brief period between the Devon Great Consols copper strike of 1844 and the coming of the Great Western Railway to Tavistock *(p 115)* in 1859. In those few years some 450 000 tons of mineral ore were shipped the 20 miles downstream to Plymouth in boats which, in most cases, only carried 50-100 tons a time. The industry and traffic were prodigious: the mined ore was brought from Tavistock by canal barges to a point 287ft above the river from where it descended by an inclined railway powered by a waterwheel, which was later supplemented by a second railway powered by steam; the quays, which had slowly evolved since the river port had come into existence in 13C, had to be developed out of recognition with tiled wharves to keep the ore and arsenic clean, and a dock constructed large enough to take six 300-ton schooners at a time. The number of villagers increased to 200; model cottages, houses, a shop, a school, a chapel, a butcher's shop, a pub, a hostelry, workshops and warehouses were built.
As rapidly as it had boomed Morwellham died: the canal was superseded by the railway; the mines became exhausted; Devon Great Consols declined; the population fell to 50.

WHAT YOU SEE TODAY

Great Dock. – Beside the dock are a log crane of the period and the restored quays.

The village. – The village has been restored with its complement of workshops, houses and hostelry. In the season, a chandler's shop, smithy, cooper's shop, assayer's laboratory, horse-drawn wagonettes and the tramway are manned by men and women in 19C period costume.

Waterwheel and millstones. – 32ft waterwheel and granite millstones were used to grind the manganese ore.

Lime kilns. – Limestone used to be burned in the kilns to extract the lime.

Central Electricity Generating Station. – The station, installed in 1933, uses water from the old canal.

Water powered threshing machine. – An example of 19C use of water power.

Canal tunnel entrance. – The canal constructed to bring ore from Tavistock *(see above)*.

Riverside tramway. – The tramway takes visitors underground into an early copper mine.

Museums. – Three small museums describe mining, the port and village life in 19C.

OKEHAMPTON   Pop 4 213

Michelin map **403** fold 34 – H and I31 – Local map pp 90-1

The market town bestrides the main A30 road from Exeter into Cornwall, where it skirts the northern boundary of Dartmoor.

Saxon in origin but abandoned, Okehampton was refounded as a strongpoint by the Normans. It became a mediaeval market town and prospered in the great wool period, only to tear itself apart during the Civil War; again it recorvered, benefitting especially as communications improved in 18-19C.

SIGHTS

Chantry Chapel. – *Fore St.* The chapel of ease on a near island site at the east end of the main street, was rebuilt in 1862 with many embellishments including obelisk pinnacles. The pulpit dates from 1626.

Through an arch behind the chapel, the old yard has been turned into professional craftsmen's studios and a shop.

Town Hall. – *Fore St. On the corner with Market St.* The town hall is in a former merchant's town house of 1685.

White Hart Inn. – *Fore St.* The refronted inn which was given an impressive portico in 18C, has held a licence since the town gained its charter in 1623. In 18-19C it served as the posting inn, the centre of local transport, and setting for Trollope-Dickensian style election schemings and celebrations – Okehampton long boasted two members, including for a time, Pitt the Elder.

The Arcade. – *Fore St – St James St, (S side).* The short, 19C shopping arcade is typical of the period with its overhead ironwork and black and white pavement.

Red Lion Yard. – *Fore St – car park (N side).* The small, open-air precinct with statuary and paved courtyard, is surrounded by arcaded, two-storey gabled buildings.

tc **Dartmoor Life Museum and Information Centre.** – *White Hart Yard, West St.* The collection is in two cottages, a mill and warehouse and an old printer's workshop, grouped round a yard approached through a granite archway. The exhibits include 1922 Bullnose Morris with a Hotchkiss engine and a farm pick-up, a farm kitchen, tools, a Dartmoor letter-box...

tc **Okehampton Castle.** – *Castle Lane.* The strategic site, the end of a spur beside the River Okement, was selected by the Normans for a motte and bailey castle, a wooden defence protected at the foot of the mound by a ditch. The Courtenays, Earls of Devon and the owners in 13C, rebuilt the castle only for it all to be slighted when Henry III executed the Earl of Devon in 1538 and attainted his property. In 18-19C the ruined castle was purchased by a politician for the parliamentary benefits it bestowed!

There remain a two-storey outer gatehouse, a barbican with the outer bailey behind it, and the gatehouse proper with its attendant guardroom, forming part of the high inner wall. The diamond-shaped inner bailey, is enclosed by the walls of 13C residential buildings, notably the hall *(right)* which communicates with the guardroom by steps and, at the far end, by means of a service room, with the kitchens. On the other side are lodgings, the chapel and another kitchen.

Climb the mound to the square keep, part 14C, part older, with a gaunt stair turret at the northeast corner to the upper rooms.

EXCURSIONS

Sticklepath. – *4m E on A30 – local map p 91.*

tc The attractive village with its slate and thatch roofed houses – two dated 1661 and 1694 – flower gardens, old low-lying inn and bridge over the River Taw, extends for half a mile along the main road. At the centre are the foundry and a Quaker Burying Ground (through an arch in 17-18C range of houses).

The Finch Foundry made agricultural hand-tools of high quality and great variety from 1814-1960 – scythes, bill-hooks, shovels, axes, cleavers, hammers, knives...

The machinery was powered by water from the river. As can still be seen in action, one water wheel drove a pair of trip-hammers and ancillary machinery including shears, a second, the fan from which air passed through underground pipes to the forges, while a third turned the grinding mill where tools were sharpened and finished.

Spinsters' Rock. – *4m E along A30 and A382; left turn by Drewsteignton.*
The megalithic tomb chamber or quoit of three large upright stones surmounted by a capstone, is visible over a gate to a field on Shilstone Farm.

South Zeal. – *5m E, just N of A30.*
The village, which lies just within Dartmoor's northern boundary, possesses from the days when it was a chartered borough, several interesting buildings along its main street and square, notably the early 16C, granite, **Oxenham Arms**, formerly the manor house, another **house** dated 1714, a third, repeatedly restored, of 1656, and one other of 15C with a **tower porch**; at the centre, the **church**, also 15C, was built as the guildhouse of the local wool trade workers.

★ OTTERY ST MARY   Pop 4 034

Michelin map **403** fold 35 – K31

Ottery, standing on the River Otter, surrounded on all sides by lush green hill slopes and well away from the main road, avoided the arterial plan and developed gradually on a hillside site as a network of winding streets, small squares and hidden corners, each lined by small 17C and medium sized Georgian houses. At the top of the hill, is the twin-towered parish church so reminiscent, in miniature, of Exeter Cathedral.

★★ ST MARY'S

The manor was given in 1061 by Edward the Confessor to a church foundation in Rouen and bought back in 1336 by **Bishop John de Grandisson** of Exeter in order that he might found in the village only twelve miles from the cathedral, a college or sanctuary for poetry and learning. This endured for 200 years before being Dissolved in 1545 by Henry VIII. The manor was presented to Edward Seymour, future Duke of Somerset but on his attainder reverted to the crown, finally being resold by Charles I.
The church, in which the villagers had always worshipped, became the parish's entirely but under the supervision of first four then twelve local residents or "Governors" – a system which continues to this day.
Henry took "all the plate jewells ornaments goods and cattalles apperteigninge to the late surrendered College".

Exterior: the towers. – The 64ft towers, dating from 14C, were the work of Bishop Grandisson who remodelled in the Decorated style the earlier church on the site. The 31ft lead covered **spire** (re-structured using the old lead in 1908) resembles one which crowned Exeter Cathedral north tower until 1752; the **weather vane,** one of the oldest in the country, is a **Whistling Cock,** so-called on account of the two tubes which run through its body and make it moan in the wind.

Interior. – The high rib and panel vaulted **nave** contains the canopied tombs of Sir Otho de Grandisson, the bishop's younger brother, in full armour (d 1359) and his wife; at the **crossing** the bishop himself is portrayed on the centre boss.
Against the wooden gallery in the south transept is **Grandisson's clock,** dating from the collegiate period, cared for in 1437-8 at a cost of 3s 4d and more recently totally rebuilt so that, like its fellows at Exeter, Wells and Wimborne Minster, it still tells the time. Note 19C mosaic **wall tiling.**
In the **chancel** the coloured vaulting changes to a curvilinear pattern to complement the window tracery. The altarscreen is 19-20C refurbishment; the **sedilia** is pure 14C Decorated Gothic. The **tomb** is that of John Haydon (d 1587), sometime "governor" of the church and builder of Cadhay *(p 85).*
Walk round the ambulatory, noting the Elizabethan **brasses** *(S side),* to pass beneath the stone minstrels' gallery into the **Lady Chapel.** This contains the church's gilded wooden **eagle lectern** dating from Grandisson's time, one of the oldest and grandest in England, also mediaeval **choirstalls** and a **corbel portrait head** *(at the opening, S wall)* of Bishop Grandisson in a mitre.
The **Outer South or Dorset aisle,** added to the church in 1520, is notable for its **fan vaulting** with large pendent bosses terminating in Tudor roses, its **corbels,** its owls on the piers at the west end and, on the second pier from the west end, an elephant's head (1520).

Green Tourist Guides

Scenery,
Buildings,
Scenic routes,
Geography, Economy,
History, Art,
Touring programmes,
Plans of towns and buildings.

Guides for your holidays

★★ PLYMOUTH

Michelin map **403** fold 33 – H32

The Hoe, Drake, Hawkins, Frobisher, Raleigh, Cooke, the Pilgrim Fathers, the Sound, R N ships of the line since the early 18C when Devonport Dockyard was laid down by William III – Plymouth conjures them all.

Plymouth developed from the amalgamation of three towns: Sutton, Dock (Devonport *see below*) and Stonehouse.

Sutton, at the mouth of the River Plym, began in earliest times in Leland's words as "a mene thing, an inhabitation of fishars". The Plantagenet period brought trade with France and the Tudor, particularly the Elizabethan, worldwide trade and prosperity, so that for a time it was the fourth largest town in England after London, Bristol and York.

The HOE and PLYMOUTH SOUND

The Hoe. – From the high hill (the old meaning of hoe) where Drake looked out across the Sound in 1588 and decided to finish his game of bowls before finishing off the Invincible Armada – or wait for the tide to turn to let him take his ships out of harbour, say some! – every visitor still looks across to the horizon, spots the Naval vessels coming in, the pilot cutters, the daily ferries to Roscoff, the twice-weekly ones to Spain (from Millbay docks, Stonehouse), the fishing and pleasure boats on the move.

The Sound. – The natural harbour lies at the mouth of the Rivers Tamar and Plym, the second giving its name in 14C to the ever more important harbour town.

tc **Drake's Island.** – The island, long a fort, is now an adventure centre.

The Breakwater. – The 19C breakwater, which marks the southern limit of the Sound two miles offshore, was constructed against the heavy sea swell which rolls in from the southwest; it is one mile in length; the engineer designer was **John Rennie**; it took 4½ million tons of local limestone to build, 29 years to complete (1812-41) and cost £1½ million.

Beside it, on an island rock, stands the round **Breakwater Fort** (*c*1860).

At either end are beacon lights *(p 17)* and, at the east end, a large iron **lobster-pot** refuge at the top of 24ft pole, into which anyone wrecked can climb and await rescue, now by helicopter.

Eddystone Lighthouse. – The lighthouse, can be seen on the skyline, about 14 miles to SW *(p 17)*.

Mount Batten. – The eastern headland is Mount Batten, now RAF rescue, marine craft repair and weather station. *(See also p 110.)*

Monuments on the Hoe

tc **Smeaton's Tower.** – The white and red painted lighthouse, replaced a beacon obelisk when it was re-erected on the Hoe in 1884 after its 123 storm-battered years on the Eddystone Rocks *(p 17)*.

Climb up the steps and ladders *(93 steps)* in the ever narrowing cylinder – note how the two bunks are fitted round the walls – to the gallery and even better **view★★**.

(R Passmore / Colorific / Cosmos)

Smeaton's Tower on Plymouth Hoe

Drake Statue. – The bronze statue by Boehm *(p 115)* was erected in 19C, west of centre, on the inland side of the wide east-west Promenade.

Armada Memorial. – The memorial stands as a pendant on the east side of the Hoe.

Naval War Memorial. – The pillar memorial, surrounded by rose gardens, bears the names of 22 443 men. The anchor in Anchor Way is from the last *Ark Royal*.

Other Monuments. – The very tall building with an inverted roof is the Civic Centre; on the Devon side, covering the headland, are the Royal Citadel and behind it the Barbican and Sutton Harbour *(see below)* and on the Cornwall side, Devonport, Millbay Dock *(Continental ferries)*, Cremyll and Torpoint Ferries and the Tamar Bridges *(p 115)*.

CITY CENTRE

New Buildings

tc **Civic Centre.** – The 14 storey centre was opened in 1962. All around, the city, which had been largely devastated in 1939-45 War, has been redesigned and rebuilt.

tc **Council House.** – Go inside to see the **engraved glass panels** in the doors and on the staircase by John Hulton and the **corporation plate**, including the four historic maces of Plymouth and the towns now incorporated within the city and a wonderful array of **modern salts**, rose bowls, candelabra and candelsticks and most notably, great silver **centrepieces.**

City Flagstaff. – The mast at the juncture of the Armada Way and the Royal Parade, is mounted on a replica of **Drake's drum** *(p 84).*

Old Buildings

tc **Guildhall.** – The building with a campanile-style tower dates from 1873, the last in a line going back to 15C; note on the Hoe side, the city's **coat of arms** transferred from 17C poorhouse.

St Andrew's. – The church, founded in 1050 but Perpendicular in style after 15C rebuilding, was reconsecrated in 1957 having been fire bombed in 1941 so that only the outer walls, fluted granite piers, chancel arch and 136ft tower were left standing.

The windows. – Six distinctive windows were designed by **John Piper** for the rebuilt church – in the tower window where the Instruments of the Passion are depicted, note how the ladder, the lance and the reed form St Andrew's cross. Below each is a complementary altar. Setting off the vivid colours of the glass is a patinaed Delabole slate *(p 71)* floor.

Among the **memorials** are 12-13C Purbeck marble effigy and a tablet to **Frobisher** and **Drake** *(N transept),* a tablet to William Cookworthy *(S wall; p 110).* Note the royal arms of Charles I, George III and George IV and, on the ledge of the first window west of the south door, the so-called **Drake crest scratching** of the *Golden Hinde* with a cord from her bow partly circling a globe. The rough engraving is believed to have been made by a mason working in the church at the time of Drake's return from his circumnavigation on 3 November 1580.

tc **Prysten House.** – The priests' house of stone, built three storeys high round an inner courtyard, dates from 15C. It may well have lodged the priests from Plympton Priory who came to officiate at St Andrew's, while the courtyard probably served as a courtroom for cases tried before the prior who held civil as well as ecclesiastical authority in the town.

Note the **window frames** and stone mullions, stone **fireplaces** and the beams – smoke-blackened from the time when, after the Dissolution, the house became, for a time, a bacon-curing store.

The Door of Unity. – The door facing the church, commemorates two US naval officers killed in action in 1813 and buried in St Andrew's churchyard.

tc **The Merchant's House.** – *33 St Andrew's St.* The three-storey timber house with limestone walls, jettied upper floors supported on stone corbels and windows extending almost the full width and height of the front, was built in the mid-16C and probably given much of its present style early in 17C when it was bought by William Parker. Parker, mayor of Plymouth in 1601-2, was a sea-captain, merchant and typical adventurer, who had amassed enough gold to buy and improve the house buccaneering on the Spanish Main *(p 15)* and possibly also as master of the victualling ship to Drake's fleet at the time of the Armada.

In the house each floor comprised a principal front room and a back room, with small bedrooms on the upper floors. Note the **pole staircase** round a 35ft shaft. The house is now a Museum of Old Plymouth.

★ ROYAL CITADEL *time: 1 hour*

tc The Royal Citadel, now garrisoned by the Royal Artillery, was built in the reign of Charles II between 1666-71. It differed from previous forts on the site and notably from its immediate predecessor of 1590-1, begun but never completed by Sir Francis Drake against marauding Spaniards, in that its cannon could be trained not only on enemy ships entering the Sound – the Dutch at that time – but also on the town – Plymouth had been Parliamentarian throughout the Civil War.

The Ramparts. – The walls, which have a circumference of about three quarters of a mile, and present a sheer face of 60ft in places (now used as a commando scaling exercise!) command **views** ★★ of the Sound, the Barbican and the mouth of the Tamar.

Main Gate. – The gate of 1670, built of Portland stone, originally contained a bust of Charles II in the niche to complement the royal arms and inscription. It was, however, considered politic to remove the head and substitute four cannon balls when the citadel was surrendered personally to William III in 1688!

George II Statue. – The statue dates from 1728. Note the **cannon** and **mortars** around the statue and on the walls, all historic, many captured in battle.

Chapel. – The small chapel was rebuilt with walls 2ft 9in thick in 1688 and enlarged to twice its size in 19C. The frescoes on the east wall were painted by an NCO in the Royal Engineers who died in 1914-18 War.

The Guard House (now the guardroom), the Governor's House, the Storeroom and other buildings, have all been rebuilt and remodelled.

The BARBICAN *time: ½ hour*

Old, historic, Plymouth survives in the Barbican, an area extending over a quarter of a mile inland from the harbourside. The quarter combines modern interests and amenities – shops, restaurants, ships' chandlers, pubs, working craftsmen's studios – with mediaeval houses, Jacobean doorways, cobbled alleys, the harbour...

Make your way to the waterfront.

Mayflower Stone. – *West Pier.* The pier, bedizened with stones and plaques, was the embarkation and alighting point for many famous voyages, notably: the **Pilgrim Fathers** sailing on 6 September 1620 in their 90ft ship, *The Mayflower* (the pavement stone is 17C); the *Tory* sailing to colonize **New Zealand** in May 1839; the *Sea Venture* voyaging to **Bermuda** in 1609; the return of the **Tolpuddle Martyrs** in 1838 *(p 143);* the safe arrival of the American Seaplane, *NC4* on completion of the first **Transatlantic Flight** in 1919; the sailing of Sir Humphrey Gilbert to Newfoundland in 1583.

On the far side of the road *(left, high on the wall by the flight of steps)* a plaque commemorates "10 Squadron **Royal Australian Air Force** stationed at Mt Batten 1939-45".

Turn N.

Fish Market. – The market is a hive of activity in the very early hours.

Island House. – The late 16C house (restored) is where the **Pilgrim Fathers** (the names are listed on a board on the wall), may have spent their last night before setting sail.

Turn right in behind the house to go up New St.

tc **Elizabethan House.** – *32 New St.* The house and its neighbour were built in the late 16C as part of a development of thirty houses for small merchants and ships' captains, prosperous from the trade in wine, Newfoundland cod, tobacco and sugar and in booty captured at sea.

The timber framed and limestone houses are distinghished by **windows** which extend across the full width of the fronts on the ground and first floors. Inside the Elizabethan House, a passage runs directly through from the front to the back and the small garden. Exposed **beams** and large **fireplaces,** stout 16-17C oak furniture, carved and patinaded with age and care, give an idea of the comforts of the time. Note the **pole staircase** fashioned round a ship's mast and where the **wooden treads** as they wore down were mended by putting another on top until it was discovered this century that there were as many as four boards to a tread!

Turn left to go to the top of Southside St.

tc **Coates Plymouth Gin Distillery.** – Go through the low, wide granite doorway into a chamber containing the onion shaped, glass lined, steel vats in which today's gin is prepared – a secret process by which 100 % raw barley spirit produced in Scotland, is transformed by distillation, flavouring and dilution with pure Dartmoor water.

Through the works is the **Refectory Room** dating from 1425 when a Dominican or Blackfriars monastery stood on the site – note the **roof** built on arch braces and resembling an upturned keel, also the prints of old Plymouth and a small herb cabinet.

Adjoining on the Blackfriars site, an inner courtyard is framed by a modern exhibition gallery, a restaurant, shops...

Cut through one of the "opes" on the opposite side of the street.

The Parade. – The quayside, lined by houses, warehouses and inns, takes its name from the days when the Royal Marines, established in Plymouth by the Board of Admiralty in 1755, used to parade on the cobbled pavement. Today one end is bright with a **giant mural** by a local portrait painter, Robert Lenkiewitz, depicting black magic in Elizabethan England.

ADDITIONAL SIGHTS

★ **City Museum and Art Gallery.** – *Drake Circus.* Plymouth was the home of the adult *tc* **William Cookworthy,** discoverer of the Cornish kaolin *(pp 67, 101),* which made the production of **hard paste porcelain** a reality in this country from 1768. The rapid development of the new material and different factory marks are displayed, also **domestic pieces** such as cider mugs, cups, sauceboats and teapots and decorative ware including human, animal and bird **figures,** vases, centrepieces with matching spoons, trellised dessert baskets all in vivid enamels and the more difficult, because flawless, pure white. Joshua Reynolds was born in Plympton in 1723 (d 1792) and the gallery has a unique collection of **Reynolds family portraits.**

The **history gallery** is distinguished by the **Drake Cup,** a silver parcel gilt globe with an astrolabe, traditionally presented to Drake by Queen Elizabeth in 1582.

tc **Plymouth Aquarium.** – *Madeira Rd.* The fish, eels and flatfish and mackerel, the sea anemones, starfish, dog-fish, crabs and other crustacea, swimming in the sea-water tanks around the gallery are almost all from local waters. The 45 kinds of fish, the 50 species of invertebrates are there primarily, in fact, for observation by the **Marine Biological Association of the UK** as part of their research on increasing the supply of food from the sea.

BOAT TRIPS

River Tamar Cruises. – To Calstock and Morwellham, depending on the tide. Landing at Calstock *(p 115, possible return by train to Plymouth)* and Morwellham *(p 105).*

Grand Circular Cruises. – Viewing Plymouth Hoe, Drake's Island, the Breakwater, the Dockyards and R N ships – *no landing.*

River Yealm and Newton Ferrers. – Across the Sound, east of the Breakwater, along the coast and to the mouth of the River Yealm – *no landing.*

EXCURSIONS

★★ **Saltram House.** – *3½m E of city centre, just S of A38 (before Plympton). P 112.*

★★ **Buckland Abbey.** – *11m NW of A386 – bear left at Yelverton; signposted from Crapstone. P 84.*

★ **Yelverton Paperweight Centre.** – *9m N on A386 (200yds along a loop road just tc off the roundabout).*
Paperweights, sparkling, in colours deep and knife edged or misty pastel, with designs, marbled, floral or swirling, made in 19 and 20C by English, Scots, French, German and Chinese craftsmen, are to be seen in the 800 strong, wondrous, collection.

tc **Mount Edgcumbe.** – *9m W by Torpoint car ferry, A374 and B3247 to Cremyll or by Cremyll passenger ferry from Admiral's Hard, Stonehouse.*
Walks through the 800-acre park and gardens and along 10 miles of coastline paths afford ever more extensive views★ across the Sound.
In 1353 William Edgcumbe of Edgcumbe, Milton Abbot, Devon married Hilaria de Cotele whose dowry was Cotehele House *(p 51)*; in 1493, their descendant, Piers Edgcumbe, married Jean Durnford, heiress to considerable estates on both sides of the Tamar and the important Cremyll Ferry; in 1539 just before he died, Piers received a royal licence to enclose grounds for the park in which his son, Sir Richard, built Mount Edgcumbe House in 1547-54.
Richard Carew in his *Survey (p 46)*, described Mount Edgcumbe as "buildid square, with a round turret at each end, garretted on the top, and the hall rising in the mids above the rest, which yealdeth a stately sound as you enter the same (and) the parlour and dining chamber (which) give you a large and diversified prospect of land and sea". This house with later additions was gutted by incendiary bombs in 1941.
When it came to be rebuilt a return was made to the original square plan and the additional 18C octagonal corner towers so that it now looks much as in Carew's description.
One family **portrait** by Reynolds is left, a **longcase clock** of 1610 (John Matchett, Covent Garden), furniture of 17 and 18C and a pair of **Bronze Age hunting horns.**
The **higher gardens,** near the house, include a wooded Amphitheatre, formal Italian and French gardens and an English garden with specimen shrubs and trees.

tc **Dartmoor Wild Life Park, Sparkwell.** – *9m E on Plymouth-Cornwood by-road.*
The collection, in large paddocks, aviaries and shelters on the edge of Dartmoor, ranges from timber-wolves to chickens, from monkeys to owls and red deer.

Devon Shire Horse Farm, Dunstone. – *9m ESE off A379.*

tc **Kitley Caves, Yealmpton.** – The caves, in a wooded setting beside the River Yealm, were discovered in the early 1800s by quarrymen blasting for limestone – a couple of ruined kilns stand near the entrance. The caves contain stalactites and stalagmites and a number of rock pools.

Turn right 1m beyond Yealmpton.

tc **Devon Shire Horse Farm Centre.** – The shires, between 15 and 20 of them, stallions, geldings, mares and foals, mostly black with blazes, white socks, characteristic feathered legs, and curved Roman noses, weigh up to one ton each. They work and, of course, dominate 60-acre farm.
The old stone farm buildings date back to 1772 with the long main stable, with the hayloft above, turning the corner opposite the house. Go through the porch into the **harness room,** gleaming with brass and leather, and **stable,** where you can walk along the far side of the manger to see those horses not at work.
The climax of every visit is the **parade** of horses, mares and foals.

SALCOMBE   Pop 2 451

Michelin map **403** fold 34 – I33
See town plan in the current Michelin Red Guide Great Britain and Ireland

Devon's most southerly resort lies on the Kingsbridge Estuary which flows out to sea between Prawle Point to the east and Bolt Head to the west.
The town, a onetime fishing village overlooking the estuary, possesses small sand beaches and coves (North Sands, South Sands, Batson Creek) within minutes of the main street and, in the street itself, more ships' chandlers than grocers. Old houses, boat-yards, the custom house and its quay, ships and a pontoon-pier, line the waterside; more modern houses sprawl back up the wooded hillside.
The estuary harbour, which extends from the sand bar in line with Sharpitor Rocks and after which Tennyson is said to have written *Crossing the Bar,* is aflutter all summer with small yachts – as many as 6 000 visiting craft have been counted in a single season.
Salcombe even has a castle, **Fort Charles,** built at the entrance to the harbour in 1544, rebuilt in 1643 and besieged by the Parliamentary troops from 15 January to 9 May 1646 when it surrendered. It is now a picturesque ruin.

tc **Ferries.** – Ferries ply the harbour estuary, crossing to **East Portlemouth** (sand beaches and paths to Prawle Point), **South Sands** and **Kingsbridge** *(p 101).*

EXCURSIONS

★ **Kingsbridge.** – *5m N by A381. P 101.*

Bolt Head. – *7m Rtn on foot, joining up with the South Devon Coast Path.* Go by the Cliff Rd, North Sands, The Moult, South Sands, left by hotel, over 400ft Sharp Tor or Sharpitor Rocks to round Starhole Bay and onto the downland head.

tc **Sharpitor Overbecks Museum and Garden.** – *2m SW.* The attraction of Sharpitor is the **view**★★ from different levels of the terraced garden. Go in the spring and the magnolias will be out, in summer the agapanthus, hydrangeas...

The last owner of the Edwardian-style **villa** of 1913 was a Dutchman, Otto Overbecks who was a research chemist with numerous other interests. He left the property to serve as a youth hostel (72 beds), an open garden and as a **museum** for his own natural history and inventive collections. To these have been added displays on old Salcombe.

Prawle Point. – *16m by A381 to Kingsbridge, A379 to Charleton and Chillington then S by by-roads to Chivelstone; continue due S through E Prawle to the end of the road then walk 200yds.*

The **views**★★★ from the point are all you could hope for.

★★ SALTRAM HOUSE

Michelin map **403** fold 34 – H32 – 3½m E of Plymouth

tc "The place is so gay, so riant, so comfortable and so everything that it ought to be" wrote the bride of 1809 of her new home. The house you see today is much as it was then.

In 1712, when the local Parker family had purchased it, it had been a Tudor mansion, in 1750 when it came to John Parker, his wife, **Lady Catherine Parker** "a proud and wilful woman", set about agrandising it. The extensions were all to her own designs which were after the Classical style with Baroque additions, notably in the interior plasterwork. Lady Catherine died in 1758; her son inherited the house in 1768.

John Parker II was an MP and man about town; he was a lifelong friend of **Joshua Reynolds** *(p 110)*, who was by then President of the Royal Academy, and at Westminster became acquainted with Lord Shelburne *(p 187)*, statesman and patron of the arts, who introduced him to the architect **Robert Adam** who was working with **Thomas Chippendale...** Between 1768-71 and 1780-81, following a fire, Adam, Chippendale, Reynolds, Angelica Kauffman, all worked at Saltram.

Only one important alteration has been made since 18C: in 1818 the local architect John Foulston, enlarged the library by adding on the music room and, at the front, he designed the balustraded porch on Doric columns, enlarged the windows above it and added to the pediment the arms of Parker III, newly created Earl of Morley. Porcelain and china were bought in the fashion of the day but not "collected", the pictures, almost all family portraits painted successively throughout their lives, are closely hung as in a family album, amenities which contribute to Saltram's being not museumlike but a house "so everything that it ought to be".

TOUR *1 hour*

Entrance Hall. – Dominant in the hall decorated with **plasterwork** of 1750 and a great marble fireplace, are the portraits of *Lady Catherine Parker* and *John Parker II, Lord Boringdon* (by Thomas Hudson). Note also the serpentine side-tables, 18C Chinese and Chinese style delftware, the Louis XIV Boulle **clock** on its original bracket.

Morning Room. – In the room hung with Genoa silk velvet, are family portraits painted by Reynolds of *John Parker II, Lord Boringdon,* leaning against a gate, *Theresa Robinson, Lady Boringdon* – with her son, John Parker III the future Lord Morley, and the boy with his sister.

The **black basalt vases** are Wedgwood of *c*1780, the **mahogany cabinets** on stands, Chippendale, the Chinese-style cabinet is English. Note the *famille rose* punchbowl.

Velvet Drawing Room. – The deep red and gold room with its original **stucco ceiling** was replanned by Adam with fluted Corinthian end pillars, giltwood tables and mirrors to serve as a prelude to the adjoining saloon. The Rococo **giltwood mirror** is mid-18C.

Saloon. – The room, a double cube of 50 × 25 × 25ft, was designed throughout by Adam, from the ceiling to the complementary carpet (£126 l), the giltwood furniture upholstered in ethereal blue and silver silk damask like the walls, the pier glasses, the torchères which support ormolu mounted tortoise-shell and blue john "candle vases".

The chandeliers are 19C. The portrait of *Lady Boringdon* is by Reynolds.

(National Trust)

The Blue Saloon

Eating or Dining Room. – Following the fire, the eating room and library were transposed and both redesigned entirely, including much of their furniture, by **Adam**. Note again the ceiling and complementary carpet, the picture frames, the marble-topped table and mirror between the windows, the curved **serving table** in the end bay.

Hall. – The hall with its cantilevered **staircase** is a return to the pre-Adam house. Of especial interest is the large **Boulle writing table** of tortoise-shell and brass which is said to have been given by Louis XIV to Sarah, Duchess of Marlborough and by her granddaughter to Lady Catherine Parker. Note also 18C **bracket clock** in an ormolu mounted case; five 18C mahogany armchairs with their original needlepoint; *The Fall of Phaeton*, by **Stubbs**, portraits of *Joshua Reynolds* and *Parker* by **Angelica Kauffmann**.

Upper Rooms. – Three rooms follow the fashion for 17-18C Chinese painted wall hangings, figured, exotic, often formally hilarious and perfectly complemented by the slender posted 18C **bed** with feathered cresting, the Chinese-Chippendale **chairs**, the painted **mirrors**.

Boudoir. – The olive-green and gold room became Lady Morley's sanctum on the death of her husband (John Parker III), in 1840. Around her she gathered the Regency centre table with a marble top, 18C mahogany secretaire **bookcase** and family portraits.

Lord Morley's Room. – Note the picture by Gardner of *Lord Morley as a Small Boy.*

Library. – The room presents a gallery of **portraits:** by the American artist, Gilbert Stuart (1755-1818), Reynolds *(Lord Boringdon* and *Sir John Chichester of Arlington, p 80)*, Northcote and Angelica Kauffman *(Self-Portrait)*.
The **tables** are functional as well as beautiful: the circular drum is a rent table with alphabetically labelled drawers, another is a writing table, another a games table and the Pembroke table opens into library steps.

Great Kitchen. – The kitchen, built in 1779, was modernised a century later.

SEATON   Pop 4 974

Michelin map 📕📕📕 fold 35 – K31

The small seaside resort at the mouth of the River Axe close to the Devon-Dorset boundary, lies back from a mile-long pebble beach between two headlands (views★★): to westward are the dramatically white 400ft cliffs of Beer Head, to the east, those of Lyme Regis *(p 134)*.
In the evening walk east along the Esplanade past the tram station *(see below)*, over the bridge and along the path round the Old Harbour to see the sunset.

SIGHTS

Seaton Tramway. – *Harbour Rd*. The swaying ride on the top of the 2ft 9in gauge, electric tram with a great iron arm reaching back to the overhead wire, the hard seats, open guard-rail and sounding bell, is fun in itself. The track, originally laid for the railway in 1868, follows the Axe Valley to Colyton *(p 87)*. The ride affords a good, view of the countryside and **waterfowl** *(p 23)* on the river banks.

The Landslip. – *Access: from the east side of the river make for the Axmouth Golf Course or Steppes Lane in Axmouth, then follow the cliff path down the face and into the slip.*
The signposted path is rough and can be slippery; it is NOT for those unaccustomed to rough walking; there are no intermediary exits and it is 5m before you come out to Underhill Farm, on the outskirts of Lyme Regis (p 134).
Minor slips occur almost annually along the length of cliff but on Christmas Day 1839 between Bindon and Dowlands Cliffs, there opened a chasm three-quarters of a mile long, 400ft across and 150ft deep, which has been known ever since as The Landslip. About 8 million tons of rock are estimated to have foundered in the one night. The area is now a woodland nature reserve.

Seaton Hole. – At the west end of the beach is Seaton Hole (sand and rock pools at low water) and above, a semi-wooded headland, from which there are wide views out to sea.

EXCURSIONS

★ **Colyton.** – *3½m by B3172, A3052 and B3161 or by the electric tram (see above; 8mins walk up from the station). P 87.*

★ **Branscombe.** – *6m W along B3172, B3174 and A3052.*

Beer. – Pop 1 328. Despite its huge popularity, Beer, with boats hauled up the shingle beach, remains essentially a fishing village, pinched into a small cove between gleaming white rock headlands.
The rock is, of course, the **Beer stone** used by cathedral, church and housebuilders since 15C also in Roman times, as a contrasting trim, the quality of the stone being such that it can be cut with a saw when newly quarried and hardens when exposed to wind and weather.
Note the spring which tumbles down the length of the village main street into the sea.
Return to the Beer turning and bear W and S, to circle Beer Head.

★ **Branscombe.** – Pop 506. The village straggles in clusters of thatched cottages at the centre of small flowered gardens, along either side of a steep and winding road which at the end of two miles arrives at the beach and a group of old coastguard cottages. The village itself, which has a recorded history dating back to King Alfred, includes old and historic houses, a **forge** of 1580, an **inn** – the Mason's Arms – of 1360 and, on the valley side, the Norman **Church of St Winifred,** built on a Saxon site in 12C. Note especially inside, the oak beamed **roof** and **Elizabethan gallery** with access from the outside staircase, the late 18C **three-decker pulpit** and box pews, the late 17C altar rail with twisted balusters and a macabre monument of 1606.

Axmouth. – *2m E along the the Harbour Rd (B3174) or the Esplanade to the Old Harbour, over the river bridge (***views ★***) then left upstream (B3172). P 81.*

Axminster. – *8m NW on B3172 through Axmouth and A358. P 81.*

SIDMOUTH
Pop 3 266

Michelin map **403** fold 25 – K32

The town lies at the foot of wooded hills which come right down to the sea where they sheer off exposing rock which is pinky-cream to the east (Salcombe Hill Cliff) and dark red to the west (Peak Hill, 500ft). The sea, as it goes out uncovers a golden sand beach and, to the west, the **Chit Rocks** and further west still **Jacob's Ladder** or Western Beach – Jacob's Ladder itself comprises three flights of wooden steps to a fort-like building on the cliff top.
The **Esplanade** and several streets and terraces are lined by Georgian and Regency houses from the time when Sidmouth had dreams of being a fashionable watering place.

EXCURSIONS

Ladram Bay. – *2m along South Devon Coast Path. Start from Peak Hill Rd.*
The path, starting by Peak Hill Cottage (thatched), goes through a glade of beeches to follow the line of the cliff edge before eventually dropping down to the small Ladram Bay with its spectacular, eroded red cliffs and offshore stacks (crowded in summer).

tc **The Donkey Sanctuary, Salcombe Regis.** – *3m NE by A3052; turn at signpost Dunscombe, Weston, Branscombe; entrance 300yds.*
In the fields, looking out of every stable door round the yard, are more donkeys than you have ever seen, rescued and now alert, inquisitive and enjoying life. In the **Slade Centre,** an indoor riding school, donkeys give rides each week to hundreds of handicapped children drawn from a wide area.

★★ River TAMAR

Michelin map **403** fold 33 – G, H31 and 32

The Tamar, for those who know it, and despite the bridges which cross it, conjures up first a mental image as the boundary between Devon and Cornwall *(p 70)*.
Geographically the river rises away up in the far northwest corner of Devon, 60m from where it flows into its estuary, known as the **Hamoaze,** and Plymouth Sound. It is still navigable at high water as far as Calstock and even Morwellham and Gunnislake *(see below)*. A thoroughfare in the Middle Ages and more importantly in 19C for ships bringing down ore from the mines *(p 115)*, the river is now peaceful with woods, undulating fields and market gardens on either bank, the haunt of avocets, herons and other waders *(p 23)*. It is beautiful along almost its entire length.

LANDMARKS: PLYMOUTH SOUND to GUNNISLAKE

Mount Edgcumbe. – Cornwall. *P 114.*
Cremyll Ferry. – The old ferry was a rich source of revenue *(p 111)*.
Mount Wise. – Devon. The memorial is to **Scott of the Antarctic.**
Torpoint Chain Ferry. – Until the opening of the road bridge *(see below)* the chain ferry afforded the only vehicle link betweem Plymouth and south Cornwall.
Royal Naval Station. – Devonport.
The base was developed as a dockyard and arsenal in the late 17C. In 1824 the name was changed from Dock to Devonport and in 1914 the town was merged with Plymouth.
River Lynher. – Cornwall. The river, which rises on Bodmin Moor, broadens out into a wide estuary where it flows into the **Hamoaze. Antony House ★★** *(p 46)* overlooks the Lynher.
The Tamar Bridges. – The bridges, one rail, one road, connect Devonport with Saltash. The **Royal Albert** was built by Brunel *(p 38)* in 1857-9 as part of the extension of the GWR into Cornwall. A combined suspension and arched bridge, supported by towering granite piers, it is an engineering feat even greater with its day-in day-out rail traffic than the more spectacular and graceful Clifton Bridge.
The **Tamar Road Bridge** was opened in 1962, replacing the centuries-old Saltash ferry. It was the model for the Forth and Severn Bridges and the Salazar Bridge in Lisbon.
Parson's Quay. – Landulph, Cornwall. The quay is one of several marking the river banks one either side. Once used to embark the lead, silver, tin, copper and arsenic mined locally, the quays now serve as pleasure-craft moorings. Parson's Quay was, in addition, an embarkation point in 15C for pilgrims setting out on the venturous journey to Santiago de Compostela in northern Spain.
River Tavy. – Devon. The river, which rises on Dartmoor, enters the mainstream beneath an eight-span railway bridge.
Bere Peninsula. – The tongue of land between the Tamar and the Tavy with **Bere Alston** as its principal town and Bere Ferrers' 13C **church** overlooking the Tavy as a local landmark, was an important silver and leadmining centre from 13-16C and again in

19C until the river burst its banks and flooded the workings in 1856. On the double bend look out for avocets as well as other waders *(p 23)*.

★★ **Cotehele and Cotehele Quay.** – Cornwall. *P 51.*

Calstock. – Cornwall. Pop 4 929.
Landing stage for most of the Tamar cruises.
The small, once important, river port, was killed in 1908 when the spectacular, 12-span railway viaduct was opened 120ft above the river.

★ **Morwellham.** – Devon. *P 105.*

Gunnislake. – Cornwall. The minute village below rock heights tunnelled by old tin mines, was famous for centuries as the most southerly bridge across the Tamar. Seven-arched, 182ft long, New Bridge was built of large regular granite blocks with cutwaters and refuges in 1520.

TRAIN EXCURSION

It is also possible to go up the Tamar Valley from Plymouth to Gunnislake by train and return from Calstock by boat. The train passes through Devonport, St Budeaux, under the Tamar bridges, over Tamerton Lake and the Tavy Bridge.

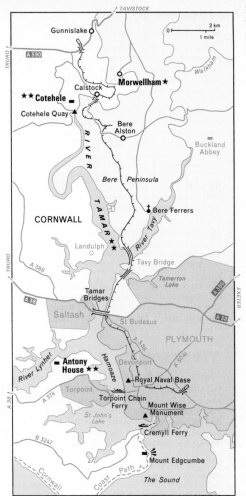

TAVISTOCK

Pop 9 271

Michelin map 403 fold 33 – H32

The modern market town constructed in the local volcanic, grey-green stone, retains many traces of its 19C days as a copper mining town and also of the monastic borough which it was from 980-1539. A bronze statue of **Sir Francis Drake** is as a reminder that he was christened in the parish in *c*1541.

The Benedictine abbey was the most resplendent house west of Glastonbury. The abbot obtained a charter for a weekly market in 1105 also an annual **Goose Fair;** at the same time **tin mining** was developing so that in 1281 Tavistock was named as a stannary town *(p 43)*. Wool and cloth brought additional wealth which resulted in the parish church, already rebuilt in 14C, being again rebuilt (1425-50) and a second south aisle, the Clothworkers' Aisle, being added while the work was in progress (1445).

In 1539 the abbey was Dissolved and the town, given by Henry VIII to **John Russell,** courtier, ambassador, counsellor and future Earl of Bedford.

With the start of the Napoleonic wars in 1790s, **mining** became the most important local industry and when in 1844 one of the richest ever **copper lodes** or veins in Europe was discovered near the surface in a pheasant covert, Tavistock became a boom town. Five separates mines in an area of 167 acres were grouped into a company known as **Devon Great Consols** whose £1 shares were quoted on the Stock Exchange three years after being launched at £800. Production was at its peak between 1848-58 then slackened as the mines became exhausted (1901); in the half century 730 000 tons of copper ore and 72 000 tons of refined arsenic – used then in dyes, paints, glass-making, ink and insecticides – had been produced at a sale price of £4 000 000. Bonuses from the new wealth were an increase in the population of the town to once and half its present size; the construction between 1803-17, with French prisoners-of-war as navvies, of the 4mile long **canal,** including 1½ mile tunnel, connecting Tavistock with the Tamar at Morwellham *(p 105)*, the remodelling in Neo-Gothic style of the **guildhall** and the Bedford Hotel (then a private house), the construction of the **pannier market** and houses for the miners and townspeople.

Parish Church. – St Eutace's 106ft embattled **tower,** built in 1430s, has doorways to north and south, having once been one of the abbey's four gateways.

Inside the church note the richer quality of the **Clothworkers' Outer South Aisle** *(see above)*, the bosses in the wagon roof, 14C oak chests, a **brass,** a bass **ophicleide,** an obsolete wind instrument from when there was a church orchestra *(tower wall)*, 15C octagonal font, a collection of early **17C pewter flagons** *(end of N aisle)* and two 16-17C tombs.

TEIGNMOUTH

Pop 13 334

Michelin map 408 fold 34 – J32

The dark red cliffs and offshore rocks, which identify Devon for so many holiday-makers appear in an almost unbroken line between the south bank of the Exe and Teign estuaries, the second distinguished by a huge red sandstone headland known as **The Ness.** *(Passenger ferries across both estuaries, also a bridge in the town across the Teign)*
The **railway,** given pride of place as it travelled west in the mid-19C, runs at the foot of the cliffs, skirting the waterline, tunnelling through the headlands and rumbling in each resort, between the flower-decked esplanades and the beaches.
Fishing for cod off the Newfoundland Grand Banks, shipbuilding and the export of dried fish brought prosperity to Teignmouth centuries ago; today its industries are offshore fishing and marketing, the handling of ball clay and tourism.

EXCURSIONS

Dawlish. – Pop 10 846. *3m N by A379.*
The town, when it expanded at the arrival of the railway to become a fashionable watering place, developed along the line of the stream which still flows through its centre.

Newton Abbot. – Pop 20 979. *6m W by A381.*
The market town, at the tidal limit of the River Teign, originated around a subsequently Dissolved monastery. The free-standing St Leonard's Tower erected before 1350, was the site in 1688 from which William of Orange first proclaimed his intention to be king.
The town's establishment as the main South Devon **railway junction** in 1846 brought it undreamed of prosperity and trebled the population. It remains the principal market in the area for both livestock and produce.
The **racecourse** is 1m NNE, off the A380.

TIVERTON

Pop 16 636

Michelin map 408 fold 25 – J31

The town between Dartmoor and Exmoor, at the confluence of the Rivers Lowman and the Exe, grew rich in 13-17C on **wool.** In Tudor times merchants settled in the town, added an aisle and chapel to the church, endowed schools and almshouses. By 18C, in Defoe's words, Tiverton had become "Next to Excester, the greatest manufactoring town in the county and, of all the inland towns, next to it in wealth and in the numbers of people": there were 55 fulling mills, 700 woolcombers.
In 19C the population grew to 10 500 and **lacemaking,** brought by John Heathcoat from the Midlands *(p 101),* had become the major industry which it remains today having diversified into net-making and modernised its manufacture.
Guarding the town from its earliest days was a castle; manifesting its continued affluence are its Perpendicular church, its mid-Victorian St Paul's Sq.

SIGHTS

tc **Tiverton Castle.** – *North Hill. Just N of the church.* In 12C Henry I created the Norman, Richard de Redvers, Earl of Devon and presented him with a great swathe of land on which to build a ring of defensive forts: Tiverton, Exeter, Plympton, Christchurch and Carisbrook. In 17C the castle was first besieged then slighted in the Civil War before, finally, being purchased at the Restoration by a rich wool merchant.
Today one enters through the massive, 14C red sandstone **gatehouse** vaulted in white Caen stone, to find oneself in a large grassed courtyard bounded by the curtain walls and towers of the old fortress overlooking the River Exe, 60ft below.
Within the gatehouse and the round tower with its conical roof, a number of rooms have been furnished with reminders of the castle builders and the special interests of the present owners which include Joan of Arc and historic clocks.

St Peter's Church. – The 99ft **tower** in pink sandstone with corner pinnacles, dates from *c*1400, when the **chancel** of 11C church was also renewed. In 1517, after the nave and aisles had long been completed, the merchant, John Greenway, enlarged the south aisle and added the **porch** and **chapel** in the fashionable late Perpendicular style with larger windows, ornamented castellations, crocketed pinnacles. The additions were in contrasting white stone and the chapel decorated with reliefs including a line of **armed merchantmen** such as shipped his woollen cloth from Devon and brought home wine and raw wool.

★ **Museum.** – *National Schools, St Andrew St.* The local museum in unpromising
tc buildings with old and new showcases, has a great wealth of material: there are early bicycles, copy-books from the old schools, trade tokens, a set of model soldiers depicting the Devon regiments from 1685-1975, Victorian laundry equipment and galleries on the canal *(see below)* and local industry.

Grand Western Canal. – *Canal Hill. Continuation of Gold St-Station Rd.* The system was intended to connect the Bristol and English Channels by way of 30-mile canal from Taunton to Topsham on the River Exe, with a spur coming off the mainstream to Tiverton. Although in 1814 the Taunton-Tiverton reach was opened, no further building was undertaken and in 1830s, when the Bristol-Exeter railway opened, the canal traffic was reduced until only locally quarried stone and limestone were carried in the horse-drawn narrowboats.
In 1960s 11½miles of the canal course were reclaimed and set to rights, wide boats and horses were found. Now you may walk or fish from the towpath or glide silently in the gaily painted *Tivertonian* drawn by amiable shires.

Old Blundells School. – *Station Rd.* The school, which stands back from the road, can be seen through a gateway above which is a tablet announcing its name and foundation in 1604 by the local clothier, Peter Blundell. The building, intended for the education of local boys, is a long single storey range in dark gold stone with a slate covered, pitched roof on the crest of which rides a small, colonnaded clock turret. Twin gables, each with a rounded doorway arch, divide the range.

The drive from the gate in the outer wall divides to approach each doorway creating before the house a grass triangle, the scene of the fight between John Ridd and Robin Snell in *Lorna Doone (p 159).* Blackmore himself was a pupil at the school.

EXCURSIONS

★★ **Coldharbour Mill, Uffculme.** – *11m E by A373 (take S fork under M5 and cross*
tc *A38) to B3391; the mill is at the end of the village.*

The working wool and worsted mill museum stands between a fast flowing stream and leat which have provided power for paper, grist and woollen mills on the site since possibly as long ago as Domesday. The last, a wool mill, which had run for nearly 200 years, flourishing at a time when the industry was moving north, closed in 1981.

The mill produces cloth and knitting yarn on sample machines, enabling the visitor to see and ask the men who work the machines about each process of combing, drawing, spinning, reducing, twisting, warp and weft winding and weaving.

★ **Knightshayes Court.** – *2m N on A396, turn right at Bolham. P 102.*

Bampton. – Pop 1 340. *7m N on A396.*
The small town with Georgian stone houses bedecked with flowers lining the main street, is the gateway to Exmoor *(p 158)* and famous for its annual October Pony Fair.

★ TORBAY   Pop 116 200

Michelin map 403 fold 34 – J32.
See town plan in the current Michelin Red Guide Great Britain and Ireland

Torquay, Paignton and Brixham all began as fishing villages. In 17 and 18C the Fleet would lie up in the bay and wives, the first tourists, would come to visit their sailor husbands. By the early 19C the population of Torquay had grown to 2 000 and when the railway came to the town in 1842, it resolved to profit from the natural advantages of a mild climate, exotic, palm-tree vegetation, sea views and wide sand beaches. Hotels, a promenade, a pier and a pavilion were built, public gardens were laid out to make the town the "Queen of English watering-places". By the turn of the century Torquay was famous and the resident population, working largely for the tourists, had increased to 25 000. Fifty years later Paignton followed Torquay's example. Brixham has remained a fishing village at heart with trawlers in the harbour and a live fish market on the quay. Also on the quay is the statue of William III who landed upon it in 1688 on his way to take the crown from James II. The force which accompanied William is outnumbered by today's tourists by tens of thousands.

In Torquay and Paignton the houses extend up the hill behind the shore; Victorian hotels and villas are now being replaced by modern apartment blocks and high rise hotels, white by day, a spangle of lights by night.

In Brixham the brightly coloured fishermen's cottages and small houses, some dating back to 1693, wind their way uphill overlooking the harbour.

Ferry. – A ferry runs throughout the summer between Torquay and Brixham, providing a good view of the modern resort area curving round the bay.

TORQUAY

★ **Kent's Cavern.** – *Wellswood, Ilsham Rd (right off Babbacombe Rd, B3199).*
tc The limestone caves run back 180yds into the hill. Excavations have shown that they were inhabited by large prehistoric animals and by men for long periods from the Palaeolithic era, 100 000 years ago, to Roman times.

The **tour** (½m) takes one through galleries with rugged roofs and walls and contrasting chambers with beautiful crystal white, red-brown and green frozen water, pagoda and organ pipe **formations**, past **stalactites** and **stalagmites** – one 54ins tall is estimated to have been more than 50 000 years agrowing.

tc **Torre Abbey.** – *Torbay Rd.* The "Abbey", in luxuriant gardens, comprises 18C house, the so-called Spanish Barn and the ruins of the mediaeval abbey.

The ivy clad house, now a **local museum**, contains collections of **English pewter**, 18-19C **glass** – wine-glasses, Nailsea flash glass *(p 34)*, old bottles, paperweights, jugs and engraved and cut crystal – marine and topographical paintings and a rare set of proof copies of **William Blake's** illustrations for the *Book of Job.*

The **tithe barn** ★ with massive buttresses along its 124ft length and at either end, dates from 1196 when its oak roof was supported on 12 ribs – increased to 17 at 1930s restoration. It became known as the Spanish Barn at the time of the Armada when it was briefly the prison for 397 crew of the flagship of the Andalusian squadron, *Nuestra Señora del Rosario,* captured in Torbay by Drake on 21 July 1588.

The **abbey** was unusually prosperous with an annual income of £396 (multiply by 30) when it was Dissolved in 1539. It had been founded in 1196, in fulfilment of a vow made for the safe return of his son by William de Briwer, the lord of the manor and a justiciar in Richard Lionheart's absence on the Third Crusade. On the king's capture, de Briwer set out to raise the 150 000 marks demanded in ransom; he found 70 000 which were sent to Austria together with 67 hostages of who one was his son.

In the event the Austrian captor was fatally injured and, on his deathbed, released his royal prisoner without benefit of the ransom.

At the Dissolution the church was razed and the pink sandstone from the monastic buildings was gradually incorporated in the "big house". There remain round the cloister garth the **ruins** of the former 168ft long **church,** the **abbot's tower** and apartment and, to the east, the still telling **wall** with an entrance to the sacristy and chapter house. Below are **undercrofts.** *(See also Cockington, below).*

Most complete, because not slighted, is the **gatehouse,** built by the monks in 14C.

PAIGNTON

★★ **Paignton Zoo.** – *½m W along A385.*

tc The comprehensive collection of **wild animals** and a luxuriant **botanical garden** extend over 75 acres with wide paths and lawns shaded by tropical trees.

There are elephants, lions and tigers, rhinoceroses and owls, penguins and giraffes, flamingos and porcupines, monkeys, camels, cranes, zebras, tortoises, reptiles and fish and even a **miniature railway** (10¼ in gauge) to give you a ride round the lake.

tc **Oldway Mansion and Gardens.** – *Torquay Rd.*

The vast, Classical mansion with a giant portico, tall Georgian-style windows and balustraded terraces overlooking formal parterre gardens, was built by the American sewing-machine magnate, **Isaac Singer** (1811-75), when he retired to Torquay in 1854.

★ **Kirkham House.** – *Mill Lane, Kirkham St. From the Esplanade take Hyde Rd, cross*
tc Torquay Rd and 25yds N continue along Littlegate Rd to Kirkham St (left).

The large **town house** of red sandstone is pre-Tudor. It belonged to the Kirkham family *(see below),* and is substantial but unpretentious. A wide cobbled passage leads from the oak front door through to the back; on the far side of wooden screens is the **hall** which, though small, rises in typical mediaeval fashion to the roof. Above, the rooms are connected by a long **west gallery.**

Note downstairs, a vivid, modern wall **tapestry.**

Paignton Parish Church. – *Church St. Opposite Hyde Rd across Torquay Rd.*

The Perpendicular church of 1450-1500, of dark red sandstone with a very tall landmark-style **tower** with pinnacles, stands amidst, houses all of the same colour. Inside, the **Kirkham Chantry Chapel,** with 15-17C family tombs, is separated from the nave by a still fine **stone screen** (mutilated at the Reformation).

Note in the nave, the Norman sandstone **font** with honeysuckle decoration, the mutilated pre-Reformation **stone pulpit** and the **dog door** complete with latch *(N door).*

tc **Torbay and Dartmouth Railway.** – *Queen's Park Station. Map p 93.* Steam locomotives afford a service on standard gauge on the former BR line to Kingswear *(6¾ m – ferry to Dartmouth, p 92),* by way of Goodrington Sands. It is both an efficient and a nostalgic ride with the old Victorian cast iron furniture on the platforms and the drivers and porters in the old uniform.

BRIXHAM

★ **Berry Head.** – *2m E by King St and its continuation, Berry Hd Rd round (S) to the old fort (ruin; car park), then 1m Rtn on foot.*

A rough stone path leads up through woods to the headland from which the **views** ★★★ become ever wider as you advance. At the top, a **viewing table** announces "from this point 190ft above sea-level about 800sq m of sea are visible" and goes on to identify every landmark from Portland Bill *(42m ENE)* around the sweep of Lyme Bay and beyond.

There have been lookouts and fortifications on the headland since the Iron Age, the most obvious now being the forts built during the Napoleonic wars in 1803 – never used, although *Bellerophon,* with Napoleon on board, did put in to Torbay in 1815 on the way to St Helena. The strange looking, modern construction is an aircraft navigational beacon.

EXCURSIONS

★ **Cockington.** – *1m W from Torbay Rd along Cockington Lane.*

The village, an entity though within the Torquay boundary, is pure picture postcard with all the **cottages** thatched above red sandstone or white-washed walls, a really ancient (now bowdlerised) **forge,** a mill pond, an **inn,** the Drum – a period pub by Sir Edwin Lutyens *(p 85)* – and horse-drawn, open carriages which will take you back to the sea front.

The Classical 19C house, **Cockington Court,** is surrounded by 270 acres of undulating wooded **parkland** and **gardens,** glowing with rhododendrons, azaleas and camellias. The **parish church,** which dates from 1196, was given a tower when it was acquired by Torre Abbey *(see above)* in 1236. Note 15C rood-screen, the old wicket door with its sanctuary ring *(p 175),* 15C font and the pulpit from Torre Abbey.

Compton Castle. – *3m W. P 87.*

Berry Pomeroy Castle. – *5m W by by-roads; turn before Berry Pomeroy village.*

The castle, erected soon after the Conquest has been falling into romantic ruin ever since the last Seymour left in 1703.

tc **Torbay Trains, Robes, Roses, Aircraft Museum.** – *High Blaydon. 3m W by A385 and by-road right.*

The aircraft, some 20 in number, and indoor galleries including displays on the German Red Baron of World War I, the Pathfinders of World War II, a long gallery of period costume from 18-20C, the OO gauge Torbay model railway and a rose garden, make a highly diversified museum.

★★ TOTNES

Michelin map **403** fold 34 – 132

The town is one of those with a narrow, rising, main street, lined by two and three-storey houses, half timbered, Georgian or 19C, built of brick or stone, slate-hung, or colour-washed. Halfway up, dividing it into Fore St and the High St, is the Arch or **East Gate**, a much altered gate-way dating back to Tudor times and a reminder that Totnes was once a walled town.

SIGHTS

Start from the Bridge over the R Dart at the east end of the town (A385). Car park across the bridge, left, then right.

The Bridge. – The bridge, rebuilt in 1828, marks the tidal and navigable limit of the Dart. The quay below is still active.

tc **Totnes Motor Museum.** – *The Quay.* The cars, motor-bicycles and even the pedal and the moto-rised cycles, housed on two floors in the old cider warehouse, are all in working order and accordingly "exercised" at races, rallies and shows. Among the cars on display are an Austin 7, Talbot Martins, Voisins, Aston-Martins and Alfa-Romeos.

(Vloo / J Alan Cash)

The East Gate

The Plains. – *Sharp left on the town side.* The open square is marked by an **obelisk** in honour of **William John Wills**, native of Totnes, who was a member of the first party to cross the Australian continent in 1860. On one corner is an old **coaching inn**, the Royal Seven Stars, built in 1660.

Fore St. – Among the houses which line the street, note on the left, **The Mansion** in dark red brick, originally the **King Edward VI Grammar School**, founded under royal charter in 1553, and refronted in 18C; in Bank Lane *(left)* the late 18C **Gothick house**; in Fore St again, **no 48**, which is 17C, **no 52**, 16C with an oversailing upper floor, and, close by, the grandest Tudor house in the town.

tc **Elizabethan House.** – *70 Fore St.* The house itself is the most remarkable exhibit in the **museum** which displays items of local life from flint weapons to Great Western Railway bygones, 15C Elizabethan and Jacobean furniture, Victoriana and a turn of the century grocer's shop.

Totnes grew to prosperity in the Middle and later ages as a wool and cloth trade town and it was in this period, *c*1575, that this rich **merchant's house** was built on four floors with a half-timbered, jettied first floor, broad windows and a full width gable pierced by the windows of the topmost, small, bedrooms.

Inside the house note the **height** and lightness of the main rooms, the **timbering**, the unevenly **wide floorboards**, 16C **fireplaces** and the number of small **closets** and corners – now all used for exhibits.

Continue up Fore St and through the Arch; immediately to your right is a flight of steps.

Guildhall. – The hall was built in 16C as a cloth merchant's hall. In 1624 it became the guildhall with a council chamber, courtroom and mayor's parlour; among the exhibits are Saxon coins pressed in the town mint in Edgar's reign (958-75).

Return to the main street, now the High St.

★ **St Mary's.** – The church which dates from 15C, has a massive local red sandstone tower.

The rood screen. – The outstanding feature is the once coloured, now white, Beer stone rood screen of 1459 which, with paired lights, carved mullions, arched panels below, cusped tracery and fan coving above, extends across the full width of the church. Before the screen hangs an, also beautiful, 18C **chandelier**.

Monuments. – Note, in the southeast chapel, the **tomb** of Walter Smythe (d 1555), founder of Totnes Grammar School, against the north nave wall, the **memorial** to Christopher Blackhall (d 1633), seen kneeling at prayer above his bevy of four wives, and against the west wall of 19C north aisle, the large **terracotta plaque** to Walter Venning, born in Totnes in 1781, who became a London merchant and was the founder of the Prison Society of Russia where he himself died of goal fever in 1821.

tc **Devonshire Collection of Period Costume.** – *10a High St.* In two rooms in a **Tudor merchant's house** with fine plaster **ceilings**, 17C windows and pastel-painted **panelling**, may be seen a changing display of costume as worn by our ancestors and ourselves from babyhood to old age between the years 1740 and 1960. The detail is meticulous from pressed pin tucks to accessories and underclothes – the presentation is dramatically staged, the collectors were "in the profession".

No 16 High St. – The house, now a bank, dates from 1585 when it was built by a salted pilchard merchant, Nicholas Ball (note the initials on the front). He died in 1586 and his widow then married a second wealthy man, **Thomas Bodley** of Exeter, scholar, diplomat and founder of the Bodleian Library, Oxford.

Civic Hall. – The modern hall has a large open forecourt on which, in summer, a pannier market is held when Tudor fare is offered by sellers in Elizabethan costume.

★ **Butterwalk.** – The granite pillared walk has protected shoppers from the rain since 17C.

tc **The Castle.** – The castle walls command excellent **views**★★★ of the Dart River Valley, upstream towards Dartmoor where the high tors rise one behind the other and downstream along the line of the estuary towards Dartmouth *(p 92)*.

The **ramparts** which encircle the central mound are 14C, a rebuilding and strengthening in stone of the motte and bailey earthwork raised in the early 12C.

The Devon Guild of Craftsmen, Totnes Community College. – *1m NW on A385, Ashburton Rd*. The annual summer exhibition has become one of the great attractions of the area. The works, which range in size from small to huge and in cost from pence to pounds, are by batik printers, potters and ceramicists, embroiderers, enamellers, furniture makers, carvers, glassworkers, weavers, lacemakers, metalworkers, silversmiths and jewellers, musical instrument makers...in all a joyful revelation of the high skills in being today.

Dartington. – *2m NW on A385 and A384. P 88.*

River Dart Boat Trips. – *P 94.*

WIDECOMBE IN THE MOOR   Pop 603

Michelin map **403** fold 34 – I32 – Local map p 91.

The embattled **tower** with tall turreted pinnacles which soars high above the moor *(p 89)*, makes the church a **landmark** for miles around; the childhood ballad about Tom Pearse's grey mare and Old Uncle Tom Cobleigh and all riding to the fair, Widecombe itself a popular legend.

(Vloo / J Alan Cash)

The Cathedral of the Moor

The village, a cluster of white-walled, thatched cottages grouped round the church, stands in a shallow valley or wide combe – hence the name – surrounded by granite ridges which rise to 1 500ft.

St Pancras. – The tower of red ashlar, 135ft high, was added, out of line, in the early 16C to the Perpendicular church which had been rebuilt in the late 14-15C with money from the Dartmoor tin-miners.

Known as the **Cathedral of the Moor,** it is a vast building 104ft long with monolithic arcades rising to plain **barrel roofs** decorated with a series of well carved **bosses.**

Church House. – The two-storey, long stone house, with its lean-to shelter outside, dates back to 1537 when it was the village alehouse. It was later converted into almshouses and, finally, the village school.

DORSET

Area 1 025 sq m Population 595 415

The beauty, the interest of Dorset, lies in its variety, the contrast between the coast and the hinterland which, even a few miles inland, seems remote from the sea.

The coast. – The cliff-lined shore is marked by arches or "doors" in primaeval rocks (Durdle), the offshore chalk stacks known as the Old Harry Rocks, by golden sand beaches, the unique Chesil Beach, towering headlands and the long Isle of Portland.

The countryside. – Between the North and low-lying South Dorset Downs, so close to the sea that the Osmington White Horse with George III upon it is best seen from a boat the countryside extends east and north in a series of barren, heath-covered, moors.
The whole area, Blackmoor Vale to the west, the part forested, part cleared Cranborne Chase to the northeast, is drained by rivers flowing north to south.

The towns. – Shaftesbury has been a historic and glorious viewpoint since the days of King Alfred; Sherborne, an attractive town, has what must be one of the most beautiful small abbeys in the country and a historic house full of interest; Lyme Regis with its impracticable main street dropping towards the sea, its fossils and the Cobb, has an atmosphere all its own – but then so has Wareham...

The Isle of Purbeck. – The so-called "Isle" is cut off from the "mainland" by a line of hills, the only gap on the skyline being filled by the gaunt outlines of Corfe Castle. Composed like Portland, of rock which has been quarried for centuries to build houses and cathedrals, the landscape is windswept on the headlands, steeply undulating and wooded just inland. The heather often gives the hills a blue-purple aspect.

Ancient Dorset. – Burial mounds, excavated finds in the county and local museums, indicate the presence of early man as does Maiden Castle (p 135).

Dorset Worthies. – The classic Dorset Worthies, including Thomas Hardy, were men of 17-19C and first quarter of 20C; in our time there have lived and worked in the county, Laurence Whistler, the glass engraver, (pp 130, 139); Reynolds Stone, the letterer on wood and stone who designed the monograms and "logos" which gave a distinctive style to print, trade-marks, bookplates, programmes and name plates for a generation; John Fowles, the novelist; John Makepiece, the furniture designer...

PLACE-NAMES IN THOMAS HARDY'S WESSEX

Thomas Hardy (1840-1928), who was born at Higher Bockhampton and whose heart lies in Stinsford churchyard, took as his literary arena an area approximately that of King Alfred's Wessex. Indeed Hardy popularised the revival of the name of Wessex; he knew its countryside in minute detail: the heaths and vales, towns, villages, the views, lanes and fields, individual houses, large and small, the churches... At times his descriptions were "straight", at times combined with place-names disguised to a greater or lesser extent: a few, such as Bath, Bristol, Falmouth, Plymouth, Chippenham, Stonehenge and Wardour Castle and some geographical features, appear under their real names; others use an old form as in Shaston for Shaftesbury.
Hardy's Wessex extended beyond the borders of this guide: for those holidaying in Dorset and the surrounding counties, we give below the geographical name, the disguised place-name and the prose works in which they occur. The lexicon below has been compiled with the learned assistance of the Secretary of the Thomas Hardy Society, J.C. Pentney.

(After Judges photo)
Thomas Hardy statue, Dorchester

KEY TO TITLES
Novels in order of publication
DR   *Desperate Remedies*
UGT   *Under the Greenwood Tree*
PBE   *A Pair of Blue Eyes*
FMC   *Far from the Madding Crowd*
HE   *The Hand of Ethelberta*
RN   *The Return of the Native*
TM   *The Trumpet-Major*
L   *A Laodicean*
TT   *Two on a Tower*
MC   *The Mayor of Casterbridge*
W   *The Woodlanders*
TD   *Tess of the d'Urbervilles*
JO   *Jude the Obscure*
WB   *The Well-Beloved*

Short Story volumes
WT   *Wessex Tales*
GND   *A Group of Noble Dames*
LLI   *Life's Little Ironies*
CM   *A Changed Man*

+ old form of place-name
? doubtful identification

EWC 6

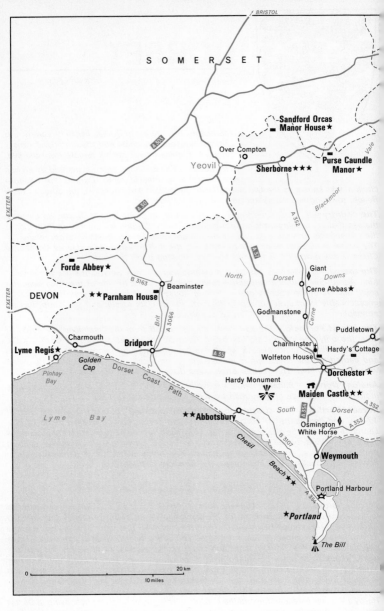

DORSET – Hardy's South Wessex

Place-name	Hardy's name	Novel
Affpuddle	East Egdon	RN
Athelhampton	Athelhall	CM
Beaminster	Emminster	FMC TD
Bere Regis	Kingsbere (sub-Greenhill)	FMC RN TM TD WT
Blandford Forum	Shottsford (Forum)	FMC TM MC W JO WT GND LLI CM
Bournemouth	Sandbourne	HE TD JO WB LLI
Brickyard Cottages, Brianstspuddle	Alderworth	RN
Bridport	Port-Brady	MC W TD WT LLI
Blackmoor Vale	Vale of Little Dairies	TD
Buckland Newton	Newland Buckton	W
Canford Manor	Chene Manor	GND
Cerne Abbas	Abbot's Cernel	W TD LLI
Chesil Beach or Bank	The Pebble Bank	WB
Church Ope-Cove, Portland	Hope Cove	WB
Corfe Gastle	Corvsgate Castle	DR HE
Cranborne	Chaseborough	TD
Cranborne Chase	The Chase	TD GND
Dole's Ash ?	Flintcomb-Ash	TD
Dorchester	Casterbridge	DR UGT FMC RN TM MC W TD JO WT GND LLI CM
Duck Dairy Farm, nr Lwr Bockhampton	The Quiet Woman Inn	RN LLI
East Holme & East Stoke	Holmstoke	WT
Easton, Portland	East Quarries	WB
Eggardon Hill	Haggardon Hill	TM

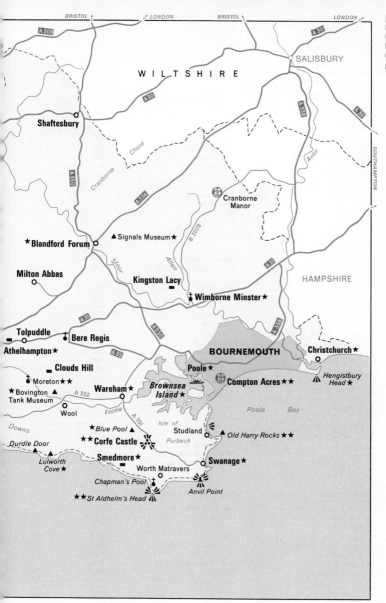

Encombe House, nr Corfe Castle	Enckworth Court	HE
Evershot	Evershead	TD WT GND CM
Farrs House, nr Wimborne	Yewsholt Lodge	GND
Fordington	Durnover	UGT FMC MC CM
Fortuneswell, Portland	The Street of Wells	TM WB
Frampton	Scrimpton	LLI
R Frome	Froom or Var	UGT MC TD CM
Frome Valley	Valley of the Great Dairies	TD
Gillingham	Leddenton	JO
Hardy's Cottage, Higher Bockhampton	Tranter Dewy's	UGT
Hartfoot Lane	Stagfoot Lane	TD
Hazelbury Bryan	Nuttlebury	TD
Higher Bockhampton	Upper Mellstock	UGT
Horton Inn	Lornton Inn	TT GND
Kingston, nr Corfe Castle	Little Enckworth	HE
Kingston Maurward House	Knapwater House	DR UGT (the Manor)
Lower Bockhampton	Lower or East Mellstock	UGT
	Carriford	DR
Lulworth Cove	Lulwind Cove ; Bay	DR FMC ; LLI
Lyme or West Bay	Deadman's Bay	WB
Lytchett Minster	Flychett	HE
Maiden Castle	Mai-Dun (Castle)	TM MC CM
Maiden Newton	Chalk Newton	UGT FMC TD GM
Marnhull	Marlott	TD UGT
Maumbury Rings, Dorchester	The Ring	MC
Melbury Osmond	Little/King's Hintock	W ; GND
Melbury House	King's Hintock Court	GND
Middlemarsh	Marshwood	W
Milborne St Andrew	Millpond (St Jude's)	FMC TD

Milton Abbey	Middleton Abbey +	W TD
Minterne Magna ?	Great Hintock	W TD
Moreton	Moreford	LLI
Norris Hill Farm ?	Talbothays	TD
Okeford Fitzpaine ?	Oakbury Fitzpiers	W
Owermoigne	Nether-Moynton/Mynton	TN WT ; DR
Pennsylvania Castle, Portland	Sylvania Castle	WB
Pentridge (also Tarrant Hinton)	Trantridge	TD
Piddlehinton	+ (Lower) Longpuddle	UGT TM LLI
Piddletrenthide	+ Upper Longpuddle (not wholly consistent)	FMC
Poole	Havenpool	HE MC LLI CM
Portesham	Po'sham	TM
Portland	Isle of Slingers, Vindilia	WB
Portland Bill	The Beal	TM
Poundbury Camp, Dorchester	Pummery +	MC
Poxwell	Oxwell	TM
Preston	Creston	DR CM
Puddletown	Weatherbury or Lower Longpuddle	UGT FMC
Puddletown Forest	Egdon Heath	UGT FMC RN TD
Ringstead	Ringsworth	DR WT
Sandsfoot Castle, Weymouth	Henry VIII Castle	WB
Shaftesbury	Shaston +	TD JO
Sherborne	Sherton Abbas	W TD GND
Stafford House, West Stafford	Froom Everard House	CM
Stalbridge	Stapleford	GND
Stinsford	Mellstock	UGT RN TD
Sturminster Newton	Stourcastle	TD
Sutton Poyntz	Overcombe	TM
Swanage	Knollsea	HE
Tarrant Hinton (also Pentridge)	Trantridge	LLI
Tincleton	Stickleford	RN TD WT LLI
Tolpuddle	Tolchurch	DR
Troy Town	Roy-Town	FMC
Wareham	Anglebury	DR HE RN MC TD WT
Waterston Manor, Puddletown	Weatherbury Upper Farm	FMC
Weymouth (and Melcombe Regis)	Budmouth (Regis)	DR UGT FMC RN TM L TT MC W WT GND LLI CM
Wimborne (Minster)	Warborne	TT GND
Woodbury Hill	Greenhill	FMC RN TM TT TD LLI
Wool	Wellbridge +	TD
Woolbridge Manor	Wellbridge Manor +	TD
Yellowham Hill, Wood, nr Higher Bockhampton	Yalbury Hill, Wood	UGT FMC LLI

CORNWALL – Lyonesse – Hardy's Off Wessex

Beeny Cliff	Windy Beak	PBE
Boscastle	Castle Boterel	PBE
Bude	Stratleigh	PBE
Camelford	Camelton	PBE
Lanhydrock House	Endelstow House	PBE
Launceston	St Launce's	PBE
Lesnewith	East Endelstow	PBE
Pentargon Bay, Cliff	Targon Cliff without a Name	PBE PBE
Penzance	Penzephyr	CM
Redruth	Redrutin	CM
St Juliot	West Endelstow	PBE
Tintagel	Dundagel	PBE
Trebarwith Strand	Barwith Strand	PBE
Truro	Trufal	CM

DEVON – Hardy's Lower Wessex

Barnstaple	Downstaple	GND
Coombe Martin	Cliff-Martin	GND
Exeter	Exonbury	PBE TM W LLI CM
Sidmouth	Idmouth	CM
Silverton	Silverthorn	CM
Tiverton	Tivworthy	CM
Torquay	Tor-upon-Sea	CM

SOMERSET & AVON – Hardy's Outer or Nether Wessex

Dunster	Markton	L
Dunster Castle	Staney Castle	L
East Coker	Narrobourne	LLI
Mells Park	Falls Park	GND
Montacute House	Montislope House	CM
Taunton	Toneborough	L GND LLI
Wells	Fountall	LLI CM
Yeovil	Ivell +	W GND LLI

WILTSHIRE – Hardy's Mid Wessex

Marlborough Downs	Marlbury Downs	GM
Old Sarum	Old Melchester	LLI
Salisbury	Melchester	FMC HE TT MC TD JO GND LLI CM
Salisbury Plain	The Great Plain	TD LLI

★★ ABBOTSBURY   Pop 393

Michelin map **403** fold 36 – M32

Abbotsbury, which takes its name from the Benedictine abbey dissolved in 1541, lies at the end of the Fleet, the lagoon formed by Chesil Beach *(see below)*. The village street is lined by reed-thatched, stone cottages.

★ SWANNERY

tc The lush bamboo and flower-filled **gardens,** the **duck decoy** with 4 "pipes" (now a ringing station), eventually lead you to the swans on the open waters of the **Fleet**. Before you will be more **Mute Swans** than you have ever seen congregated together in your life. Founded 650 years ago by the monks it is the only managed colony of swans and numbers more than 400 birds plus their cygnets; they are not pinioned but are ringed, from which it has been discovered that they live some 20 years, and return regularly to the same nesting sites on the two-acre meadow where they are prepared to do battle against upstarts.

★★ CHESIL BEACH

The unique beach curves round in a silver scimitar of **shingle,** joining Portland to the mainland and continuing for another ten miles. The cannon-ball sized stones at Portland decrease to pea-gravel at Abbotsbury whilst the ridge itself rises to 50ft in places. The sea rolls and rustles the pebbles, crashes against them, overtops them in winter but never tears the bank apart. In the lee lies the **Fleet Lagoon,** a shallow tidal waterway which is the habitat of the Abbotsbury swans, of herons and cormorants, also the little tern and overwintering and migrant waterfowl. Parts of the beach, a Nature Reserve, are closed during the nesting season.

★ SUB-TROPICAL GARDENS

tc The woodland gardens lie in a hollow, a geological fault, protected from the salt-laden winds by bands of holm-oak. Within the 20 acres is a semi-formal, walled garden laid out in 18C adjoining a now vanished castle. The gardens are famous for their camellias and rhododendrons, their specimen **trees** and modern plantings: oaks, palms, myrtles, a 70ft tall tulip tree, Virginia creepers with massive trunks, trees from Chile and Australia. There are also a recreated 19C **bog-garden** and eucalyptus walk; a beautiful golden false acacia, a rare Caucasian wing nut...

ADDITIONAL SIGHTS

Abbey ruins. – In 1541 after the Dissolution, the abbey lands were leased on condition that all "edifices being within the site and precinct of the late Monastry.... be hereafter thrown down and removed"; the church was reduced to mere footings, the monastic buildings converted into a private residence (burned down in 1644).

St Nicholas Church. – The parish church, in local buff stone with Portland stone dressings, was built between the late 14-17C. Note the **plaster vault** of 1638 above the two east bays; 18C, pedimented and Corinthian columned **altarpiece** with a vineleaf frieze; 15-16C, stained **glass panel** of the Virgin; 18C **chandelier** and the plain Jacobean testered **pulpit** with a back panel in which are two bullet holes from 1644 skirmish after which the Royalist, Sir John Strangways, owner of the abbey lands, was imprisoned in the Tower.
Finally, as you leave, salute the 14C standing stone figure of a monk in the porch.

Tithe Barn. – The barn dates from c1400, when it measured 272ft long by 30ft across; today, although only half roofed, it remains a spectacular building with close standing buttresses, a west gable and wide porch *(not open)*.

★ St Catherine's Chapel. – ½m uphill; 30mins Rtn on foot.
tc The chapel, small, rugged and windblown on its 250ft downland crest, is the only 14C monastic building to remain. The walls are thick, the stair turret octagonal with lancets, the flat-topped buttresses stout for such a small building until inside you see that the roof is a stone **tunnel vault**. The Perpendicular windows are later.
The church probably served as a seamen's lantern.

EXCURSION

Hardy Monument. – 3¾m E by B3157 and by-road.
The strange, 70ft tall, stone tower standing on Blackdown and visible for miles, commemorates **Admiral Hardy** (1769-1839), Nelson's flag-captain who spent his boyhood in the village of Portesham. It was erected in 1844. Panoramic **views** from the tower foot *(tower not open)*.

★ ATHELHAMPTON

Michelin map **403** fold 36 – N31

tc The house dates from early Tudor times when the then Lord of Athelhampton, Sir William Martyn, Lord Mayor of London, whose family came originally from Tours in France and claimed descent from St Martin, was given permission to enclose 160 acres of deer park and build himself a towered and battlemented mansion. To this house with its porch, upper room, and great hall were added a gabled parlour wing in the same creamy limestone, new fronts and gables and, as a final embellishment, the gardens – the magnolia grandiflora on the front of the house is believed to be about 200 years old.

TOUR ¾ hour

Great Hall. – The hall is remarkable for its roof, its oriel and linenfold panelling: the roof is built up on braces and collar-beams, the whole given character by the pointed cusps; the **oriel** is vaulted with cusped ribs and illumined by tall, two-light, two-transom windows on each side again with the cusp motif – note among the mediaeval painted glass, the Martyn crest, a chained ape or, in heraldic parlance, a martin. The ape, now with a Saxon crown and carrying a mace has been adopted by the present owner as his heraldic badge – the crown being a reference to the manor's situation in the realms of Athelhelm and Athelstan, the mace to the family service in Parliament. The **brass chandelier** with the Virgin is 15C; the **tapestry** is Flemish; the chests are of 14 and 15C and 1681 (dated), the **love-seat** of the time of William and Mary.

Additional rooms. – Note the oak **panelling**, the Pugin and William Morris **wallpaper** and silk fabric wall hangings and in the gallimaufry of treasure which ranges from 17C furniture to examples of metalwork and manufactures from 1851 Exhibition, a Henry VIII period **credence cupboard**, a painting on glass, *The Misers,* by the Flemish artist, **Quentin Matsys** (1465-1530), a collection of wine glasses, Chinese and Chinese-style cabinets and mirrors, 200 **19C china jugs** and Westminster mementoes.

GARDENS

Individual gardens surround the house, so planned as to lead from one to another, often through graceful iron gates, and all so that the focal point of every **vista** is a fountain or statue fountain.

There are a **Great Court Garden** with twin pavilions and giant pyramidal yews, a **Private Garden** with lawns and a fishpond and a **White Garden.**

Rarest of all is the **Corona,** an Elizabethan-style, circular garden, distinguished by an undulating stone wall topped by slender obelisks and banked with flowers; at the centre an urn gently brims over into a small basin.

On the far side of the house are the **Octagon,** a pleached lime cloister and a circular, 15C **dovecote** with a renewed hammerbeam roof and lantern and 1500 nest-holes.

BERE REGIS
Pop 1 979

Michelin map **403** fold 36 – N31

The church, but little else, was saved in 1788 when the last in a series of fires devastated the village – the communal iron hooks of *c*1600 used to pull away burning thatch from cottages on fire, still hang above the church door.

★★★ **St John the Baptist.** – Inside the Perpendicular church is the finest wooden **parish church roof** in Dorset and probably in England. It was the climax in the then 500-year old church's rebuilding, made possible by the gift in 1475 of a huge sum by the locally born Cardinal Morton (1425-1500), Archbishop of Canterbury and Lord Chancellor to Henry VII.

The roof. – The roof is a structure of oak tie beams and braces, crown posts and queen posts, outlined by cresting, filled with tracery, decorated in gold and rich reds,

(After AF Kersting photo)

The apostle roof

browns, blues, the meeting points masked with bosses, the not-in-fact hammers disguised by almost lifesize carved figures of the **apostles.**

Easily recognisable are John (holding a book or gospel), Judas (with a money bag), Matthew (holding a book), Philip (with a staff) and Peter (with mitre and keys). In 1738 the entry appears in the church wardens' accounts "Paid Benjamin Moores for Cleaning and Oyling the Apostles 4*s* 0*d"*.

In the roof also are four **bosses** celebrating Cardinal Morton: the head at the east end is said to be a portrait; the arms are of Canterbury of which he was archbishop; the Tudor rose is in honour of Henry VII and the fourth symbolises the marriage Morton arranged between the king and Elizabeth of York. Note the **capitals** in the late 12C arcade with carved figures in an agony of toothache, sore throat...

The south aisle, since 14C, has been the Chapel of the Turbervilles – after who Hardy modelled the family in *Tess of the d'Urbervilles.*

★ BLANDFORD FORUM   Pop 3 957

Michelin map 403 fold 37 – M31

The town rose within 30 years of a disastrous fire in 1731 "like the Phoenix from its ashes, to its present beautiful and flourishing state". Houses were rebuilt along the old street courses in the latest 18C style, the church, in new guise, rose on its early site...

SIGHTS

Market Place. – The square, the wide juncture of West and East Sts with Salisbury St coming in at the northwest end, is the town centre.

Town Hall. – The 18C hall, on the north side, stands over a three-bay arcade, filled with iron gates and lanterns and crowned by stone urns matching those on the church.

St Peter and St Paul. – The large stone church of 1733-9, has a west tower rising squarely to a pierced balustrade, stone urns and an open, domed, turret.

The interior, which is filled with light from the tall, rounded, typically Georgian windows, has Portland stone columns with Ionic capitals which soar to a moulded entablature and groined vault. Note, amidst the box pews, the **Mayoral Chair** of 1748, canopied, carved and plush lined, the **17C pulpit** and the **memorial** to the Bastard family who were responsible for much of the rebuilding.

Old Greyhound. – The former inn of vast size, (now a bank) has an ornate front comprising giant pilasters, a pediment, decorated window frames, plasterwork grapes and a greyhound.

Red Lion. – Note the wide, central carriage entrance between the pilasters.

26, Market Place. – The house on the corner was built by **John Bastard** for himself and given an integrated façade with the house next door (no 75, East St) which he also built. (East St itself escaped the fire and contains several older houses.)

Town Houses. – The area north of the main road is a network of winding streets and alleys which are marked by several attractive houses. In Church lane are **Old Bank House, Lime Tree House,** of unusual purple brick with red brick dressings and vertical decoration between the windows, and **Coupar House,** "The finest post-fire in Blandford", built of purple bricks laid as headers, relieved by a full complement of stone dressings.

Bear right.

The Plocks. – The street was the gathering place for sheep to be sold in the market.

Continue through the triangular, oak planted, Tabernacle.

Old House. – *The Close.* The house of 1660, stands high, rambling and disjointed, built of red brick, ingeniously cut and moulded to decorate the round-arched entrance, form balusters and colonettes, and fill every space with a decorative motif...

Ryves Almshouses. – *Salisbury St, E side.* The range of 1682 is distinguished by a small centre gable, dominant chimneys and an ornate shield of arms.

Bridge. – The stone bridge at the west entrance to the town (A354), which spans the River Stour with six arches, dates from 1783.

EXCURSIONS

★ **Royal Blandford Signals Museum.** – *Blandford Camp. 2m NE off B3082.*
tc Less than 150 years separates the invention of the Morse code (1835), the first electric, single needle telegraph (1837) and micro-circuit transmitters and receivers. Chronologically there have been smoke and water signals, beacons, heliographs of metal and mirrorglass, messengers, pigeons, flags and lanterns and despatch riders on horseback and motor cycles. Field telephones date from Ladysmith in 1899; now radio keeps contact with units in the field, guerilla forces and in 1939-45 with POWs who, against all the odds, made wireless sets in camps in Europe and Asia.
In this **Royal Corps of Signals' Museum,** the equipment is displayed stage by stage in interesting detail but still comprehensibly to the woefully ignorant!

Milton Abbas. – *9m SW off A354. P 135.*

BOURNEMOUTH   Pop 145 704

Michelin map 403 fold 37 – 031
See town plan in the current Michelin Red Guide Great Britain and Ireland

Bournemouth, between two pine covered hills at the mouth of the Bourne River, began to develop as a summer and winter resort in the mid-19C. The arrival of the railway made it easily accessible; amenities were increased with the construction of **two piers,** the pavilion, wintergarden and theatre, with the laying out of the always colourful **public gardens.** By 1890s the population had reached 37 781 and Bournemouth had become fashionable – Queen Victoria recommended it to Disraeli. Today the population has multiplied five-fold, the number of hotels runs to several hundred...

★ BOURNEMOUTH MUSEUMS

tc **Rothesay Museum.** – *8 Bath Rd.* Each room is filled with objects so diverse that it could furnish a small museum on its own: there are **majolica** and **delftware,** 19C **Whitby mourning jet, toby jugs** and **Staffordshire figures,** 17C English furniture, 16C polygonal virginal, Victorian bygones, African spears, Ghurka kukris, Limoges enamels, and upstairs, **hand guns** from 16-20C...
One gallery is devoted exclusively to a collection of **typewriters:** 300 machines mark the developments from 1870s to 1980s, from the Swinging Sector and Radial Strike Plunger to electric machines.

tc **Russel-Cotes Art Gallery and Museum.** – *Russell-Cotes Rd.* East Cliff Hall, was the museum-home of Sir Merton Russell-Cotes, hotelier, theatre-goer, JP, mayor and intrepid traveller.

Each room, with its massive Victorian furniture, palms, painted ceiling, wallpapers of the period, is filled with pictures (**William Frith's** *Ramsgate Sands, Venus* by **Rossetti**), English fine china (part of a Rockingham tea-service once owned by the Prince Regent, Coalport and Worcester, Wedgwood plaques, Parian ware), silver and gold ware, mementoes of Napoleon (a death-mask) and Sir Henry Irving, a personal friend.

From abroad there are Dresden miniatures, finds from Egyptian tombs, swords, oriental armour, bronzes, Buddhas, a bronze incense-burner in the style of a cock, a silver and gold elephant with a crystal ball, inlay and lacquerwork, ceramics and lanterns...

tc **Shelley Museum.** – *Shelley Park, Beechwood Av, Boscombe.* The evocative collection, in part from the the Casa Magni where Percy Bysshe Shelley (1792-1822) was living at the time he was drowned, includes letters, the revolutionary leaflets, poems, notebooks, portraits and miniatures.

EXCURSIONS

★ **Poole.** – *2m W. P 136.*

★ **Hengistbury Head.** – *7m E by the panoramic road. P 129.*

tc **Cranborne Manor Gardens.** – *18m N on B3078.*

The tall house, a former royal hunting lodge in Cranborne Chase, took on something of its present appearance in the early 17C when Robert Cecil, first Earl of Salisbury, received the manor from James I whose accession he had elped to secure.

The garden including avenues of fine trees, was laid out by **John Tradescant** (1570-1638), designer, and plantsman. Among the several areas enclosed by old walls and high hedges are an Elizabethan **knot garden** and a rare Jacobean **Mount Garden** where three low, circular grass tiers surround a central mound white outer beds with old fashioned roses, peonies and foxgloves spandrel the corners.

BRIDPORT   Pop 6 921

Michelin map **403** fold 36 – L31

Bridport is a name recalled because, as was said as early as 1505, it has been making ships' ropes and cordage "for time out of mind". In 15C Henry VII decreed that all hemp grown within a five-mile radius of the then river port should be reserved for the king's ships. Changes in rigging, the development of a fish and submarine netting industry, the substitution of nylon for hemp have brought reorganisation; nevertheless the trade remains the town's mainstay.

The TOWN

Bridport is T shaped, the early, walled Saxon river port, where South St now runs, expanding north and then east-west in Georgian times along the Dorchester-Exeter road.

South St. – The town's original street is lined by the oldest houses, seamen's cottages and inns and the Perpendicular St Mary's church with its many 19C additions.

tc **Museum.** – The museum of local bygones, is in 16C stone-fronted house with a prominent porch, known as the Castle.

Unique exhibits include a display of lace, fishing net-making frames and the wheals and hooks on which ropes were made in the streets in olden times and which gave rise to the common name for many an alley of the Rope Walk.

West St. – The Georgian street and its continuation, East St, are overlooked by imposing houses, built for merchantand professionnal men, and former coaching inns.

Note **Granville House,** built in the mid-18C *(N side)* opposite a Venetian windowed house, and, at the bottom end of the street, the late 18C stone **Rope and Net Factory.**

East St. – The chemist's, no 9, with bow-fronted shop windows and a centre door, smaller, domestic bow windows above and a proud fascia, is late 18C; the **Unitarian Chapel,** with Ionic columns supporting a semicircular porch, is also 18C, the classically columned Literary and Scientific Institute, now the **Library,** 19C.

EXCURSIONS

★★ **Parnham House.** – *6m N on A3066. P 136.*

Beaminster. – Pop 2 380. *1m N of Parnham House.* An undulating countryside of woods and trees surrounds Beaminster (pronounced Bemminster) which, at its centre, presents a triangular square with an old-style, pyramid roofed **market cross** (1906) and a number of thriving old family **shops.** All were rebuilt after fires in 1644, 1684 and 1781, had reduced the town to the "pityfullest spectacle".

The **church,** to the southwest, is distinguished by its very tall, castellated **west tower,** built in 1503 in a local ochre stone with a rare number of canopied niches, statuettes and carvings and a spectacular thrust of crocketed pinnacles. Inside, the **arcades** have narrower bays to the east and foliated capitals to the west; the Purbeck marble **font** is 12-13C, the **pulpit** Jacobean. Note the monuments to members of the Strode family, owners of Parnham House *(p 136).*

★ BROWNSEA Island

Michelin map 403 fold 37 – 031 – Poole Harbour

tc The island, 1½miles long, half a mile across and covered with heath and woodland, has inviting beaches along its south shore. Its 500 acres might be considered as two nature reserves one on either side of **Middle Street**, the island's central spine.

The **north reserve** is a sanctuary for waterfowl and supports a heronry, blackheaded gullery and a colony of common tern *(p 23)*.

The **open reserve,** south of Middle Street, allows you to wander at will (and picnic) by 19C church with its painted angels and memorials tablets, in the **Peacock Field,** where there will probably be more birds than you have ever seen before, in the **Daffodil Field** *(steps to the beach from paths at E and W ends of the field),* to continue west to the **Baden-Powell Stone,** commemorating the first exprimental Boy Scout Camp of 1907. The stone is also the island's principal viewpoint, affording a **panorama★★** from Poole Bay, to the Purbeck Hills with Corfe Castle *(p 131)* just visible in the Gap.

When walking, and even more when sitting still, look out for **red squirrels.**

The island's "castle" was built on the site of one of Henry VIII's forts in 18C.

★ CHRISTCHURCH   Pop 37 986

Michelin map 403 fold 37 – 031

The wide, shallow harbour with its narrow outlet to the sea, pleasure-craft and little bandstand, the water meadows, the old streets, bridge and ferries, the Rivers Stour and Avon flowing into the harbour, the Norman priory which Henry VIII dissolved, the Norman castle which Cromwell slighted, make Christchurch attractive to wander around.

Early history. – Ten years after Domesday the village was given by William Rufus to his chief minister, Ranulf Flambard, the builder of Durham Cathedral. He pulled down the existing Saxon church and was about to start the construction of a great Norman church when William II died (1100) and he, Flambard, was put in the Tower; Henry I gave the patronage to his cousin, Richard de Redvers, Earl of Devon, who after Flambard had been pardoned in 1107, encouraged him to complete the church.

★ The PRIORY *time: ½ hour*

Augustine canons worshipped in the choir, allocated the nave to the parish, and erected monastic buildings abutting the north wall. In the early 13C the crossing tower collapsed leaving only the nave and west and end walls of the transepts; rebuilding proceeded slowly until 16C by which time the church presented a sequence of architectural styles: Norman in the **nave** – note the fish-scale decoration; EE in the **clerestory;** 14C Decorated for the **choirscreen,** Perpendicular at the east end in the **choir** and **Lady Chapels** – note the cusped and pinnacled arcading in the chapel also the canopied reredos with the *Tree of Jesse.*

The **choirstalls** are late 15C with an excellent set of **misericords** (one, 13C), depicting everything from a jester to a salmon's head, an angel to Richard III.

Chantry Chapels. – The finest, again Perpendicular, is the **Salisbury chantry** *(N chancel aisle)* carved in Caen stone by the Renaissance sculptor, **Torrregiano,** with tiers of enriched canopies and fan vaulting but empty because Margaret, Countess of Salisbury, was executed in the Tower by order of Henry VIII in 1541.

The traces of **paint** to be seen on the stonework throughout the interior would once have been a blaze of colour, high-lighting every decoration.

The priory legends. – It was originally intended that the priory be built on a hill about a mile away but every morning materials taken up the hill the previous day would be discovered mysteriously brought down to the sacred Saxon site until, finally, the builders decided that this was divine intervention. When building began on the town site, the masons and carpenters were joined by an extra, unknown, workman who received no pay and was not seen at meals. One evening it was discovered that a beam had been cut too short to span the walls and the men went home disconsolate; when they returned in the morning, however, they discovered that it had "grown" in the night and that the stranger had vanished. All were convinced it must have been the Carpenter from Nazareth and the church, and subsequently the town, were renamed Christ's Church.

ADDITIONAL SIGHTS

The Castle. – The castle keep, built to dominate the countryside from its artificial mound, was originally of wood but by the late 13C had walls of stone 30ft high and 10ft thick. The fort was contested in the Civil War and was razed in 1650.

The Constable's House. – The ruined house at the castle's foot is late 12C.

Town Bridge. – The old stone bridge with its pointed cutwaters dates back to 12C.

tc **Red House Museum.** – *Quay Rd.* Among 18C houses in the network of streets round the priory, 19C Red House, long and solid in red brick, has been made into a **local museum** which displays, among many items, the **seine fishing nets** once used to catch salmon in the harbour and the fine 19C **chains,** for which the town was famous.

EXCURSION

★ **Hengistbury Head.** – *4m by B3059; bear left at Tuckton for Southborne.*
From the head there is a wide **view★★** over Poole Bay, and east to The Needles and the Isle of Wight. (Less extensive panorama from the **panoramic road** from Bournemouth.)

CLOUDS HILL

Michelin map **403** fold 37 – N31 – 9m E of Dorchester

tc **T E Lawrence**, Lawrence of Arabia, rented then bought Clouds Hill for his own, "a ruined cottage in a wood near camp". In 1923-25 he was a private in the Royal Tank Corps at Bovington *(p 145)* and from 1925-35, in the RAF; throughout this time and in the few weeks before his death in May 1935 in a motorcycling accident, he described in letters to his friends how the cottage became "the centre of my world".

"I put the (Greek) jape, «Why worry» upon the architrave. It means that nothing in Clouds Hill is to be a care upon its inhabitant. While I have it there shall be nothing exquisite or unique in it. Nothing to anchor me" (18/X/32). "I look forward to settling there in a year's time, for good" (26/III/33). "The whole place is designed for just a single inhabitant. Panelling; bookshelves; bare wood and undyed leather. A queer place, but great fun. No pictures and no ornaments" (5/3/34). "Two rooms; one upstairs for music (a gramophone and records) and one downstairs (23/XI/34). "I think everything, inside and outside my place, approaches perfection" (23/XI/34). "Wild mares would not at present take me away from Clouds Hill. It is an earthly paradise" (8/V/35). (*The Letters of T E Lawrence*, edited by David Garnett; Jonathan Cape, 1938).

EXCURSION

★★ **Moreton Church.** – *3½m by B3390 and by-roads left.*
T E Lawrence is buried under the cedar in the cemetery entered through the lychgate. St Nicholas itself is a graceful, small Georgian Gothick church with sparkling windows; it dates from 1950. Ten years before it lay in ruins, destroyed by a bomb jettisoned by a German aircraft. The new church discarded much done in accordance with Victorian taste and reverted to 18C church plan.
The entrance is beneath the pinnacled tower, trimmed, like the apse and aisle rooflines, with a narrow, lacelike balustrade. Inside, the wide nave, beneath a coloured vault, leads the eye to where the altar stands at the centre of the circular apse. The walls are pierced on all sides so that the church is an ethereal lantern.
The engraved **windows** – the first, it is believed, in the outside walls of any church – were executed by **Laurence Whistler** *(p 139)* between 1958 and 1980. The design is a celebration, in festive style, of spiritual light and the church's dedication to the patron saint of children and Christmas: St Nicholas. You see candles, ribbons, the emblems of the Passion, trees, a Christmas tree, the church in ruins and rebuilt, the Cross...

★★ COMPTON ACRES

Michelin map **403** fold 37 – 031 – 3m SE of Poole

tc The 15-acre garden, or series of **gardens,** set in a rift or *chine* in the sandstone cliffs, is famous for having flowers brilliantly in bloom at all seasons.

Italian Garden. – The Classical canal and fountain, statues and vases, are highlighted by quantities of flowers, carpets of bedding plants, roses, rhododendrons, clematis...

Rock and Water Garden and Woodland Glen. – The gardens are informal with cascades, pools, iris, agapanthus, eucalyptus, mimosa, palms, jacarandas, a Judas tree...

English Garden. – The garden lies open to sunsets and a westerly view★★★ of Poole Harbour, Brownsea Island and the Purbeck Hills.

Heather Dell. – The dell presents a wonderful shading of every imaginable purple.

Japanese Garden. – The very big garden is lavish with garden ornaments, animal and bird statuary, and brilliant with flowers and ornamental trees reflected in the waterfall and pools traversed by stepping stones and bridges.

(Vloo / J Alan Cash)

Corfe Castle

★★ CORFE CASTLE

tc Corfe Castle has dominated the landscape since 11C, for the first 500 years as a towering stronghold and since 1646 as a gaunt ruin. It stands on a high mound in the single break in the line of the Purbeck Hills, the **Corfe Gap**. The **views**★★ are spectacular.

History. – In 978, the 17 year-old King Edward, the son of Edgar, went to visit his half-brother at the castle. Still mounted, he stopped at the inner gate-house to greet his stepmother, Queen Aelfryth who handed him a cup a wine. As he drank the poisoned wine, the boy king was stabbed to death. The body was removed to Wareham and, in 980, to Shaftesbury; in 1001 the king was canonised as **St Edward, King and Martyr**. Ethelred the Unready took his place as monarch.

In 1635 the castle was purchased by **Sir John Bankes** whose wife was alone in residence when it was twice besieged by the Parliamentarians. Lady Mary resisted the first siege but in 1646 she surrendered. The castle was slighted. At the Restoration, Lady Bankes recovered the family estates; in 1663-5, her son, Sir Ralph Bankes, built a new house at Kingston Lacy *(p 134)*.

★ DORCHESTER

Pop 14 225

The small county town, Hardy's home town, possesses still the house lived in by the Mayor of Casterbridge, the Old Crown Court where the Tolpuddle Martyrs were tried and the half-timbered house known as Judge Jeffreys' Lodgings, where the judge stayed during the Bloody Assizes when he came to "try" 290 of Monmouth's local supporters *(p 175)*.

It also bears the imprint of the Romans, who in 3C AD, built the hilltop town they named Durnovaria either side of the London-Exeter highway, of 16-17C when new houses were erected along the High St, and of 18-19C, when those houses were refaced or rebuilt. Every owner decided his own style, producing façades of infinite variety.

MAIN STREETS

High East St. – The **town hall** of brick and stone with a steepled **clock tower** is 19C.

The King's Arms. – The inn is 17C, re-faced with Doric columns during 19C Classical Revival; the house and shop opposite, **no 24**, is of the same date.

Nos 31-33 and no 9. – The shopfronts are all 19C.

Borough Arms, nos 45 and 7-7a. – The inn and houses are all 17C.

Nos 36 and 17-18. – The houses, much altered, date back to 16C.

South St. – The street is marked at its opening by **Cornhill**, a pedestrian precinct characterised by a stone **obelisk** (town pump) and 16-19C, **Antelope Inn** *(see below)*.

No 10 (now a bank). – The three-storey, late 18C house of lustered brick headers with redbrick dressings, is where the Mayor of Casterbridge lived in the novel of that name by **Thomas Hardy** who, when he left school, worked at no 62, an architect's office, before he went to London.

Napper's Mite. – The bell gabled almshouse was founded by Sir Robert Napper in 1615.

High West St. – The street opens with the much restored **St Peter's Church,** with 12C doorway and multi-pinnacled tower and, inside, 14C **military monuments** and 17C **pulpit** and communion table.

Before the church is a statue of **William Barnes** (1800-86), schoolmaster, linguist and pastoral poet in English – *Linden Lea* – and the Dorsetshire dialect; buried in the porch is the Puritan rector, **John White** (1575-1648), who organised a refuge for North Atlantic Dorset fishermen which led to many settling in the future Massachusetts.

No 6, Judge Jeffreys' Lodgings. – The judge made his way from the house to the assizes at the Antelope by a secret passage, it is said, for fear of the mob. The house with its gabled roofline and jettied upper floor, is the town's only half-timbered building.

tc **Old Shire Hall.** – Inside the Classical style hall of 1797 is the **Old Crown Court** with the dock in which the six **Tolpuddle Martyrs** *(p 143)* stood on 19 March 1834.

The benches, judge's chair and George III royal arms are 18C.

Old Ship. – The inn was built as a coaching inn in 1600.

No 62. – The shopfront is mid-19C, the original bay window above fifty years older.

No 16. – The house is the same but with two upper bays.

No 58. – The house with a rounded doorway is early 19C.

Thomas Hardy Memorial. – To the right at the West Gate roundabout at the top of the street, sits the figure of Thomas Hardy, a posthumous portrait bronze (1931) by **Eric Kennington** *(illustration p 121)*.

MUSEUMS

★ **Dorset County Museum.** – *High West St.* Three unique collections combine to make
tc the museum outstanding: the Thomas Hardy Memorial, the Maiden Castle Gallery and the fossils.

Thomas Hardy Memorial. – The archive (1840-1928) together with memorabilia of other **Dorset worthies** – William Barnes *(see above)*, the painters Alfred Stevens (1818-75) and James Thornhill (1675-1734) and Admiral Sir Thomas Hardy (1769-1838; *p 125)*, are displayed in a splendid **Victorian gallery** with slim, cast iron, painted pillars supporting a balcony and high glass roof; Roman mosaics pave the floor. Furniture and pictures from the house Hardy built himself on the Dorchester-Wareham road, and where he lived from 1885 until his death, original drawings for the novels, attract the visitor to the actual **study from Max Gate** which stands reconstructed as on the day the writer died, 11 January 1928.

Maiden Castle Gallery. – The castle, its history and the artefacts discovered when it was excavated in 1930s are displayed in the context of other sites in the county of the same active period *(p 135)*.

The fossils. – Lyme Regis *(p 134)* is the great fossil area of England: on display are fossil outlines of leaves and fish imprinted on rocks, ammonites, ichthyosaurus and plesiosaurus, also maps and diagrams of current prospecting and **oil exploitation** in the county.

tc **Dorset Military Museum.** – *Bridport Rd*. That combination of the historic, the heroic and the personal, which is a regimental museum, is seen here in the battle honours, log-books, despatches and diaries telling of campaigns fought under Clive in India, in the Napoleonic wars, in the War of Independence, in 1914-18, 1939-45, in Ireland, Korea... Colour is provided in the old barracks gatehouse by dress and battle uniforms – extraordinary headgear! – kettledrums and cartouche boxes, regimental silver, swords, arms, insignia, trophies. The proud record runs from the raising of 39th Foot in 1702 to the formation of the **Devonshire and Dorset Regiment** in 1958 to today.

ROMAN REMAINS

Roman Villa. – *N of High West St, behind the County Hall*. A rich man's town villa has been excavated to reveal the walls and a number of mosaics.

Maumbury Rings. – *Weymouth Avenue (A354) – Maumbury Rd crossroads*. The rings, a Neolithic henge, were remodelled by the Romans to provide seating, pens for wild animals and an arena. In 17C, the Parliamentarians converted the rings into a gun emplacement.

EXCURSIONS

★★ **Maiden Castle.** – *2m SW off Weymouth Rd (A354). P 135*.

tc **Hardy's Cottage, Higher Bockhampton.** – *2½m E along A35 plus ½m S up a minor road, plus 10 mins walk from car park*.
The "small low cottage with a thatched pyramidal roof, and having dormer windows breaking up into the eaves, a single chimney standing in the midst" was built by Hardy's great grandfather early in 19C. Downstairs are the modest living rooms, and the office from which the early Hardy conducted his business as local builder and smallholder; upstairs are the bedrooms in one of which Hardy was born and given up for dead until rescued by the midwife. The garden is pleasant with herbs and simples.

★ **Athelhampton.** – *6m NE on A35*.

Puddletown. – Pop 946. The village lies back in an oasis of calm: the "square" of small houses, neatly white-painted or colour-washed, the grey stone, Perpendicular **church★** with a pinnacled and crocketed tower, a few yards away.
The interior is remarkable for its **17C furnishings** and its **monuments**: the oak box pews,

three-decker pulpit and prayer-desk, Norman beaker-shaped font, the west gallery with the arms of England and France and 16C black-letter texts on the walls.
From 1485, when Sir William Martyn came to Athelhampton, part of the church became a family chantry for which Sir William had his own, very fine, **funeral effigy** carved in alabaster some twenty years before his death in 1503.

★ **Athelhampton.** – *P 125*.

The A35 E continues to Tolpuddle (p 143) and Bere Regis (p 126).

★ **Cerne Abbas.** – *8m N by the Sherborne road (A352)*.

Godmanstone. – Pop 117. The village has what is reputedly the **smallest inn** in the kingdom, the Smith's Arms, 17C flint and stone building of one room, snug and warmly thatched.

Cerne Giant. – The figure, in outline only, stands 180ft

(After J Salmon photo)

16C houses in Abbey Street

tall. He carries a club 120ft long, his shoulders measure 44ft across, his head and eye respectively 23ft 6in and 2ft 6in – note how the feet are in profile. The theories are innumerable, but in truth no one knows the giant's origin or his date *(see also p 183)*.

Turn round and take the first turning on the left.

★ **Cerne Abbas.** – Pop 573. The village main street, bordered by shops and a couple of very old inns, is joined by Abbey St where there stands a beautiful **range of 16C houses,** timber framed upon brick coursed flint; carved corbels support jettied upper floors. The Benedictine abbey, after which the street is named, was founded in 987 and Dissolved in 1539.

The house (*not open*; much rebuilt after a fire) aligned to the street, with a centre gable and angle buttresses, was built as the main gateway to the abbey of which the ruined porch to the abbot's hall remains in the undergrowth in the wood to the right.

In *c*1300 the monks gave the village a **church,** St Mary's, of which the EE chancel was retained when the nave and aisles were rebuilt in 15C. The spectacular Ham Hill stone **tower** with its statue of the Virgin and Child is 16C.

Of note inside are the **arcades** of attached columns with ring capitals, the **table altar** of 1638 *(S aisle),* the **testered pulpit** of 1640 and Jacobean **communion rail,** 18C **chandelier,** 14C wall paintings *(chancel)* and the **stone screen,** dating from 15C.

Charminster Church. – *1½ NW by A37 and first turning right.*

Charminster Church. – St Mary's has a splendid **west tower** of three stages rising to battlements and crocketed pinnacles, presented by Thomas Trenchard of Wolfeton House *(see below).* Relish in the carving property of the Ham stone appears in the profusion of gargoyles, grotesques, corbels, angels and the double T monogram of Thomas Trenchard. The body of the church with its round **chancel arch** and massive circular pillars dates back to 11-12C; note the **nail-head decoration** and, at the northeast end of the nave, the purple-pink **pomegranates,** which being similar to those in Seville Cathedral, are said to have been stencilled by craftsmen sent over after Philip of Habsburg and his wife, Joanna, daughter of Ferdinand and Isabella of Spain, had sheltered from a storm at sea in Wolfeton House in 1506.

tc **Wolfeton House.** – A **gatehouse** of massive, but dissimilar, round towers guards the entrance to the former Elizabethan manor house, built by Trenchard in 16C.

In the house, the **screens passage** with a stone-groin **vault** above linenfold panelling, is embellished by a **stone staircase** of *c*1580 with a pierced balustrade and stone caryatid, also by two Jacobean **porch doorways,** robustly carved with Romans in sandals, moustachioed and carrying cutlasses also a club-carrying ancient Briton.

The stairs lead through 16C pedimented doorway to the **Great Chamber** where a floor-to-ceiling stone fireplace of *c*1600, exotically carved with Red Indians and Orientals, remains from a once fine room.

The Jacobean porches open into the plaster-decorated parlour and dining room.

Go through to the garden to look at the early 16C **south front** with its candle-snuffer buttress, stair-turrets, transomed windows...

★ FORDE ABBEY

Michelin map **403** fold 35 – L31 – 4m SE of Chard

tc The abbey is a synthesis of three major building phases in a garden which has taken owner-gardeners three centuries, notably 20C, to perfect.

The Cistercian monastery was 400 years old and still very much abuilding under its 32nd abbot, **Thomas Chard,** when it was Dissolved in 1539; the following century of neglect ended only in 1649 when the estate was bought by **Sir Edmund Prideaux,** Cromwell's Attorney-General. In the next seven years he saved, knocked down, rebuilt Forde Abbey until it looked much as it does now. In 19C the abbey was bought by ancestors of the present owners.

TOUR *¾ hour*

Exterior. – The range extends from west to east with the main entrance at the centre beneath the Perpendicular **tower;** to the left with its tall windows lies the **Great Hall;** beyond were the abbot's lodgings, remodelled by Prideaux in 17C when he also castellated the front. To the right of the entrance lay the cloisters of which the north gallery remains, now glazed and superimposed by an upper storey; between the tower and cloister gallery, Prideaux inserted on the site of the west cloister, a loggiaed and balconied two-storey block where he placed his **saloon.** On the far right is the **chapel.**

Interior. – As you walk to the entrance, look at 16C tower's **two-storey oriel** with its mullioned and transomed windows and friezes matching those above the Great Hall; just inside, look up again to see the fan vault, still unfinished as at the Dissolution.

Great Hall. – The hall has its original, panelled ceiling but has lost its early proportions, the west end having been walled off in 17C to afford a separate dining room. Note the oak refectory table of 1947; the royal arms, 18C chandelier, 16-17C chairs.

Grand Staircase. – The staircase is spectacular, possessing an enriched **plaster ceiling** of 1658 and a carved **bannister** of which a mirror image has been painted on the surrounding walls.

The Saloon. – The room has a coved ceiling, moulded with fruit and flower garlands, small pendants and the Prideaux arms enriched with gold. Note the side panels of the *Slaying of Abel* and *The Sacrifice of Isaac* in which everyone is in Commonwealth dress! The **Mortlake tapestries** are after the Raphaël Cartoons now in the Victoria and Albert Museum.

Library. – The former refectory was created as a second eating place in 15C when the Cistercian order was permitted to eat meat; as not all the monks approved the concession, the community had two refectories. Note the recess for the reader's desk and 15C roof; 19C Gothick windows *(p 21)* and fireplace and the end screen made out of Breton box-bedsteads.

Monk's Dormitory. – The dormitory range, above an 11-bay undercroft, is 160ft long with lancets along the outer wall. It was divided down the centre in 19C when it was also given a new vaulted ceiling. The **gun** is 18C French pinnace gun.

Return to the ground floor.

The Chapel. – The chapel, with, Norman rib vaulting, round columns and scallop capitals, has been repeatedly remodelled, most strenuously in 17C.

KINGSTON LACY

Michelin map **403** fold 37 – N31 – 3m NW of Wimborne Minster

tc The house, built by Sir Ralph Bankes in 1663-5 *(p 207)*, was altered and encased in Chilmark stone in 19C. It was left to the National Trust in 1982 together with its contents which include a collection of master paintings (Sebastiano del Piombino, Velasquez, Murillo, Rubens, Titian, Van Dyck), furniture, books and Egyptian antiquities.

★ LYME REGIS   Pop 3 464

Michelin map **403** fold 35 – L31

tc "The remarkable situation of the town, the principal street almost hurrying into the water, the walk to the Cobb skirting round the pleasant little bay... the Cobb itself, the very beautiful line of cliffs stretching out to the east of the town, are what the stranger's eye will seek", as Jane Austen wrote in *Persuasion*.

The town's name dates from 14C when Edward I gave the manor to his second queen.

Fossilling. – The areas where fossils are found are west of the Cobb and **Monmouth Beach** (where the Duke landed in 1685), round the point and in Pinhay Bay *(2m)*, east of the town, below 450ft high **Blue Venn Cliffs** (Charmouth; *2m)*, **Stonebarrow** and **Golden Cap** *(4 ½m)*.

FIND OUT *(in Lyme or Charmouth)* the time of HIGH TIDE – the sea comes in fast to the foot of the cliffs and there are no gateway paths; DO NOT CLIMB THE CLIFFS or cut out fossils embedded in the cliff faces – you would probably break them anyway! The cliffs are not stable, rock falls are frequent, especially after rough weather. Do not enter closed areas; always beware the tide. Good hunting!

SIGHTS

Broad St. – The main street is lined along its steep sides by late Georgian houses with shops below, and inns of earlier date, including the Royal Lion, bay windowed above a pillared porch. At the bottom are the sea and the **views**.

Bridge St. – The street, bearing left, crosses the outlet of the Lyme and before it turns uphill, overlooks a ledge known as the **Gun Cliff** from the days when the town was besieged by the Royalists (1644).

Museum. – The collection of **lace,** particularly point lace, the 1710 Sun Insurance **fire engine**, are overshadowed by the **fossils** found in this, the prime fossil area in England. The greatest "finder" ever was **Mary Anning** (1799-1846) whose father, a carpenter, imbued her with his skill and passion for fossilling. Early on she found a good ammonite which she sold for *2s 6d;* at the age of 11, after a violent storm had brought down tons of cliff rock between Lyme and Charmouth, Mary Anning found the first complete fossil of the 180 million year-old **ichthyosaurus**. In 1824 and 1828 she made further unique finds, first of a **plesiosaurus** then a **pterodactyl**.

St Michael the Archangel. – The church, truncated at its west end by the road and ever in danger at its east end of sea erosion and landslip, has nevertheless survived since Norman times – one of the bells is inscribed "O Sea spare me". The 58ft west **tower** was the crossing tower of the Norman church, the present porch that church's nave. When the larger, Perpendicular church came to be built, the Norman chancel was demolished and replaced by a wide nave and aisles.

Note the difference in level from west to east, the **piers** with their shield and foliate carving in place of capitals, the plain, tested **Jacobean pulpit** presented by a Mercer and Merchant Adventurer in 1613, the **gallery** of 1611 with the borough arms and the **window** to Mary Anning *(see above)*.

Marine Parade. – The houses lining the parade, pink washed, pantiled and many with upper observation window bays, are 18 and early 19C; note on the house between the hotel and Library Cottage, the huge **ammonite fossils** embedded in the walls.

★ **The Cobb.** – The Cobb is a breakwater, a curving 600ft long stone jetty, with its back braced against the Atlantic swell and a small harbour on its lee side. It lies half a mile west of the town, built of boulders and rocks at the end of the Marine Parade. Neither the origin of the name, nor the date of the first wall of rocks in which fossils can still be seen embedded, are known although it is recorded that repairs were being carried out in 14C. It is Lyme's focal point and the dramatic setting used by novelists from Jane Austen to John Fowles.

The Landslip. – *P 113.*

Michelin map **403** *is the map to use for the West Country.*

Michelin map **404** *for South East England,*
                    the Midlands and East Anglia.

Michelin map **402** *for Southern Scotland,*
                    the Lake District and Northern England.

Michelin map **401** *for Scotland.*

★★ MAIDEN CASTLE

Michelin map 403 fold 36 – M31

tc The massive, grass-covered **earthwork ramparts**, three miles long as they follow the hillside contours to enclose fifty on the saddleback down, have commanded a **view★** of the surrounding countryside for more than 2 000 years. The importance of Maiden Castle is that it is the finest earthwork in Britain.

Building periods. – A Neolithic settlement was established on the site in *c*3000 BC. The existing fort was begun in *c*350 BC when 16 acres on the east knoll were enclosed by a single rampart with entrances to east and west. At the end of the century the west knoll was added to the enclosure, now some 47 acres.

In *c*150 BC the rampart was rebuilt to twice its original size and augmented by 50ft deep ditch; additional fortifications were constructed to north and south.

The **final phase** came in 100-60 BC, when the appearance of the sling with a range of 100yds, caused the outer ditches and ramparts to be remodelled and the gateways, always well protected by inner and outer walls, to be made even more of a chicane. Inside, the walls, huts, storage barns and metalled streets were kept in good order, ammunition dumps of 20 000 beach-pebbles for use as sling stones were kept prepared. In **43 AD**, however, the future Roman Emperor, Vespasian, in his campaign to subdue southern England, invested Maiden Castle. The Roman infantry advanced up the slopes, cutting their way through rampart after rampart until, in the innermost bay, they reached the huts which they fired. Under cover of the smoke, the entrance was forced, the inhabitants put to the sword.

At the end of 4C a Romano-British **temple** and adjoining priest's house and hut were built (foundations uncovered on the east knoll), since when the site has been deserted. All the finds from the 1934-8 excavations are in the Dorset Museum *(p 132)*.

*Europe on a single sheet: **Michelin map 920**.*

MILTON ABBAS   Pop 433

Michelin map 403 fold 36 – N31

Henry VIII Dissolved Milton Abbey in 1539; Lord Milton, Earl of Dorchester, removed the village with equal autocracy two and a half centuries later.

The property was valuable and Henry sold it for £1 000, to his proctor, Sir John Tregonwell, who constructed a house amidst the conventual buildings, while the village adopted the abbey as a parish church. **Lord Milton** in 18C, would have none of this: he rebuilt the village (1771-90) out of sight of the abbey, knocked down almost all the remaining conventual buildings and built himself the house (now a boys' school) at the centre of a park he had planned by **Capability Brown.**

tc **The ABBEY** *time: ½ hour*

Massive as it is – it is 136ft long – the abbey was never completed. The first church, was struck by lightning in 1309 and almost destroyed; building re-started in 1331 in the EE – Decorated styles, but virtually ended at the Black Death in 1348. The abbey, therefore, comprises an aisled presbytery, the crossing with its tower and the transepts.

Transepts. – The contrasting tracery in the windows is late Decorated *(S)* and Perpendicular *(N)*. The *Tree of Jesse* is by Pugin; the white marble funeral monument was designed by **Robert Adam.**

Presbytery. – The height of the stone vaulting, the size of the presbytery or chancel, recall that this was intended to be a great mediaeval abbey. In 15C the monks erected the **reredos** of three tiers of canopied niches; Dissolution, Reformation and Puritanism have stripped it of brilliant colour and saintly figures, so that today it stands bone-white, like a piece of lace.

Furnishings. – The mother-of-pearl **Crucifix**, the tall, hanging **tabernacle** with an octagonal spire of carved and once painted wood, the **panel painting** of the King Athelstan, founder of the abbey, are all 15C; the bust of the pilgrim St James is 16C.

tc **The HOUSE** *time: ½ hour*

Lord Milton, future Earl of Dorchester, commissioned **William Chambers,** future architect of Somerset House, to design his new mansion: the style outside was of the plainest to complement to the abbey.

Staterooms. – The most impressive of the typical 18C staterooms with their plasterwork **ceilings** and white **marble chimneypieces,** are the **library,** where the bookcases are framed by paired pilasters, and the **ballroom** which is covered by a tunnel vault with Adam-style moulding.

Abbot Middleton's Hall. – The hall, the one part of the old monastery to remain, dates from 1498. Beginning with plain panelling, the walls rise through a clerestory interspaced with angel-supported stone shafts, to a **hammerbeam roof** with panel tracery.

★ MILTON ABBAS VILLAGE

The village was rebuilt by Lord Milton as twin lines of identical **thatched cottages,** well spaced on either side of the grass verged main street. Marking the centre are the **church,** erected in 1786 with stone and timber from the abbey tithe barn and the **Tregonwell Almshouses,** a rebuilding of 16C houses of the original village.

★★ PARNHAM HOUSE

tc Parnham combines a mellow stone house in a wooded garden setting and beautiful furniture, each of their time: Elizabeth I and Elizabeth II. The **house** is of Ham stone, E shaped, many gabled, finialled and multiple chimneyed, mullioned, emblasoned on the oriel above the entrance. Balustraded steps lead to the **gardens** and riverside.

The house was begun around a Great Hall built by Sir Robert Strode in 16C. In 17C the mansion was overrun by Cromwell's soldiers, who murdered Lady Anne Strode in that same Great Hall. After centuries of neglect it was restored, enlarged and crenellated by John Nash and finally was purchased in 1976 by John Makepeace, who set it to rights once more and established it as the **John Makepeace Furniture Workshops**, the School for Craftsmen in Wood, and an exhibition gallery for modern furniture and living art.

Makepeace is considered to be among the country's outstanding furniture designers; pieces are commissioned, a few may become prototypes of limited editions, most are unique pieces, often celebrationary, as is the fourth centenary table at Longleat *(p 196)*.

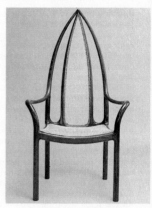

Chair by John Makepeace
in ebony and nickel silver

★ POOLE

Pop 119 316

Poole overlooks one of the largest natural harbours in the world.

The port, with ships sailing to foreign parts, appears to have been well established by 12-13C when it took the ascendancy over Wareham as the channel silted up. Warehouses such as the Town Cellars were built, Henry VI granted the town the status of a **Custom Port** and **Port of the Staple**, so licensing it to export wool and woollen cloth, then Dorset's and England's richest product *(p 13)*. As trade increased in 16-17-18C, particularly with Newfoundland, the town knew even greater prosperity which resulted in the refacing or rebuilding of many houses to give the Georgian style still evident – in Market St is a house *(not open)* of Tudor origin which was divided. The owners, presumably of different fortune, in the one case kept their frontage unaltered with exposed beams, their more prosperous neighbours in 18C had their frontage classically refaced.

The **Poole fleet,** carrying cod and salt fish to Spain and Portugal, continued to expand until by 1802 it had 80 ships on the Newfoundland run and more than 200 engaged elsewhere. In the mid-19C trade shifted to Scandinavia (timber, coal and clay).

Poole however, has always cared less for the past than posterity; in recent years it has become one of the most popular **yachting havens** in the country; now, in addition to bulk traffic in grain, fertilizer, timber and clay, it is developing into a major lorry and heavy vehicle **roll-on-roll-off port** with transporter parks, entrepot sheds and as many as three ferry sailings daily for the continent (Cherbourg). On the landward side Poole has attracted big business so that now, stacked behind the quay, are the modern office blocks of national and multinational enterprises. The human dimension is on the **Quay**, in the **Old Quarter** and in **Poole Park**, this last containing a saltwater lake and amusement facilities.

The QUAY and OLD QUARTER

The Quay. – The quayside is lined with yacht chandlers, inns and restaurants.

tc **Poole Pottery.** – Moulding and throwing, glazing, firing and decorating are seen and explained as you are conducted through the working area to the old plant where tiles decorate the walls and there is a museum of commemoration pieces.

tc **RNLI Museum.** – Large models show developements in the design of lifeboats and the heroic deeds of the men since the institution's foundation in 1824.

The Old Quarter. – The quarter extends inland to the church and Old Guildhall. On the quay stand the late-18C **Customs House** of red brick with a doorway at the top of twin stairways, and old the Town Cellars *(see below)*.

Bear back from the quay to the church.

St James' Close. – The close, a green and flowered triangle, frames the large **church** of 1820 with high windows and a tall doorway in its west tower. All around are **18C town houses** each in its own garden.

★ The THREE MUSEUMS

tc **Maritime Museum.** – *Town Cellars.* Models of the old sailing ships, modern dinghies and canoes, lights, anchors, tools, medals, charters and seals, vividly describe Poole's past in the historic building with its fine **timber roof**. The **iron roundel** of a galleon, outside, is a replica of the borough's 14C silver seal.

tc **Scalpen's Court.** – The discovery and recovery this century of the Tudor house beneath the accretions of years, is a romance in itself. Today it displays a modest **Edwardian** parlour complete in every detail, and a **Victorian kitchen**.

tc **Guildhall Museum.** – The hall was built in 1761 at the then high cost of £2 260 14s 0d. What makes it so very special a building are its **perfect proportions:** the balance of curve or circle, versus a straight line: the round clock-face in the triangular pediment; the circular-headed windows and door, square porch and flat topped windows; the **horseshoe staircase** with plain iron railings.

Inside, the **hall,** with its ornate, twin balconies, fluted pilaster doorway with a pediment containing a 14-15C version of the borough and pre-Stuart **arms** *(over the fireplace),* served as the corporation meeting hall, quarter sessions courtroom, and, until 1835, the court of admiralty – the court which determined values and prize money, salvage rights and dues.

The town possesses a rare collection of town seals dating back to 14C and rich corporation regalia which are, on occasion, incorporated in the local history displays now housed in the hall.

EXCURSIONS

★★ **Compton Acres.** – *3m E by B3369. P 130.*

★ **Brownsea Island.** – *P 129.*

Sandbanks. – *2m E by B3369.*
The promontory runs like a mile-long, built-up breakwater to enclose Poole Harbour. At the point is a roll-on, a roll-off **chain ferry** to Studland *(p 143).* The boats which cross to Brownsea Island *(p 129)* call at Sandbanks.

★ PORTLAND   Pop 10 915

Michelin map 📗 fold 36 – M32

The Isle of Portland, a peninsula 4½ miles long, which in winter stands defiant amidst the Channel storms, its name mentioned almost daily in gale warnings in the shipping forecasts, in summer becomes a place where visitors head for **The Bill,** the southernmost tip, to stand in the sun on the springy turf and idly watch the horizon.

Portland stone has been quarried all over the island since the Middle Ages – hence the numerous worked-out quarries which pock-mark the landscape. The pure white limestone is both soft enough to carve yet durable – Wren selected it for St Paul's. On Portland itself everything is built of the stone: the prison and borstal, houses, garden walls...

SIGHTS

Portland Bill. – The Bill, in addition to being a splendid **vantage point** ★★, is distinguished by three markers: **Portland Bill Lighthouse** *(p 16),* the **Bird Observatory,** a former lighthouse, and the **Obelisk** of Portland stone, erected as a day-mark in 1844.

tc **Portland Museum.** – The museum, Avice's House in Thomas Hardy's *The Well-Beloved,* presents a history of the island with exhibits from 19C days when the convicts worked the quarries, built the prison (1848 – now the borstal) and St Peter's Church.
The **Pulpit Rock** affords an invitation to the energetic to perch high above the waves.

tc **Portland Castle.** – The castle was built in 1539-40 at the water's edge on a Saxon site as one of **Henry VIII's forts** along the south coast. The fabric is Portland stone, the cost was a stupendous £4 964 19s 10¼ d, it being the finest of all the castles erected. Additions were made to the building in Elizabeth's reign, in 17C and again in 19C during the Napoleonic wars.

Portland Harbour. – The harbour Henry VIII's castle was designed to defend, comprised an anchorage protected on three sides but wide open to the east. In the mid-19C work began on the system of breakwaters and channels which, after 20 years' construction by convicts was to provide one of the largest (3 sq m) and safest harbours in the world.
Today it is occupied by the **Admiralty Underwater Weapons Establishment.**

★ PURSE CAUNDLE MANOR

Michelin map 📗 fold 27 – M31

tc The introduction to the house is by way of a delightful small, late 15C **oriel,** riding high on a gable wall on the lane. Go through the courtyard gates and circle the silver-grey, stone walls of the house to come to a rounded porch, added this century. The house, L shaped in 15-16C, extended to an Elizabethan E in 17C, rises to gables crowned with the slim square chimneys known to be the hallmark of a group of local Dorset builders who flourished between 1600-30.

Among the more outstanding rooms are the **Great Hall** and, above, the **Great Chamber.** In the hall the lofty roof is archbraced, re-inforced with tie-beams below the original wall plates, and built up with struts and king posts to produce a forest of timber. Comfort came in 16C with the introduction of the massive fireplace in the main hall and a smaller version in the dining bay. The panelling and the gallery balustrading are 17C.

In the first floor chamber where the roof is barrelled, the walls are amazingly deco-rated with a Chinese painted wallpaper. Off the east end is the oriel one sees from the lane.

★ SANDFORD ORCAS MANOR HOUSE

Michelin map 403 fold 36 – M31

tc The story of the house is as straightforward as the house is attractive in its setting amidst the gently undulating countryside and a terraced garden with long flowered borders. It was bought, newly built, two centuries ago by the present owner's family as a farming property and leased to careful tenants. Since 1870s the family has begun to live in it and return it to life.

TOUR ¾ hour

Exterior. – The long and rambling house of the 1560s, which is built of brownish Ham Hill ashlar, is many gabled with every point the perch of a heraldic monkey, lion, or other beast. The **windows** are hoodmoulded, stone mullioned and transomed, those to the Hall and Great Chamber above, wide bayed to let the light flood in through plain and armorial glass. Slim square **chimneys** crown the stone roofs.

The **entrance porch**, off-centre and advanced under its own small gable, is framed by slim octagonal shafts topped by minute obelisks.

The Hall. – The chamber is single storeyed with oak panelling, a **fireplace** with a Ham stone lintel and an overmantel displaying the full range of Jacobean carved fantasy. On the walls are **Gainsborough** family portraits; among the furniture, examples of the periods represented in the house: Tudor, Jacobean, William and Mary and 18C.

Upper rooms. – At the top of a **spiral stone staircase**, the Great Chamber, closets, landings, bedrooms, are furnished with **marquetry chests**, English and Dutch, opening to reveal ever smaller, decorated drawers, cupboards and hidden recesses.

The **testered beds** range in date from Elizabethan to slender 18C; note the two **embroidered covers**: one in natural silk on silk appliqué, the other a William and Mary work, all glistening greens and brown.

SHAFTESBURY   Pop 4 951

Michelin map 403 fold 27 – N30

The **views** ★ remain: from Gold Hill and paths round the crest of 700ft spur on which the town stands (Park Walk and Love Lane) one looks out south across the Blackmore Vale, west to Somerset – Glastonbury Tor is visible on a clear day – north towards the Salisbury Plain. Not for nothing did Alfred make the site a strongpoint in his struggle against the Danes, but of his or earlier hillforts nothing worthy remains.

SIGHTS

★ **Gold Hill.** – The hill behind the church descends as a very steep, curving, cobbled, road, down to the valley below. One side is lined by a massive, 13C, ochre-coloured **wall**, high and buttressed, the other by small **16, 17 and 18C houses**, thatched, tiled, built of stone or brick, all sitting on each others' shoulders.

★ **Local History Museum.** – Go along the garden path to the house which, in 19C was
tc a barber's shop and before that a doss-house. Inside is an interesting and amusing miscellany of bygones.

tc **The Abbey.** – The Benedictine house of 100-140 nuns stood within 4-acre precinct; today in a walled garden not quite the extent of the great abbey church which measured 240ft from east to west, the excavated footings look somewhat like a rockery.

The abbey was rich from its foundation in 888 when King Alfred endowed it with "100 hides of land" (9 000 acres). In 948 it was given the hinterland and the "right of wreck" along the coast west of St Aldhelm's Head *(p 143)*; thirty years later it became the centre of the cult of St Edward, King and Martyr, murdered at Corfe Castle *(p 131)*. In 1368 the abbess was granted a licence to crenellate the church and campanile and in the same period, took the rank of baron, keeping seven knights in fealty to protect the monarch and sending a representative to parliament.

Among the abbesses was **Marie de France**, 12C Anglo-Norman lyric poet, half-sister to Henry II, Plantagenet; among visitors, **Canute**, who died in the abbey in 1035.

It was said in 15-16C that if the Abbess of Shaston (Shaftesbury) were to marry the Abbot of Glaston (Glastonbury) their heirs would own more land than the king! In 1539 Henry Dissolved both abbeys.

> *18C Ringer's Rhyme*
>
> *Hark how the Chirping Treble Sings most Cleare*
> *And Covering Tom coms rowling in the Rear*
> *We ring the Quick to Church, the dead to Grave*
> *Now up on end at Stay come let us see*
> *What Laws are best to keep Sobriety*
> *To swear or Curse or in a Choleric mood*
> *To Strike or Quarrel, tho he draw no Blood*
> *To wear a Hat or Spur to ore turn a Bell*
> *Or by unskiffull (sic) handling marrs a Peal*
> *Such shall pay Sixpence for each single Crime*
> *What Forfeitures are due as here it is Exprest*
> *Here is a Box to take the same when ye have Trangrest*
> *And we the whole society of Ringers do agree*
> *To Use the same in Love and Unity.*
>
> *(Fowey Church)*

The town, in triumph, bought back the abbey as its parish church at the Dissolution, paying 100 marks for the fabric and 400 for the roof timbers, lead and bells, or £ 330 in all. It was a goodly sum but represented victory in the feud with the Benedictine community and Sherborne, a prosperous market in a wool and sheep area, was about to become one of the principal cloth towns of the West Country.

★★★ The ABBEY *time: ½ hour*

Construction. – The abbey began as a **Saxon stone church,** which grew mightily in importance in 705 when Ine, King of Wessex, appointed as first bishop, **St Aldhelm** *(p 196),* of who it was said that "by his preaching he completed the conquest of West". Gradually the church was rebuilt by Aldhelm's 26 successors until by the Conquest a large Saxon cathedral stood on the site. In 998 a Benedictine community had replaced the earlier, secular canons and in 1121, 50 years after the see had removed to Old Sarum *(p 203),* the church had become an independent abbey with the east end reserved for the monks, the west for the townsfolk. During 12C the church was rebuilt in the Norman style but west of the nave St Aldhelm's original church probably survived until it was replaced in 15C by a chapel of ease. All Hallows.

In the century before the Dissolution, 1420-1504, the monastic church was again rebuilt, this time in the Perpendicular style but EE Lady Chapel and Norman porch, both of which survive in part, were left intact. As the chancel was nearing completion in 1437, a quarrel arose between the townsfolk and the monks over the narrowing of the doorway between All Hallows and the abbey. The townsfolk rioted and "a priest of All Hallows", according to Leland, "shott a shaft with fire into the top of that part that the monks used (the chancel) from that which the townsmen used (the nave); and the partition, chancing at the time to be thatched in the roof (while the rebuilding was going on), was set afire and consequently the whole church, the lead and the bells melted, was defaced". The chancel limestone walls remain to this day reddened by the heat of the fire. All Hallows was demolished in 15C.

Exterior. – The abbey is built of **Ham Hill stone**: deep honey-gold in sunlight, dark ochre on a grey day, old gold by floodlight. The Perpendicular windows rise in two tiers along the south front, divided midway by the great eight-light transept window. The **crossing tower,** on massive Saxon-Norman piers and walls, lifts to a final stage on thinner, recessed, 15C walls with bell openings in pairs below a parapet and twelve crocketed pinnacles. A parapet outlines the roofs; flying buttresses support the chancel.

Go through the porch and rounded **Norman doorway** with its zig-zag decoration.

Interior. – The **fan vaulting** is breathtaking and full of subtleties.

The choir. – In the early 15C choir the **vaulting** is polychrome; the shafts shoot from the floor without a break, framing the arcade arches and clerestory windows directly above before breaking into fan ribs and the network at the crest. It is the earliest large scale, fan vault in the country, but is almost flat and despite the flying buttresses, after 400 years the ridge had dropped 7ins and so vault and buttresses were rebuilt exactly in 1856.

The nave. – The late 15C nave **vault,** even more beautiful, is slightly arched and so stands proud after 550 years.

The nave builders' problem was not the vault but a shortage of funds! The Norman aisle walls, Saxon west wall and arcade piers were, therefore, all retained; the piers were, however, neither opposite one another nor evenly spaced, the north file being 14ins to the west, making impossible a facsimile of the chancel fan vault with shafts rising from the ground to meet at the crest. Instead, a well marked string course, emphasised by angel corbels, was inserted, a regular clerestory built above – the windows are out of line with the arcades – and the shafts sent from on high on their upward sweep to a cobweb of ribs in which only the bosses are coloured.

Chancel arch. – A splendid, unadorned Norman tower arch divides the nave and chancel.

North aisle. – The **Saxon doorway** to the original Saxon church can still be seen at the end of the aisle. In an open coffin, at the east end, is the skeleton of one of the **Saxon Kings** Ethelbald or Ethelbert (850-60 or 860-6), elder brothers of King Alfred.

Lady Chapel. – In the chapel is an engraved **glass reredos** by Laurence Whistler *(p 130).* The chapel, with its flanking chapels, was converted into a house for the Master of the School *(p 141)* in 1560 and occupied as such for 300 years, hence the arms of Edward VI, the school's founder, on what is now the outside south wall of the abbey.

Choir. – The stalls are modern with humourous mediaeval **misericords** and **arm-rests.**

South transept. – The tomb by **John Nost** is of **John Digby,** 3rd Earl of Bristol (d 1698; *p 140)* a man, according to the epitaph "naturally inclined to avoid the hurry of public life, yet careful to keep up the port of his quality".

★★ SHERBORNE CASTLE

tc **Raleigh and Elizabeth.** – The Old Castle *(½ m E)* is a **ruin** proudly, if somewhat indecipherably, erect *(see Museum below).* At the outbreak of the Civil War, the Digbys, Earls of Bristol, moved into the old castle, but in 1645, after being pounded by artillery fire and mined while under siege, it was ordered by Parliament to be slighted.

It was constructed in 1107-35 by Bishop Roger of Salisbury *(p 200).* At the end of 16C, **Sir Walter Raleigh** saw it from the London-Plymouth road and, to persuade Elizabeth to buy it for him from the church, gave the queen a jewel of the estimated value of the castle, namely £260. The jewel, or more probably a slightly smaller sum of money (!) was passed to the bishop, and the queen obtained the castle which she first leased and finally gave to her favourite. The favourite, however, had committed the cardinal sin only a few weeks before of marrying one of the queen's ladies-in-waiting, Bess

Throckmorton. On discovering the marriage, Elizabeth in a jealous rage, banned them from the court for ever – although Raleigh returned after five years – and threw them, separately, into the Tower. They were released after five weeks and journeyed to Sherborne.

By 1594 Raleigh had decided, after spending lavish sums, that the castle could not be made into the type of house he wished to live in and he built Sherborne Lodge, the nucleus of the present castle on the far bank of the River Yeo.

James I and the Digbys. – James I, who repossessed Sherborne Castle in 1608 when he imprisoned Raleigh, gave it to Prince Henry, then to his favourite, Robert Carr, who, however, soon fell from grace; the king next offered it for £10 000 to **Sir John Digby**, long employed in trying to arrange a marriage between the future Charles I and the Spanish infanta. Digby, created Earl of Bristol, purchased the house, which had an intrinsic attraction and the sentimental link of Digby's grandmother and Raleigh's wife both being Throckmortons. It has remained in the family ever since.

The Castle Builders. – When he came to build the new castle, **Sir Walter Raleigh** created a four-storey house beneath a Dutch-style gable and balustrade; each angle was marked by a hexagonal turret and each turret angle alternately by a tall, plain, square chimney or heraldic beast. The fabric was Ham stone with rendered walls.

Sir John Digby, in 1620-30, between missions abroad, and using the same style and materials, enlarged the castle to the typical H plan mansion of the time and its present appearance. The interior, by contrast, has rooms decorated in the styles and furniture of every period from 16-19C. "I imagined it to be one of those fine old seats... but this is so peculiar", wrote Alexander Pope in 1722, "and its situation of so uncommon kind, that it merits a more particular description".

The GROUNDS

The drive through the deer park to the house, passes by a 50-acre **lake**, created after a flash flood in 1757 made the river overflow and the then Lord Digby determined to make the effect permanent; **Capability Brown** was called upon. The Adam-style stables and **dairy** constructed in stone from the Old Castle are also 18C.

Raleigh's Seat, a stone bench under the trees on the far side of the lake, is said to be where Sir Walter was enjoying a quiet pipe when his servant, bringing him a drink, grew alarmed at seeing him supposedly on fire and doused him with ale! Among the trees are giant Virginia cedars grown from seed brought back from the colony.

The HOUSE *time: ¾ hour*

The first three rooms epitomise the house's kaleidoscope of styles.

Library. – The gallery was redecorated in 18C in Strawberry Hill Gothick *(p 21)*; the furniture is Georgian. Note **Raleigh's** *History of the World* (1614), and the portrait of *Sir Kenelm Digby* (1603-65), traveller, founder member of the Royal Society.

Solarium. – The Raleigh parlour was converted in 19C into a Victorian dining-room. The **heraldic chimneypiece**, installed at the time of the conversion, includes the ubiquitous family **ostrich**, adopted some 350 years ago for reasons unknown but present everywhere even on the weather-vanes in Sherborne town. The **monkey supporters** sometimes to be seen with the arms, originate from the time when monkeys, kept as pets in the house, alerted a nursemaid of a fire in the children's rooms.

Red Drawing Room. – The plaster **ceiling** is 17C, the furniture Georgian.

Among the pictures are a portrait by **Cornelius Jansens** of *Sir John Digby*, first owner of the present house, *Sir Kenelm Digby*, his wife and children and the historic painting of 1600, of Queen Elizabeth.

(By courtesy of Mr Simon Wingfield Digby, Sherborne Castle)

The Procession of Queen Elizabeth

Sporting and Porcelain Rooms. – Prints, trophies, Meissen and Chinese figurines show the family's interest in the chase and as founders of the Blackmore Vale Hunt. In adjoining rooms pieces of 17C Chinese Transistional and 17-18C K'ang-hsi periods make a proud display.

Green Drawing Room. – Raleigh and Digby arms appear in the decoration: Raleigh's five lozenges in shields on the ceiling; the Digby fleur-de-lys over the fireplace. The walnut **despatch box**, is said to have held the would-be English-Spanish marriage contract *(see above)*. Note the French **kingwood writing-table**, the late Georgian commodes, and, among the portraits, that of Col Stephen Digby, "Mr Fairly" in Fanny Burney's diary.

Blue Drawing Room. – The room, so-called from the original colour of the wallpaper, is crowded with fine English and French **18C furniture**, Chinese and Japanese **lacquer** and **porcelain**. Among those portrayed is *Sir Jeffrey Hudson*, Henrietta Maria's Dwarf, Henry, 1st Earl of Digby, by **Gainsborough** and John Digby, 3rd Earl of Bristol, who received the future William III on his journey from Brixham to London in 1688.

The Hall. – The hall, in 16C part of the house, still has the **studded door** and **lattice windows** from when the end wall was the outer wall of Raleigh's house.

Small Dining Room. – Tudor and Stuart oak furniture are seen through the Elizabethan doorway.

Oak Room. – The room with 1620 **panelling**, contains two, remarkable, draft proof, **Jacobean inner porches**, decorated with fluted pilasters, pierced parapets and heraldic beasts (note the **wooden spring** on one of the door latches). The prehistoric antlers above the wide fireplace were found in Ireland; the mediaeval helmet is a tilting helm; the portrait is believed to be of Sir Walter Raleigh.

ADDITIONAL SIGHTS

Walk in the town centre. – The abbey lies at the centre of the town west of the main, Cheap St. This is marked at its start by an open square in which stands the **Conduit** *(left side)*, the transposed lavatorium from the abbey cloister. On the same side *(corner of Abbey Rd)* are 17C **stone houses** and a combined wood framed and stone house with three advanced, half-timbered, gables.

Long St. – The wide street leads off right to Sherborne Castle *(see above)*.

Newland. – The third road on the right curves southeast to join up with Long St. It and the two before it are lined by 18, early-19C **houses** built in irregular terraces in stone with period doors and windows.

St John's Almshouses. – The 15C foundation comprises a **chapel** (mediaeval glass), a **hall**, two-storey houses and a cloister, surrounding a low walled courtyard. To the rear is the **Abbey Close**, ringed by modest 16-18C houses.

tc **Sherborne School.** – The school was granted a royal charter as a Free Grammar School by Edward VI in 1550 *(p 139)*.
It had grown to only 30 boys by 1850; 27 years later there were 278 and now 650. The buildings, including the Gatehouse and Great Court, are predominantly 19-20C but follow the Jacobean style and are in the same Ham Stone where they abut such areas as the **Jacobean Schoolroom** (Old School Room) of 1660 and 1670 **Library**.

tc **The Museum.** – *Abbey Gate*. Life in the almshouses, Victoriana, a model of 12C castle which makes the ruins comprehensible *(see above)*, exhibits on the local 17-18C silk and present glass fibre industries, comprise a museum of unusual exhibits.

EXCURSIONS

★ **Sandford Orcas Manor House.** – *4m N by B3148. P 138.*

Worldwide Butterflies, Over Compton. – *3m W off N carriageway, Sherborne-Yeovil Rd, A30.*

tc **The Butterflies.** – Tropical butterflies in brilliant velvet colours with wingspans of 6-9ins, fly freely amidst jungle plants growing in glass enclosures which each fill a whole room in the ancestral house. As you watch you see the smaller ones, the better camouflaged; in the Palm House in high summer, you walk amidst them. On the first floor, are the silk-worms which, maintaining the tradition of the **Lullingstone Silk Farm**, founded in 1932 and now at Compton, supply silk for famous royal occasions.

Compton House. – The setting for the butterflies is the part-19C, part-16C Tudor-style mansion, built on the foundations of houses dating back to pre-Domesday.
In the garden are tall cedars of Lebanon and a small **church** with a high, pinnacled and embattled tower. Its several periods were "beautified" in 1882 by Robert Goodden, ancestor and namesake of the present owner, who had his **statue** sculpted and set inside the church three years before he died; it is carved to the life.

★ SMEDMORE

Michelin map ⁴⁰³ fold 37 – N32 – 7m S of Wareham

tc The first view of Smedmore after the drive along uphill, downhill, narrow, turning lanes affording views of the wooded Isle of Purbeck countryside, the cliffs and the sea, is of 18C house of grey Purbeck stone with great rounded, bow windows rising two storeys to a plain parapet and stone tiled roofs. The dignified northwest range represents the last major addition to the house which was described when first built in c1620 as "a little new house beautified with pleasant gardens". The land on which the house and garden stand has been in the same family since 1391; the ever-present owners are as conversant over furniture and pictures as over the garden.

SMEDMORE★

The GARDENS

The gardens today, increased since 17C by small gardens planted between the walls of old outbuildings, are more than "pleasant" with rare and colourful flowers, herbs, wistarias, clematis and, especially superb, banks of deep pink hydrangeas.

The HOUSE *time: ¾ hour*

The outstanding feature in the house is 17-18C **Dutch marquetry furniture**, inherited through a family connection from a noble and wealthy Dutch family whose most distinguished member, a soldier who won several important victories in Ireland, was created Earl of Athlone in 1692 by William of Orange.

The "Cedar Room". – The room, a part of the original house, oak panelled in 18C, presents piece after telling piece of **marquetry**, intricate with outer doors and inner drawers and little secret cupboards, and beautiful with different inlaid, floral, oysterwork and geometrical designs. All are Dutch with the exception of an English **writing-desk** and French **secretaire**.

Dining Room. – Note the high **chest** with leaf-patterned outer doors lined with oysterwork, marquetry enriched **chairs** and pedimented display **cabinets** in which are delightful small **Dresden figures, dessert plates** handpainted with brilliantly plumed birds or gilt and trellis-bordered. The gold rimmed **Bohemian table glass** is 18C. The **elbow chair** belonged to Napoleon.

Drawing Room. – The painted furniture is, 19C, Italian; the satinwood card-table by Sheraton.

Hall. – The deeply carved **chest** is Italian; the two large Dutch, early 17C walnut marquetry cabinets contain Dresden figures and florally decorated dessert plates. The clocks are 18C: a Parliament clock of 1797 in a black lacquer case, the other a French mantel timepiece.

Staircase Hall. – Note the **stair balusters** and the two pairs of **library steps** which convert respectively into a chair and a pole.

★ SWANAGE

Pop 8 822

Michelin map 403 fold 37 – O32

The quarry town and harbour from which stone and marble were shipped to build Westminster Abbey and the Cathedrals of Exeter, Lincoln and Salisbury, was transformed by the arrival of the railway, into a "pleasant little watering place with a good beach".
Some years before, **John Mowlem**, a native of Swanage, had begun to beautify the town. He had started as a local quarry boy before setting out for London where he founded a construction firm for which he imported stone from Purbeck and granite from Cornwall, Aberdeen, Guernsey and Leicestershire, to accomplish the massive Victorian rebuilding of the City and the resurfacing of roads and bridges with granite sets. The sailing ketches which brought the stone to London returned to Swanage in ballast with unwanted **street furniture**, dressed and carved stone, even **monuments**.

SIGHTS

Mowlem Institute. – *The Parade.* The modern complex on the front stands on the site of the institute presented to the town by John Mowlem in 1863.

The Pier and **Wellington Clock Tower.** – The small pier was built in 1896; the landmark-like tower, stood at the south end of London Bridge until 1863 when it was pronounced an "unwarrantable obstruction". Mowlem offered to remove it and shipped it home! It never included a statue of the duke.

Turn inland up the High St.

Queen's St. – *Left.* Several City of London **bollards** are to be seen used as gateposts.

Old Millpond. – *Church Hill. Right off High St.* The old millpond with a couple of ducks, is surrounded by 18-19C cottages and houses, pretty with flowering creepers.

St Mary the Virgin Church. – The church, rebuilt for the third time in 1859, has a **tower** which dates, in its lower half, from 12-13C when it served as a refuge for local townsfolk from marauding pirates – note the arrow slit windows. Originally there was no door at ground level, entry being by means of a ladder to the first floor.

Return to the High St.

Town Hall. – The ornate **17C stone front** of the hall originally stood in Cheapside in the City of London as the façade of the Mercers' Company; when Cheapside was widened, it was decided that it would be less costly to reproduce the stone front than to clean it of its "London black" and re-erect it – London, therefore, has 19C replica, Swanage Town Hall the original 17C stone which Mowlem shipped home and which, for good measure, the sea air has gradually cleaned.

Our Lady of Mercy Convent. – The house in Scottish baronial style, built by Mowlem's nephew, George Burt *(see below)*, incorporates columns from old Billingsgate Market, statues from the Royal Exchange, tiles from the Houses of Parliament...

Durlston Country Park. – *1m S by Lighthouse Rd.*
The headland, from which there is a panoramic **view**★★, the castle-folly-restaurant, Great Globe, London bollards and the lighthouse, today make up the country park George Burt had in mind when he purchased 80 acres (now 260 acres) in 1862.

The Castle. – The folly is built of Purbeck stone with a full complement of towers, turrets, battlements and bastions; the stalwart **granite bollards** at the entrance are prototypes of those which delimit Trafalgar Sq. The interior is designed as a winter garden.

Take the path down towards the head. Note the London **bollards.**

★ **The Great Globe.** – Mowlem had the globe made in his yard at Greenwich. It is 10ft in diameter, 40 tons in weight and is made up of 15 segments of Portland stone held in position by granite dowels.

Anvil Pt Lighthouse. – *¾ hour circular walk.*

The path to the all white lighthouse *(p 17)* passes the **Tilly Whim Caves,** a former cliffside quarry. The **view★★** extends from St Aldhelm's Head to Portland Bill, Hengistbury Head and The Needles; inland are the Purbeck Hills.

EXCURSIONS

★★ **St Aldhelm's Head.** – *4½m SW by B3069.*

Worth Matravers. – Pop 525. This small village of stone houses round a duck pond, was once the quality centre of the quarry industry being where marble such as that in the slender shafts in Salisbury Cathedral came from. In 1506 Swanage took precedence.

The **church** of rubble stone with ashlar dressings and 19C pyramid roof to its ancient square **tower,** possesses several Norman features including, outside, the enriched south doorway and the **corbel table** which runs the length of the eaves, carved with grotesque heads of birds and beasts.

Inside, the **chancel arch** with its chevron moulding above round columns is mid-12C, and at the west end, the plain **tower arch,** even older.

Continue through the village 1½m SSW along surfaced roads and farm tracks.

St Aldhelm's Chapel. – The chapel, dedicated to the local saint *(p 196)*, stands squat and square on the windswept clifftop, the shallow, pyramid roof surmounted by a turret which must once have held a fire cresset, or basket, as a sailors' lantern. It was built between 1150 and 1200. The rounded, Norman doorway leads into a 30ft sq chamber reminiscent of an undercroft with a square pillar supporting rib vaulting.

★★ **St Aldhelm's Head (or St Alban's Head).** – The headland, at 352ft one of the highest in the area, affords a grandiose, circular **view★★★** from Portland to the Old Harry Rocks, Hengistbury Head and The Needles. Behind you, as always, are the Purbeck Hills. Just below the headland to the west is the dark, circular **Chapman's Pool** eroded by the sea out of the Kimmeridge Cliffs.

Studland. – *5m N by Victoria Avenue and Northbrook Rd to B3351, bear right.*

tc Studland is the promontory closing Poole Harbour from the south. A chain ferry runs from the promontory end, South Haven Point, to Sandbanks *(p 137).*

Studland Beach. – The two mile arc of sand below a narrow band of shingle is crowded in summer; the bay is wide and shallow; the **view★** vast across Poole Bay.

Studland Village – Pop 559. The village is small and scattered, the houses half-hidden in gardens, with, not far from the water's edge, **St Nicholas Church★,** early Norman and fortress solid with a low tower. Note the **corbel table** with monstrously grimacing heads, the lancets, the **leper squint** peering through the south chancel wall (glazed 1881). Inside are a **groined vault** and plain Norman arches on **cushion capitals.**

★★ **Old Harry Rocks.** – The two stacks of gleaming chalk were once part of a continous shoreline from The Needles but are now separated from the mainland and even from each other; Old Harry is the larger and three-legged, his wife slimmer by the day.

TOLPUDDLE   Pop 280

Michelin map **403** fold 36 – N31

Tolpuddle, the village whose name has entered the language as a symbol of workers' rights to form a trade union, lies at the centre of Dorset's farming country. In 1830 an agricultural labourer's wage was 9*s* a week; in the next two years it dropped to 8*s* then 7*s*... The villagers met, according to tradition, under the now named **Martyr's Tree** to form the Friendly Society of Agricultural Labourers.

Fear of militant trades unionism and riots brought arrest of the six ring-leaders, their trial at Dorchester Crown Court *(p 131)* and the sentence of seven years transportation. The cause of the Six Martyrs, as they soon became known, was taken up by Robert Owen, by Cobbett in the House, and at mass rallies, until in 1839 the men were granted a free pardon though not before they had worked in Australia in penal settlements and Hammett had been "sold like a slave for £1". Hammett was, in fact, the only one to return to the village where he died in 1891.

tc **TUC Memorial Cottages and Museum.** – *N side of A35 just before W end of the village.* The cottages were erected in 1934, a line of six with, at the centre below the middle of the gables, a memorial **museum** hall.

In the centre of the village *(just beyond the garage)* is the **cottage** of one of the men, Thomas Standfield *(plaque).*

Methodist Chapel. – Five of the six were Methodists. The **arch** to the chapel bears the **affirmation** handed to the judge immediately before sentence was passed.

St John's Church. – The parish church of flint with stone trims, despite remodelling in 1855, retains elements of earlier sanctuaries: a Perpendicular tower, Norman doorways, late 13C chancel and transept arches, a Decorated north arcade and a **tie-beam roof** of 14C with struts and crown posts. Earliest of all, in the north transept, is a carved Purbeck **marble coffin-lid** of one, Philip, a priest of 1100 AD.

★ WAREHAM

Michelin map **403** fold 37 - N31

The town is immediately recognisable by its long High St which runs in a straight line from the River Frome to the small upraised Saxon Church of St Martin; on either side are Georgian and Victorian houses, tightly packed, most with shops below. They date from 1762 when a disastrous fire destroyed 133 houses in the town centre. It was the last in a long series of fires which began in 9C when the **Danes** used the port as a base from which to make incursions inland and each time would fire the town before being driven off – **Canute** mounted his invasion of southern England in 1015 through Wareham and also fired it.

The prosperity which developed in the Norman period and continued for centuries with trade in wine, fruit, olive oil, wool and woollen cloth, cereals and foodstuffs was marred in 17C first by the Civil War, when the town changed hands a number of times, and then by Judge Jeffreys' arrival to scourge those who had supported Monmouth in his Rebellion. By 18C when the fire occured, trade was in decline as Poole Harbour and the River Frome had silted up making Wareham inaccessible to shipping.

SIGHTS

★★ **St Martin's.** – The church at the north end of the High Street, epitomises one's idea of an Anglo-Saxon church. It dates from *c*1030, the Danes having destroyed an earlier church which, if legend is to be believed, was built by St Aldhelm *(p 196)* in 678 AD. Traces of **Anglo-Saxon building** remain in the "long and short" work in the external angles at the east end of the nave and chancel, the nucleus of 11C church.The **chancel arch** was rebuilt, the **north aisle** added by the Normans, the arcade rebuilt in 13C, the south wall pierced and the elegant **window** inserted in 14C; finally, in 16C, although some hold that it dates from 11-12C, the **tower** was erected with its saddleback roof and round doorway.

Decorating the walls are 11-18C **paintings**, faint, faded, clear and indistinct by turns, of St Martin dividing his cloak, the arms of Queen Anne superimposed over those of Charles II, the Commandments... In the north aisle lies the posthumous marble effigy, by **Eric Kennington** of Lawrence of Arabia *(p 130)* in his desert robes, his hand on his dagger.

High St. – Three buildings especially mark the street: the square **Red Lion Hotel** at the crossroads, typical of the rebuilding in brick after 1762 fire; the **Manor House** of 1712 in Purbeck stone which escaped the fire; and the **Black Bear** of *c*1800 with bow windows and a columned porch, plinth for its emblematic black bear.

The Quay. – The quay, where pleasure-craft now tie up, is lined to the east by an ancient russet-red brick **granary**, three storeys high (restaurant) and, adjoining **18C house** also of brick with tablet stones above the windows.

tc **Local History Museum.** – The collection includes a number of cuttings and photographs on T E Lawrence *(p 130)* and his motor-cycles, notably the Broughs.

Lady St Mary Church and the Priory. – Rising behind the buildings at the east end of the quay is the battlemented tower of the parish church. Adjoining it was one of England's oldest priories, a Benedictine nunnery reformed by St Aldhelm in the late 7C, destroyed by the Danes in 876, rebuilt by one of King Alfred's sisters in 915, and sacked by Canute in 1015. It was rebuilt only to be Dissolved in 16C.

The church foundation went back equally far, the first being built before 700 AD. The erection of the second on the churchyard of the first, resulted in the unearthing of the uniquely **engraved stones** of 6-7C pre-Saxon, British chieftains and landholders *(N aisle)*. This second church, unlike the priory, was not sacked by the Danes and survived more than 1 000 years as one of the largest and most magnificent **Saxon churches** in the land until 1842 when it was substantially rebuilt "on the grounds that the oratorical qualities of the then rector deserved a better setting"!

Interior. – In the nave on 13C Purbeck marble pedestal, stands a very fine, late 12C **lead font**, one of only 29 surviving in England and unique in being hexagonal; in the aisle is the stone coffin traditionally associated with the murdered King Edward *(p 131)*. In the chancel there are examples of bar tracery (12-13C) to the north, reticulated to the east (13-14C). Among the memorials are **brasses** *(S wall)* and two 13C knights in chain mail and surcoats with crossed legs.

EXCURSIONS

★★ **Corfe Castle.** – *5m SE by A351. P 131.*

★ **Blue Pool.** – *3m S on A351 and right (W), at signpost.*
tc The heavenly blue, three-acre lake is encircled by silver birch and pine woods and a circular path *(1m; 45mins)*. The blue-green colour comes from the diffraction of light on minute particles of clay suspended in the water which flooded in to a depth of 36ft when the pit ceased to be used to mine blue-ball clay. On many a summer's day the pool is bluer than the sky!

★ **Smedmore.** – *7m S by A351 and by-roads. P 141.*

★ **The Tank Museum, Bovington.** – *7m W on A352. Turn left on to B3071 to Wool.*
Wool. – Pop 5 219. The railway line separates the small expanding town from the mediaeval **packhorse bridge** with pointed cutwaters which rise to the parapet as pedestrian refuges. Over the bridge can be seen **Woolbridge Manor**, a three-storeyed house with a brick front and projecting porch, which dates from 17C when it was owned by the Turbervilles. As **Wellbridge Manor** it was the setting for the ill-fated wedding night of Tess and Angel Clare. *(Not open.)*

Bear right across the railway and over the bridge; Bovington Camp is signposted.

★ **The Tank Museum.** – The 140 and more tanks, massive, darkly camouflaged ironclads, *tc* which make up the museum, afford a crowded panorama of the historical and technical development of armoured fighting vehicles from 1915 to the mid-1970s. The ranks of tanks include British, American, French, Russian, German, Japanese, South African, Italian and Swedish machines. In the adjoining Alan Jolly Hall are armoured cars, airborne light tanks and guided missiles and in odd corners and on the walls, souvenirs from the field, maps and field orders, models, insignia and battle honours.

(BTA)

The Cove

★ **Lulworth Cove.** – *11m SW along A352, B3070 to West Lulworth.*
The cove, which is a perfect circle, is almost closed by the downland cliffs.

Durdle Door. – *Access: on foot from Lulworth Cove along the Dorset Coast Path, 2½m Rtn or continue on B3070 through West Lulworth to Toll Gate/Newlands Farm.*
Durdle Door lies to the west, beyond Dungy Head, at the far end of St Oswald's Bay. The whole area of headlands and scalloped bays has been likened to a "crash course in geology" with Durdle the dramatic climax, for whereas elsewhere the geological material is mostly lias (at Lyme Regis), oolite, Purbeck stone, Portland limestone and chalk (Old Harry Rocks), at the Door, impermeable folded strata were forced up on end to produce a **cliff archway** of quite different appearance.

WEYMOUTH

Pop 7514

Michelin map **403** fold 36 – M32

Weymouth, a port with roll-on ferry services to Cherbourg and the Channel Islands, is a Georgian town associated with **George III** who was the first monarch to stay in a seaside resort and chose Weymouth for the experiment: "The preparations of festive loyalty were universal", Fanny Burney wrote in her diary in July 1789, "think but of the surprise of his Majesty when, the first time of his bathing, he had no sooner popped his royal head under water, than a band of music, concealed in a neighbouring machine, struck up God save great George our King".
The sovereign returned many times; in 1810, "the grateful inhabitants" erected the **statue** on Esplanade which remains the town's major landmark.

The Esplanade. – The Esplanade beyond King George's statue, punctuated some 200yds further along by Queen Victoria's Jubilee Clock, follows the sweep of the bay. Facing the sea are terrace houses of the late-18, early-19C with first floor iron balconies, sash windows (some with slender glazing bars), canopies, copings and good proportions, notably at the harbour end.

The Old Town. – Situated close to the old quay, now extended to 2 000ft, is the heart of the old town which began on the far side of the inlet on **North Quay** and, as the town grew, spread to the mainland from the promontory on which Sandsfoot Castle had been erected in 16C and Nothe Fort in the early 19C.

Custom House Quay. – The quayside is lined with boat repair shops, inns and houses with windows overlooking the pleasure-craft, the Sealink Ferries and the swans.

St Alban St. – The street, parallel to the quay, cuts through from the Esplanade to the wide St Mary's and St Thomas' shopping streets; it is very narrow with old houses seeming to touch overhead, small shops, people, inns and atmosphere.

★ **Boat Trip.** – Weymouth Bay and Portland Harbour.

EXCURSIONS

★★ **Abbotsbury.** – *9m NW along B3157. P 125.*

Osmington White Horse. – *6m E along A353.* George III on his horse, which, with Uffington, is the only animal facing right, is unique in having a rider. The figure is popularly supposed to be the king, patron of Weymouth from 1789; an alternative version credits engineers, stationed at Weymouth in case of invasion in 1815, with the carving, whereupon the rider would be Wellington; Hardy, in *The Trumpet Major,* described it as a memorial to Trafalgar... The figure is the largest of all being 323ft high by 280ft long. *(See also pp 132, 183.)*

★ WIMBORNE MINSTER Pop 5554

Michelin map **403** fold 37 – O31

Wimborne Minster, glimpsed across the water meadows, needs explaining for its size, its disparate towers, its extraordinary, chequered stonework.

The MINSTER *time: ½ hour*

The foundation dates from 1043, when Edward the Confessor established a college of secular canons on a site occupied by a Benedictine nunnery until it was sacked by the Danes in 1013. In 1318 Edward II declared the church a **royal peculiar**; in 1537, as a collegiate church, the community was Dissolved by Henry VIII and the church given to the parish.

Exterior. – The **stone** is local and varies in colour from grey to pinky-brown and cream; the **towers** are Norman of *c*1120-80 at the crossing, with round-headed and lancet windows, and Perpendicular at the west end, the latter being built in 1448-64 to take a peal of bells. The church had, by then, taken on its present appearance and size there having been extensions in 13-14C.
Before entering look on the south wall of the west tower, at the **quarter-jack**, installed in 1612, originally a monk but since the Napoleonic wars, a grenadier, who strikes the two bells every quarter of an hour.

Interior. – The Decorated outer walls of 1307-77 fit like a glove round 12C Norman church which forms the core of the present 190ft long minster.

The Crossing. – The round columns with plainly **scalloped capitals** are Norman, also the triforium with small rounded arches and Purbeck marble columns. The **eagle lectern** is 17C.

The Nave. – The **arcades** march west from the crossing, the first bays with rounded arches; above are the small round windows of the Norman clerestory although the actual **clerestory** is Perpendicular. In the north aisle are an **almsbox** let into the nearest pillar to the door, and a small tablet to one, **Snodgrass**, who with **Wardle** *(in the tower)*, furnished Dickens with two famous names.

Tower. – The octagonal black Purbeck **marble font** on marble shafts is late Norman (all decoration was stripped from it during the Commenwealth); the **astronomical clock** *(pp 95, 107, 179)* dates from 1320, pre-Copernican times when the earth was shown as the still centre of the universe with the sun, the hour hand, revolving round the outside of the dial face and the moon, also revolving to show the lunar phases. The present works are of 1792 – the model is modern. The **royal arms** on the wall are of Charles II – a relimning at the Restoration of those of Charles I which had been painted out.

East End. – The east window of three tall lights surmounted by foiled circles dates from *c*1220 extension of the church, the *Tree of Jesse* is 15C Flemish glass.
In the **sanctuary**, adjoining **chapels** and the cusp-arched **crypt**, are a **brass** of King Ethelred (d 871), elder brother of King Alfred, and a number of **tombs** including Sir Edmund Uvedale (d 1606), a coloured Renaissance figure, restored to have two left feet, the **Bankes** of Corfe Castle and Kingston Lacy *(pp 131, 134)*, **John de Beaufort**, Duke of Somerset and his duchess, the grandparents of Henry VII, Anthony Ettricke, 17C eccentric, who is buried in a wall recess, so that he is neither within nor without the church and who had a final date of 1693 carved ready on his coffin but lived on, as the altered numbers show, to 1703! There are also old **chests**, one Saxon with a recess in the solid oak for relics...

The TOWN

Bridges. – The town is compact and still lies largely within the bounds of its three bridges: the **Canford** on the Poole road (A341), constructed of Portland stone with three bold arches in 1813; the **Juliana**, to the west (A31), over the River Stour with eight pointed arches and refuges in the brick parapet, which dates from 1636 (widened 1844), and the **Walford** to the north (B3078) which was originally a mediaeval packhorse bridge over the River Allen (widened in 1802).

High St. – The street leading to the minster is one of the town's earliest streets.

tc **Priest's House.** – This early-16C house is Wimborne's most complete mediaeval dwelling; additions were made in 17 and 18C so that now it has 18C refronting with 16C face forming the rear of the "front" room, which in addition combines a Tudor moulded **plaster ceiling** with a Queen Anne **fireplace**. Go through to the garden at the back to see the original **Tudor gables**.
The **local history museum** which now occupies the house, displays finds from excavations, blacksmith's and tinsmith's forges, toys, books, horse brasses, Victoriana and a smiling-solemn, Celtic 3-faced head carved in stone.

The Cornmarket and Square. – The old street and former market square are overlooked by 17-19C houses.

Westborough. – The wide street leading north out of the Square was the principal area of expansion in 18C and is therefore distinguished by **Georgian houses**.

SOMERSET

Area 1332 sq m Population 427 114

Somerset is a county to take slowly: quaff the cider but take time to look at the landscape, to become familiar with the outlines and curves of the downland hillsides so that you can tell at a glance which are the Quantocks, the Mendips, the Brendons, the Blackdowns or the Polden Hills; to explore Exmoor from its open heaths to its wooded valleys and the coastline which is its northern border; to climb Glastonbury Tor – a matter of minutes – and look out across the ancient "levels". Go to see the Cheddar Gorge in as un-leafy time as possible, visit the agricultural Vale of Taunton and the south of the county in spring, summer or autumn to admire the longstanding fertility and good husbandry of one of the great farming areas of England – as long ago as 12C Henry II was buying Cheddar Cheese.

Church Building in Somerset. – Somerset ranked fourth in wool production when England was the premier wool producing country in the world. As an area it possesses fine, workable, **building stone**: the pink-red and deep red Quantock stone, grey Doulting, the tawny gold of Ham Hill.

In this county where some claimed that Glastonbury had been founded by Joseph of Arimathea, the mediaeval wool prosperity coincided with 13-16C period of church renewal and rebuilding, the Gothic Perpendicular period. The local lord of the manor or squire funded the church chancel and family chapels; the parishioners, the nave, the aisles and transepts. Construction, furnishings and embellishment were executed by bands of travelling masons, stone-cutters, carpenters and skilled carvers in stone and wood.

Towers, which in Norman churches rose above the crossing and were crowned with spires, were shifted to the west end and ceased to support often dangerous, tapering cones. They were the last area of the church to be built and marked the triumphant culmination of local enterprise – they became objects of very considerable local rivalry.

The requirement of a west tower to include a belfry was universal but as first one and then another tower was built, it became evident that there were a seemingly infinite number of ways of combining in the upper parts blank lights, bell lights, buttresses, pinnacles, castellations, friezes and pannelling, of rising tier upon tier, ever higher...

A unique ornament was the filling of the upper lights with **Somerset tracery**, uniformly carved screens of the tractable stone.

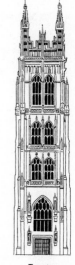

Bishop's Lydeard	Batcombe	Evercreech	Bristol	Taunton
p 176	p 174	p 174	p 35	p 175

The travelling masons must have carried ideas from site to site; villagers undoubtedly went to see and report back what was being erected in the neighbouring parish ! Today, between 4-500 years on, partisanship is still strong. There are 100 or more towers, 60-80 outstanding, 30 described in the following pages: start collecting !

Church roofs. – The churches inside demonstrate the skill of the woodmen: the carpenters in the wagon, hammer-beam, tie-beam, king and queen post roofs; the carvers in the moulding, the cresting, the wall plates, the infinitely various bosses, the panelling and tracery, and most notably, the life-size angels.

Earlier than the parish churches had come the great glory that is Wells Cathedral.

Houses and Gardens. – The houses in the villages are transformed by being built of stone with roofs of stone or the local style terracotta tiles.

The manor houses, the great houses, dating from Queen Elizabeth's reign to Georgian times, in stone, and in several cases decorated inside with outstanding plasterwork, nearly all rejoice in beautiful gardens.

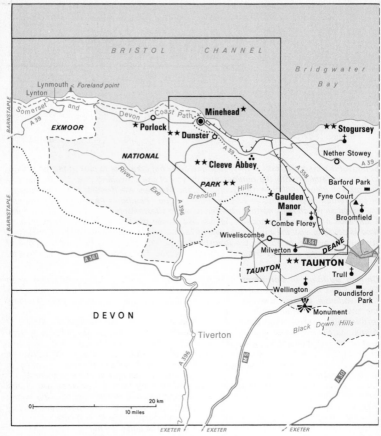

B R I S T O L   C H A N N E L

B r i d g w a t e r
B a y

★★ AXBRIDGE

Pop 1 724

Michelin map 408 fold 26 – L30

The Cheddar Rd leads directly into the irregular Square, used since Saxon times as the market place and now ringed by tall 17-18C houses, the pedimented, early 19C town hall, several 18C refronted pubs of earlier vintage and, on the far corner, two half-timbered houses with oversailing upper floors – the legacy of highly prosperous mediaeval wool and cloth merchants.

★ **King John's Hunting Lodge.** – The house, an example of a timber framed building, dates from the late 15C – the name is purely notional derived from such facts as the Mendip Forest having been a royal hunt and the town's first royal charter being granted by King John. The king's head carving outside at the angle, probably dates from 17-18C when the building was the King's Head Alehouse !

The lodge is now a **museum** with exhibits including a "nail" *(p 36)* and two early mayoral maces.

The house is most interesting, however, for the revelation inside of its **structure.** It stands on a stone sill from which it rises through a ground floor, once an open arcade of shops, to upper living and bedroom floors and, finally, an open timber roof of collar beams, wind braces and rafters made from trees from the onetime royal forests.

Note the all-important **corner post,** the wall plates, peg-holes and slots, wattle and daub partition walls, panelling, the original windows and doorways and 15C staircase with oak stairtreads round a slim, one-piece **newel,** where the 500 year-old carpenters' adze marks remain visible on the beams.

★ **St John the Baptist.** – The church, on a mound on the north side of the square, was rebuilt in the Perpendicular style at the height of the town's prosperity in the early 15C: aisles, nave and transepts were built tall with wide windows, the crossing tower was raised to three stages and crowned with a pierced parapet and enriched pinnacles.

Inside, through the notable **south porch,** the eye is immediately attracted to the nave **ceiling** – a rare example in a church of the moulded plasterwork which decorates the great houses of the early 17C: George Drayton, a local craftsman, was paid ten guineas for the St John's roof in 1636. In contrast to the snowflake pattern, the crossing is fan vaulted with, hanging from the centre, a beautiful branched **candelabrum,** bought in Bristol in 1729 with the enamelled wrought ironwork above it, at a cost of 21 guineas.

Also of interest are 15C **font** with its circle of carved angels, hidden during the Commonwealth in a plaster casing and only rediscovered centuries later when a sexton, waiting for a baptism, iddly picked away some of the cracked plaster; the charity **bread cupboard** *(W of S door)*; the oak bier, the brass to Roger Harper (d 1493) and his wife *(S chapel)*; the **altar frontal** of 1710 embroidered with contemporary altar furnishings.

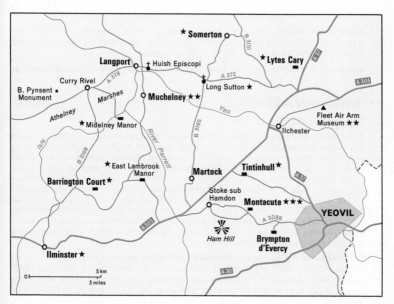

★ BARRINGTON COURT

Michelin map 403 fold 26 – L31 – 3½m NE of Ilminster

This is one of the countless beautiful houses built in 16C in Ham Hill stone which suffered decline and a long period of use and abuse as a farm and outbuildings before it was rescued... Now it stands proud once again: a mellow, honey, gold house, rising to spiral chimney stacks and as many as seven gables on one front, each topped and flanked by spiral shafts and shaggy ball finials.

tc **The garden.** – The garden on three sides, divided by walls and high hedges into rose, lily, iris and kitchen gardens, formal in design with pools and terraces, still bears the imprint of **Gertrude Jekyll** (1843-1932; *p 22*).

tc **The house.** – The house was constructed in 1550-60s, to the standard E plan with long outer wings enclosing a forecourt, and a slightly off-centre porch all facing south – the present, north, entrance is modern. Finialled gables, each advanced to a different degree, afford a lively skyline and provide an ever changing play of light and shadow. In 1920, the house which by then was a mere shell, was taken over by Col A A Lyle whose hobby was collecting oak panelling and interior fittings.

TOUR ½ hour

Great Hall. – The linenfold panelling is English, the screens doors and Italianate ceiling beams were from the Lyle collection, the Ham stone fireplace especially designed.

Staircase. – In the main staircase, which surrounds an open well, the bottom newel is 17C and provided the pattern for those which had to be made to complete the bannister. The splendid **timber ceiling** above is late 15C.

Library. – The room, probably at one time, the "best parlour", contains an original **overmantel** dating from *c*1625 and still with its early paintwork on the Ham stone, it shows the arms of the house's 17C merchant owner, William Strode and his wife.

Bedroom. – The bedroom, furnished with a Jacobean four-poster, contains a second 17C overmantel illustrating the *Judgment of Solomon*.

Kitchen. – The Tudor kitchen occupies the entire ground floor of the southwest wing. Note the baronial **fireplace** on the end wall with two 8ft long Ham stone lintels, each 3ft deep and 1ft thick which stand on the massive piers which also support the arch from which pots and kettles were hung over the fire. The charcoal **braziers** recessed below the left window were also used for cooking. The eight legged kitchen **refectory table** is 22ft long. Also in the kitchen is an exceptional collection of **pewter** – plates, chargers, lidded flagons and measures.
The fireplace is built against the wing's end wall; the flues are bent round to come out in chimneys on either side of the gable outside where for the sake of symmetry a dummy window was inserted in the wall (all visible from the garden).

Small Dining Room. – The room which is finely panelled, is remarkable for the inner wall of early 16C **latticed lights** and the wooden ceiling, which forms a deep honeycomb of star patterns. All is from a house in King's Lynn.

Buttery. – The outstanding Jacobean **panelling** was again from Col Lyle's collection.

★ BRIDGWATER   Pop 26 132

Michelin map 403 fold 26 – L30

Bridgwater was involved in the Civil War when its castle, under a Royalist governor and with a garrison of 2 000, was besieged, captured, slighted and the surrounding area set on fire: otherwise the town has progressed steadily from being a settlement at the first crossing point on the River Parrett, to Somerset's second largest town. In the earliest times it was surrounded on all sides by marshes, or "levels" as they are known locally, which the people drained by open ditches or "rhines" and traversed by log and brushwood surfaced tracks. By 1200 the town had a charter, by 1350 a population of 850, a castle, a church rebuilt on older foundations and a flourishing river port trade in saltfish, wine, iron, barley, wheat, peas and wood for dyeing cloth. In 18-19C the Bridgwater – Taunton Canal, the dock and quays were constructed only to be superseded by the railway.

The Battle of Sedgemoor. – **Monmouth**, the natural son of Charles II born in the Netherlands in 1649, returned four months after the death of his father in 1685, landing at Lyme Regis on 11 June with 82 followers. He proceeded to Taunton, where he was proclaimed king and advanced, gathering 5-6 000 followers, to Bristol, only to find the royal forces encamped before the city; he turned, fought a rearguard action at Norton-St-Philip, where he stayed at the George *(p 171-2)*, and, with his army reduced to 3 500, confronted the king's force less than three miles from Bridgwater in a night attack on Sedgemoor (6 July 1685).
The aftermath was more cruel than the two-hour battle in which 300 of Monmouth's men and 25 king's men died: summary execution was carried out on the rebels on the field and in the surrounding villages and within a week James II had despatched **Judge Jeffreys** (1648-89) on the notorious **Bloody Assizes** *(p 175)*. Monmouth himself was captured two days after the battle and executed on Tower Hill on 15 July 1685.

SIGHTS

West Quay. – The quay is overlooked by warehouses, a pub and 18-19C houses.

★ **Castle St.** – *Off the West Quay.* The town's most attractive street is lined by 18C houses built of brick with stone trims, segment-headed windows, pillared and pilastered doorways and parapets rising to the street's incline.

King Square. – At the top, on the site of the slighted 13C castle, is the never completed King Sq, comprising two sides of 18C houses and a much altered country farmhouse.

★ **St Mary's.** – The day before the battle, the **Duke of Monmouth** climbed 60ft red sandstone tower to survey through his spyglass (in the museum), the disposition of the Royalist troops camped on Sedgemoor.

The embattled **tower** belonged to an EE church of *c*1200. The Ham Hill stone **spire** was added in 1367 from monies collected in thankfulness at Bridgwater's not having been decimated by the Black Death; it took a year to build, cost £143 13*s* 5 ½*d* and stands, octagonal and distinctive, 113ft tall with 2ft 3in weathercock at the summit which served for centuries as a landmark to shipping on the Parrett.

Interior. – A late 17C Bolognese painting of the *Descent from the Cross* provides a striking altarpiece. Also of interest are the octagonal, rose decorated **font** of 1460, the Queen Anne **royal arms** of 1712 *(W wall)*, 15C **oak pulpit**, the former rood screen of 1420, now behind the choirstalls, the Jacobean **altar-table**, the marble monument in the chancel of Sir Francis Kingsmill (d 1620), leaning on one elbow.

★ **Admiral Blake Museum.** – *Blake St.*

tc The **Commonwealth Jack** flown by Admiral Robert Blake and adopted by the Commonwealth, flies above the museum, the house in which he was born in 1599. **Blake** entered parliament in 1640 where he joined the Commonwealth cause. He played an active part in the Civil War before, as General-at-Sea, embarking on a campaign against the Dutch admirals, Tromp, De Ruyter and De Witt, proceeding to do battle with pirates off North Africa and finally, sailing his fleet of 12 ships into Santa Cruz harbour, Tenerife. There he sank 16 Spanish galleons, sacked the port and set sail for Plymouth; he died entering the Sound on 7 August 1657.

In the museum are a diorama of the Battle of Santa Cruz and a quantity of Blake memorabilia including his sea-chest, compass and log-books.

Other galleries display, in a Shipping Room, models of all the sailing rigs in use in 19 and early 20C, Victorian bygones, mementoes of three Bridgwater families, topographical drawings and water colours.

An exhibit on the "levels" shows how the timber trackways crossed the marshes. The **Battle of Sedgemoor** is described in the Monmouth or Sedgemoor Room: there are pistols, swords, billhooks, armour, cannon balls, the spyglass *(see above)*, proclamations – £5 000 was offered by James II to anyone "Who shall bring in the person of James, Duke of Monmouth alive or dead".

EXCURSIONS

★★ **Stogursey Priory Church.** – *14m WNW by A39 and by-roads.*

tc **Coleridge Cottage, Nether Stowey.** – Pop 1 133. Coleridge lived from 1797-1800 with his wife, Robert Southey's sister, and small son in a cottage at the end of the village. It was then a pretty thatched cottage with "a clear brook" running before the door. One sees the former kitchen now furnished as the parlour containing mementoes, photographs and early editions of the poems and prose works. While at Stowey, Coleridge wrote *The Rime of the Ancient Mariner* and *Kubla Khan (p 172).*

Take a by-road N for 3m from the far end of Nether Stowey.

★★ **Stogursey Priory Church.** – *Pp 174-5.*

Barford Park. – *5m W by by-roads.*

Durleigh Reservoir. – The 80-acre lake is the haunt of waterfowl and migratory birds.

tc **Barford Park.** – The Queen Anne house, low-lying by comparison with the trees all round, is extended on either side by wings curving out from the centre. Inside, are earlier kitchens, a modern garden room and panelled and cornied rooms of 18C – hall, dining and big music room, highlighted by contemporary furniture, porcelain and silver.

In the **garden** the informality of a woodland walk contrasts with a semi-circular, walled garden bright with flowers and enlivened by peacocks.

Athelney Marshes. – *10m S by A372 and A361.*

Westonzoyland. – Pop 1 548. St Mary's, the Perpendicular parish **church ★★**, was the prison after Sedgemoor *(p 150)* for 500 of Monmouth's men, "of which", according to the parish register, "there was 79 wounded and five of them died of their wounds in our church". The splendid 15C **tower** rises by four stages to 100ft through a west doorway and window, two traceried bays and a triple-light, bell stage, to a crest of pierced battlements, pinnacles and sub-pinnacles.

Inside, the dark oak **roof**, a construction of braces and king-posts on crested beams, dressed overall with panelled tracery, mouchette bosses, pendant posts on bone thin beams, is everywhere aflutter with **angels** and **half-angels**...

Bear right at Ottery into A361.

Burrow Mump. – In this area of flat marshland and water meadows, Burrow Mump, a hillock of 250ft, is a major landmark.

A castle stood on the mump in 12C and before that possibly an Alfredian fort. Today what remains is a church tower, mediaeval in origin but altered in the early 18C.

Athelney Marshes. – The marshes may or may not be where **King Alfred** burned a cottager's cakes; what is certain is that it was his hidden retreat after his first running campaign against the Danish invaders and the place from where he advanced some months later to open the campaign which was ultimately to sweep them out of Wessex and subdue them across the greater part of England.

The first campaign began as a successful skirmish in December 870 only to be followed by defeat in 871, a victory at Ashdown in Sussex and further defeats. In 876 and 877 the Danes pillaged Wareham and Exeter; both towns were freed by Alfred who was then surprised at his palace in Chippenham (878). It was at this point that the King sought refuge in Athelney *(illustration p 181).*

In May 878 the king set out from the marsh, defeated the Danes at Edington *(p 192)* and signed the Peace of Wedmore *(see below)* which cleared the invaders from west of Watling St and had as a condition that Guthrum and 29 of his chief men accepted baptism. In 884, however, the Danes invaded again; at the same time Danes already settled in East Anglia rose; Alfred moved east. In 885 he recaptured London and signed a second treaty with Guthrum.

Never daunted the Danes returned in 890 and 894, the second time again investing Exeter which was freed by Alfred in what turned out to be the last major battle. Alfred the Great died, aged 53, in 901; he is buried at Winchester.

Broomfield. – *10m S and W by A38 and by-roads.*

North Petherton. – Pop 3 792. The **church tower**★★ is outstanding even for Somerset. It rises to 109ft, in silver-grey stone in three stages: a west door superimposed by a frieze and a large window with tracery at the transom as well as the apex; a three-light, decorated window; paired, bell openings and a panelled wall area. Finally, there is an embattled parapet from which pinnacles and sub-pinnacles fountain skywards.

Fyne Court. – The manor house was the residence of Andrew Crosse (1784-1855), a scientific investigator into the electricity of the atmosphere, who was known locally as the "Thunder and Lightning Man". The house, largely destroyed in a fire in 1898, is now the office of the **Somerset Trust for Nature Conservation.**

Broomfield. – Pop 202. The **Church of All Saints,** which has a grin of gargoyles and a modest three-stage tower was built in *c*1440 before the great tower rivalry began. Inside are yellow Ham stone columns and the original **wagon roofs,** supported by 47 angels. Note 16C bench-ends, Queen Anne's royal arms, and, in the porch, a list of charities which includes the provision of free tools to honest workmen who had not pawned previous gifts! The kitchen type table *(by S door)* with a copper band across it was Andrew Crosse's workbench; his obelisk memorial stands in the churchyard.

BRYMPTON d'EVERCY

Michelin map ▨▨▨ fold 27 – L31 – 2m SW of Yeovil

tc Brympton d'Evercy, a house of Ham stone with slate and stone tile roofs, is attractive not least in the contrast between its west, entrance front, which is Tudor, and the south front, which is late 17C and strictly regular. Surrounding the entrance forecourt are 14C parish church and stables.

The house's history is a saga of construction, devotion, decline and rescue repeated now for the third time since the original Evercys purchased the property in 18C. Note in the great **entrance hall** the rug made after an old engraving of the estate and the **needlework hanging** of the family tree.

BURNHAM-ON-SEA   Pop 14 920

Michelin map ▨▨▨ fold 26 – L30

Two special recollections remain after a visit to the seaside resort on the Bristol Channel: the lighthouses *(pp 16,17)* on stilts and the Grinling Gibbons carvings.

The Lighthouses. – In the shallows on the seven mile beach, beyond the sunbathers, sand-castle builders and donkeys, there stands a lighthouse on stilts – a pair with one behind on the sand dunes; in line, they serve as a navigation bearing for ships in the channel; both are vertically striped red and white, the upper one shows a light.

The Parish Church. – St Andrew's stands just back from the beach, its 14-15C **tower** noticeably "leaning" out of the vertical. Inside are a delightful gathering of **cherubs** and two expressive **angels** carved by **Grinling Gibbons** (1648-1700) and Arnold Quellin, for the Whitehall Palace chapel. After the palace fire of 1698, the altarpiece found its way to Westminster Abbey before being transferred, in part, to Burnham in 1820.

EXCURSION

Wedmore. – Pop 2 758. *9m E on the Wells rd B3139.*
The village, with its lantern-headed market cross, is historic as the signing place of the treaty between King Alfred and the Danes in 878 AD *(see above).*
The crossing **tower** of the Perpendicular **Church of St Mary Magdalene** was inspired by that of Wells Cathedral. Inside, the tower **roof** is fan vaulted, the pulpit Jacobean, the **wall painting** of St Christopher 16C and the **chandelier** 18C.

CHARD   Pop 11 797

Michelin map ▨▨▨ fold 26 – L31

The town has long been known as a market centre: for tanning in 13C, wool cloth in 15C, coarse linens, cloths and serges for the East India Co in 17-18C, lace early in 19C and now engineering, food processing, textiles and animal feed.

Fore St. – The main street and High St, reflect the town's 17-19C prosperity in a number of substantial Georgian houses and public buildings: the town hall of 1834 with a two-storey portico; the **George Hotel;** the Elizabethan **Manor Court House** built partly of flint, the adjoining Waterloo House. Finally there is the Grammar School *(E end, N side),* which, when it was founded in 1671, took over a house of 1583.

St Mary the Virgin. – The church, which lies south of the main street in the oldest part of the town, reflects local wealth in 15-16C, notably in the tower. This rises to a two-light bell opening filled with Somerset tracery, battlements and pinnacles.

EXCURSIONS

★ **Cricket St Thomas Wildlife Park.** – *3m E by A30. Pp 154-5.*

★ **Clapton Court Gardens.** – *11m ESE by A30 and B3165.*

Crewkerne. – Pop 5 340. The town centres on the wide Market St and the **Market Sq,** overlooked by the Jacobean-style Victorian Hall and Georgian houses.

The **parish church** ★ is a Perpendicular rebuilding with immense windows, of an older church. At the time of rebuilding the substantial piers at the crossing were kept to support a new 80ft tower which includes Somerset traceried bell openings extending through two stages to gargoyles, pinnacles and a pinnacled stair-turret. Battlements and gargoyles appear along the main rooflines and gargoyles in close frills around the twin, **octagonal turrets** which mark the west front.

Inside, the piers are tall and slim beneath a wagon roof on angel figures while the north transept and chapel have rich, panelled ceilings. Beneath the tower there is a fan vault. Note, at the west end, the early 19C galleries, the square, Purbeck marble font which is Norman and in the chancel, on the south wall, a brass to Thomas Golde, a knight of 1525, at prayer.

★ **Clapton Court Gardens.** – The ten acre garden comprises formal terraces, spacious lawns,
tc a rockery, rose and water gardens and a woodland garden with natural streams and glades.

With flowers in bloom throughout the spring and summer and the colours of the trees in the autumn, Clapton Court is a garden for all seasons. Many seats allow one to appreciate vistas, colours, scents, at leisure.

★ **Forde Abbey.** – *Dorset. 4m SE on S bank of the R Axe. Pp 133-4.*

★★ CHEDDAR GORGE

Michelin map **403** fold 27 – L31

The "deep, frightful chasm in the mountain, in the hollow of which the road goes" as Defoe described it 18C, has been a tourist sight since 17C.

★★ The GORGE *car and coach parks near the bottom*

The gorge, which is two miles long, is 1:6 gradient – come down it, for preference. Wide and squeezed narrow by turns, is twists and turns in its descent from the high Mendips. The cliffs are of limestone, lush with greenery in places, gaunt and grey where the fissured walls and pinnacles rise vertically 350-400ft. From its course, the rift must once have been a river-bed – it is even believed that Cheddar may have been used as a quay by barges taking lead down from the Mendips by way of the Rivers Yeo and Axe to Uphill on the Severn, from where the Romans shipped it to Italy.

tc **Jacob's Ladder.** – From almost the foot of the gorge a staircase of 322 steps *(rest benches)* leads up to the plateau level from which there is a panoramic **view** ★ of the Mendips, the Somerset moors and the Quantocks.

★★ The CAVES *time: 2 hours*

The caves are near the gorge bottom on the east side *(right going up).* Cox's Cave was discovered in 1837 by George Cox when quarrying limestone, Gough's Cave, in 1890, by Richard Cox Gough. Both caves were opened to the public soon after their discovery. The series of chambers follow the course of underground streams through the porous limestone; the formations increase by 1 cubic inch in every 400 years.

tc **Gough's Cave.** – The stalagmites and stalactites, the lace curtains, frozen falls and pillars coloured by the minerals in the limestone, are every one a different, glistening hue from white to alabaster, amber, rust-red (iron), green (manganese) and grey (lead). Among the fancifully named, but nonetheless beautiful formations are the nine-tier Fonts, the Swiss Village and Aladdin's Cave, both with mirror pools, King Solomon's Temple with its stalagmite cascade and the blue spotlighted, Black Cat – the only feature in the caves not lit with a white light.

tc **Cox's Cave.** – Among the formations note the Transformation Scene, the Marble Curtain, the ringing stalactites known as the Peal of Bells and the Speaker's Mace.

tc **Fantasy Grotto.** – The cave, by contrast is hocus-pocus with fountains, coloured lights and melodramatic, moving models.

tc **Museum.** – Weapons, utensils in flint, bone and antler horn, iron and bronze, pottery and the skull of Cheddar Man indicate that the caves were inhabited intermittently from the Palaeolithic to the Iron Age – 20000-500 BC – and even Roman times.

The TOWN

The town (pop 3 798) straggles from the foot of the gorge, through a crossroads-square to the parish church at the far end of the main street.

tc **Chewton Cheddar Cheese Dairy.** – To the rear of the shop a demonstration factory shows cheese-making from the vat being filled with milk, starter and rennet to curd cutting, pressing and the bandaging of the cheese truckles – Henry II bought 80cwt of cheddar in 1170AD declaring it to be the "best cheese in England".

The Market Cross. – The cross was originally a preachers' cross around which a hexagonal colonnade was built in 16C, converting it into a market centre for which travelling merchants paid rent to sit under cover.

Hannah Moore's Cottage. – *Venn's Close.* The cottage *(not open)* is where Hannah Moore, writer and philanthropist (1745-1835), who spent her later life improving the physical and mental welfare of the people of the Mendips, opened her first school.

★ **St Andrew's.** – The Perpendicular church, the fourth on the site, dates from 1380-1450. The typical Somerset **tower** rises 110ft through four stages from a west door and window, flanked by carved heads believed to be those of Henry V and Queen Catherine, to a window between the Annunciation figures of the Archangel Gabriel and the Virgin, a second two-light window and a bell stage; finally there are a pierced parapet with enriched pinnacles and a staircase turret with a spirelet roof.

Inside are coffered **oak roofs** on arch braces supported on **corbels** carved with kings' and bishops' heads – possibly an allusion to Mendip Forest having been a royal manor until sold by King John in 1204.

Among the furnishings are an early 14C **font** with a Jacobean cover, 15C stone **pulpit** coloured as in mediaeval times, an **altar-table** of 1631, the tombchest and large brasses of Sir Thomas Cheddar and his wife (dd 1443, 1460) and, in 15C Fitzwalter Chantry *(off S aisle),* a pre-Reformation **altar-stone** and a painting of *The Last Supper* by Jan Erasmus Quellinns of Antwerp (1629-1715).

EXCURSION

★★ **Axbridge.** – *3m NE; bear left off the by-pass (A371) ½m before the village. P 148.*

★★ CLEEVE ABBEY

Michelin map 403 fold 26 – J30

tc The red sandstone abbey ruins are particularly interesting since they comprise the buildings most often destroyed, the monks' quarters.

Cleeve was colonised by an abbot and 12 monks in 1198 when building began on the church. Construction was in two main phases: 1198-1297 and 1455-1537. In the first phase the community increased to nearly 30 monks, a pilgrimage chapel was built at Blue Anchor *(p 169)* and land in the area was brought under cultivation; the second phase was a period of renewal and improvement verging on the luxurious with the provision of sets of rooms decorated with wall paintings for the monks. All was abrogated at the Dissolution.

TOUR ½ hour

Go through the two-storeyed gatehouse and across the 3-acre outer court to what was the west end of the priory church and now exists only as footings; walk up the nave and through the arch just before the south transept.

The Cloister. – Despite the destruction of all but one arcaded wall along part of the west gallery, the enclosed feel of the cloister remains with the church occupying one side and the high dorter and frater ranges still standing on the east and south sides. Note the **collation seat** in the centre of the church wall, from where the abbot presided over the reading before Compline.

The dorter range. – The doorways led, respectively, to the **library**, the **chapter house**, the parlour and the slype or passageway to the commonroom *(sharp right).*
Mount the stairs to the dormitory or **dorter**, a vast room, 25ft across and 137ft long. It was built to accommodate 36 monks, had a lime and mortar floor supported on the vaulting of the ground floor rooms and was lit by lancets. Note the night stair into the church *(left of the two doorways in N wall).*

The frater range. – The range is 15C rebuilding of an earlier construction.
The original refectory, of which the splendid **tiled pavement** remains, lay on the far side of the range *(go through the barrel vaulted passage at the corner).*
The tiles, from their heraldry, date from 1272-1300 and show in still bright red, yellow, black and white, in three main compartments, the **three leopards** of England as borne by Henry III (1216-72), the **lion** of Poitou and **border** of Cornwall of Richard, Earl of Cornwall (1209-72, second son of King John) and his son, Edmund – both abbey benefactors – the **double-headed eagle** of Richard who also held the title King of the Romans, the central **diamond** of Cornwall flanked by those of England...
Return to the cloister.
The later **frater**, through the wide 13C doorway and up the stairs, is a hall 51ft long by 22ft wide, lit by 9 transomed windows with traceried heads – note how the north windows are blank below, where the cloister roof once abutted the wall.
The outstanding feature of the hall is the **roof**, a great timber construction, supported on stone corbels, with archbraced collars, trusses, purlins, richly moulded and further decorated with 50 deeply undercut, foliated bosses and crowned angels. The roof is unfinished, being intended as a boarded-in barrel; also it was never painted.
The lobby at the top of the stairs opens onto an office while the gallery alongside the cloister wall leads to small rooms decorated with still visible wall paintings.

★ CRICKET ST THOMAS Wildlife Park

Michelin map 403 fold 26 – L31

Cricket St Thomas lies amidst the rolling south Somerset countryside, extending along the banks of a tributary of the River Axe and up towards Windwhistle Hill.

tc **The house, church and gardens.** – The early 19C colonnaded house (not open), and the small church, are fronted on the river side by trees, tall dark hedges and flower gardens as decorative and brilliant as the free-flying macaws.

The animals. – The animals – elephants, lynxes, leopards, servals, monkeys, deer, wallabies, llamas (the females produce 6½-9lbs of wool a year), sheep, camels, wapiti and sea-lions, birds and reptiles, are in enclosures in the house and church area, in the old walled vegetable garden and in large paddocks on either side of the stream. Cows from the home farm are milked each afternoon in the **milking parlour** off the walled garden *(enquire as to time)*.
There is also a **Heavy Horse Centre** with working shires at the far right end of the park.

★ **Country Life Museum.** – *Off the walled garden.* The specialised collection comprises hand tools from Somerset, Dorset and Wiltshire displayed to show the local differences in shape and set of spades used in land drainage and the cutting of rhines in Somerset and Wiltshire, in peat cutting in Dorset, the Shetlands and the Western Isles, in foot, breast, and animal drawn ploughs, in bill-books and trimming hooks, in shepherds' crooks...

★ DOWNSIDE ABBEY

Michelin map 403 fold 27 – M30 – Stratton-on-the-Fosse

Downside is the senior Benedictine monastery in England.
The Community of St Gregory the Great was founded in 1605-7 at Douai in northern France by English and Welsh Benedictine monks who had been trained abroad since the Reformation. Among their number were priests who travelled to England on missionary work.
In 1793 Douai University was suppressed by the French Revolution, the Benedictines were put under guard and the monastery was ransacked. Although Catholicism was still officially proscribed in England, the penal laws were not being enforced and in 1794 the Community crossed the Channel and, after a brief interval, settled (1814) at Stratton-on-the-Fosse.
The community today numbers 50 members; the school about 550 boys. The buildings, which include 17-18C mansion, known as Old House, have multiplied in every architectural style current in the last 150 years *(not open)*.

★ The ABBEY ½ hour

tc The abbey church, built between 1870 and 1938 is steadfastly neo-Gothic in style, only the tower, which rises to 166ft taking cognisance of the Somerset tower tradition. The proportions inside are cathedral like, the French 13C style rib vaulting being 74ft high, the length 330ft. Colour is provided by the windows, pictures and statuary.

North Transept. – The transept contains the altar and shrine, a gilt oak casket, of **St Oliver Plunkett,** hanged in 1681, the last Catholic to die at Tyburn. Note the windows with St Aldhelm and St Dunstan.

Holy Angels Chapel. – The Flemish school triptych of the *Adoration of the Magi,* is 16C.

St Placid Chapel. – Note the old oak **statue** of the Madonna, a Spanish 16C **reliquary** and a very old oak **statue** (copy) of the Notre Dame de Foi of Dinant, Belgium.

St Sebastian Chapel. – A 15C Italian painting of a bishop hangs in the chapel by Sir Ninian Comper (1864-1960).

St Sylvia's Chapel. – The chapel contains a modern relief of the Crucifixion.

Lady Chapel. – The all-gold chapel was decorated by Sir Ninian Comper.

Sacred Heart Chapel. – The ceramic panels are again modern.

St Benedict's Chapel. – The **ivory figure** on the Crucifix is attributed to Andreas Faistenberger (1646-1735); the **bosses** on the groined vault depict the arms of the 54 Benedictine abbeys and priories Dissolved by Henry VIII.

South Aisle. – Both the **Virgin and Child,** from the Upper Rhineland, and the statue of **St Peter** *(W end)* are believed to date from 15C.

★★ DUNSTER   Pop 793

Michelin map 403 fold 25 – J30

Dunster is a singular old town in a beautiful setting on the northern edge of Exmoor. Its name derives from *torre*, a fortified tower, and *dun* or *dune*, a ridge of hills; its landmark is the Conygar Tower, an embattled folly, high on a hilltop; its cipher, the dormered Yarn Market which stands in the centre of the High Street.
Dunster had developed by 1197 into a chartered borough with a flourishing coastal and continental trade exchanging beans and barley for Bordeaux, Spanish and Italian wine and Welsh wool; by 15-16C the sea had retreated – it is now two miles distant – and the town had become a wool market and weaving centre.

★★ The CASTLE

tc The red sandstone castle, high on its tor, dominates the town, its rugged appearance of towers and battlements belying its age but not its history: a fortification has stood on the site for over 1 000 years. In Saxon times the hilltop probably served as a frontier fortress against the Celts and Northmen. The present castle, however, is very largely 19C.

The de Mohuns and the Luttrells. – Two families only have owned the castle throughout the centuries: William de Mohun (d 1155), who accompanied the Conqueror and was rewarded with the office of Sheriff of Somerset, built a Norman style fortress upon the tor and a priory in the town. By 1374, however, the de Mohun line was dying out and the castle, three manors and a hundred were sold for 5 000 marks (£3 333) to Lady Elizabeth Luttrell. After possession by successive Luttrells who preferred action on the field and in politics to husbandry in Somerset, the castle in the late 16C came to George Luttrell who reconstructed the residential quarters within the mediaeval walls and in the town, rebuilt the Yarn Market and remodelled the Luttrell Arms.

17-19C. – The castle defences were put to the test in the Civil War: first Thomas Luttrell, a Parliamentary sympathiser capitulated, paid a fine and allowed the Royalists to occupy the stronghold; then, in 1645 Robert Blake *(p 151)* laid siege to it until after 160 days, peace was negotiated. Parliament gave orders that Dunster was to be slighted: the curtain walls fell but destruction of the house and gateways was stayed – the owner paid a hefty fine and swore allegiance to Cromwell.

A new phase opened in the late 17C when **Col Francis Luttrell** and his rich bride, Mary Tregonwell of Milton Abbas, Dorset *(p 135)*, inherited the castle. They spent extravagantly on clothes and on the decoration of the house; but in 1690 the colonel died and all work ceased.

Apart from construction of the **Conygar Tower** folly in 1765, little was done until 1867 when **George Fownes Luttrell** inherited 15 374-acre property. He promptly called in the architect, **Anthony Salvin**, to enlarge and reconstruct the castle to its present appearance of a fortified Jacobean mansion.

Tour ¾ hour

The Gatehouse. – Walk through the gatehouse, which is 15C and was part of the mediaeval castle, and the forecourt, formerly the castle lower ward.

The Halls. – The combination of periods of construction evident throughout the castle begins in the first hall, which was created in 19C.

The portrait of **Oliver Cromwell** is contemporary, the wooden overmantel a Jacobean pastiche.

The second, **inner hall,** is 16-17C adaptation of the mediaeval castle's great hall, complete with the original Jacobean spider-web **plaster ceiling** and **overmantel**, decorated with the Luttrell arms. On the wall between the hall archways hangs an **allegorical portrait** (1550) by **Hans Eworth** of *Sir John Luttrell*, in which, like a triton, he dominates the Scottish storm or forces who had opposed Henry VIII.

Dining Room. – The panelled room displays one of the most beautiful moulded **plaster ceilings** in southwest England. It was installed in 1681 by Col Francis and Mary Luttrell *(see above)* whose portraits hang over the fireplace and whose arms are displayed in the frieze. Adjoining is a small panelled **serving room** with another remarkable **ceiling.** The black lacquer long-case clock has 1730 movement.

Grand Staircase. – The staircase with another great **ceiling**, forms the climax of Francis and Mary Luttrell's alterations: the stairs rise in three shallow flights around a square well; a flower-filled vase stands on each newel post, a handrail frames the 4in thick elm **balustrade**, carved and pierced to illustrate a swirling pattern of acanthus leaves and flowers, inhabited by cherubs and hounds at the chase – a pile of Charles II silver shillings dates the carving as 1683-4. The portrait of an unknown *Young Cavalier* is by Edward Bowyer *(pp 46, 61)*.

Upper rooms. – After the stairhall, the upper rooms are an anti-climax except for the **views★** from the windows. Among the furnishings, nevertheless, are late 18C **mahogany seat furniture** reputed to be by Thomas Chippendale (Morning Room), hand tooled and coloured **leather wall hangings** depicting the meeting of Antony and Cleopatra, the former moustachioed and both ringletted and costumed in 17C fashion (Gallery), 1620 overmantel illustrating the *Judgment of Paris* (King Charles' Room), a great arched fireplace in the Billiard Room and late-18C satinwood tables and painted seat furniture (Drawing Room).

(National Trust / J Gibson)

The Luttrell Staircase

Circle the castle and walk down through the gardens beside the R Avill or, if the castle is closed, along Church St, West St and Mill Lane to the mill.

★ **Dunster Castle Water Mill.** – The mill machinery runs throughout the open hours. The mill, rebuilt and improved at intervals since Domesday, ground corn until the late 19C when it was abandoned. In 1939-45 it came back into temporary wartime use;

in 1979-80 it was rebuilt and restored by the present tenants – a task involving re-roofing with 20 000 random Delabole slates *(p 71)*, copper nails and roof lead, re-making the overshot water-wheels, rebalancing the phospher-bronze bearings, re-dressing the stones... a modern saga of 12 months' work, applied knowledge and craftsmanship.

Water power. – The diagram is applicable to all water-wheels and to windmills with the obvious difference that in the latter the main vertical shaft is powered from above. At Dunster the two overshot water-wheels, both fed by the one chute controlled by a sluice gate (1), are 12ft in diameter by 3ft 6in wide, with oak spokes and shrouds and 40 elm wood buckets each holding about 10 gallons of water (100lb approx); 16 buckets are full at one time so that each side of the wheel carries just under 1 ton of water; it turns 4-6 times a minute.

The **pit wheel** (2) turns the wallower (3) and main vertical shaft 4 times to the water-wheel's once; the **spur wheel** (4) with applewood cogs, drives the stones' gear 7 times faster – the running stone, therefore, turns 4 × 4 × 7 or 112 times a minute to produce 1cwt of flour in 15-20 mins or 1½ tons a day per pair. Mills often used one pair of stones for flour, a second for animal feed.

WATERMILL

BIN FLOOR

STONE FLOOR

GROUND FLOOR

Belt

Grain

Main vertical shaft

Vibrating shoe

Running stone

Bed stone

Grain

Flour

Water chute

Water wheel

The **stones**, 4ft across, each have an "eye" and one also a "swallow", to receive the grain from the runner; both are "dressed" or "feathered" and "furrowed" – a highly skilled incising to reduce, grind and finally expel the flour.

Mill-stones were made of one piece or of many lumps or burrs of particularly hard rock, principally from quarries in Derbyshire. The burrs would be fitted together and bound with a number of iron hoops which would be put on white hot. As the hoops cooled they cinched the rock into a solid mass; as the stones wore down the hoops would be removed – old mill-stones, sometimes seen in farmyards, are often quite thin. Note how quietly the mill runs.

Before returning to the town, turn left off Mill Lane to go through the car park.

Ahead may be seen the twin arched **packhorse bridge** leading to the open Exmoor countryside.

The TOWN

High St. – The long, very wide street, characterised by the unique yarn market, is bordered on either side by 17-19C houses with shops on the ground floor.

Yarn Market. – The octagonal, dormered market was most recently rebuilt in 17C.

Luttrell Arms. – The inn dates back to *c*1500. Inside all still centres on the **Great Hall** with its hammer beam roof, twelve-light window and huge fireplace with 17C overmantel.

tc **Molly Hardwick Doll Collection.** – *Memorial Hall, right side.* Among the 700 dolls, some date back two centuries.

Church St. – The street is marked by buildings related to the priory founded in 1090 *(see above)* and Dissolved in 1539.

Nunnery. – The so-called building, slate roofed with slate-hung floors above a stone ground floor, dates in part from 14C when it was built as the priory guest-house.

Priest's House. – The half-timbered house of the same date was over-restored in 19C.

★ **Dovecote.** – The dovecote, which stands beyond the gate in the end wall of the Priory Garden behind the church, is a 20ft high, early mediaeval pigeon house, round in shape with a conical slate roof.

Inside are over 500 L-shaped **nest holes** set in 4ft thick stone wall. They are reached by a **ladder** attached to two arms fixed to a central, 400 years' old **pole** made of ash. A 3in long, solid metal cone has been lodged at the pole base enabling it to revolve upon 7in, dome-headed pin set in the oak floor beam. At the top a pin protrudes from the pole to revolve in a replaceable oak shoe fastened to the exact centre of the cross-beam.

Pigeons pair for life and have a breeding life of 7 years; for most of the year, the breed kept for food layed and hatched two eggs every 6 weeks; the squabs were removed at 6 weeks when they weighed 16oz. Meat production, in a good year, could have amounted to 3 tons.

★ **St George's.** – The red sandstone parish church of early Christian origin was rebuilt by the monks in the Norman style, then again in 15-16C in the Perpendicular style. A contract of 1443 remains for 110ft **tower** which stipulated that it should have a "batylment and pynacles... three french botras (buttresses) and gargoyles", all of which it duly has. A carillon plays different tunes at 9am, 1, 5 and 9pm each day.

Interior. – Inside are **wagon roofs** and a 54ft screen which extends across the nave and aisles to divide the church in two – a deliberate contrivance ordered by Glastonbury in 1498 to settle a long running dispute between the priory and the parish.

The **screen** is a quite splendid example of local carving with blank panels below cusped and traceried openings separated by slender columns which open out into a strongly sinewed fan vault and richly carved friezes. Being not a rood in origin, it survived both Parliamentarians and Puritans.

Note also 16C Perpendicular **font** with quatrefoils carved with Christ's wounds; 18C **chandelier** and its wrought iron suspension; the three 12-13C iron-bound chests *(S aisle, E end)*; the Charles II royal arms; 19C bench-ends; 20C reading desk and, among the **funerary monuments**, a lady of *c*1300 in a wimple beneath a canopy *(chancel)*, the gravestone with a foliated cross of Adam de Cheddar, Prior of Dunster *c*1345-55 *(S transept)*, 20in brass of John Wyther (d 1497) and his wife *(nave, W end)*, a Jacobean tomb of 1621 and the Luttrell tombs, notably that of 1428.

EXCURSIONS

★★ **Cleeve Abbey.** – *5m SE on A39. P 154.*

Combe Sydenham Hall. – *10m SE on A39 and B3188.*

tc The house, beyond the gatehouse which incorporates a stone arch believed to be of *c*1450, was built to a typical Elizabethan E shape by Sir George Sydenham, father of Elizabeth (d 1598, *p 84*), who Sir Francis Drake married as his second wife in 1585. Expansion, demolition, rebuilding, further neglect, sum up the history of the hall until its rescue by the present owners who are gradually restoring the house, gardens and grounds, the mill, trout stream, fishponds and a birds of prey care centre.

An earnest of the future can already be seen in the **Great Hall**, 18C staircase and panelled sitting room and in work begun on the Restoration banqueting room.

On the stone flags in the Great Hall is a cannon-ball which weighs over 100 lbs and may be a meteorite, but is known locally as **Drake's cannon-ball**. Legend has it that although Drake had wooed her before going to sea, Elizabeth Sydenham was at the church door when the ball hurtled through the air to fall between the would-be bride and stranger groom. Drake sailed into Plymouth on the next tide...

★★ **EXMOOR**
National Park

Michelin map **403** fold 25 – I and J30

The moor, within an area of 265 sq m, is very various in scenery and beautifully in scale: the bare, upland ridges, covered in blue moor-grass, bracken, deer sedge or heather, ripple away as far as the eye can see; here and there a great hollow opens out, a wide valley is enlivened by a stream trickling over the stones, a wooded ravine, silent except for birdsong and a rushing torrent, invite exploration.

Exmoor is the smallest of the National Parks extending into Devon along its western limits but lying for the most part in Somerset as a 1200-1700ft ridged plateau west of the Brendon Hills. Three of its rivers, descending 1500ft in 4 miles, drain into the Bristol Channel.

Exmoor Forest. – In the early Middle Ages the forest was one of many unenclosed, uncultivated tracts of land where game, notably red deer, was preserved for the royal hunt; by 1300 the Royal Forest had been reduced to 20 000 acres around the headwaters of the principal rivers; since 1508 much of the land has been leased out to pasture – as many as 30 000 sheep and additional cattle now graze it between March and October and ponies all the year round. The stock has always belonged to local farmers, for the moor has been settled since prehistoric times.

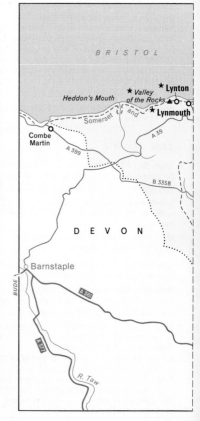

In 1818 the last 10 000 acres of the Royal Forest were sold at £5 an acre to John Knight, a Midlands ironmaster who set about revolutionising farming on the moor: by the end of the century a pattern had been set of isolated farmsteads breeding beef and sheep on the uplands for finishing in the valleys. Between 1800-1940, when agriculture everywhere in England sank into decline, the moor looked as though it would take over once more; since 1945 however, the pattern has resumed, with owner-occupiers and tenants farming 50-300 acres with flocks of breeding ewes and small herds of cattle.

The ponies. – The ponies, brown, bay or dun in colour, have a characteristic **mealy coloured muzzle** and inside ear. The quick intelligence and distinctive head show clearly the Exmoor pony's direct descent from the horses of prehistory.

The red deer. – The deer on Exmoor are also descendants of the animals of prehistoric Britain. It is estimated that there are now between 500-600 on the moor. They live in the woodlands close to the deeper river valleys and are wild, elusive and seldom seen.

The cattle. – The cattle, usually in herds of 25-30, are horned Devon Reds, known as the "Red Rubies" of the West Country.

The sheep. – The sheep, in flocks of 200-250, are for the most part the traditional Exmoor Horn breed or the Devon Closewool.

LANDMARKS, TOWNS, VILLAGES on the Moor

Allerford. – *P 169.*

Combe Sydenham Hall. – *P 158.*

Combe Martin. – *P 105.*

★ **Doone Valley.** – *Access from Oare: 6m on foot Rtn, 1½ hours.*
The valley came to fame with the publication in 1869, of R D Blackmore's *(p 117)* novel *Lorna Doone,* based on tales surrounding a group of outlaws and cut-throats who settled in the Badgworthy Valley in 1620s and were only expelled in 1690s. The path from Oare *(see below),* still trodden it is estimated by 30 000 visitors a year, passes beside **Badgworthy Water** and **John Ridd's Waterfall** to reach the coomb.

★ **Dulverton.** – Pop 1 301. Sited 450ft above sea level amidst beautiful scenery, the "capital" village of the area is characterised at one end by an upstanding **church** on a hillock with a plain 13C west **tower** (rest of the church rebuilt in 19C) and, at the other, by an old stone bridge with five arches between cutwater piers above the glittering River Barle. Between, the **main street** and **market square** are appointed with shops, 19C market-house, stone terrace houses, and colour-washed cottages, some thatched, others with broad chimneys built up from ground level. Along a back path to the church is a terrace of small Georgian houses.

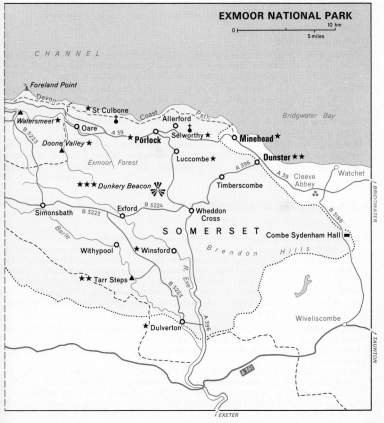

★★★ **Dunkery Beacon.** – *Access from A396: turn W into B3224 at Wheddon Cross, left then right to Dunkery Gate, then follow the path, 3m Rtn.*
The 1706ft beacon, the highest point on the moor, is visible for miles around and from its summit commands **views**★★★ of sixteen counties.

★★ **Dunster.** – *P 155.*

Exford. – Pop 409. The village is grouped around the central green with the occasional farmstead and cottage on the surrounding hillsides. It is the home of the Devon and Somerset Staghounds and at the centre of the hunting country.
The **church**★, to which the blacksmith in 1532 left £3 towards "the makying of an yled" – now the only ancient part of the building – contains 15C oak **rood screen** with panelled coving and a cornice of richly carved friezes, and 14C octagonal **font** with quatrefoils. The choirstalls were presented by Queens' College, Cambridge.

Heddon's Mouth. – *P 105.*

★ **Luccombe.** – Pop 179. The village, on the hills below Porlock, is a centre from which one can walk to the Dunkery Beacon *(see above)*, also along woodland paths to Webber's Post, a well known local viewpoint *(7m Rtn)*. It is attractive in its own right with cottages, shops, a post office and 16C Perpendicular **church**★ with a tall embattled tower and a barrel **roof**, decorated with large bosses carved with solemn faces.

★ **Lynmouth and Lynton.** – *P 104.*

Oare. – Pop 85. The village in a green valley only a couple of miles from the sea, owes its fame entirely to *Lorna Doone (see above)*. The 14-15C **church** with a tower rebuilt in the mid-19C when much else was restored, is the one in which John Ridd and Lorna Doone were married and the north window the one through which Carver shot at Lorna. Note the 18-19C **box pews, pulpit** and desk, 18C painting of Moses.
Blackmore's grandfather was a typical, mostly absent, rector of Oare in 19C.

★ **Porlock.** – *P 172.*

★ **Selworthy.** – *P 169.*

Simonsbath. – The village, the centre of John Knight and his son's operations in 19C *(see above),* stands on the River Barle where the Lynton road meets the main east-west road across the moor. The church, with its slate-hung west wall, the school, many of the houses, even the east windbreak of mature beech trees, owe much of their form to the Knights. The **hotel** was built as a royal hunting lodge.

★★ **Tarr Steps.** – *Access from B3223; parking only in carpark, then 6 minute walk down steep path – car turning point only at the bottom or continue through the ford.*
The finest **clapper bridge** in the country crosses the River Barle at the centre of an open, wooded valley. The 180ft causeway of 15 "arches" built of flat stones laid upon uprights in the stream bed with many of the stones weighing 2 tons or more and not local in origin, dates certainly from the early Middle Ages and probably centuries earlier. It has often been swept away by floodwaters and as often been rebuilt.

Timberscombe. – Pop 380. The village of reddish stone houses with slate roofs, straddling the A 396 just south of Dunster, has a Perpendicular **church**★ with an early 18C castellated west tower which was crowned in 19C with a pyramid roof. Inside, beneath the wagon roofs, note the **rood-screen** with carved dado, coving and cornice.

★ **Valley of the Rocks.** – *P 105.*

★ **Watersmeet.** – *P 105.*

Wheddon Cross. – The crossroads and minute village which stand at 1 200ft, the highest point reached by roads on the moor, are a good **vantage point**★ from which to view Dunkery Beacon *(3m W)*, the Brendon Hills and deep, wooded valleys.

★ **Winsford.** – Pop 340. Streams run on all sides through the village with the result that within yards there are **seven bridges**, the oldest being the **packhorse bridge** over the River Exe *(by the vicarage)*. The **green**, shaded by huge trees, is marked by old thatched houses and cottages and the Royal Oak which has a thatched roof which folds and turns as it tucks up every corner of the rambling old inn.

Withypool. – Pop 231. The centres of interest in the village, which stands beside one of the only two commons on the moor, are the church largely rebuilt in 1901 but with its ancient Norman font, and the old **bridge**, one of only four across the Barle.

★ **FARLEIGH HUNGERFORD CASTLE**

Michelin map **403** fold 27 – N30

tc The castle **ruin** stands guard on the Wiltshire-Somerset border.
In 1369-70, Sir Thomas de Hungerford, a Wiltshire squire and onetime Speaker of the House of Commons, bought Farleigh manor house which he fortified, transforming it into a rectangular walled castle with five-storey angle towers with conical roofs. In 1420-30, Sir Thomas's son increased the castle to the south by the addition of an Outer Court enclosed by a new wall, towers and the two-storey East Gate by which one still enters. Also enclosed by the new perimeter was 14C St Leonard's Chapel, formerly the parish church.

★ **St Leonard's Chapel.** – Go through 16C west porch and down the steps into the nave of 1350 where there are a chaplain's funerary stone of *c*1480, 12C font and, to the right of the east window, a giant **wall painting** of St George killing a no longer visible dragon.
Under the wide, semi-circular arch in the chantry chapel added by Sir Thomas in 1380-90, are the remarkable **Hungerford funeral monuments** of Sir Thomas and his wife (dd 1398, 1412), he in chain mail, she in a cloak and mantle and, just beyond, the Parliamentarian, Sir Edward Hungerford (d 1648) and his wife, very beautifully carved in white marble.

FROME

Michelin map **403** fold 27 – N30

SOMERSET

The town, at a crossing on the river of the same name, was from 685 AD until 19C an important market and wool cloth town.

Streets. – Market Place and Bath St, which lead up steeply from the bridge, are lined with shops beneath older 17-19C upper floors and skylines punctuated by gables. It is in the side streets, however, that the chief interest lies: in 18C houses and two and three house terraces; a **Blue Coat School** and **almshouses** of 1726; the picturesque **Cheap St** with 16-17C shops, lamp standards, bay windows, oversailing upper floors, swinging iron signs lining either side of the cobbled pathway divided at the centre by a swift running stream; the paved and winding **Gentle St** with larger 17-18C houses and a gabled 17C inn...

St John's. – The church, overlooking Cheap St and standing on a Saxon site, is 14-15C restored in 19C. The castellated **tower** and recessed octagonal **spire** are of the same date.

EXCURSION

★ **Farleigh Hungerford Castle. –** *11m. Take A361 going NE; bear left into A36; turn right opposite the Red Lion, Woolverton.*

tc **Tropical Bird Gardens, Rode. –** The 17-acre park and the wooded flower garden, which descend to a cascading stream, provide a setting for strutting ornamental pheasants, free-flying macaws, penguins and flamingoes and large aviaries containing more than 180 different species: there are eagles, owls and other birds of prey; finches and canaries; parrots, parakeets and cockatoos; birds from the jungle and from Pacific Islands...

Return to Woolverton and take B3110.

Norton St Philip. – *P 151.*

Take A366 due east.

★ **Farleigh Hungerford Castle. –** *P 160.*

★ GAULDEN MANOR

Michelin map **403** fold 35 – K30 – 9m NW of Taunton

tc Gaulden Manor, a two-storey 16C red sandstone manor house with quite exceptional **plasterwork** inside, stands between the Brendon and the Quantock Hills. It is surrounded by tall trees, an immense old monastic fishpond bordered by poplars and by individual small gardens, quiet, secret, shaded, brilliant with flowers or scented with herbs.

In 1560s the house was chosen, most understandably, as the place to end his days by **James Turberville**, Bishop of Exeter (d 1571), after he had refused to take the oath of supremacy to Queen Elizabeth I and suffered a spell in the Tower of London.

In 1618 the house and farm were bought by a mercer from Wellington, whose son, **Henry Woolcott**, emigrated to America in 1630 and founded a family which has since become so extensive that the members have formed a descendants' society.

In 1639 the bishop's great nephew, **John Turberville** repurchased the manor where although at first there was "scarce a chamber yet ready to lodge myselfe or my friends", he soon had it entirely refurbished and his arms implanted on the overmantels.

TOUR ½ hour

The porch and iron-studded oak door lead into the screens passage.

Dining Room. – The former kitchen has a huge fireplace complete with a bread oven and salt niche.

Throughout the house are choice pieces of **furniture** of all periods from 17C refectory tables to early ladder-back and Hepplewhite-style chairs, 16-17C and late-18C oak chests, English and Meissen **porcelain, modern needlework...**

Great Hall. – The hall has a splendid **plaster ceiling** of three garlanded roundels, the centre one descending in a solid ribbed pendant, the others showing reliefs of King David with his harp and an angel blowing the last trump. Round the room, a deep **frieze** continues the Biblical theme and, possibly in reference to Bishop Turberville's misfortunes, includes the scales of justice and a tower from which it has been surmised that the ceiling and frieze and the considerable decoration over the Tudor fireplace date from 16C although the decoration on the overmantel itself, since it shows John Tuberville's arms impaling those of his wife, is, obviously, 17C – if all the plasterwork is 17C it could have been done using older moulds.

At the far end of the room, 17C panelling and a line of lesser pendants, screen a smaller room with its own 16C fireplace, known as the chapel.

The Stairs. – As you mount the stairs with their original **oak treads**, note the old crooked **window** with bottle green glass which dates back to 17C.

Turberville Bedroom. – The room, records the house's 17C associations with the **Turberville arms** over the fireplace and a **Wolcott window** and brass plate. The mirror is by Chippendale.

*The **Maps Red Guides** and **Green Guides** are complementary publications. Use them together.*

★★★ GLASTONBURY

Pop 6 807

Michelin map **403** fold 27 – L30

Although there has only been a ruin on the site for the past four and a half centuries, the name immediately conjures up the great abbey, its existence for centuries as one of the richest houses in the land *(p 138)* and as a centre of learning.

The town which grew up round the abbey has never ceased to revolve around it.

★★★ The ABBEY

tc **Legend and history.** –
Glastonbury Tor and the Polden Hills were once islands rising out of the marshes which were connected by tidal channels to the open sea; by the Iron Age (450 BC) the hilltops were occupied by forts – the name Glastonbury means hillfort of the Glastings people – hut settlements being built above the waterline. Eventually timber trackways were laid across the "levels" *(p 175).*
The abbey foundation appears most likely to have been as 4-5C Celtic monastery and church – a supposition that by 12C had developed into a tale that it had been

(Pitkin Pictorial)

The transept piers

founded by St Patrick in person! Other legends developed: that Christ's disciples established the monastery and, most famous of all, that **Joseph of Arimathea** landed in Somerset one Christmas morning (some said returned, having come originally with the boy Jesus), bearing the Holy Grail. Joseph, according to the legend, set foot on a hill known as Avalon and later rested on a second hill, Wearyall, where he stood his staff upright in the ground; it promptly sprouted and flowered and has been known ever since as the **Glastonbury Thorn** – *Crateagus Praecox.* The original tree was cut down by the Puritans but descendants still bloom twice a year in December and May in the abbey grounds and in St John's churchyard *(see below).* Joseph was given land by the local ruler, Arviragus, and constructed a wattle and daub church on the site of the abbey Lady Chapel.
Another legend concerned **King Arthur** *(p 71),* who, it was claimed, after being mortally wounded at the Battle of Camlan in 537, sailed away to the island of Avalon or Glastonbury where his and Guinevere's bodies were "discovered" in the abbey cemetery in 1191 and re-interred in the chancel in 1278. The tomb survived until the Dissolution; the site is now marked by a plaque.
"Disputable matter", as William of Malmesbury *(p 197)* termed the various theories of the abbey's foundation when he began to write its history in 1120, is replaced by "solid fact" from 7C. In 688, **Ine**, King of the West Saxons, who had by then driven the Celts from Somerset, in consultation with **Aldhelm** *(p 196),* built an additional church to that already on the site; in 943 Dunstan was appointed abbot.
Dunstan was the son of a West Saxon noble and was born in *c*910 near Glastonbury where he was educated, before he entered the household of his kinsman, Athelstan (925-39), whose policy, in the tradition of Alfred, was the supremacy of Wessex against the Danes. When Dunstan lost favour at court, he went to Winchester where he became a Benedictine. Successive kings recalled him to court; appointed him abbot of Glastonbury which he enlarged and rebuilt spiritually and physically and which, during his abbacy (943-59) became famous as a centre of learning. He was recalled as a political administrator, suffered royal displeasure and outlawry before Edgar appointed him Bishop of Worcester of London, and in 961, Archbishop of Canterbury in which capacity he crowned **Edgar** first King of England in Bath Abbey (973). Edgar died and was buried at Glastonbury two years later.
The abbot appointed to Glastonbury after the Conquest considered the church inadequate for the richest abbey in the land and, in the manner of Norman prelates of the time, began to rebuild it. The task was completed by his successors only to be destroyed entirely in a fire in 1184. Rebuilding began immediately with the St Mary's or Lady Chapel, which was completed within two years, and then proceeded slowly over the next two centuries. It was at this period and that immediately following, that the abbacy was taken over by the ambitious Bishop Savaric (d 1205) of Bath and Wells and the abbey church declared to be a cathedral; it was also at this time that the abbey began to acquire vast manorial holdings *(p 138)* and great riches and that **Abbot Richard Bere** (1493-1524), who was a great populariser as well as a great churchman and builder, developed the cult of Joseph of Arimathea.
The Dissolution in 1539 brought annihilation: the abbot, Richard Whiting, despite having taken the Oath of Supremacy, was brutally executed with two brothers on Glastonbury Tor, the other forty-five monks and 120-130 lay servants were dispersed, the manors were confiscated and the buildings encouraged to fall into ruin.

162

TOUR ½ hour

The ruins, extending far across the lawns, stand tall amidst majestic trees. The tower piers, arches, south nave wall, even the relatively complete shell of the Lady Chapel, give no idea of what the abbey church must have looked like during the short years of its prime – the relics in their glorious setting, nevertheless, are unforgettable.

St Mary or **Lady Chapel.** – The chapel, in Doulting stone, has a **corner turret** and walls decorated with blind arcading and a modillioned cornice; the west end has three stepped lancets. The **doorways** are rounded, that to the north being enriched, possibly later, with **carved figures** of the Annunciation, the Magi and Herod.

The chapel stands on the site of the first wattle and daub church; all subsequent churches, including King Ine's (which measured 42ft), have been built to its east. Enter to see the embrasures with zigzag decoration and arcading, to glance into the St Joseph Crypt (c1500) and east through the arch in the chapel wall *(see below.)*

Nave. – Look east through the crossing tower piers to the distant chancel walls and the site of the Edgar Chapel beyond – the nave, chancel and retrochoir together measured 375ft, the full length of the abbey was 555ft – longer than Salisbury and Wells Cathedrals, shorter than Winchester.

Bishop Bere's rebuilding was completed in the early 15C with the construction of the **Galilee** which joined the main church to the Lady Chapel through the arch in the chapel wall.

The **Edgar Chapel**, a rebuilding of a mausoleum for the Saxon Kings, who the abbey also claimed as founders, was undertaken early in 16C.

Throughout, the style was Gothic which became slightly more ornamented with time; each area, shortly after it was completed, would have been painted directly on the stone. (A **scale model** in the museum gives an idea of the completed church.)

Abbot's Kitchen. – The 14C kitchen, the sole building to survive intact, is square with an eight sided roof rising to superimposed lanterns which served to draw the smoke from the corner fires in the kitchen up the flues in the roof.

Glastonbury Thorn Tree. – The large thorn tree *(labelled)* stands north of the abbey.

St Patrick's. – The church was built in 1512 to serve no longer extant almshouses.

The TOWN

The town comprises two principal streets, the High St and Magdalene St which intersect at the Victorian-Gothic, Market Cross.

Magdalene St. – The street contains a number of attractive, small 17-19C town houses. South of the abbey entrance are the pedimented town hall of c1814, the mid-18C Pumphouse *(not open)* from the days when Glastonbury aspired to be spa, and a group of mediaeval almshouses (restored) and 13C chapel.

St Benedict's. – The pinnacled tower glimpsed *(west)* at the top end of the street just before the market cross, belongs to a Perpendicular church of c1500. It was built on an older site by Bishop Bere, whose mitre and initials may be seen outside the north porch and whose rebus is carved on one of the roof **corbels** in the north aisle.

High St. – The street is overlooked by two buildings formerly connected with the abbey, the tribunal or old courthouse and a hotel, founded in 14C and nobly rebuilt in 15C by an abbot to ensure that there was suitable accommodation for the pilgrims, lawyers and other respected visitors to the abbey.

tc **The Tribunal.** – The building dates from 14C when it was timber fronted; the fine ashlar stone face, the canted bay, stone mullions and doorway were added by Bishop Bere in 1500; the latest additions were made in Elizabethan times when it had ceased to be abbey property. Today it houses a **museum** of excavated antiquities from the Iron Age **Lake Villages** *(p 175).*

The George and Pilgrims Hotel. – Interesting features of the hotel front include its actual height below the embattled roofline, the heavy **string courses** to emphasise the width of the building, the intricate, **panel style decoration** and asymmetrically placed **entrance** decorated with the abbey arms, those of Edward IV and one blank. Inside are the original **oak panelling**, beams, doorways, an early fireplace and old Dutch tiles.

★★ **St John the Baptist.** – The 134½ft **tower** of the church is one of the finest in Somerset with its "crown" of principal and secondary crocketed pinnacles which rise through buttresses and shafts from the lower stages to stand high above the battlements of two tiers of pierced arcading.

The church was rebuilt in 15C in part because of the collapse of the earlier, Norman, crossing tower. The **nave** of seven bays has a clerestory, making the interior "lightsome" as Leland declared, beneath its 15C Somerset oak **roof** on angel corbels.

Note especially the finely carved Charles II **royal arms**, the **chest** bought second hand in 1421, the **domestic cupboard** of 1500, **15C glass** *(chancel N window)*, 15C **tomb chests** of the wealthy cloth merchant, Richard Atwell, and his wife *(transepts)* and another with an alabaster effigy with angels and camels round the base.

In the churchyard is the **Glastonbury Thorn Tree** from which the Queen is sent a sprig in bloom each Christmas.

At the end of the High St turn right down A361 Shepton Mallet Rd-Lambrook-Chilkwell St; turn off right into Bere Lane; 550yds in all.

★★ **Somerset Rural Life Museum.** – The museum illustrates two aspects of rural life *tc* in 19C; dairy and outdoor work on the farm and the domestic daily life of an agricultural labourer.

The barn. – The barn measures 93 × 33ft and is small by comparison with many but the **stonework** and the **roof**, outside and in, make it outstanding.

The walls are buttressed, the ends gabled as are the transepts containing the massive, double doors; the windows at either end have intricate moulding; each gable is decorated with a roundel carved with the symbol of one of the evangelists and the point with an animal finial; above each corner buttress is a carved human head. The roof has always been stone tiled.

The interior is a skilled example of mediaeval carpentry in which superimposed cruck beams span the width and support the braces and laths which take the weight of the tiles.

In the barn and the adjoining byres are the wagons, ploughs, machines and tools which after centuries of slow development are now historic farm relics.

The house. – The house with its kitchen, larder and upstairs rooms filled with day-to-day items of life from the cradle to dead-cart, by way of school-desk and copybook, clothes, kettles, sugar cutters, ornaments, furniture, rag rugs, registry entries and photographs, presents John Hodge's long life in the village in heart-warming detail.

Return to Chilkwell St; turn right (250yds).

tc **Chalice Well and Gardens.** – The well, a natural spring pouring out 25 000 gallons of water a day at a constant temperature of 11°C – 52°F has long been associated with the abbey legend of Joseph of Arimathea who is said to have hidden the Grail or Chalice beneath the spring waters, whereupon they flowed red.

Wellhouse Lane, just beyond the well, leads to the Tor. Park the car at the bottom and take the steeper path or continue 250yds up the lane to the alternate path.

★ **Glastonbury Tor.** – Climb it if you can – it is a landmark visible for miles around and the sense of achievement as you continue to tour the county is ludicrously pleasurable! The Tor is 521ft high. The tower at the summit, is the last remnant of a Church to St Michael, built in 14C on a hillfort and Saxon church site.

On a fine day, the **view** ★★★ includes the Quantocks and Bristol Channel *(WNW);* the Mendips – Wells Cathedral, 5m, *(NNE);* the Marlborough Downs and possibly Salisbury *(ESE);* and the Polden Hills *(SW).*

EXCURSION

★ **The Shoe Museum, Street.** – Pop 8820. *2m SW on A39.*

tc In a setting of lawns, trees, a clock tower and a Henry Moore bronze sculpture, near the centre of the town, stands Clark's Shoe Factory founded in 1825. In the oldest part of the factory are displayed hand-tools for making shoes, 19C machinery, fashion plates and showcards, tally books and a collection of shoes from Roman times to the present: button boots, dancing slippers, postillions' boots, children's shoes...

In the town *(between the shopping centre and car park)* is a modern stone mosaic-mural of familiar heights, towers and the landscape of central Somerset.

HATCH COURT

Michelin map **403** fold 35 – L31 – Hatch Beauchamp, 6m SE of Taunton

tc The square Georgian house of Bath stone, graced by a tall arcade of columns at the top of a shallow flight of steps, small end pavilions with pyramid roofs and a pierced balustrade, dates from 1755. It was designed by Thomas Prowse, MP, a substantial landowner and amateur architect.

In front is a small park with a herd of fallow deer. There is no association with Jane Austen but it once proved a perfect setting in which to film one of the novels.

TOUR ½ hour

Hall and Staircase. – The hall is planned with great style to lead through a screen of fluted Ionic columns to the **staircase** which rises to a half-landing where it divides and returns; the **landing** above, columned, triple-arched and with a groined vault, sweeps round behind a curved balustrade.

Note in the hall, 9ft 6in **oak table** of *c*1630 and rare, contemporary **walnut benches**.

Drawing Room. – The room possesses its original **plasterwork ceiling**. The Japanese silk embroidery of peacocks is 19C.

Library. – The **bookcases** follow the line of the walls in a graceful arc.

Orangery. – The gallery is curved to enhance the house's exterior appearance.

Museums. – Two rooms, converted into small museums, contain **English fine china** including a dark green set of Minton dessert plates with birds in white relief, and mementoes of **Princess Pat's Regiment** (Princess Patricia's Canadian Light Infantry) and of early aviation.

St John the Baptist's. – The church behind the house was rebuilt on an older site in 15-16C when it was given its embattled tower of blue lias which is overtopped by its stair turret and the surrounding trees.

Join us in our never ending task of keeping up to date.

Send us your comments and suggestions, please.

Michelin Tyre Public Limited Company
Tourism Department
81 Fulham Road, LONDON SW3 6RD.

HIGH HAM
Pop 722

Michelin map 403 fold 26 – L30

The village, which stands 300ft above the surrounding Sedgemoor levels, is reached by a series of short climbs; on the way and from the village itself there are **views**★★ of the Polden and more distant Mendip Hills *(NE)*, Bridgwater Bay and the Severn Estuary *(NW)*, the Quantocks *(WNW)*, Taunton Vale *(WSW)* and even of Dunkery Beacon on Exmoor.

At the centre is the **village green**, shaded by tall trees and overlooked by a scattering of stonebuilt 17-18-19C houses and the parish church.

★ **St Andrew's.** – The church is notable for its high **clerestory**, a run of wide Perpendicular windows above the battlements and **gargoyles** which mark the aisle roofs – among the gargoyles are a fiddler, a piper and a trumpeter, a listener with his hand behind his ear, a stone thrower and a chained monkey nursing a baby.

The embattled tower is 14C whilst the remainder of the building "was builded anew from the foundation and finished within the space of one yeare, 1476".

Interior. – With so many windows, the **roof** above the nave can be clearly seen with its tie-beams, king posts, bosses and arched braces rising from angel figures. The high **oak screen** which widens out into a panelled coving and ornate cornice, was carved by Glastonbury monks in the early 16C.

Note also the Ham stone **pulpit** of 1632; the **lectern** with turned balusters and linenfold panelling; 15C **poppyhead pews** and round Norman **font** with cable moulding.

tc **Windmill.** – ½m E along Stembridge rd.

The mill of 1822, which worked until 1910, is unique in having a **thatched cap**, at the summit of its blue lias tower.

Inside, climb to the top to see the rail on which the cap turned enabling the sails to face into the wind *(p 199)*.

Among the outhouses, note the **bakehouse** with wooden gutters.

★ ILMINSTER
Pop 3 722

Michelin map 403 fold 26 – L31

The Ham stone town on the south side of the London-Exeter road *(A 303)*, originated in Saxon times, was listed in Domesday as possessing both a minster and a market, and grew to prosperity in 15-16C on wool – Ilminster was a named cloth. New houses were built, old houses refronted in Georgian times, the town's well-being depending, as it still does, on being at the heart of some of England's best agricultural land, both dairy and arable.

★★ **St Mary's.** – The climax of the church outside is its **crossing tower**, modelled on that of Wells Cathedral *(p 178)*. It rises through two stages of bell openings – paired and three abreast with intervening shafts, transoms, tracery and Somerset tracery; it continues to a crest of gargoyles, fountains of pinnacles and spirelet upon the stair turret.

Interior. – Inside are a tie-beam and king-post **roof**, a **fan vault** at the crossing and **the Wadham Chapel**. This remarkable "glass lantern" was built in 1452 to contain the **tomb chests** (inlaid on the lids with large brasses) of Sir William Wadham (d 1452) and his wife, and Nicholas (d 1618) and his wife, the latter the founders of Wadham College, Oxford.

Market Square. – The square is characterised at its centre by the single storeyed Market House, open on all sides and last rebuilt in 1819.

EXCURSION

★ **Barrington Court.** – *3m NE by B3168. P 150.*

LANGPORT
Pop 947

Michelin map 403 fold 26 – L30

The town, at the tidal limit of the River Parrett, was for centuries, a small but important centre for traffic sailing upstream into the heart of Somerset and down to Bridgewater and even overseas. Its main street, Bow St, which crosses the River Parrett by an iron bridge, follows the ancient course of a Roman causeway.

The town's architectural hey-day was in 18-19C, the late Georgian period, when Palladian-styled, Tuscan-pillared houses were erected along Bow St and Cheapside.

All Saints. – The church, rebuilt in the late 15C, retains from the Norman church on the site, a **stone relief** *(over S door)* carved in *c*1200 with a lamb and cross supported by twin angels and saints.

The **tower**, buttressed, battlemented and pinnacled, with a taller stair turret, rises from the door and west window, through transomed windows with Somerset tracery and flanking niches and a bell stage of three windows abreast, the outer ones blind, the centre traceried. Embattling marks the rooflines; pinnacles add to the height of the chancel which is enriched with tall windows handsomely traceried at apex and transom.

The **east window** contains largely mediaeval glass.

Buried in the churchyard is Langport's famous son, **Walter Bagehot** (1826-77), economist, banker and author of *The English Constitution*.

The Hill (A372) continues east, the road bridged at the town boundary by the **Hanging Chapel**, 16C guild or corporation chapel, constructed over a vaulted gateway which effectively frames the view of the one mile distant Huish Episcopi *(p 166)*.

EXCURSIONS

★★ **Muchelney.** – *2m S by a by-road. P 171.*

★ **Long Sutton.** – *4m E by A372.*

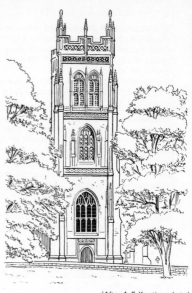

(After A F Kersting photo)

St Mary's Tower

Huish Episcopi. – Pop 1 550. St Mary's church **tower**★★ is one of the great jewels in the Somerset crown.

Built in 15C of local blue lias and mellow Ham stone to perfect proportions, it rises, supported by stepped and pinnacled buttresses, to pierced battlements and fountains of crocketed, intermediate and corner pinnacles. Each stage is underlined by panel tracery or a quatrefoil frieze: the Somerset traceried and transomed three-light window is flanked by pinnacled niches, the paired bell lights are divided and framed by shafted pinnacles... The height to the top of the pinnacles is 99ft.

The Norman **west doorway** of 1150-1200, with zigzag decoration was "fired" to a dark rust-gold in a disaster in the early 1300s when much of the church perished.

The parish is said to have served Trollope as the model for Plumpstead Episcopi in *The Warden.*

After 2m turn right off A372.

★ **Long Sutton.** – Pop 800. The parish **church**★★ at the village centre dates from 1490. The **tower**, with a taller stair turret, rises through three stages from the spandrelled door and west window with tangential arcs instead of transoms, to a window with framing niches, three belfry windows, the outer ones blank the centre filled with Somerset tracery and, finally, an embattled crest with every feature ending in a pinnacle.

Inside are an outstanding **roof** of tie-beams, king posts and angel figures, a coloured **rood screen** with slender tracery between the mullions and a contemporary 16-sided, coloured **pulpit** with small 19C figures filling the original canopied niches.

★ **Midelney Manor.** – *4½m W by A378 and by-road.*

Curry Rivel. – Pop 2 582. The Perpendicular **church** which incorporates earlier features within its walls has strangely banded **buttresses** and a tall tower with a taller stair turret built of blue lias with Ham stone dressings. Note the quatrefoil frieze and transomed, Somerset traceried, bell openings.

The urn-crowned column in the vicinity, is the **Burton Pynsent Monument.** Built of blue lias faced in Portland stone, it was designed by Capability Brown and erected in 1765 by William Pitt the Younger to Sir William Pynsent, who left the statesman his Elizabethan manor.

Turn round at Curry Rivel and bear right towards Drayton.

★ **Midelney Manor.** – The manor dates back to King Ine's charter of 693 under which he granted Muchelney, Midelney and Thorney – Great, Middle and Thorn Islands which rose above the surrounding marshlands – to the Benedictines. The abbot built a hunting lodge on Midelney which, by 16C, was let to a John Trevilian whose sons built the present house which is still occupied by the family.

The grey stone house's classic H plan was disrupted by the brothers' quarrelling when it was under construction: no central porch but two separate entrances in opposite corners of the forecourt were built and inside a massive partition wall which was only pierced in 1926! Trevilians in the east wing enlarged and improved their range, notably in 18C when the interior was remodelled in the Queen Anne style.

Inside are Georgian and Louis XV **furniture**, porcelain and **armorial china**, paintings and family portraits and **mementoes** including high sheriffs' banners and city freemans' presentation caskets – one of which, in silver, is a model of the house. A fund of stories highlights the intertwined histories of the manor and the family.

In the flower-filled garden is an early 18C **falcons' mews.**

High Ham. – *4m N. P 165.*

Guard against all risk of fire.
Fasten all gates.
Keep dogs under proper control.
Keep to the paths across farmland.
Avoid damaging fences, hedges and walls.
Leave no litter.
Safeguard water supplies.
Protect wild life, wild plants and trees.
Go carefully on country roads.
Respect the life of the countryside.

★ LYTES CARY

tc Two 16C oriels in Ham Hill stone beneath swan and gryphon finialled gables and an attached chapel, distinguish the manor house which was occupied by fourteen generations of the Lyte family from the time when William Le Lyte, Sergeant-at-Law under Edward I, built the first house on the site in 1286. *(Illustration p 18.)*

The Lytes of 16-17C were interested in botany and genealogy: Henry made a garden at Lytes Cary and published (1578) as an enlarged translation from the Dutch, a work which became widely known as *Lyte's Herbal;* his son traced the genealogy of James I from Brutus, which earned him the king's pleasure and award of the Nicholas Hilliard miniature of the king set in gold and diamonds now to be seen in the British Museum.

In 18C the house was sold and fell into decay. Only in 1907 was it rescued by Sir Walter Jenner, son of the physician, who restored the fabric, furnished the interior with 17-19C pieces and textiles in character, and laid out Elizabethan topiary gardens in the original forecourt, a parterre garden, a yew alley...

TOUR ¾ *hour*

The Hall. – The hall, which was added to the original house in *c*1453 has a typical Somerset **roof** of arch braces, cusped wind braces and an ornate cornice marked by supporting half-angels holding shields bearing the Lyte arms.

The 15C **fireplace** is original, the landscape above it is by Jan Wyck (17C).

Of especial note among the furniture and furnishings are two oak **refectory tables**, one with the massive turned legs of *c*1600, the second with the fluted frieze of the mid-17C, the pair of late 17C **delft tulip vases** and the late 18C **mahogany cheese coaster.**

Oriel Room. – The room, which served as the family dining room, was heated by a miniature version of the hall fireplace.

The **oak bird cage** dates from 18C. Note the copies of pages from the *Herbal (see above).*

Great Parlour. – The parlour, with the bay and other windows overlooking the garden almost filling one side, is notable for its original 17C **panelling** with fluted Ionic pilasters and pillared chimneypiece.

Among the wealth of beautiful oak and walnut 17-18C furniture, note the laburnham oyster **parquetry sidetable** on six legs, a red tortoise-shell **bracket clock** (London, 1700) and, in contrast, a Chinese lacquer bureau cabinet (*c*1700).

Little Parlour. – The small room, a carpenter's shop until restored by Sir Walter Jenner whose portrait hangs on the wall, was probably the study of the antiquarian-botanist Lytes of 16-17C.

Among the furnishings are a pair of 18C **jardinières**, 17C brass **lantern clock** (Taunton), 18-19C glass, and a semi-circular mahogany **drinking table** with a wheeled decanter trolley, which enabled both wine and imbibers to be warmed by the fire.

Great Chamber. – The great room at the top of the stone newel staircase is embellished by the upper part of the parlour bay window and a **plaster ceiling**, coved and ribbed; on the end wall are the **arms** of Henry VIII.

Chapel. – The detached chapel, dating from 1343, is the oldest feature of the house. The **frieze** of coats of arms was added by the genealogist member of the family in James I's reign.

MARTOCK   Pop 3 749

The glory of Martock, a village built entirely in its older parts of Ham Hill stone, is 15-16C church and the glory of the church is its **angel roof.**

★★ **All Saints.** – The west **tower** marked the completion of the church's reconstruction in 15-16C. It rises from a shafted door and five-light window which starts below the string course and fills the second stage. The elevation then continues through a bay and paired, transomed bell openings, all tracery filled, to a typically pinnacled crest.

Interior. – Above the arcades of Ham Hill stone and the clerestory, the **roof** presents an ordered arrangement of embattled tie-beams, purlins, king posts and braces, of secondary braces and posts descending in carved pendants, enriched with tracery and pierced coffering – 768 panels in 6 different patterns. As a final embellishment in 1513, 67 **lifesize angels** were added in wood and stone.

Note the five stepped windows at the east end, relic of the EE church on the site. The clerestory was originally glazed with heraldic glass: ten shields to each window, "about 120 coats" a 17C diarist calculated, before in July 1645 the Parliamentarians came to Martock, held a thanksgiving service for the capture of Bridgwater and smashed the lot. The windows were reglazed in plain glass and, after the Restoration, the niches painted with the figures of the apostles in 17C dress.

The main street. – Among the houses lining the main street close to the church are: the **Treasurer's House** of 13-14C, so-named because the rector of Martock was treasurer of Wells Cathedral; the many gabled, 17C manor house, much rebuilt after a fire in 19C and **Church House**, a long low building of two storeys with mullioned windows in which the door is superimposed by the date, 1661, and a composite inscription in English, Latin, Greek and Hebrew from the time when it was the local grammar school.

Also in the main road are the **Market House**, a small Georgian building with a Venetian window, upraised upon arcades which once sheltered market stalls, and a market cross in the form of a Doric column.

★ MINEHEAD

Pop 5 955

Michelin map **403** fold 34 – J30

Minehead was the chief port in the area from 14-17C, trading with Ireland (in wool), Virginia and the West Indies. In 19C, with the coming of the railway, it became a "seaside watering place"; today money comes from local light industry and above all from the large summer holiday camp to its east.

SIGHTS

The Esplanade and Quay St. – The wide roads follow the curving line of the sea wall round to the harbour jetty and the small harbour filled with pleasure-craft and rowing boats. Lining the side of the road, at the foot of the wooded slopes of North Hill, is a thread of colour-washed and stone seamen's cottages dating back to 17-19C.

Higher Town. – The community of houses on North Hill is linked by steeply rising and turning roads, winding lanes and stepped alleys; the houses, many thatched and with round-cornered cob walls, appear to stand each upon his neighbour's shoulders.

★ **Church Steps.** – *Access: on foot, by Church Path, an opening off Quay St; by car, up Quay Lane, at the juncture of the Esplanade and Quay St. In both cases keep bearing right to come into St Michael's Rd.* Explore Church Steps, for preference, from the top!

★ **St Michael's.** – The church of light grey sandstone, with a buttressed and battlemented **tower**, 87ft high, has stood on the hill since 14-15C when it replaced a Norman building in turn probably successor to a Saxon church.
Inside is 16C, coved **rood screen** with a foliated crest which remained intact throughout the Commonwealth because, fortunately, the churchwardens were Parliamentarians! The octagonal **font** with a kneeling figure, possibly the donor, dates from *c*1400; the brass of a young woman and effigy of a priest *(both E end)* are late 15C; the pulpit is 17C as is **Jack Hammer**, the clock jack; the **chandelier** is 18C.
The **royal arms** on the north wall and over the south door are of Queen Anne, George II and Charles II, at whose coronation the churchwardens, at a time when beer was less than *Id* a pint, provided 16*s* for beer for the refreshment of the bellringers! Look back at the tower as you leave: on the north face is God holding a Crucifix, to the east St Michael weighing souls with the Virgin tipping the scales in our favour!

★ WEST SOMERSET RAILWAY

The WSR, which owns one of the longest private lines in Britain, operates diesel business and shopping services and, in the holiday season, services by **steam trains** which puff and whistle along the line to the abiding joy of passengers of all ages – *timetable at Minehead; bus connection Bishop's Lydeard – Taunton.*
The line, which opened in 1862, was extended to Minehead in 1874; the track, originally the Great Western Broad Gauge of 7ft 0¼ in, was converted within ten years to standard size. In 1922 the West Somerset became part of the GWR, in 1948 of BR and in 1971 the line was closed. This was not the end, however, for in March 1976, under "new management" the West Somerset Railway Co re-opened for business.

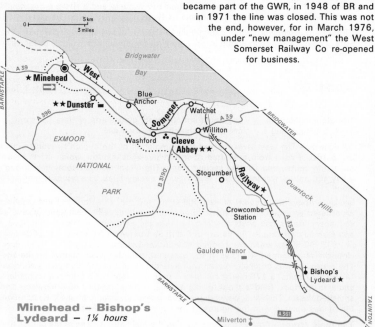

Minehead – Bishop's Lydeard – *1¼ hours*

The following stations and landmarks characterise the 20 mile journey:

★ **Minehead.** – Platform long enough to take 16-coach train; signal box from Dunster and water tower from Pwllheli, N Wales; restoration depot. Holiday camp, sea on left.
Conygar Tower. – *P 156.*

★★ **Dunster Castle.** – *P 155.*
The line follows the shore round the bay – view of Hinkley Point Power Station and the Welsh coast on a clear day;

Blue Anchor. – Signal box; seaside village with caravan site; sand and pebble beach.

Washford Bank. – 1:65 gradient; Washford *(p 169)*; restoration depot.

★★ **Cleeve Abbey.** – *P 154*.

Watchet. – Pop 3074. On the hilltop – 15C tower of St Decuman Church and below a large papermill at the entrance to the town. Watchet, home port of Coleridge's *Ancient Mariner (p 151)*, is the oldest commercial harbour along this part of the coast still in active trade. The line approaches to within feet of the cliff. Helwell Bay is popular with fossil-hunters.

Williton. – Pop 2472. Brick-built signal box, second water tower from Pwllheli (steam trains often take on water – halfway point), goods shed and siding. Views of the Quantocks *(left)* and Brendons *(right)*.

Stogumber. – Pop 632. Village with red sandstone church with 14C tower *(1m)*.

Crowcombe Station. – Village – pop 412 *(1¾ m)*. 400ft above sea-level, the topmost point of the line, beautiful countryside, walking centre for the Quantocks.

★ **Bishop's Lydeard.** – Signal box, goods shed, renovation depot. *P 176*.

EXCURSIONS

★ **Porlock.** – *10m W by A39*.

★ **Selworthy.** – The white-walled thatched cottages and ancient stone tithe barn, make a perfect setting for the small, embattled Church of All Saints.
The 15-16C **church**★★, white-walled with dark stone trims, is entered through a two-storey porch set between finely traceried windows. The door is linenfold panelled. The interior is light, with slender piers. Walk over to the **south aisle** of 1538, known for its original wagon roof embellished with a multitude of carved **bosses** and **angel wall plates**. Note the slender turned balusters of the **communion rail** of *c*1700.
As you leave, look southwest across Exmoor, for a **view**★★ of Dunkery Beacon *(p 160)*.

Allerford. – The village of a few houses and a pub nearly all built of local red sandstone, is known for its ancient **packhorse bridge**.

★ **Porlock.** – *P 172*.

★★★ MONTACUTE HOUSE

Michelin map **403** fold 36 – L31

tc Ham Hill *(p 182)* a few miles away, provided the stone for Montacute House, the village (pop 734) and for the Perpendicular parish church, casting its glow upon the house and enriching to a tawny-ochre, grey-brown the modest houses, inns, and small bay-windowed shops which surround the Borough, or large village square.

The House. – The Elizabethan H shaped mansion of three storeys was built in 1597-1601 by Sir Edward Phelips, a successful lawyer, Speaker of the House of Commons (1604) and Master of the Rolls (1611). Nearly two centuries later, in 1786, Sir Edward's namesake and his wife attended a "Sale of the Materials of Clifton House then Pulling Down" and bought "The Porch, Arms, Pillars and all the Ornamental Stone of the Front to be Transferred to the Intended West Front of Montacute".
The **early house**, true to the Elizabethan style, rose majestically and symmetrically on either side of a porched entrance front, through tiers of transomed windows to an open balustrade, obelisks and small, round gables. Flanking either side were taller, shaped gables and columnar chimneys; bay windows gave subtle relief to the lower walls. In deference to Renaissance fashion, there was a modest entablature and niches filled with nine roughly carved worthies in Roman armour. The rear, west face, between advanced wings, was plain with pointed gables and square chimney stacks.

The "Intended West Front". – The front was a key part of 18C Edward Phelips decision to reverse the house: instead of entering from the east through the balustraded forecourt with its twin pavilions with ogée roofs crowned by open stone spheres, he determined on a new approach through the west face, which, however, needed to be dignified for the role – hence his attendance at the Clifton House sale.
The Ham stone from Clifton matched perfectly. Phelips utilised his purchase as a shallow infilling between the advanced wings to produce a new west front. On the new **porch** at the centre he implanted his own arms, on either side fluted and spiral shafting, pierced balustrading, a Noah's ark of heraldic animal finials...

Land, farms, furniture and possessions were accumulated and sold as the Phelips family fortunes rose or declined; from 1911 Montacute was let – the most famous of the tenants being **Lord Curzon** (1915-25) who entrusted the redecoration to the novelist, Elinor Glyn. In 1931, the house in a sad state of dereliction, was purchased by the National Trust.

TOUR *1¼ hours*

Ground floor

You enter through the original, pre-18C, east doorway into the screens passage.

Dining Room. – The room was created by Lord Curzon out of the old buttery from which dishes were once carried in ritualistic procession through the Great Hall and up the stairs to the formal dining room *(see Library below)*. The Elizabethan style chimney-piece bears the **Phelips arms** of 1599; the **tapestry** of a knight against a *millefleurs* background is Flemish (Tournai); the walnut **refectory table**, Italian 16C. Among the **portraits** are Mary, Queen of Scots, James I and Robert Dudley, Earl of Leicester.

Great Hall. – The hall, the communal living room until after the Restoration, retains from 16C its **panelling**, the **stone screen** with rusticated archways and pillars with ramshead and acanthus leaf capitals and a roughly carved crest, and the **heraldic glass** in the window which includes Queen Elizabeth's and Sir Edward Phelips' arms.
The plaster relief or **Skimmington frieze**, at the far end of the hall, of a hen-pecked husband taking a drink while minding the baby and later being paraded astride a pole around the village, is early 17C.

(After Erik Pelham / National Trust photo)

The Skimmington Frieze

Parlour. – The room retains its original Ham stone **fireplace**, Elizabethan **panelling** and **frieze** of nursery animals. Among 18C furniture are a Gobelins tapestry of 1788, *The Hunter*, a settee and chairs with needlework covers, a giltwood table, Gothick longcase clock, a centre table of beautiful simplicity by Thomas Chippendale the Younger and, from 17C, the portrait by Cornelius Johnson of an *Unknown Cavalier*.

Drawing Room. – The room serves as the setting for a memorable **Joshua Reynold's** *Portrait of a Lady*, chairs covered in red damask made in 1753 by Walter Linnell for Sir Richard Hoare *(p 206)*; a giltwood **side-table** with eagle supports, a George I walnut **card-table**, a Boulle brass and tortoise-shell **chest** and Chinese porcelain lion dogs and birds.

Staircase. – The staircase, of which each **tread** is a single 7ft block of stone, rises by straight flights around a stone core – the intermediary stage between spiral stairs and Jacobean wooden staircases built around open wells. The tapestries are 15-16C.

First Floor

Lord Curzon's Room. – The room, besides his lordship's bath neatly stowed in a "Jacobean" cupboard, contains 17C **overmantel** of *King David at Prayer*, 18C bed, a Dutch oak drop-leaf table and 18C, japanned, skeleton mirror.

Crimson Room. – The room, so-called since 19C when red flock wallpaper replaced the tapestries which once hung below the plaster frieze, is furnished with a sumptuous oak **four-poster**, carved with the arms of James I.

Library. – The library, formerly the dining room and the goal of the dishes brought in procession from the distant kitchens, is chiefly remarkable for its brilliant **heraldic glass** – a tourney of 42 shields displaying the Phelips arms, those of the sovereign and, by way of a compliment, those of Phelips' Somerset neighbours and friends at court. Other features from the time when this was a stateroom are the monumental Portland **stone mantelpiece** and **plaster frieze**, the Jacobean **inner porch**, 19C the moulded plaster ceiling and bookcases. The library steps date from 1770.

Top Floor

Long Gallery. – The 172ft gallery with oriels at either end, occupies the whole of the floor and is the longest in existence. Today it provides a perfect setting through 90 **portraits** (on loan from the National Portrait Gallery) for a panoply of **Tudor England** and the early Jacobean Age.
In the main gallery contemporaries, friends and rivals stand together, kings and queens *(centre bay)* and full length portraits of Drake, Lord Burghley, James I as a boy with a falcon, Prince Henry, Charles I as a boy, Francis Bacon, Philip Herbert, 4th Earl of Pembroke *(p 209)*. Five dependent rooms are filled with the personalities of the Reign of Henry VIII, Elizabeth and her Court, The Elizabethan Age, The Early Stuart Court and The Jacobean Age.

The Royal Arms, once displayed in every church, originated in the reign of Henry VIII to mark the cleavage with Rome and the king's position as supreme head of the church. A new order to set up the royal arms came after the Commonwealth at the Restoration.

Michelin map 403 fold 35 – L30 – 2m S of Langport

The abbey ruins, 15C parish church, a mediaeval priest's house and a village of attractive 17-18C cottages many, obviously, incorporating dressed stones from the abbey, make an attractive group.

tc **The Abbey.** – The abbot's lodging, in part, is the area remaining of the Benedictine monastery which was founded in 693 AD on what was then an island *(p 162)* at the centre of the frequently flooded marshland. It was destroyed by the Danes in 870s, refounded in *c*950 and finally Dissolved in 1538.

The abbey's annual income, recorded in Domesday as being £51 16*s* had risen by 16C to £447, an increase which contributed, at the expense of the spirit, to the brothers' temporal well-being: after a visitation in 1335 they were charged with living too well, leaving the church in disrepair, riding about the country and keeping unfit company, dining in private, owning costly utensils and ornate beds. Whether the house reformed or not, the abbot's lodgings were rebuilt in Tudor Gothic manner and remain as testimony to the grandeur of monastic life-style in 15-16C.

After the Dissolution, the domestic quarters were occupied as farmhouses for some 200 years while the church, which measured 247ft, and conventual buildings were ruined and looted for their fabric. Backing onto the south cloister walk, which remains, would have been the refectory, and in the corner, the abbot's lodging.

Kitchen. – Go through the gabled and battlemented south front into the kitchen, a long, lofty room with a massive, double-sided **fireplace**, 17ft wide by 7ft deep.

Walk up the stairs at the far end.

Guestroom. – The fine **door** *(right)* leads into the large guestroom which has a coffered **oak ceiling**, mullioned windows and a stone fireplace.

Return to the ground floor and walk up the wide stone staircase.

Parlour. – The **Abbot's Staircase** leads through a decorated **archway** to the parlour. This room, which served as a waiting and meeting room, is lined with **linenfold** panelling and equipped with a large **panelled settle** before stone mullioned and transomed windows. It also contains an impressive **stone fireplace**, ornamented with enriched quatrefoils, friezes of fruit and foliage and, high on the framing shafts, a pair of couched lions.

★★ **Parish Church.** – The early 15C Perpendicular church on an older Norman or even Saxon site, stands within three feet of the north transept of the former abbey church. The massive **tower** rises through three stages from the west door and window to a window flanked by canopied niches, a belfry stage of two bays framed by shafts springing from lower buttresses and continuing like those at the centre through the battlemented crest to end as secondary pinnacles to those at the angles.

Inside, the wagon roof was transformed between 1600-25 by a local man into a full colour, **painted ceiling** of smiling, bare bosomed angels in Tudor costume enjoying the heavenly life!

Note also the panelled arch to the west tower; 15C octagonal **font** with carvings of the Crucifixion; 19C **barrel organ** still capable of playing 25 hymns and 3 double chants; 17C Netherlandish stained **glass roundels** *(chancel windows)*; and, in the chancel and around the font, 13C **tiles** from the abbey Lady Chapel.

Priest's House. – The thatched house of 14-15C has a mediaeval two-storey hall and 16C Gothic window *(not open)*.

tc **Muchelney Pottery.** – *1m S of the village.* At the pottery John Leach, son of David, grandson of Bernard, produces the handthrown, wood-fired domestic stoneware to be seen not only in Somerset but also in shops and exhibitions in many parts of the country.

NORTON ST PHILIP Pop 781

Michelin map 403 fold 36 – N30

The village, on the main road to Bath, was known for centuries for wool and cloth merchants who came twice a year to what were amongst the biggest cloth fairs of the West Country.

Charters to hold the fairs were obtained, in the first place, in 13C by the Carthusian monks who had built a monastery on land nearby at Hinton, given them by Ela, Countess of Salisbury, the founder of Lacock Abbey *(p 193)*. The charterhouse which was called *Atrium Dei*, was dedicated to the memory of her husband, William Longespée (d 1226; *p 201*), natural son of Henry II and halfbrother to Richard Lionheart.

By 18C the local speciality, in Defoe's words, was "fine medley, or mixed cloths such as are usually worn in England by the better sort of people and are exported in great quantities to Holland, Hamburg, Sweden, Denmark, Spain, Italy etc."

At the centre of the main street, lined by old stone houses, stands the famous inn.

★★ **The George Inn.** – It was built in *c*1223 as the monks' hostel while they were constructing Hinton Charterhouse. When the priory was complete the hostel became the priory guesthouse and inn and eventually a storehouse for wool from sheep raised on the priory lands. It was, at first, just a single storey building in the local stone with a wide **central archway**; in 15C two storeys were added, half-timbered and oversailing with three attractive **oriel windows**.

At the Dissolution, while the priory lands passed to the crown and the priory itself was encouraged to fall into ruin, the inn continued to provide hospitality to wool merchants and clothiers – Norton had become a weaving centre. After the decline of the industry in the early 18C, it remained as a welcome halt for travellers such as Samuel Pepys and his wife, who passing by on 12 June 1668, commented "dined very well, 10*s*".

(A F Kersting)

The George Inn

Ten days before the Battle of Sedgemoor *(p 150),* **Monmouth's** men fought a running battle with the king's force in the fields outside the town. The duke, who had a price on his head, was surveying the scene from the inn, when a sniper fired but missed, at which, according to a local ballad, he "gaily turned him round and said: My man you've missed your mark and lost your thousand pound".

Go through the arch to see the old beamed rooms and the flowered **courtyard** at the back with a long **mediaeval gallery** running down one side.

★ **PORLOCK**   Pop 1 368

Michelin map **403** fold 34 – J30

Porlock is an attractive village despite the crowds. It is surrounded on three sides by the Exmoor hills and has a narrow winding main street marked by a church with a lopped spire and thatched and creeper-covered houses. **Porlock Hill** to the west with a superb **view**★★ at the start, remains as notorious as ever with 1:4 gradient and "the man from Porlock", who interrupted Coleridge as he began to write *Kubla Khan,* remains as unknown a character as ever.

★ **St Dubricius Church.** – The church has a truncated, octogonal **spire** covered in oak shingles set on a solid 13C stone tower. It is not known whether the tower was ever completed and subsequently destroyed in a storm or whether it was abandoned halfway – one story has it that the workmen left to follow the hunt as it passed through the village and never returned from the moor !

Inside, **EE arcade, east window** of three tall lancets under one arch, the double piscina and arch at the west end of the nave, are all 13C; the Perpendicular windows were inserted during 15C reconstruction. Note the remarkable **canopied tomb** with alabaster effigies of John, 4th Lord Harington and his wife (dd 1417, 1461).

The dedication and tradition of foundation by St Dubricious or Dyffrig is a reminder of the work in the southwest of Celtic missionaries from Wales in 5-6C; Dubricius, a legendary figure who died aged 120 in *c*612, is said to have been a friend of King Arthur and present at the Battle of Bladon Hill in 517.

Porlock Weir. – *Take the by-road on the right at the end of the village.*

The small harbour filled with pleasure-craft, is overlooked by white-washed cottages and old inns.

EXCURSION

★ **St Culbone.** – *2m along the Ashley Combe Toll Rd to the old farm toll gate; park the car and continue on foot – 3m Rtn: go armed with insect repellent or a fly whisk.*

The irregular path is through broad leafed woods which extend back from 400ft cliffs towards the Exmoor hills – you are always within sound of the sea.

Suddenly, in a dell with a rushing stream, there is the church.

The 12-13C **church**, the smallest complete church in England, is 12ft 4in across by 35ft long. The walls of rubble stone are intended to be rendered and whitewashed; the roof is of slate also the spirelet, added in *c*1810. Walk round to look on the north side, at the possibly **Saxon window** of two lights, cut out of a single block of sandstone, decorated at the top of the mullion with a relief of a catlike face !

Inside, the chancel has had a too large east window inserted and a neo-Gothic reredos, but the **rood screen** was carved with foils and cusps by 14C craftsmen. The family pew is 17C, the **benches** are pre-Reformation and the circular **font** is possibly Saxon.

Shepton Mallet, with Wells and Glastonbury, was a stocking knitting town, in 17-18C and a wool town producing pure wool cloth, serges, sailcloth and silk in 18-19C with as many as 4 000 people employed in the giant mills.
Situated in the valley at the foot of the Mendip Hills, the town has always been and remains a livestock centre and market close to main highways including the Roman Fosse Way and the roads to Bristol, Frome and Ilchester.

SIGHTS

The Market Place. – The Market Place *(pedestrian precinct)*, enclosed by 17C inns, shops, 18C houses and a new public library, is distinguished by a Market Cross, a tall pinnacle of 1500, encircled by 18C hexagonal arcade and by the shamble.

Market Shamble. – First built in Shepton in 1450, it is an obvious development from a little shed – the Anglo-Saxon meaning of the word. The shed developed into a permanent line of roofed stalls, which, in time, became a street of open fronted shops mostly butchers, sometimes fishmongers – from the disorder of whose backyards, slaughterhouses etc, the modern meaning evolved!

Walk through the modern buildings to the parish church.

★ **St Peter and St Paul.** – The west **tower** with its capped spire remains as testimony to an architectural change of fashion. Constructed in the local Doulting stone on a Norman base in *c*1380, it is the earliest in the Somerset style, yet being intended to support a spire, among the most solid: pairs of set back buttresses at the angles strengthen it as it rises from the west door through stages marked by a big six-light window, statuary niches, a clock bay and a bell tier of three paired openings, to reach the pierced balustrade and solid buttress pinnacles at the crest.

An eight-sided **spire** was begun, halted, capped and never completed. It is said that spires ceased to be built because the Black Death (1348) so depleted the number of masons and craftsmen that people got used to seeing spireless towers, that Shepton Mallet tower was so beautiful anyway it needed no addition. It must also have occurred to many that spires were hazardous constructions both architecturally and as lightning attractors – the number of Norman spires which collapsed is countless.

Inside, the church of Saxon origin, Norman and 13-17C rebuilding and enlargement, has suffered Puritan depredations and a thorough-going Victorian remodelling. Nevertheless there remain a circular **Saxon font,** knights in chain mail, the **pulpit** of Doulting stone, richly carved in 1550 with niches, Renaissance cornucopia and flowers and, greatest of all, the "richly wrought" **roof** of 1450.

The roof is a barrel vault of 350 carved panels and 1400 leaves caught into nearly 400 bosses and half bosses: "the most glorious of all wagon roofs in England".

Town Houses. – Take time to walk round the town to discover the **Georgian houses** with pedimented doorways and well proportioned windows; the **Strode Almshouses** of 1699 *(S of the church);* to explore the narrow, stone-walled, lanes *(left)* leading to **Leg Sq** and 18C clothiers' houses, **Eden Grove** and **The Hollies,** with their columned doorways. There are the half-timbered **King's Arms** which supplied ale to the prison opposite; **Peter St** with its Georgian houses and, in the lane to the left, the old **Grammar School,** founded in 1627 with its uncompromising Latin tag on the wall of the Georgian annex, *Disce aut discede* – learn or get out! *(N side of the church).*

On the far side of the Market Place and Town St, **Great Ostry** is lined by 17C, three-storey terrace of seven identical houses with mullioned windows, built for no one knows who. Continuing through the lanes you will see more of the old mills 17C, gabled weavers' cottages, pocket handkerchief sized gardens.

tc **Museum.** – *High St.* Exhibits illustrate local archaeology and the town's history.

EXCURSIONS

★ **Oakhill Manor.** – *4m N off A37, right at B3135 crossroads.*
tc The visit opens at a stone-built, country-style station from which you ride ¾ mile through the grounds to the house. An N gauge railway, with open carriages, gathers steam and takes you, with all the correct clickety-clack, through woods and cuttings and, to the accompaniment of whistles and the reminiscent smell of steam and coaldust, under bridges and through a "long tunnel".

The house. – The house, which stands 700ft above sea-level, is 19C Tudor-style rebuilding on an older site – the two cedars of Lebanon in the garden are about 200 years' old or nearly twice the age of the house.
The interior has become the setting for the owner's model collection of transport which covers ships, aircraft and, most notably, steam locomotives.

★ **Downside Abbey.** – *5m N off A37 and A367. P 155.*

★ **Nunney.** – *9m W on A 361.*

tc **East Somerset Railway, Cranmore.** – *½m S of main road.*
The station has been restored to a modest Victorian appearance; the signal box serves as an exhibition gallery for the African wildlife paintings and prints of David Shepherd. The depot, built in the tradition of Victorian train sheds, is a repair workshop for the stock which includes as jewels of the collection, the locomotives Bluebell (P/0-6-0T/1910), Green Knight (4MT/4-6-0/1954) and Black Prince (9F/2-10-0/1959).
The East Somerset Railway opened in 1858, became part of the GWR and ultimately of BR. It was closed in 1967. The private line now extends for just under 2m.

Return to A361. Nunney is ½m N of the main road.

★ **Nunney.** – Pop 804. The village of 17-18C stone houses and cottages and an inn sign spanning the main street, surrounds a moated castle and small church.

tc Dating back to 1393, **Nunney Castle**, which was slighted in 1645, remains as a picturesque ruin, its tall towers reflected in the waters of the moat.

The **church**, vigorously restored in 19C, is 13-16C. Note the spirally fluted Norman **font** with a Jacobean cover, 14C arcades with no capitals between the piers and arches. Among the **tombal effigies** are Sir John Delamere (d 1390) who built the castle, Richard Prater and his wife who bought it in 1577 and their Cavalier grandson who lost it to the Parliamentarians. Note the castle model.

Evercreech. – *4m SE by A371 and B3081.*
Dominating the village square and mediaeval market cross, the **church tower ★** *(p 147)* rises between shafted and pinnacled buttresses to immensely tall, twice-transomed bell-lights – the lower bays blind, those above tracery filled. Pinnacles and sub-pinnacles continue the vertical lines ever higher above the crest. Inside is a tie-beam roof of angels and bosses richly gilt and coloured.

Batcombe. – *7m SE. After Evercreech, continue by by-roads 3m E.* The tower of 87ft is a complete contrast to others in the county *(p 147)*, the profusion of pinnacles being all below the skyline.

★ SOMERTON   Pop 4 375

Michelin map **403** fold 36 – L30

The small town with an arcaded market cross, boasts of having been the capital town of Wessex in 10C and the county town in 13-14C; now it is blissfully off all main routes and closely surrounded by rolling, wooded farmland.

The houses and inns along the two main streets which form an L, are of the local blue lias or limestone with Ham stone trims, mullioned windows and stone tile roofs.

Houses and Inns. – Note particularly in the **Market Place ★**, the unique 17C arcaded **cross ★**, the Town Hall of the same date but much altered, and the White Hart on the site of the town's early castle. East of the church are several **17-18C houses**, **16C house** with symmetrical oriels and dormers in the tiled roof, a **round-cornered house** with a Tuscan porch (now a bank), and, closing the street, the **Red Lion**, 17C coaching inn with a rounded archway entrance superimposed by a pedimented Venetian window.

The tree shaded **Broad St**, by contrast, is lined by substantial 18C houses.

(After BTA photo)

The Market Cross

★ **St Michael's.** – The octagonal south **tower** which dates from 13C, is the oldest part of the church which inside was transformed in *c*1450 by the addition of a clerestory and a wonderful **tiebeam roof** with kingposts and castellations, tracery, foliage, carved wall plates, 640 identical quatrefoil panels, dragons, and, of course, angels, all now highlighted in gold. Note the **barrel** *(lft long, bunghole downwards, N side of centre beam, 3rd oblong from W end)*, said to celebrate local beer and cider-making.

The **pulpit**, the **altar**, carved upon its legs with symbols of man's fall and salvation, the **panelling** behind the altar, are all Jacobean; the **bishop's chair** is said to be from Glastonbury; the brass **candelabra** are 18C.

EXCURSION

★ **Lytes Cary.** – *4m S by B3151 and E from Kingsdon. P 167.*

★★ STOGURSEY Priory Church

Michelin map **403** fold 25 – K30

From outside St Andrew's Church with its octagonal, slate covered, spire rising from an early crossing tower, gives little indication of its interest.

The history. – The church, on land given by the Conqueror, was founded as a daughter house of the Abbey of Ste Marie de Lonlay in Normandy.

By *c*1107 a priory church had been built; by *c*1180 the religious had so increased that the church had to be considerably enlarged. The community prospered but later declined to a prior, one monk and a few servants. In 1414 under the Alienation Act, Henry V sequestered the priory; in 15C it became a **parish church.**

The interior. – Go through the **Norman doorway** and walk up the nave with its Perpendicular windows, 19C **Friendly Society boards** against the walls and 31 **benches** carved in 1524-30 with a pelican, double-headed eagle, a spoonbill, a green man...

The crossing. – At the crossing, wider than it is deep, the church's 11C date becomes obvious in the circular **Norman arches** with dog-tooth and zig-zag decoration, the **arcade** of great round pillars and remarkably carved **capitals** of Ham Hill stone.

As completed in *c*1107, the priory church comprised the crossing, a single bay chancel with a rounded apse, transepts with round apsed chapels and a mimimal nave. In 1180 the chancel and transepts were extended eastwards converting the latter into three-bay, chancel aisles. Four **mediaeval angels** were retained at the corners of the nave at the time of 19C restoration.

The furnishings. – The **chandelier** was made in Bridgwater in 1732; the **tub font** *(N transept)*, decorated with cable moulding, four mysterious faces and St Andrew's crosses at the rim, is Norman; the encaustic **floor tiles** are mediaeval. The **sanctuary ring** was attached to the southeast crossing pier in 13C when a murderer sought sanctuary in the church but absconded before his trial, leaving the priory liable for his fine! (The provision of a ring was intended to enable any future miscreant to be chained to it while awaiting trial – the right of sanctuary was abolished in 1623.)

Verney Chapel. – 18C wall monuments and tablets surround William Verney (d 1333), who lies holding his heart, and John Verney (d 1472), the local squire, a rumbustious character summoned to Canterbury in 1442 to answer charges of interrupting the Latin service and preaching in and out of church in English. Seventy years after his death there appear in the accounts for 1540, entries for the purchase of a Great Bible (Cranmer's Bible) for 10*s* 6*d* and 4*d* for a chain to secure it safely in the church.

★★ TAUNTON
Pop 45 326

Michelin map **403** fold 35 – K30

Taunton's recognition as the county town in 1850s when the Shire Hall was built, was an acknowledgement that after 1000 years of steady development, it had become the most important marketing and administrative centre in Somerset.

In the millenium it had progressed from being a battlefield where King Ine of Wessex won a victory against the British in 710, to an agricultural and livestock market at the heart of one of the nation's most fertile regions, the Vale of Taunton *(p 176)*. For more than six centuries it had also been an important cloth weaving town: it was the first to introduce the fulling mill to this country in 1218 and so start the shift from cottage industry to company mills – in 1702 Defoe described Taunton as a "large, wealthy, and exceedingly populous town (that had) so good a trade that they had 1100 looms going for the weaving of sagathies and duroys" (fine wool and silk and coarse woollen cloths).

SIGHTS

The Castle. – **Perkin Warbeck** passed through Taunton on his rebellious expedition against Henry VII in 1497 and was brought back to stand trial in the castle Great Hall. Nearly two centuries later the **Duke of Monmouth** also passed through the town; after the Battle of Sedgemoor in 1685, 526 of his followers were brought before **Judge Jeffreys** in the selfsame hall. Jeffreys condemned 508 – how many actually died of those condemned in the **Bloody Assizes** is not known; estimates range from 3-500 with between 800-1000 transported to the West Indies – there was a brisk trade in pardons. The Bloody Assizes remain a green memory in the southwest.

The Civil War, between the two uprisings, put Taunton and the castle in particular, under siege three times, most notably in 1645 when the town, under Robert Blake *(p 151)*, resisted the Royalist forces for three months. In 1648 Parliament ordered the castle and manor to be sold – the sum realised was £9210 17*s* 0½*d*; in 1662 the Royalist government ordered the castle to be slighted.

The 11-12C castle remained a ruin after the slighting until 18C when it was rescued. The east gatehouse is now incorporated into a hotel; 15C **gateway** which leads through the south range into the inner ward, serves as the entrance to the museum.

★ **Museum.** – In the **Great Hall** hangs a contemporary portrait by Kneller of **Judge Jeffreys**. Among the displays note especially the one on **wooden trackways**, laid in 2900 BC across the "levels" or marshlands, the prehistoric dug-out canoe and finds from the **Lake Villages** around Glastonbury; the Roman mosaic of Dido and Aeneas; the **ceramics collection** with pieces of Eltonware *(p 40)*, Wrothamware, local Donyatt and 19C Martinware, the Nailsea glass collection *(p 40)*; the bequest of Chinese pottery, highlighted by Han dynasty vases (206 BC-220 AD) and a robust T'ang tomb figure (618-906 AD).

The **17C silver collection** displays a set of apostle and seal top spoons and beakers. A separate gallery recalls the Somerset Light Infantry, with battle honours, uniforms and mementoes including a Stars and Stripes captured in 1813.

★★ **St Mary Magdalene.** – The church with its soaring tower closes quite perfectly the vista along Hammett St.

The Tower. – The **tower**, which was completed in 1514 after 26 years abuilding, was the joy and climax to 15C reconstruction of the parish church on its ancient Saxon site. At a period when the county was the third or fourth most densely populated in England and amongst the wealthiest, it represented the final flowering of what has remained Somerset's great contribution to church architecture.

It is of Ham Hill stone, and is marked at every stage by crocketed pinnacles on set back buttresses. From the door and a transomed west window it mounts to a frieze surmounted by the first of three similar sets of paired openings each of three lights with transoms, tracery and Somerset tracery, divided and framed by pinnacled shafts; the top pair, the bell openings, are longer, the pinnacles set diagonally, the walling above, panelled; higher still are a fourth frieze, spouting gargoyles, another frieze and the great **crown** of pierced battlements, pinnacles and, at the angles, four tiers of arcading and pierced, crocketed pinnacles flaunting iron wind-vanes – 163ft in all, the top pinnacles 32ft and pierced to minimise wind resistance. The vanes were added, as their 3½in numerals indicate, in 1682 *(illustration p 147)*.

The church interior. – The interior is almost square with a narrow nave and double aisles; the outer aisle and arcade on the north side only were not rebuilt in 15C and are EE. The **roof** is typical of Tudor Somerset with crested tie-beams, king posts, moulded arch braces, panelling, small oak leaf bosses and **angels**, recently gilded and painted for the first time. **Angels** re-appear, delightfully, in the arcade capitals while hilarious **mediaeval masks** decorate bosses above the light brackets, the inner aisles and the chancel arch (N side possibly Henry VII), otherwise the statues are 19C replacements of those destroyed by the Puritans.

★ **St James.** – The church, again except for the north arcade and aisle, is 14-15C.

The tower. – The 120ft tower of Quantock red sandstone with Ham stone decoration, which many believe to be the forerunner in design to St Mary's, rises from the doorway and six-light west window, in stages marked by pinnacled buttresses and diagonally set pinnacles, to a bell stage with transomed openings filled with Somerset tracery. Above are a **crest** of gargoyles, a pierced parapet, pinnacles and an overtopping **staircase tower** with a pyramid roof.

Near by is **Vivary Park,** like St James, in the former priory grounds. Named after, the monks' fishpond or *vivarium,* it possesses an incredible Victorian fountain.

Public buildings and streets. – Among the more notable buildings are the **Shire Hall** of 1855-8 in early Tudor style which brought county town status to Taunton *(see above);* the **Tudor House** of 1578 (Fore St) with its carved timbers and oversailing gable with multi-light oriel windows; the red brick **Market House** of 1770s with a pediment spanning its full width which stands at the centre crossroads.

On the Bristol Road are the two-storeyed, brick, **Gray's Almshouses** dated 1635, with nine chimney stacks with two diagonally set chimneys in each and the thatched single storey, **St Margaret's Leper Hospital,** (now Somerset Guild of Local Craftsmen and Social Security offices) founded in 12C, rebuilt early in 16C and converted into almshouses in 1612 *(Gray's, south side of East St; St Margaret's at far end of East Reach – continuation of East St).*

Finally, in 1977, there opened in a transformed 19C warehouse building by the river the **Brewhouse Theatre.**

The most appealing streets are **Hammett St★** of 1788 with twin lines of dark brick **terrace houses** with pillared and pedimented porches attractive in themselves, making the perfect frame for St Mary's *(see above)* at the street's end; **The Crescent★** of 1807 *(westerly parallel to the High St),* designed as a single undertaking; **Bath Alley★** *(between the High St and the end of Corporation St),* in which every house, cottage and shop was built in 17-18C to a different design. Finally, the wide High St *(pedestrian precinct),* leisurely with late Georgian-early Victorian houses, shops and pubs...

tc **British Telecom Museum.** – *38 North St (next to PO).*

The small museum contains early telegraph and cable systems: 100-year-old telephones and manual, automatic and early electronic exchange equipment.

EXCURSIONS

Poundisford Park. – *5m S by the Trull and Honiton Rds and Trull-Pitminster by-road.*

Trull. – Pop 4 122. The **church★**, which is Perpendicular with 13C tower, is known for its **wooden pulpit** which is carved all round with figures of saints and guardian angels wearing 1530s style clothes.

Take the by-road towards Pitminster.

tc **Poundisford Park.** – The house was built in the former deer park fo Taunton Castle in 1546-50 by William Hill, a Taunton merchant.

The garden front is traditional, three floors high with advanced wings and gables crowned by tall square chimney-stacks or ball finials and outlined by buttresses, rainwater heads and pipes. Flat hood moulds emphasise the mullioned windows. Inside, the **hall** has an enriched **plaster ceiling** with the ribs forming a star pattern around a fine pendant. Note the enclosed **gallery** with its oriel window.

Late 16C ceilings also decorate the screens passage, gallery and a bedroom in which are displayed porcelain and costume collections.

Hatch Court. – *6m SE on A358. P 164.*

TAUNTON DEANE

Michelin map **403** fold 35 – K30

Taunton Deane or the Vale of Taunton lies west of the town, a beautiful diamond of fertile agricultural and cider apple country, watered by the River Tone and ringed by the moorlands and hills which characterise the county: the Quantocks to the northeast, the Brendons to the northwest and the Blackdowns to the south. At the feet of the hills are a number of small market towns, an old manor house and, on the Blackdowns, a monument.

TOWNS in the Vale

★ **Bishop's Lydeard.** – Pop 3 520. The **houses,** some still thatched, the **almshouses** of 1616 with mullioned windows and curved doorway arches, the church, all in local **red sandstone** reflect the village's situation below the Quantock Hills.

The **church★** in true Somerset tradition, is notable for its west **tower** of *c*1470 which rises from a transomed west window to the bell stage where the flourish begins with a three-light opening, transomed, traceried and Somerset traceried, flanked by buttress pinnacles; above are a collar of gargoyles, a pierced parapet and countless more pinnacles *(illustration p 147).*

Inside, is an early 16C **rood screen** in which the elaborate tracery complements the fan vaulting and has a unique decoration of **lead stars**; note the finely carved **cornice**. The carved **bench-ends** of the same date are coloured the better to show the windmill and flying birds, the ships and symbols of the Passion. The pulpit is Jacobean.

In a wall cabinet *(light switch)* is the town's **market charter** of 1291 sealed by Edward I.

★ **Combe Florey.** – Pop 180. The picturesque small village in a valley at the feet of the Brendon Hills, is romantically named after 12C knight, Hugh de Flori.

Almost every building is in the local pink-red, Quantock sandstone, most noticeably the **church** where a particularly deep coloured stone has been employed for the embattled and pinnacled tower and for the trims and window tracery. Inside, note the **angels** at capital height *(tower arch and N arcade)* and the early 14C **tomb** with a lifesize effigy of a cross-legged knight and, presumably, successive wives.

★ **Gaulden Manor.** – *P 161.*

Milverton. – Pop 1 324. The town, with the Brendon Hills to the northwest, surrounds a hillock crowned by the parish **church**, 14-15C building in the local red sandstone. The Perpendicular tower with a square stair turret, rises to bell openings filled with Somerset tracery and a crest of battlements and pinnacles.

Inside, the **north arcade** is 14C, the **font** with cable moulding and a frieze of crosses is Norman, the **rood screen**, as can be seen from the date, was made in 1540. The **stalls** and **benches**, which date from 15-16C, are attractively carved with poppyheads, the twelve apostles, local characters, the arms of Henry VIII...

The **village** itself is a mixture of Georgian houses (North and Fore Sts and south Sand St), small cottages and 19C houses, spiced with the occasional 17C house and, east of the church, 15-16C parsonage.

Wellington. – Pop 10 623. The town had become a market and cloth centre by 15C. In 19C its communications were revolutionised by the construction of the Bridgwater-Tiverton Canal and, in 1840s by that of the Bristol-Exeter railway. The houses, the town hall of 1833, the Baptist Chapel, even the Friends' Meeting House, reflect the late Georgian – early 19C prosperity.

The 15C **church**★ possesses a fortress-like **tower** of red sandstone which rises through three stages from a west door and four-light window to bell openings filled with Somerset tracery and a final outpouring of gargoyles, battlements and pinnacles, of which there are three to each angle and nine on the stair turret.

Inside, are an EE **east window** of three stepped lancets below encircled quatrefoils, a **lily crucifix** carved into the centre mullion of the east window of the south aisle and the **funerary monument** of Chief Justice, Sir John Popham (d 1607, *p 194*), who presided at the trials of Guy Fawkes and of Sir Walter Raleigh, and is shown recumbent on a chest, beneath a canopy ornate with achievements and obelisks.

Wellington Monument. – *2m S by-roads.* The Duke of Wellington, on being granted his title,took the town's name as being the nearest to his family name of Wellesley but otherwise had no connection with it. Nevertheless the townspeople erected in his honour on the Blackdown Hills, 175ft tall, grey stone monument in the form of a bayonet which can be seen from miles around.

From its base there are **views**★★ across Taunton Deane to the Polden Hills, the Quantocks, the Brendons and Exmoor and into Devon *(viewing table)*.

Wiveliscombe. – Pop 2 120. *(Pronounced wivvel-iss-cum)*. The most westerly of the vale market towns dates back to pre-Roman times when there was an early Britisth fort on Castle Hill to the north. By 14-15C the village was prospering from occasional visits by the bishops of Bath and Wells to their manor house of which the gate still remains *(SE of the church)*.

Developments in cloth-weaving transformed the village: it became with Frome, one of the most important in the county its speciality by the late 18C being Penistones, the strong blue cloth popularly used for clothing slaves in the West Indies. The cloth was produced in such quantities that a Taunton carrier made £6000 one year transporting it to London. More than 60 Quakers lived on the town in 18C.

Prosperity brought rebuilding so that today houses and public buildings are almost all 19C. Note in the **Market Sq**, the red tile-hung public library, once the **Court House**.

★ TINTINHULL HOUSE

Michelin map **403** fold 36 – L31

tc The **house**, comprising the present east front with a cross wing at the south end and only one room deep, was built as a farmhouse in *c*1600. In 1630 Thomas Napper rebuilt the south wing completing the gable with an **initialled datestone**; nearly a century later, his grandson increased and reversed the house to its present appearance with a new **west front** and a **walled forecourt** which he intended to be the formal entrance. This 18C pedimented front in Bath stone, dignified by giant pilasters and with a corresponding pedimented doorway, nevertheless retains such 17C touches as stone mullions and transoms in some of the windows.

The two-acre **garden** is so planned that borders, flowering and foliage trees, and shrubs and colour schemes can be viewed from a number of angles and so planted that there is something to enjoy at all seasons.

Begin with the individually enclosed, formal gardens, laid out in line with the west front: the **Eagle Court** (named after the birds on the piers marking 18C forecourt), the **Azalea Garden** and the **Fountain Garden** where white flowers stand starlike against outlining yew hedges.

Off the view line are a Cedar Lawn, Pool and Kitchen Gardens.

Enjoy the planting, so arranged that colours contrast, are massed or shade from the darkest to the palest tone, texture is varied with flowers and foliage, outlines with climbers, trees and shrubs, the exotic and the everyday...

Michelin map **403** fold 36 – M30

In England's smallest cathedral city the streets and square bustle with shoppers and a twice weekly market while just inside the precinct gates calm reigns as the Cathedral Green spreads out before the unique west front, that panoply of the church displayed through the famous of all ages from Christ in Majesty, the apostles and saints, kings of the Bible and this land, queens, holy women, bishops, hermits and knights in armour.

★★★ The CATHEDRAL

History and Construction. – The cathedral is 800 years old, the bishopric of Bath and Wells 1000 years, the foundation by Ine, King of the West Saxons 1200 years and the site as one of Christian worship possibly 1600 years, being Roman or even Celtic. Of the early churches nothing remains above ground. In 1091 Bishop John de Villula (d 1122), having purchased the city and abbey of Bath, removed the throne; a successor, Bishop Savaric (d 1205), equally power hungry, seized Glastonbury and omitted Wells from his title. Glastonbury, in time, regained its autonomy; the title of Bath and Wells was re-adopted and the throne returned to Wells.

The cathedral took more than three centuries to plan and build, from c1175 to 1508.

c1175	Building began – Wells was the first cathedral church in EE style. Three bays of the choir and the greater part of the transepts were completed under Bishop Reginald de Bohun (d 1191).
1239	Cathedral consecrated. Nave completed, west front partly built and many statues carved under Bishop Jocelyn (1206-42).
Before 1250-1306	Chapter house built in successive stages as finance allowed.
1315-22	182ft, central crossing tower constructed and separate Lady Chapel built beyond the east end.
1338-48	Scissor arches inserted to counteract tower subsidence on the west side.
c1320-40	Choir completed; retrochoir built to link east end and Lady Chapel making the cathedral 415ft long from west to east. East, Golden Window glazed c1340.

The 125ft west towers were added in 1384-94 and c1430; the cloisters rebuilt in stages, c1420-1508.

TOUR

Exterior

West Front. – Before you rises the west front. Long ago it would have been blazingly dramatic, the figures coloured and gilded; it would have resembled an illuminated manuscript or a magnificent tapestry. Today we see it in sunlight and shadow, tinted at sunset and gilded by floodlight.
Despite much destruction by the Puritans, it is England's richest display of 13C sculpture.
The screen front is nearly 150ft across, twice as wide as it is tall, extending round the bases of the west towers – strange constructions which continue the gabled lines of the screen in slim and soaring pinnacled buttresses and tall paired lancets, only to stop abruptly. It may have been felt that elaborate cresting would detract from the screen with its near 300 statues, half of them life-size, which rises to a climax in the centre gable with a frieze of apostles and Our Lord.
Continue round to the north side of the cathedral.

North Porch. – The porch leads to a twin doorway with a central pier of ringed shafts; on either side is a display of 13C delight in pure line as exemplified in shallow tiers of subtly varied blank arcading.

Chain Gate. – The "gate" dates from 1459 when it was built to afford a covered way from the oriel led **Vicars' Hall** of 1348 to the cathedral – it emerges inside the cathedral at the top of the chapter house stairway *(p 179;* Vicars' Close: *p 180).*

Quarter-Jack. – *W wall of N transept.* 15C knights strike the bells with their pikes at the quarters.

Cathedral Roofs, Crossing Tower, Chapter House. – Continue a few yards to look up at the pinnacled and balustraded **roofs** of the east end, at the **crossing tower** with paired lights, shafted buttresses, a pierced balustrade and fountains of pinnacles, and at the octagonal **chapter house** again buttressed, pinnacled, arcaded and balustraded above wide, foil-traceried windows. (Another beautiful view of the east end is from the Bishop's Palace garden – *p 180.*)

Interior *time: 1 hour*

Straight ahead is one of the **scissor arches** inserted to west, north and south when the west piers of the crossing tower sank; whether considered graceful or gaunt, they were an outstanding and successful solution to a nightmare problem and have become a hallmark of the cathedral.
The constant features, the **roof vaulting** and the **pier shafting**, are subtly varied in design in each cathedral sector – the vaulting reaches its climax in the star in the Lady Chapel and the piers, in the slender clustered column in the chapter house...

The Nave. – The **piers** are topped by stiff leaf **capitals**, crisply carved and deeply undercut at the west end.

At the top end of the nave, the stone **pulpit** dates from c1547 and the adjoining **Sugar Chantry** from 1489 – a pair in hexagonal plan with that opposite of Bishop Bubwith of 1424, but enriched with fan vaulting, angel figures in the frieze and an ogée arched doorway.

Crossing. – Pass under the west scissor arch to see the **fan vaulting** of 1480.

Continue up one of the chancel aisles to enter the choir.

Chancel. – Immediately striking are the **vista** east through the three pointed arches behind the high altar to the retro-choir and Lady Chapel, and on high, of the Jesse or **Golden Window** of mediaeval glass.

Note the **bishop's throne** made of stone, the tapestry bishops' banners and stall coverings of 1937-48 workmanship and the **Bekynton Chantry** of 1450, with the bishop, Keeper of the Privy Seal to Henry VI, in full vestments and as a cadaver.

Return to the crossing.

(BTA)

The scissor arch at the end of the nave

South Transept. – The **capitals**, less sharply carved, have men's heads and animal masks hidden among the leaves or digress to show a man with toothache or tell the tale of two caught in the act of robbing an orchard *(SW pillar)*. The **corbels** also portray figures including an angel.

The circular **font**, with a Jacobean cover, is the only relic of an earlier cathedral on an adjacent site.

Among the **tombs** note that of Bishop William de Marcia (d 1302), possibly a true portrait effigy, on a low chest encircled by a frieze of heads.

St Calixtus Chapel. – The **tomb chest** of Thomas Boleyn (d 1472) is panelled with Nottingham **alabaster** impressively carved to represent God the Father and the Annunciation.

South Chancel Aisle. – The chancel aisles are the resting place for **tombs** convincingly carved in 1220-30 to resemble seven early **Saxon bishops**.

Retro-Choir. – The **piers,** few in number with shafts almost separated, produce a forest of ribs to support an intricate **tierceron vaulting**. Note 13C cope chest and three of the cathedral's **misericords** which show respectively, a left-handed man killing a wyvern or dragon, Alexander the Great being lifted to heaven by two griffins, both mediaeval carvings and 17C illustration of a boy pulling a thorn from his foot.

Lady Chapel. – At the centre of the unequal octagon which is the Lady Chapel – it enters spatially into the retro-choir – a finely **painted boss** forms the climax to the **star vault**. Much of the glass, destroyed at the Reformation, has been replaced in its fragmentary state.

North Transept. – In the transept are 1955 **lifesize carving** of Christ rising from the tomb on Easter morning and an **astronomical clock** of 1390 with the sun and a star revolving round the 24 hour dial. Above is a **knights' tournament** which circles at every quarter hour, one knight being struck down every quarter. At the quarters, also **Jack Blandiver**, a seated figure at gallery level, kicks his two quarter bells and on the hour, strikes the bell in front of him. (The mechanism is silent during services).

Chapter House. – The grace of the chapter house begins at the **steps** – a wide flight curving in a quarter circle, laid in c1290, the shallow treads worn since by several million feet. The direct continuation is the extension to 15C Chain Gate *(see p 178)*. The octagonal **chapter house** is supreme with its clustered **centre pier** from which 32 ribs fan out to meet those rising from each angle in an encircling octagonal rib. The traceried windows superimpose gabled stalls, each crocketed and cusped gable resting on a **figured corbel** – an opportunity taken by the mediaeval masons to carve portrait heads!

Cathedral Precinct

Mediaeval Gates. – Three 15C gates lead through from the city streets to the calm of the Green: **Brown's Gate,** a tall gatehouse (now a hotel) from the narrow Sadler St, **Penniless Porch,** the massively towered gatehouse built by Bishop Bekynton in 15C which affords access from the Square *(NE corner)* and got its name from the mediaeval beggars who used to crowd it, and the **Bishop's Eye** a polygonal towered archway from the centre of the east side of the Square.

Cathedral Green. – The Green, a forecourt from which to view the cathedral exterior, is marked on the north side with the Liberty behind it by 17-18C houses, including the **Old Deanery**, buttressed, battlemented and turreted in 15C and remodelled in the late 17C and the Chancellor's House, remodelled in 18C **(local museum)**.

★ **Vicars's Close.** – The close at the east end of the Green, is entered just beyond the Chain Gate through a gateway beneath the Vicars' Hall. It is a 150yds long street of **identical cottages** built in c1360 for members of the cathedral in minor orders. The houses, to which the walled front gardens were added in c1415, have been continuously occupied and altered except for **no 22**, which has retained its original outward appearance.

At the end – the street narrows for the sake of perspective – is 15C **chapel**.

★ **Bishop's Palace.** – The palace, on the south side of the Green, stands stoutly walled
tc and encircled by a moat patrolled by swans.

The approach is through the Bishop's Eye *(p 179)* and an inner, 14C gatehouse, square, castellated and formerly preceded by a drawbridge.

Inside are walled gardens, the welling **springs** from which the town gets its name – 3 400 000 gallons a day or 40 gallons a second – the mellow ruin of the old palace (known as the New Hall), the present palace and a beautiful **view** ★★ of the east end of the cathedral.

The **palace** itself is 700 years old. The walls with bastions and angle towers (rampart walk) and the moat were constructed in 14C as a status symbol.

The oldest part of the palace proper is the centre block with its undercroft of 1230-40, re-ordered and re-decorated inside in 19C when a top storey was also added. The chapel dates from in c1280.

At the end of 13C as a final enbellishment, the **New Hall**, 115 × 60ft, was built of red sandstone with corner turrets and great traceried windows. In 1552 the roof was stripped of its lead (the proceeds going to the king) whereupon the roof timbers rotted and fell in. Part of the remaining walls were removed in 19C to make "a picturesque ruin".

ADDITIONAL SIGHTS

Market Place. – The bustling town centre has been equipped since the Middle Ages with a **conduit** bringing water from the springs in the palace garden *(see above)*; the **Gothick** fountain is a late 18C replacement of earlier fountain-heads.

Along the square's north side is a range of houses erected in 1453 by Bishop Bekynton and still known as the **New Works** (Nova Opera). There have been repairs but the range appears still much as described in a document of 1480. Marked on the pavement is Mary Rand's record long jump of over 22ft achieved at 1964 Olympic Games.

High St. – The short High St is lined above 20C shopfronts by houses with uneven rooflines which date from 15-17C; the King's Arms still has 14C roof; the **City Arms**, a low, half-timbered building surrounding a small courtyard served as the city goal from 16-19C.

St Cuthbert's. – St Cuthbert's 122ft **tower** is distinguished by its slender stepped buttresses framing enormously tall bell openings, a crest of blind arcading between corner buttresses and pinnacled turrets.

A Perpendicular church, it succeeds an EE church (transept chapel window) and a Saxon building of which only the dedication remains – Cuthbert was an English monk and Bishop of Lindisfarne in 685-7.

Inside the typical Somerset style wooden **roof**, with tie-beams, cresting, coffering and a chorale of demi-angels, was vividly restored to its true mediaeval colouring in 1963. Note also the **piers,** elongated to take the clerestory and with differently carved capitals, the **royal arms** of Charles I and Charles II *(N aisle and N transept chapel)*, the late Jacobean **pulpit**, exceptionally carved with scenes from the Old Testament (Jonah and the Whale, David and Goliath), two much mutilated **13C altarpieces** *(transept chapels)* also the **contract** for the altarpieces' erection in 1470.

Two massive **silver flagons**, presented in c1639, make a gleaming display in their south pillar niche.

Outside, at the east end, stands **Priest Row**, a line of Victorian cottages on the site of former priests' lodgings, delightful with neat porches and flowered garden.

★★ WOOKEY HOLE

Michelin map **403** fold 36 – L30

tc "Just under the hills, is the famous and so much talked of Wokey Hole" wrote Defoe in 1686. Since his day many more caves have been discovered but the stalactites he saw and that you will see, will have grown only one inch apiece.

The approach is through wooded pastureland at the foot of the Mendip plateau.

Mill buildings, trees and greenery, surround the hole in 200ft cliffside from which the River Axe pours out in a 12 million gallon a torrent. The river has no visible source: two miles away up on the plateau the soil composition alters from impervious shale to permeable carboniferous limestone through which rainwater percolates, collects in rock faults and wears a course which forms the passages and caves which comprise the Hole.

★ **The Caves.** – The river is always present in the caves, in echoing, although mostly unseen, cascades and in deep green-blue-black pools, mirroring the walls which vary in colour from iron rust-red to leaden-grey and green-white. The caverns and narrow fissures through which one walks for some 350yds, represent less than one tenth of the explored passages.

Stalactites, stalagmites, frozen falls, translucent pools, cliff faces of different coloured rock, the stone outline of the witch, which one legend even claims was killed by King Arthur, ferns growing beside the arc lights, present an immutable world. In their 500 million year lifecyle the caves have been inhabited by Iron Age man in 300 BC and later by Romano-British and Celtic peoples.

★ **The Papermill.** – Handmade rag paper with body, texture and a watermark, has a unique quality of simple luxury and is fascinating to watch being made. Paper, which has been made in England since the Middle Ages, was first made at Wookey Hole in *c*1600; the mill supplied paper for the Confederate banknotes issued at Richmond, Virginia.

★ **The Fairground Collection.** – The gloriously garish collection of gallopers, spinners, old bioscope fronts, fascias, gods, horses, deer, dragons and peacocks, were made for the travelling fairgrounds of 1870-1939. Many are beautifully carved, painted and signed. You walk among them expecting a clock to strike and all to come whirlingly alive.

Mme Tussaud's Storeroom. – A Bosch-like array of the funny, the famous and the unspeakable line the shelves. There are the known and recognisable; the unrecognisable; the altogether forgotten; those recalled only by their labels; and a few, including Mme Tussaud herself and Marat, not modelled but truly sculptured.

(West Country Tourist Board / Mike Weaver)
Fairground galloper

The towns and sights described are shown in black on the maps.

YEOVIL

Pop 27 359

Michelin map **403** fold 36 – M31

The bustling town, the base of Westland Aircraft, the centre of the dairy farming industry, also remains the glove and leather centre which it has been since 14C when gloving was a cottage industry, the skins then coming from sheep on the Polden and Quantock Hills – there is still a Glovers' Walk in the town.

Big increases in the population came after 1853, when the railway link with Taunton was opened. The **buildings**, therefore, are principally 19-20C with a few, scattered 18-19C, Georgian houses and older inns, most notably in **Princess St**, the **High St** (two old inns), **Silver St** (inn sign on a fine wrought iron bracket). **Church House**, in brick, west of the church, is Georgian.

★ **St John the Baptist.** – The parish church stands tall upon the central hillock around which the town grew up, the 90ft **tower** a dominant landmark since it was erected in the late 14C. Severe and stoutly buttressed, it rises from a plain doorway and five-light window, through an opening and a belfry bay to a high, pierced parapet.

The church itself, an early Perpendicular, much pinnacled structure, was entirely constructed of grey lias with Ham Hill stone dressings, between 1380-1400. All the **windows**, and there are 18, have five lights and measure 9ft wide by 20ft high, from which the church has come to be known as the "lantern of the west".

Inside, the **roofs** above the tall, slim, clustered arcades, have retained their original **bosses**, a strange collection of human faces and animal masks, many of the men, in the aisles especially, apparently in full African tribal warpaint possibly inspired by the travellers' tales of returned crusaders.

Below the chancel is a **crypt** with rib vaulting resting on a central, **octagonal pier**; it was once used as a charnel house and is approached from the chancel through an ogée arched doorway decorated with a wreathed skull.

The **lectern** and **font** are both 15C, the former one of only four to remain from 1450. It stands 6ft 6in high, has lion feet and a triangular section reading desk engraved with the figure of a friar whose face was obliterated by the Puritans in 1565.

As you leave look up at the dragon and other savage gargoyles.

tc **Yeovil Museum.** – The museum is in an 18C coach house of mellow brick with Ham stone angle quoins and Venetian upper windows. The collections include **gloving tools** from when the industry was a local staple, a bequest of 18-19C **glassware** with wine and cordial glasses and Nailsea pieces *(p 40)*, a special display of **firearms** and a **Petter oil engine**, the invention of a local man in 1895.

(After LC Hayward / Yeovil Council photo)
The Alfred Jewel

Also in the museum is a reproduction of the **Alfred Jewel**, discovered in 1693 close to Athelney *(p 151)*, believed to be the handle to a pointer, and depicting Christ, in *cloisonné* enamel on gold plate, holding two gold sceptres. The letters in the filigree frame spell out, in Anglo-Saxon, "Alfred had me made".

EXCURSIONS

★★★ **Montacute House.** – *4m W on A3088. Pp 169-70.*

★★ **Fleet Air Arm Museum, Yeovilton.** – *8m NW by A37 and Ilchester by-road.*

Ilchester. – Pop 1 768. The triangular **green** with its Tuscan column and ball finial erected in 18C, the **square** overlooked by Georgian houses – among which is the **town hall** – and by the **parish church** with 13C fortress-like octagonal tower, hint at the town's long and varied fortunes.

Its importance began with the Romans who, under the name Lendinis, made it a cantonal capital at the junction of the Fosse Way and the road from Dorchester; the Saxons maintained it as a centre and by 950 it had become a royal burgh. In 11-12C, it possessed a flourishing market and a mint; by 1327 it had taken over from Somerton as the county town, a position it maintained until 19C when Taunton took its place.

Turn right in Ilchester. The airfield is beside the road (A303).

★★ **Fleet Air Arm Museum.** – *Royal Naval Air Station.* More than a quarter of a million visitors
tc each year come to see the 60 historic and present-day **aircraft**, the battle honours, paintings and photographs of famous actions including 1982 Falklands War. As back-up there are models, photographs of auxiliary services, of training, reconnaissance, rescue... Visitors of all ages come also to see the flying – routine and training most days, acrobatic and breathtaking on special display days. *(Local announcements.)*

★ **East Lambrook Manor.** – *12m W. Take A3088 W out of Yeovil.*

Ham Hill. – The 425ft hill is a notable landmark and commands **views**★★ of the rolling countryside for miles around. It was once crowned by a prehistoric hillfort but is, of course, famous as the **quarry** from which limestone has been cut to build churches, beautiful houses, and small cottages throughout Somerset and the southwest. The stone varies in colour from creamy white and grey to yellow, gold and brown ochre depending on the ferrous deposits in the ground. The quarries after more than a thousand years are exhausted and stone is now only found for repairs.

Continue ½m along A3088.

Stoke sub Hamdon. – Pop 1 825. The village, which is in two parts and built almost entirely of the Hill stone, has an attractive collection of 17-18C houses and cottages.

The **parish church**★ stands amidst trees near a stream at the bottom of the hill. A mixed building, it dates from 12-16C: the **tower,** on the north side, is 13C at the base, 15C above, with battlements, a cornice and gargoyles; the chancel and nave in Ham stone, comprising the Norman church, were erected in *c*1100 – note the corbel tables along the chancel walls; the north transept was added in *c*1225, the south in 1300; the two-storey, north porch in *c*1325 though the **doorway** is Norman.

Inside, the **chancel arch** in dark Ham stone, is carved with three orders of zig-zag and lozenge decoration above small columns. Note the Norman **font** with cable mouldings and frieze, Jacobean pulpit and **hour-glass** and 17C **communion rail balusters.**

Continue W by by-roads across A303 to South Petherton; turn N.

★ **East Lambrook Manor.** – The visit is primarily to the **garden** – a garden of "cottage mixtures",
tc of exotic, old fashioned, foliage and simple plants, lacking vistas but showing the close-up beauty of plants in separate gardens which extend round two sides of the rambling, stone and brick house, once thatched and now Somerset tiled.

When it was built in *c*1470 the house probably belonged to a minor squire, a merchant or a prosperous yeoman; in 1938, when discovered by Margery Fish and her husband, it was derelict and rat infested; the garden, of course, was a wilderness.

Mrs Fish, before she died, converted it into the **plantswoman's** garden which it has remained. It is attractive throughout the year, very modest in size – about 2½ acres – but filled with ideas and plants which we can all grow: hydrangeas, salvias, achilleas, alyssum, primulas, lavender, ivies, vines, double daisies...

Brympton d'Evercy. – *2m W off A3088. P 152.*

Cadbury Castle. – *11m NE by A359.*

Queen Camel. – Pop 785. The small village possesses a parish church with a severe 14C west tower which rises to battlements and pinnacles, overtopped by the stair turret.

Continue along A359 to Sparkford; bear right into A303 and right again at Chapel Cross.

Cadbury Castle. – The castle with commanding **views**★★, crowned a hilltop 500ft above sea-level. Nothing remains on 18-acre site which was excavated in 1966-70.

Cadbury, which began as a prehistoric settlement, was converted in the Iron Age into a hillfort. It was still occupied at the time of the Roman invasion in 43AD and was re-fortified in the late 5C.

The names of the River Cam to the west and Queen Camel have given rise to a belief that the Battle of Camlann was fought nearby, that the builder could only have been King Arthur *(p 71)*, that Cadbury was, therefore, the fabled **Camelot.**

WILTSHIRE

Area 1344 sq m Population 518 545

Wiltshire is beautiful with the distinctive Marlborough Downs along its eastern border and open country to the south and west. There are woodlands and the small but soaring Savernake Forest, the Wylye and other river valleys. It possesses beautiful gardens and great houses and manor houses, contains England's classic prehistoric monuments and many would say, England's finest cathedral. In contrast, there are small and friendly market towns and villages with wide main streets, picture postcard villages, tithe barns and village greens.

Yet because of its network of roads which dates back from today's M4 to trunk roads and coaching roads, turnpikes and post roads, mediaeval, Saxon and Roman roads, even the prehistoric Ridgeway Path, because of the railway since the mid-19C, almost everyone has "passed through" Wiltshire and, unless they have found themselves in camp on Salisbury Plain, they have failed to stay in the county and enjoy it. The places of interest are well scattered but the distances are not great.

The Chalk Downs. – The downlands throughout the ages have provided a crest for the Ridgeway Path, grazing for hundreds of thousands of sheep and, in modern times, arable and farm lands and sites for a number of chalk hill figures.

CHALK HILL FIGURES

Hill figures cut into chalk escarpments are an idiosyncratic feature of the region although they are not unique to it. They date from the year 0 to 20C; most are in Wiltshire – 7 horses still visible plus other figures – although the oldest are actually outside the county: the Uffington Horse on the Berkshire Downs (Oxon), the Cerne Giant in Dorset (p 132), and the Long Man of Wilmington in E Sussex.

All the figures, because of their size and consequent foreshortening, can only be viewed from a distance, therefore viewpoints as well as the location are listed below. Because it is interesting (just once!) to see a figure close to, where there is easy access this is also mentioned.

NB several figures are on private land, others may be enclosed because of erosion; in addition some figures may be difficult to see if overgrown with grass and awaiting scouring, but the majority, most of the time, are white and cheerful.

Uffington White Horse. – White Horse Hill (856ft), Berkshire Downs. Location: *500ft up overlooking the Vale of the White Horse. Illustration p 210.*

Viewpoints: *Ashbury/Wantage rd (B4507), Swindon/Faringdon rd (A420) and the Vale Rd (B4508), also the railway between Swindon and Reading.*
Access: *by car – B4507* (signpost); *on foot – from the Ridgeway Path (p 199). NB: the horse is not visible from the Ridgeway.*
It is possible that both the Uffington Horse and the Cerne Giant had a religious significance originally; the date of the horse is unknown but it has been put at 100 BC to 100 AD. The sculpture is 365ft long and, with Osmington (p 145), is alone, in facing right.

Westbury White Horse. – Bratton Down. Location: *facing west.*
Viewpoint: *1½ miles along B3098 from Westbury.*
Access: *continue along B3098 almost to Bratton village, turn right* (signpost) *up a steep track to Bratton Castle (p 208) and the horse.*
The horse, near the end of the steep west facing, chalk down measures 166 × 163ft high and is Wiltshire's oldest having been cut in 1778 by a connoisseur of horseflesh who had been irritated for many years by an earlier figure on the same site! This animal, smaller, daschund-like in form and facing the other way might possibly have been Saxon, but was more probably of 17-18C date. The 1778 figure, now secured by stones and concrete, has sired a long line.

Cherhill Horse. – Cherhill, Calne. Location: *facing north.*
Viewpoints: *Calne/Marlborough rd (A4) just east of Cherhill, Calne/Melksham rd (A3102) just out of Calne.*
Access: *a path from A4 leads to Oldbury Castle hillfort (¾ m) and the chalk figure. The horse, which measures 131ft by 123ft from nose to tail, dates from 1780. The obelisk on the skyline beyond its tail was erected by Lord Lansdowne in 1845 (p 187).*

Marlborough Horse. – **Viewpoint:** *200yds beyond the College, on the south side of the Bath rd (A4); look left across the field to the low escarpment.*
The horse was designed and cut in 1804 by boys from the local town school. He is 62ft long, 47ft high and perky with a docked tail and round eye.

Alton Barnes Horse. – Old Adam Hill, Pewsey. **Viewpoints:** *the horse looks south over the Vale of Pewsey and can best be seen from the small road running west from Alton Barnes-Allington or the parallel Woodborough-Beechingstoke rd.*
The figure was cut on a gradual slope in 1812 after the outline of the Cherhill horse and measures 166ft by 160ft long; its dominant feature, probably due to weathering and scouring, is its enormous eye which is 11ft long by 8ft deep.

183

Hackpen Horse. – Hackpen Hill, Marlborough. Location: the far side of the Ridgeway Path from Marlborough.

Viewpoint: B4041 rd between Broad Hinton and junction with A361 and again on A361 Devizes-Swindon rd before the Wootton Bassett turning.

Access from the Ridgeway Path (pp 199-200).

The horse is said to have been cut in celebration of Queen Victoria's coronation in 1838. Its dimensions, 90ft x 90ft may be an attempt to overcome the lack of hillside incline; the slenderness of the neck and legs is unusual, the round eye is possibly after Alton Barnes.

Broad Town Horse. – Wootton Bassett. *Viewpoint:* from Wootton Bassett take the Broad Town rd (B4041). The horse is said to have been cut in 1864 by a farmer which perhaps explains its proportions (78ft long by 57ft) and more naturalistic appearance except for the eye.

Pewsey Horse. – *Viewpoint:* Pewsey-Salisbury rd (A345) just out of the town, and closer to, Pewsey-Everleigh side road.

The trotting horse was commissioned by the town council to celebrate the coronation of King George VI in 1937.

It replaced a late 18C, almost obliterated, horse and after being pegged out by the designer, was excavated and chalk-filled by the local fire brigade. It measures 45ft × 66ft long.

Regimental Badges. – Fovant Down. Location: on the escarpment behind the military camp south of Wilton-Shaftesbury rd, A30.

Viewpoint: off the road east of Fovant, a signpost on A30, indicates a footpath which gives a closer view of the badges.

The frieze of military crests was cut by successive companies of soldiers in camp in Fovant in 1916. As a sign of changing times, they and all other hill figures were covered over in 1939 to prevent their use as navigational bearings.

Among the figures from east to west, are: a map of Australia, and about 4 on, a rising sun and a kangaroo (all Australian), RAMC badge, YMCA triangle, 6th City of London Rifles, London Rifle Brigade, the Rifle Brigade, Devon Regiment (towered castle), 7th Royal Fusiliers, Royal Warwickshire Regiment (a deer).

Bulford Kiwi. – Beacon Hill, Bulford Barracks, Amesbury. Location: on the escarpment.

Viewpoint: the kiwi faces NW and is best viewed from the Bulford-Tidworth side road off A303 (Amesbury-Andover rd).

GLOUCESTER

GLOUCESTERSHIRE

★ Malmesbury

Castle Combe ★★

Sheldon Manor ★

AVON

★ Biddestone

★★★ Corsham Court

Chippenham

BATH

★ Lacock

★ Great Chalfield Manor

★★ Bradford-on-Avon

★ Westwood Manor

Trowbridge

Steeple Ashton ★

Edington

Westbury

Bratton Castle

Westbury

Chalcot House

Frome

Warminster

Heytesbury

Longleat ★★★

Wylye

SOMERSET

★★★ Stourhead

★ Wardour Castle

DORSET

WEYMOUTH

BRISTOL

YEOVIL

TAUNTON

EXETER

EXETER

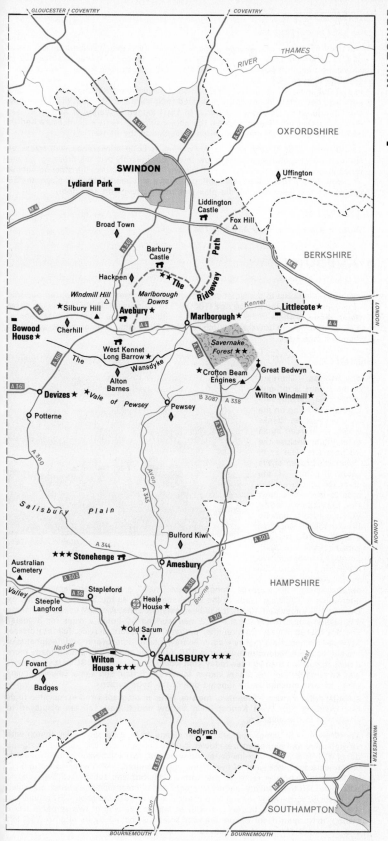

The bird is vast, being 420ft long and covering 1½ acres of ground; the letters NZ below the bill are 65ft high and the bill itself 130ft long. It was designed by a NZ engineer to commemorate the troops' stay in the barracks and was cut in 1918. Note especially the brilliant foreshortening which makes the bird instantly recognisable from a great distance and many angles.

AMESBURY

Michelin map **403** fold 28 – 030

The town at a major road crossing beside the Avon and the church are descendants of a centuries-old market and an abbey. According to legend it was to a nunnery at Amesbury that, in 5-6C, Guinevere fled from the court of King Arthur and remained until she died *(p 162)*.

In 979 Queen Aelfthryth *(p 131)*, in expiation of the murder of King Edward IV founded a Benedictine abbey in Amesbury dedicated to St Mary and St Melor, the Breton boy saint murdered by his uncle. The abbey in 1501 lodged Catherine of Aragon on her way to London but, like the queen, the abbey suffered Henry's displeasure and in 1539 it was Dissolved and the church presented to the parish.

The Church. – St Mary's, built largely of flint, is EE in appearance with traces of Norman and Perpendicular work; a low tower sits squarely over the crossing. Inside, note the small two-tier piscina *(S aisle)*, the two fonts, one Norman the other octagonal and even older, 16C oak beams roofing the nave and carved when in place, the EE vaulting in the Jesus Chapel, the plain oak rood screen with 16C door.

EXCURSION

Bulford Kiwi. – *4m E by A303. P 184.*

★ AVEBURY

Michelin map **403** fold 28 – 029

Avebury, in contrast to the isolation of Stonehenge, presents superimposed patterns of occupation from the Bronze Age (1800 BC) to the present. Thirty to forty-ton **sarsen stones** rise everywhere in the fields, loosely encircling a village of small houses, shops, 17C pub, a square towered church, a Tudor-Elizabethan manor house and 17C thatched tithe barn.

SIGHTS

★ **The Stones.** – The plan of the stones is difficult to decipher, the only vantage points being on the circular earthen banks which, re-inforced by an outer ditch, enclose the 28 acre site. The earth "rampart", broken at the cardinal points of the compass to provide access to the centre (now the Devizes-Swindon (A361) and the High St-Downs roads), encloses a **Circle** of 100 Ice Age sarsens from the Marlborough Downs and two inner rings. From the south exit an **Avenue** of

(Vloo / J Alan Cash)

The Avenue

approximately 100 pairs of stones, square "male" and slender "female" stones alternating in each file, leads to the burial site known as the Sanctuary *(1 ½ m)*, on Overton Hill (excavated 1930). It has been estimated that Avebury henge took some 1 ½ million hours to construct – 200 men working 60 hours a week for 3 years? The 4 ½ thousand year old site, after perhaps 1000 years' service, fell into disuse; eventually it became a quarry – John Aubrey, exultant discoverer and designator of the site as a pre-historic monument in 17C, was able to show Charles II many more stones in position than you see today. One would-be quarryman, 13C barber-surgeon, was carrying on him the oldest known scissors in Britain and some Edward I coins when he was crushed as he toppled one of the huge sarsens.

tc **Alexander Keiller Museum.** – Models of the site, aerial photographs and exacavated finds from Avebury, the West Kennet Long Barrow and Silbury Hill are displayed to advantage in the museum.

★ **The Church.** – St James appears, at first glance, to be a Perpendicular church with an embattled and pinnacled west tower, but the doorway with colonettes and zig-zag decoration is Norman and inside, at the west end, two solid walls extend forwards which were the outer walls of the original Saxon church. Aisles were added in 12C. In 19C a local builder removed the Norman columns and substituted Tuscan-style pillars, but left the possibly mediaeval arches and circular clerestory windows which are believed to be Anglo-Saxon. The chancel arch is 13C, the choir 19C rebuilding. Among the furnishings, the **tub font**, with an intricate carving of two serpents and a bishop, is Norman if not Saxon; the rood screen is topped by its original 15C loft and crocketed parapet of vine leaves.

tc **Avebury Manor.** – The Elizabethan manor house is sharply gabled on its oldest, east side. Inside are oak panelled rooms, coved plasterwork ceilings and still complete with period furniture, staterooms visited by Charles II and Queen Anne.

tc **Museum of Wiltshire Folk Life.** – *Great Barn*. The collection includes agricultural implements, cheesemakers' churns and presses and complete sets of tools of such craftsmen as tanners, smiths and stone-masons.

EXCURSIONS

★ **Silbury Hill.** – *2m on N side of Marlborough rd (A4); lay-by car park; no direct access.*
Silbury, which covers 5¼ acres, was built in four stages, beginning in c2500 BC,
using human muscle, reindeer antler picks and oxen shoulder blade shovels only to
pile up its million cubic yards of chalk. The final, 130ft high, grassy mound, with its
distinctive 100ft wide flat top, is, even today, the largest manmade hill in Europe.
Its purpose remains a mystery despite shafts sunk to its centre in 18C, tunnels pierced
in 20C...

★ **West Kennet Long Barrow.** – *3m on S side of the Marlborough rd (A4), plus ¾ m
field footpath – signposted from lay-by car park; take a torch and boots, if weather
at all wet.*
No mystery surrounds the burial barrow, England's finest, which dates from
3500-3000 BC. The entrance to 340ft long by 75ft wide, earth covered mound **(view)**,
is at the east end between giant sarsens.
On either side are dependent burial vaults and, at the far end, a hall, roofed with
massive capstones supported on upright sarsens and drystone walling. Some 50
skeletons of the late Mesolithic builders, farmers and their families were discovered
in the vaults.

The Wansdyke. – *Access: 4m by A361, Devizes rd; there is no public right of way
along the Wansdyke though many stretches are open.*
The frontier earthwork, built possibly in 5 or 6C by the Romano-Britons or Saxons
of south Wiltshire to protect themselves from incursions by Saxon settlers in the
Thames Valley, runs for some 14 miles in a west-east direction.

Windmill Hill. – *4m NW on foot Rtn from the church by a lane and a path.*
The hill is famous, archaeologically, as the causewayed camp after which the earliest
Neolithic culture in Britain is named. It comprises three concentric ditches and
embankments in which the livestock herds were gathered before the annual autumn
meat slaughter.

★ BOWOOD HOUSE

Michelin map **403** fold 28 – N29

tc The house was still abuilding when **Lancelot Brown** was first summoned to Bowood
in 1757 and, for a fee of 30 guineas, gave his opinion of the "capability" of the park;
in 1762-8 he returned to execute his plans which centred on the creation of the
idiosyncratic lake and woodlands and the planting of specimen strees including the
now 140ft tall cedar of Lebanon. As the park matured, the house, begun in 1725
and sold, still uncompleted, in 1754 to the first Earl of Shelburne, father of the future
Marquess of Lansdowne, underwent change upon change by a succession of famous
architects. Throughout it suffered the disadvantage of absentee owners: the
Marquesses of Lansdowne were political men holding high office in government at
home and as ambassadors, governors and viceroys – the marquisate was created in
1784 for negotiating peace with America at the end of the War of Independence.
Their principal residence in England was Lansdowne House in London. In 1955 the
"big house" at Bowood was demolished except for the Orangery and its attendant
pavilions which were retained as a residence and sculpture gallery.

The GROUNDS

Three paths from Temple Gate *(50yds from the car park)* lead: ahead to the front of
the house; left, through glades of trees, across lawns characterised by specimen
beeches, cedars, elms, to the timber-built adventure play area; and right, to the far
end of the lake (cascade, 18C Doric temple), circling through woods and coppices
in a 2 mile arc.

The Terraces. – The 100yds long terraces enclosed by low balustrades and
punctuated by clipped yews, glow throughout the summer with red roses. The centre
path was originally the approach to the now demolished 18C house.

Woodland Garden. – *Entrance off A432, nearer Sandy Lane.* In May and June visit
the garden to drift through the acres of bluebells, rhododendrons and azaleas.

The HOUSE *time: ¾ hour*

Entrance to the house is now through the Orangery, classically designed by **Robert
Adam** in 1769 with an important pedimented and giant columned, centre doorway.
Inside, the briefest Ionic colonnade leads across the gallery to the chapel.

Laboratory. – *Right.* The small room is where **Joseph Priestley** discovered oxygen in
1774 and Jan Ingenhouse (d 1799) the process of plant photosynthesis.

Library. – The end room by C R Cockerell after Robert Adam, is warm with a gilded,
coved and coffered ceiling, portrait medallions of Greek writers, Josiah Wedgwood
Etruscan vases, a white marble fireplace of 1755 from the old house, beautiful
bookcases and shield back chairs. Look through the windows at the **view★** of the park.

Sculpture Gallery. – The gallery, which extends the length of the Orangery, is the
setting for chosen pictures, statuary and tapestries from Lansdowne collections past
and still in the making – the head of Hermes, the Florentine sleeping cupid, the
Diskobolos, portraits by Reynolds, a Gainsborough landscape, gilded, marble-topped
console tables, porcelain, a gilded French clock with a blue face framed by a mirror
and torchères.

BOWOOD HOUSE★

Exhibition Galleries. – *Far left end of Sculpture Gallery.* Surprises in the upper galleries range from the **Albanian costume** in which **Byron** was painted in 1814 (given by the poet to the mother of 4th marchioness as fancy dress!), 18-19C furniture and small possessions, an immensely rich and colourful assembly of objects collected by 5th Lord Lansdowne when Viceroy of India (1888-94), and a glittering display of family honours, orders, swords, insignia, fabulous jewels...

★★ BRADFORD-ON-AVON   Pop 8 968

Michelin map **403** fold 27 – N29

It is the houses rising tier upon tier up the hillside from the river and the old mediaeval bridge with its weather vaned chapel, which give the town its character, not any one building. The larger houses were built in the local creamy-yellow ochre limestone by 17-18C clothiers, by Paul Methwin (d 1667; *p 190*) and his contemporaries, some of who, Daniel Defoe estimated early in 18C, were worth between ten and forty thousand pounds a man. In the same streets are terraces of weavers' cottages, including those of 17C Flemish craftsmen and, in the shopping streets, alleys and shambles, 17-18C houses above 18-19C shopfronts.

SIGHTS

★★ **Saxon Church of St Lawrence.** – The church may date from 7-8C, the time of St Aldhelm *(p 196)*, who is known to have founded a convent on the site between 672 and 705 AD. In 1001 church and convent were given to Shaftesbury Abbey *(p 138)* but by Domesday the convent had disappeared. From 12-19C the church was used as a cottage, a school, a charnel house.

The minute building of stone, tall and narrow with steeply pitched roofs, and a blind **arcading decoration** on the walls, is believed to have been erected in a single phase. It has not been enlarged or altered since, apart from three windows pierced at the west end in 19C. The orientation is east-northeast with the chancel slightly "skewed" a feature made more obvious because the arch at the end of 25 x 13ft nave is only 9ft 8in x 3ft 6in. The "floating" angels and assembled altar-stones are Saxon.

★ **The Bridge.** – The town developed around the regular passage across the river at the broad ford. The first pack-bridge was built in 12C. In 1610, when the wool and cloth trades were booming, a wider bridge with round arches was erected with upon it the *tc* small, square, domed **chapel** topped by an Avon gudgeon **weather-vane.**

Tithe Barn. – The vast stone barn (Crafts Centre) with gabled doorways, oak doors on long iron hinges pinned with possibly the original **nails** and a forest of **timberwork** inside, was probably built in the early 14C by a tenant of Shaftesbury Abbey. The tenant paid the abbey £6 13*s* 4*d* a year rent, a vicar £5 a year's salary and let out the land from which he collected tithes worth some £46 13*s* 4*d.*
The adjoining granary is later.

Holy Trinity. – The church was consecrated in 1150 having been built possibly because St Lawrence was too small, more probably because 12C was a great period for church building and Bradford was prosperous: Domes-

(After West Country Tourist Board / Mike Weaver)
The Bridge and Chapel

day records that there were 126 burgesses – with their families, labourers and servants this would mean a township of, possibly, 1 000 inhabitants. In the early 14C the chancel was extended, in 15 and 19C the entire church was remodelled and embellished. There are, therefore, Norman features (chancel windows, arcade piers), a mediaeval **wall painting** of the Virgin being taught to write *(N of E window)*, a **squint,** possibly the longest in England, cut in 13C when the chancel was lengthened, Flemish glass *(S window in the nave)* presented by an 18C clothier, memorials and brasses to clothiers and, at the west end, 13C **sculpture** of a young girl in a wimple.

WALK to the TOP OF THE TOWN

Start from the Bridge.

Silver St. – The road crosses the Bridge to become the main shopping street.

Market St. – *Wide, centre left fork.* The street, which is lined with 17-18C houses with later shop fronts, goes straight up the hill.

Church St. – *Sharp left.* The road, which leads circuitously uphill, opens with two Georgian frontages with Venetian windows, the one Church House, the other a fashionable refacing in black and white of 16C inn; beyond are 19C converted mill

– one of 32 once at work in the town – Old Church House (now a hall), built in 17C by the clothier Thomas Horton (brass in the church), Dutch Barton, 18C front on 17C foundation, Hill House, home of the Druces, early-18C Quaker clothiers, 18C Abbey House with a profusion of pediments, and 18C **Orpin House** *(just NNW of the church)*, the house of Mr Orpin who was parish clerk for 40 years and lies in a tomb mid-way between his house and the church. The two Chantry Houses are 16C, Barton Orchard and the terrace of **weaver's houses**, 18C.

Newtown. – The so-called Newtown is 17-18C.

Middle Rank. – The street is marked by a chapel and gabled terrace houses.

Top Rank Tory. – The road runs along the crest past 18C houses and terraces and a very special row of 17C **weavers' houses**, to the town's highest point and the **hermit chapel** of St Mary Tory (12C rebuilt in 1877).
From the hilltop a circular **view**★ extends round from the Marlborough Downs towards Bath, Bristol, the Severn and Somerset. At your feet is the town with the River Avon and the Kennet and Avon Canal *(p 40)*, the railway and the tithe barn.

> *It is possible to reach St Mary Tory by car by taking the road at the right (E) end of Newtown, Conigre Hill, and bearing second left into Tory.*

CHIPPENHAM   Pop 18 696

Michelin map **403** fold 28 – N29

In 20C, by way of main roads and the M4 motorway, since 1837 by the railway steaming west along its high striding viaduct, since 1474 along Maud Heath's Causeway and, since Saxon times, by pack horse to the first settlement at the bend in the River Avon, people have come to Chippenham to trade. At the top end of the town are the church, a street of houses of every degree and age, and the half-timbered town hall.

SIGHTS

★ **Yelde Hall.** – The 15C half-timbered hall, on an island site beside the former standing
tc place of the local gallows, pillory, stocks and whipping post, served as the office of the bailiff and burgesses of the Hundred. Inside are a panelled courtroom over a blind-house or lock-up and adjoining, beneath an open timber roof, the old town hall.

St Andrew's. – The many times remodelled Perpendicular church stands on the site of the Saxon church in which Alfred's sister, Aethelswitha, married the King of Mercia in 853 AD. Go inside to see a flatly **carved effigy** of a beautiful, mysterious woman of 13C *(S chapel)*, 13C **vestment chest** with bird and animal carved panels and an outstanding 1730s oak **organ case**, pedimented, turretted, intricately carved and surmounted by trumpet-blowing angels.

St Mary's St. – The long street behind the church is lined with cottages, terrace and large town houses, timber-framed, small windowed and low-lying, or tall and ashlar faced with graceful doors and windows, pediments and parapets.

Maud Heath's Causeway. – Maud Heath, 15C widow, farmer's wife or spinster property owner, no one knows, left houses and land in the town for the construction and, most importantly, the maintenance of a causeway so that local producers could come to market dryshod. The pathway, 4½ miles long, still exists, running from Wick Hill, where an inscribed stone and 19C pillar crowned by statue of Maud Heath mark the start, through East Tytherton, Kellaways and Langley Burrell to the former outskirts of the town. A 1698 end stone is now in Barclays Bank in the Market Place; a film-strip on the causeway may be seen in the Yelde Hall *(see above)*.

EXCURSION

Round tour. – *14 miles; leave Chippenham W by A420; bear right, B4039; bear left.*

★★ **Castle Combe.** – Pop 347. The picture postcard village is approached along a wooded valley, the road coming out from beneath the trees straight into **The Street**, as it is known. Punctuating its length and contrasting with the stone cottages on either side, are the Upper Manor House of *c*1700 with a shell hood above the door, **mounting blocks** and a **market cross** with a solid pyramid roof.
The **church,** with a tall pinnacled tower, was built in 13-15C when the village was a rich wool market. Inside are 15C font with an integral lectern, 16C pulpit, a royal coat of arms with seated lion and unicorn supporters, a wall tablet of 1588 in mixed Latin and English and a mediaeval knight.
Still further along The Street are the **pack bridge** and, opposite, **Water Lane** circling a widening out of the stream into a pool which mirrors the former weavers' cottages bordering the lane. Gardens, trees, flowers, the stream, complete the picture.

> *Continue along the by-road to Ford; turn left in A420 and right at Giddeahall.*

★ **Biddestone.** – Pop 479. The village centre is a large green complete with a duck pond; all around 16-18C houses and cottages, many with stone mullioned windows, are set in spacious array. One, behind 18C wrought iron gate and railings, stands in a modest perfection of two storeys with angle quoins, segmented bays and, above the door, an open pediment framing the date, 1730.
The manor house just off the green, is 17C, with stone walls and roof, gables ending in ball finials, mullioned windows and a brick gazebo poised upon the garden wall.

> *Continue 2m E along the by-road towards Chippenham.*

★ **Sheldon Manor.** – *P 203.*

> *Return to Chippenham.*

tc Corsham Court, an Elizabethan house of 1582, was bought by Paul Methuen in the mid-18C to house in due grandeur, a collection he was to inherit of 16 and 17C Italian and 17C Flemish **master paintings and statuary.** At the end of 19C the house was enlarged to receive a second collection, purchased in Florence at the end of the Napoleonic Empire, principally of fashionable Italian masters, rare Italian primitives and stone inlaid furniture.

Paul Methuen (1732-95), was a great-grandson of Paul Methwin (d 1667) of Bradford-on-Avon *(p 188)*, and a grandson of John Methuen (1650-1706), ambassador and negotiator of the **Methuen Treaty** of 1703 with Portugal – a treaty which gave us our "oldest ally", permitted the export of British woollens to Portugal (heretofore prohibited) and allowed a preferential 33⅓% duty discount on imported Portuguese wines – so bringing about a major change in English drinking habits! Field Marshal Lord Methuen (1845-1932), who became famous in the wars in Africa against the Ashanti and the Boers was the father of 4th baron, Paul Methuen (1886-1974), the painter.

The architects involved in the alterations to the house and park were successively **Lancelot "Capability" Brown** in 1760s, **John Nash** in 1800, and Thomas Bellamy in 1845-9. Brown set the style by retaining the Elizabethan stables and riding school (now occupied by the Bath Academy of Art) but rebuilding the gateway, retaining the great, gabled, Elizabethan stone front and doubling the gabled wings at either end and, inside, by designing the east wing as stateroom-picture galleries... The park he planned to include a lake, avenues and specimen trees such as the Oriental Plane, now with a 200yd perimeter.

Nash's work, apart from embellishments such as the octagonal corner towers and pinnacles has largely disappeared; Bellamy's stands fast, notably in the hall and staircase.

TOUR   *1½ hours*

Four state rooms, music and dining rooms provide the setting for the outstanding collection of 150 and more **paintings, statuary, bronzes** and **furniture.**

Picture Gallery. – The triple cube of 72 × 24 × 24ft with a white coved ceiling, is hung with crimson Spitalfields damask which was used also to upholster the Chippendale furniture. Note the pier glasses and tables by the **Adams brothers,** the girandoles attributed to **Chippendale** and the white marble fireplace.

The gallery is hung with the **classic paintings** in the collection by Fra Bartolomeo, Caravaggio – *Tobias and the Angel* – Guido Reni, Strozzi, Salvator Rosa, Tintoretto – *Adoration of the Shepherds* – Veronese – *Annunciation* – Rubens – *Wolf Hunt* – Van Dyck – *Christ's Betrayal* – and by Sofonisba, a portrait of the *Three Caddi Children*.

Cabinet Room. – Among the pictures are **Fra Filippo Lippi's** *Annunciation* (1463) and Cesari's cartoon of a *Flying Cherub*. The side tables with porphyry tops are attributed to **Chippendale**, the pier-glasses are by **Adam** and the inlaid commode and torchères by the cabinet marker, **James Cobb**.

State Bedroom. – The four-poster and serpentine mahogany chests are by **Chippendale** the oval mirrors framed with vines and bushy tailed squirrels are by **Thomas Johnson**. The 18C bracket clock is Italian. Note also the games table and two pictures: the *Infant Christ* by **Guercino** and the *Duke of Monmouth* by Lely.

The Octagon Room. – Highlight of the room designed by Nash in 1800 is **Michaelangelo's** *Sleeping Cupid* (1696). Among the paintings are a Claude, an Elder Breughel flower piece, a Caracci self-portrait and an extraordinary allegorical portrait of *Queen Elizabeth* as a seated old woman with death close by and cherubs bearing off the emblems of sovereignty.

Music Room. – The pianoforte of 1807 is by **Clementi**. Note also the aeolian organ and harps and, among the furniture, the Regency mahogany chairs and matching horseshoe shaped **wine-table** with a hinged coaster. On the showcase are 19C medicine chests and inside Derby, Rockingham and Minton ware and a big "tea-pot" which is, in fact, a rare 18C Liverpool or Derby creamware **punchpot**.

Dining Room. – The room is hung with the finest family portraits: *Paul Methuen,* the purchaser of the house, by **Reynolds** and two delightful children's portraits by the same artist also one of the girl twenty years later by **Romney.**

★ **DEVIZES**   Pop 10 649

Devizes, in 20C, connotes the army – more precisely the red brick barracks in the London Rd on the town outskirts. From mediaeval times until 19C it denoted an important cloth market which specialised in the narrow woollen suiting known as "drugget" – hence the number of well disposed 18C town houses, many on 17C timber framed foundations: there are more than 500 listed buildings in the ¼ square mile of the town centre.

In the earliest years of the period it was a flourishing sheep market, from which it gained its broad Market Place, and evolved the mediaeval **street plan** which, uniquely, has been neither added to nor reduced over the past 800 years. Before even these times the spur west of the present Market Place was selected by the Normans as a strongpoint on which to build a castle which, in the early 12C, was rebuilt by Bishop Roger of Old Sarum *(p 203)*. This fortification eventually became "ruinated" and was finally demolished by Cromwell's forces in 1645. The castle now on the site is 19C fantasy *(not open)*.

SIGHTS

★ **The Market Place.** – The long, half moon shaped Market Place with its 19C cross and fountain, is overlooked almost entirely by 18C houses and a rare number of old inns – the town stands on an old coaching road.

The Bear. – The inn, part 16C, part 18C, was known in 18C for the portrait sketches of customers drawn by the landlord's young son, **Thomas Lawrence** (1769-1830).

Northgate House. – The brick house with a handsome porch (Council Offices), was the King's Arms coaching inn before becoming the house of the family for who George Eliot worked as a governess while living next door at the giant pilastered, Sandcliff.

The Black Swan. – The three-storey, pilastered inn, on the curving east side of the Market Place, is again 18C.

Parnella House. – *No 23*. The house was built in *c*1740 by a doctor who decorated the front with a somewhat odd, roughly carved statue of Aesculapius, the Classical god of medicine (modern copy).

No 32. – The house was the White Hart.

No 40. – The Victorian-Florentine style bank is 19C rebuilding of the former White Swan.

Corn Exchange. – The giantly arcaded and balustraded building, crowned with the gilded figure of Ceres is 19C.

Old Town Hall. – The hall, facing the Market Place from the far end dates from *c*1750 when it was built with an open ground floor to serve as a butter, cheese and poultry market beneath Ionic columned and pedimented upper halls and offices.

Town Hall. – The "new" hall of 1806 on an island site at the end of St John's St, is an elegant building with a rusticated ground floor with arched windows, a rounded back and a wide bow to the front, dignified by tall Ionic columns.

★★ **St John's.** – The parish church, through the churchyard, is robustly Norman with a mighty oblong **crossing tower,** which inside has round arches towards the nave and chancel and pointed ones towards the transepts. The broad mouldings, sharp with zig-zag decoration, the spandrels and walls covered with fish-scale patterning, are enhanced by the local golden stone. The chancel has low rib vaulting and walls densely patterned with intersecting arches. The Norman corbels in the chapels are carved with human faces and monster masks.
Later additions include the Perpendicular aisles, the tracery panelled ceiling over the nave, the acanthus leaf carved organ case.

★ **Devizes Museum.** – *41 Long St.* The museum possesses geology and natural history
tc collections, an art gallery with a stained glass window by John Piper (1982) and a long-famous **archaeological department** in which are clear, progressive models of nearby Stonehenge and Avebury. Among the finds on display are axe and arrowheads, daggers, pots, urns, glassware, the Stourhead Collection of gold ornaments, small sculptures and a round and a smiling Celtic Janus head.

The Brittox. – The shopping street with modern fronts on older houses existed in 1386 when it served as the palisaded entrance to the castle (the meaning of the Norman-French *bretasche* from which the name derives).

The Shambles. – The old dark street still serves as a twice-weekly market *(p 173)*.

St John's Alley. – *Obliquely across from the Town Hall.* The alley is lined by a complete range of half-timbered, compact Elizabethan houses with jettied upper floors.

EXCURSION

Potterne. – Pop 1590.
2m S on A360.
The village of 18-19C houses of all shapes and sizes with shops below, is aligned along a main street.
The **Porch House**★★, at the south end, is a house to end all porch houses. It has black and white half-timbering, the beams all vertical, gables with neat ball finials, stone tiles, a two tier hall window, an

(Vloo / J Alan Cash)

The Porch House

oversailing upper floor and the porch itself, well advanced with an oriel window beneath its independent gable *(not open)*. It was built when Henry VIII was on the throne.
Adjoining is a second house, gabled, stone-tiled and with the later 16C "cross-gartered" half-timbering.

*Three Michelin Green Guides for North America:
Canada, New England, New York City.*

EDINGTON
Pop 686

Michelin map **403** fold 28 – N30

Edington is where, in 879 **Alfred** defeated the Danes finally *(p 152)*. It is also where William of Edington, Bishop of Winchester (1345-66), Treasurer and Chancellor to Edward III, was born and decided in 1351 to rebuild the existing church as a chantry, soon afterwards enlarged into an Augustinian monastery. The monastery was Dissolved, the church given to the village.

★ **St Mary, St Katherine and All Saints.** – The church, which is 150ft long, was built in the transitional period between the Decorated (reticulated tracery) and Perpendicular periods (upright, straight-sided panel tracery).

A massive, low, crossing **tower**, a three-storey porch and at the west end, a twin turreted gable framing a wide perpendicular window over a processional door, are the striking exterior features.

Inside are great clustered columns in golden stone, 17 and 18C pink-and-white and all-white plaster **ceilings** and a double **chancel screen** or monastic pulpitum of *c*1500 with seats between the trellises and a gallery above. The **chancel**, the Decorated part of the church, has a combined Decorated-Perpendicular window and 14C canopied niches with lively figures. In the north transept, the Crucifixion window is 14C.

The furnishings are principally Jacobean: the testered pulpit – the stairs are 18C – the font cover, the **communion rail** with alternating flat and turned balusters and a row of points possibly following Archbishop Laud's injunction to keeps "dogs and cows" away from the altar. The monuments are older: three early 14-15C knights, one with his lady, and a partly coloured tomb *(S transept)* of a blue robed monk with his feet on a barrel or tun and sprigs of bay suggest a rebus of his name – Bayton.

★ GREAT CHALFIELD MANOR

Michelin map **403** fold 27 – N30 – 2 ½ m NE of Bradford-on-Avon

tc The manor, surrounded on all sides by park and farmland, was originally fortified with a moat, curtain wall and bastion. In 1430s Thomas Tropnall, steward to Lord Hungerford, MP and landowner, entered on thirty years of disputes and lawsuits to possess the house which had been in his family since the Conquest but had passed to another branch; in 1467 Great Chalfield was his. Two years earlier he had purchased a stone quarry near Box, so that almost immediately he was able to begin work on the house, rebuilding and extending it and ordering the north face to its present most attractive, mellow gold appearance of paired but dissimilar gables, finials, chimneys, buttresses and most particularly two oriels, one three sided with a small pyramid roof surmounted by his coat of arms with supporters, the other semicircular, poised on corbels and a buttress and coroneted with a strawberry leaf decoration. To complete the forecourt, Tropnall erected a bellcote and added a crocketed spire to the parish church.

TOUR ¾ *hour*

The Porch. – Note the vaulting, Tropnall's arms and the squint through which visitors were surveyed before being admitted through the wicket in the oak door.

Great Hall. – As you enter the hall, which measures 40 × 20 × 20ft, the game of detection begins: what is 15-16C, what 20C, for in its 500 years the manor passed from owner to tenant farmer, from being a prize possession to a Parliamentary garrison. At length, in 1836, the absentee owner had a survey and drawings made but then lost interest; finally in 1905, a new owner, using the meticulous 19C drawings, began removing accretions, rebuilding, putting in a carved oak screen and collecting stout examples of 16-17C refectory tables, benches, stools, chests, Cromwellian chairs, court cupboards, Jacobean small tables, Carolean chairs...

Dining Room. – The panelling and ceiling are of 1550. Note the squint to the porch, and wall painting of a man with five fingers and a thumb, possibly Tropnall himself.

Bedroom. – The bedroom, at the top of the stone staircase, includes the three-sided oriel window one sees from the front of the house. It is adjoined by a closet built over the porch where a maid or page would have slept.

★ **The Church.** – The 14C All Saints received from Tropnall in 1470 not only its spire bul also the **panelled hood** which forms the porch and the wagon roofed chapel named after him: the chancel and vestry were added in 16-18C. Note 17C **three decker pulpit**, the consecration crosses on either side of the door, 17-18C chandeliers, the tub font, 15C crested **stone screen** with painted Tropnall arms and, in the chapel, the wall paintings of St Katherine. (Tropnall himself is buried at Corsham.)

★ LACOCK
Pop 1 289

Michelin map **403** fold 28 – N29

The calm, attractive, stone and brick-built village has always been under special patronage: first of the abbey, then the Talbots and now the National Trust.

LACOCK VILLAGE

The village comprises four streets which form a hollow square.

★ **The High St.** – The wide thoroughfare, often blocked in mediaeval times by the three-day fair and weekly wool and produce market, leads to the abbey. On either side mellow roofs of tile and stone, cover cottage-shops and houses of every height and size, as various in date as design.

Porch House. – The gabled, black and white half-timbered house is 16C.

The Inn. – The building is old and was refaced with red brick in 18C.

Tithe Barn. – The barn with its timber roof, on the street corner, dates back to 14C.

West St. – The street at right angles and also wide, marked the old village's perimeter.

George Inn. – The inn is the oldest in this village of at least one pub to each street.

The Brash. – The high, upraised **pavement** which turns the street corner, is named after the loose broken rock used in its foundation.

Church St. – The street, which runs parallel to the High St, leads to the church.

Cruck House. – The house is named after the exposed beam supporting in a fashion common enough in 14C, both roof and wall.

The Angel. – The inn, which dates from 1480 is named after the gold coin of the time bearing the figure of the Archangel Michael. Go down the horse passage to the old coaching yard to enter the beamed interior.

Market Place. – The street towards Church St's end opens out into what was the village's original market place – Lacock's first market charter was obtained by Ela, Countess of Salisbury and abbess in 1241 *(see below)*.

King John's Hunting Lodge. – The so-called lodge dates from 16C.

The Tanyard. – The yard includes a drying loft for skins and a gaunt 19C workhouse.

East St. – The fourth of the village's four streets, is narrowly enclosed by 16 and 18C houses and onetime shops.

★ **St Cyriac.** – The Perpendicular church, is a "wool church" from the time of Lacock's prosperity in 14-17C as a wool and cloth market on the London-Bath road.
Distinctive features outside include the large embattled and pinnacled **porch** fronting an older **tower** which was crowned, in the early 18C, with a recessed, octagonal spire; the Perpendicular tracery of the north aisle west window; and, on the south side, which is decorated with amused gargoyles, a mullion windowed **cottage**, added in c1615.
Inside is the **Talbot** or **Lady Chapel** which has 15C lierne vaulting with rib encircled pendants and arches decorated with carved masks and small animals, all of rare craftsmanship. The **tombchest** in the chapel is also remarkable: dating from 1566 and set up for Sir William Sharington *(see below)*, it is ornamented with carved strapwork, cartouches, panels, little vases of flowers, cherubs and a shell crest.
In the south transept is a brass to Robert Raynard (d 1501) in armour and heraldic tabard, his wife in a kennel headdress, and their 13 sons and 5 daughters.

★ **Fox Talbot Museum of Photography.** – The museum, in 16C barn at the abbey
tc gate, celebrates, on the upper floor beneath spendid roof timbers, the work of photographers of today and, on the ground floor, through his notes and letters, his equipment, early cameras and collotypes and his awards from all over the world, **William Henry Fox-Talbot** (1800-77), the inventor of modern photography.

★ LACOCK ABBEY   *time: ¾ hour*

tc "A grand sacrifice to Bacchus" was held by **John Ivory Talbot** to celebrate the opening in 1755 of the new entrance hall to the abbey, constructed in the Gothick style recently made fashionable by Horace Walpole at Strawberry Hill, Twickenham. The house had been in the family for two centuries having been purchased at the Dissolution in 1539 from Henry VIII by Talbot's ancestor, **William Sharington** *(see also above)*, for £783 and repurchased by him from the crown for £8 000 in 1550s, after unsuccessful political intrigues and coin-clipping at the Bristol mint had put him in the Tower! On Sharington's return to Lacock he built the tower on the south front and the Stable Court which includes domestic quarters, a bakehouse, dairy, brewhouse and hay lofts, beneath large dormered roofs, decorative chimneys and heraldic beasts.
As Talbot followed Talbot (Sharington's niece married the first), alterations followed in the style of the day: Ivory Talbot continued his Strawberry Hill Gothickisation *(p 21)*, three oriels were added to the south front in 1827-30 by **William Henry Fox-Talbot** whose first successful photograph was of the centre window.

House interior. – Of particular interest inside are the Gothick entrance hall with "not expensive terracotta performances" in the niches and arms on the vault; a massive bronze **pestle and mortar** engraved with Sharington's name and scorpion crest; an exceptionally carved **stone fireplace** and a modern copy of 1225 edition of *Magna Carta,* probably sent to William Longespée *(p 201)* as Sheriff of Wiltshire and kept by his wife, **Ela, Countess of Salisbury,** when she succeeded him in the office – the only woman sheriff in the county's history.
In **Sharington's Tower**, built as a belvedere, is a **stone table** of c1550 in which the octagonal top is supported on the shoulders of four grinning satyrs.
Finally in the South Gallery or Drawing Room note the prints from Fox Talbot's **original negatives** of the centre oriel and the shelves of china.

> Leave the house and walk back to S front; the entrance to the cloisters is below the centre oriel.

The Convent. – The nunnery buildings date from the abbey's foundation in 1232 by Ela, Countess of Salisbury.
The 15C **cloisters** with carved bosses of the pelican and lamb, a mermaid, jester, angels and animals, were adapted as offices and lodgings by Sharington in 16C, hence the decorated chimneys and dormer windows. Leading off each gallery would have been, the church (destroyed 1540) containing the countess' tomb, now in the gallery, 13C sacristy with two chapels *(E end)*, 15C chapter house *(entered through the triple arch)*, and the big warming room, the nuns' only room with a fire – the cauldron was made in Malines in 1500.

★ LITTLECOTE

Michelin map **403** fold 28 – P29

"The Knight, was brought to his tryall, and to be short this judge had this whole house, parks and manor, and (I thinke) more, for a bribe to save his life" – the knight was Sir John Dayrell; the crime, the murder of his newborn, bastard baby; the judge, the future Lord Chief Justice, Sir John Popham *(p 177)*; the house, Littlecote; the date, the late 16C.

The house was already misnamed being the full length of the multi-gabled north face, built of flint relieved by brick courses, stone tiles and with the fine oriel window through which there is a good view from the gallery. Sir John increased the house, constructing a south front in deep rose brick with stone dressings outlining the large windows and centre gables.

tc The HOUSE *time: ¾ hour*

The feature of the house which gives it the particular atmosphere of richness and solidity, of royal feasts in the great hall, of mystery and plots in dark corners and corridors, is the **oak panelling** variously in Tudor squares, decorated with fluted pilasters, carved cornices and friezes. It is complemented by the massive furniture of the time except in three rooms where 18-19C reign supreme.

Great Hall. – The hall, which measures 46 × 24ft and is 25ft high, is decorated upon the walls with 17C **buffcoats**, breast plates and helmets and a rare display of **firearms**, also a painting of Littlecote in 17C; there are portraits of **Sir John Popham** and his grandson, Col Alexander Popham, a Parliamentarian. Note also 30ft **shuffleboard table** complete with catchnets and the prehistoric Irish **elk antlers** (7ft 6in from tip to tip) on the wall.

Drawing Room. – The room is the first of 18-19C rooms. It is notable for the hand-painted Chinese paper upon the walls, an **Aubusson carpet** from Versailles with Louis XV's coat of arms, a **long case clock** by James Reith of London (1715), Chippendale chairs, tables, mirrors and torchères.

Library. – The library, which is oval-ended, is again 18C in style with a second Aubusson carpet and **Sheraton** satinwood furniture. Among the books are the annotated law books of Lord Chief Justice Popham.

Dutch Parlour. – The room was decorated with contemporary scenes by early 17C Dutch prisoners of war.

Brick Hall. – The small hall with a brick floor has outstanding carved **panelling**.

Cromwellian Chapel. – The dignified chapel at the heart of the house, has no altar in accordance with Puritan practice; the upraised pulpit is also of the period.

Haunted Corridor and Haunted Bedroom. – The corridor, in which there is a large fireplace and the panelled bedroom, with a fourposter with crewell embroidered hangings, remain eerie, despite the fact that the crime happened so long ago. In those dark days a handmaid was delivered of a son by Dayrell by a local midwife; when she took the newborn baby to the father in the corridor outside he put it on the fire; the mother remained masked throughout her travail; the midwife, after two years, told a justice of the crime and Dayrell was brought to trial before Sir John Popham.

Long Gallery. – The gallery on the north front is 110ft long and oak panelled with great windows and the early oriel affording views of the wooded countryside. Within the room are Georgian **crystal chandeliers**, French and English 18C **furniture** – inlaid commodes, cabinets, a Queen Anne needlework carpet, Chippendale chairs – **porcelain** from China and the Nether-lands, glass, collections of paperweights and cow cream jugs...

tc MOSAIC PAVEMENT

(BTA)

The Roman Mosaic

Centuries before the house was built, Romans or Romano-Britons dis-covered the gently undu-lating parkland site and built there a villa and, it is believed, a Temple to Orpheus of which the glorious mosaic pave-ment remains.

The pavement was "lost" until 1728 when a steward on the estate discovered it and his wife embroidered a panel of the design (now hanging outside the New Chamber); the pavement was then covered over and lost again until 1978 when excavations revealed the pavement and foundations of adjacent buildings.

tc FRONTIER CITY

The city is make-believe, being a full-blooded, full-size manned, guns a-banging replica of a Wild West town.

★★ LONGLEAT

Michelin map **403** fold 27 – N30

Longleat is a cornucopia of treasure: the grand Elizabethan house in a glorious, wooded, lakeside setting, is built in golden stone in the Italian Baroque style, rising through three tiers of windows to a skyline of balustrading, ornamental chimney-stacks, turrets and statues; close by are formal flower gardens; at a distance an azalea and rhododendron drive. In the grounds, without impinging on the views from the house, are 15in narrow gauge railway and a maze. To one side is the lake where safari boats accompanied by leaping, honking sea-lions, sail past gorillas and hippos; there is a pub; there is coarse fishing; there are, of course, the lions and the safari park.

(R Passmore / Colorific / Cosmos)

Longleat House

tc SAFARI PARK

African elephants, white rhinos, rhesus monkeys, giraffes, zebras, eland, deer, buffaloes, camels, long horned cattle, Canadian timber wolves, Shetland ponies, Siberian tigers and the lions, note every passer-by through their enclosures, eye each car with apparent indifference, curiosity or predatory, monkey, inquisitiveness.

PARK and GARDENS

It was **Capability Brown**, in 1757, who landscaped the park with dense woods on the hillside, and specimen trees in the foreground, who transformed the early 18C "canal" made out of the original ponds or "long leat" in the valley, into the present tree fringed, Half Mile Pond.

The flower gardens, developed since Brown's day, lie enclosed by high yew hedges and wistaria covered walls. A conservatory displays exotics amidst pools. In the garden white doves coo, shimmering peacocks display, seats invite one to linger among the blossom-covered trees, roses and hydrangeas.

tc LONGLEAT HOUSE

The house is four centuries old; the contents – portraits, furniture, porcelain, books, embroideries, silver – range over the whole period, reflecting the diverse interests of the unbroken line of Thynnes from Sir John, purchaser in 1541 for £53, of the site of 13C Augustinian priory from Henry VIII, to the present Marquess of Bath – the family tree from 1215 is at the foot of the Grand Staircase.

Exterior. – The house was completed in 1580, Sir John Thynne, "an ingenious man and a traveller", acting as his own architect. Life at court, as brother-in-law to Sir Thomas Gresham, the financier and builder of Osterley Park, and, more especially, as adjutant and steward to the Duke of Somerset on the latter's travels abroad, on the battlefield, during the remodelling of Syon Park and construction of the original, Renaissance-style Somerset House, had all given Thynne many ideas which he proceeded to draw up into plans for his own new house in Wiltshire. The result has been justly termed "the first great monument of Elizabethan architecture".

Interior. – It was Sir John's idea that the rooms at Longleat should look not, as was 16C custom onto inner courts, but out over the park.

In 19C seven rooms along the east front were transformed in their decoration. The transformation was the achievement of 4th Marquess, a traveller and connoisseur, who visited Florentine, Venetian and Roman palazzi and returned with ideas, artefacts and craftsmen, with roundels, cameos and painted ceiling panels, Baroque plaster-work, wall hangings and furnishings. Against this background are set family portraits, master paintings, English, French, Portuguese furniture, ceramics from Europe and the Orient, silver and crystal, splendid centrepieces...

LONGLEAT★★★

TOUR *1½ hours*

Great Hall. – Note especially in the hall, the **fireplace** pillared by five terms, in the ceiling the Gresham golden **grasshopper crest**, galleries displaying the **arms** of Sir John Thynne, and his patron, the Duke of Somerset, panelling hung with trophies and vast hunting scenes by 18C painter, John Wootton... Note also the 30ft **shuffleboard** table of *c*1600, the oak and steel treasure chests, 17C armchairs, inlaid writing-tables...

Ante-Library. – The first of the transformed rooms, which is furnished in the French Empire style, contains a portrait painted in 1971 of 6th Marquess by **Graham Sutherland**.

Red Library. – The long gallery, which houses some 6 000 of the 39 000 volumes in the Longleat collection, is furnished with Florentine **bookcases** of inlaid walnut, 17C inlaid **secretaire**, 18C **writing desk** and a laburnham, holly and robinia **table**, 1980 piece created by John Makepeace *(p 136)* to celebrate the house's 400th anniversary.

The Breakfast Room. – The room is hung with yellow damask and furnished with Chippendale style chairs set round a table laid for breakfast. On the walls are family portraits including that of 5th Marquess by William Orpen *(over the fireplace)*, 4th Marquess, who Italianised the house, his wife by G F Watts (full length in a dress to be seen in the collection displayed in the Corridor on an upper floor).

Lower Dining Room. – The table gleams with a gilt 17C **steeple-cup,** silver-gilt wine flagons, crystal, silver, Sèvres china. Chairs and furniture are of 17C Portuguese ebony and ebonised mahogany. On the panelled walls hang portraits of 1st marquess by Lawrence *(over the fireplace),* **Sir John Thynne,** the builder *(left)*, Thomas Thynne *(window alcove)*, friend of the Duke of Monmouth, known from his riches as Tom o' Ten Thousand, assassinated in Pall Mall in 1682.

State Dining Room. – In the first of the state rooms, the table stands arrayed with a silver **centrepiece** (1837) of 1 000oz, representing the last charge in the Civil War Battle of Landsdown Hill, silver **salt-cellars** of the *Cries of London* (1851) and 18C silver plates. The walls are covered with Cordoba leather and hung with 17C portraits.

Saloon. – The 90ft Elizabethan Long Gallery with a wall of windows onto the park, a massive **marble fireplace** and alabaster doorcases, contains fine small **furniture:** 17 and 18C Sicilian and French clocks, 17 and 18C French tables – note the mirror pair of tortoise-shell and brass – James II chairs with their original rose brocade...

State Drawing Room. –The end room in the series of transformed rooms overlooks the hall through an embrasure. It is rich with ceiling panels after Titian and Veronese and 17C Genoese velvet from which the gold thread disappeared on the journey from Italy ! The paintings are Italian except for a portrait by Hans Eworth of *Master John,* son of Sir John the builder, at six months *(by the door)*. Note especially among the furniture the French **inlaid tables** with gilt mounts by Boulle, a **writing-table** made for Louis XVI and acquired by Talleyrand, 18C galleried, marquetry **bonheur du jour**...

LYDIARD PARK

Michelin map ▨▨▨ fold 28 – 029

tc **The House.** – The mid-18C stone house, two storeys high, eleven bays wide with pyramid roofed pavilions, overlooks spreading cedars and distant avenues. The rooms are notable for their proportions, moulded plaster and white-painted woodwork – note how funds ran out before the gold leaf highlighting the library ceiling was complete ! Furniture and fine china of 18-19C have been assembled, together with family portraits of the St Johns, owners of the manor for 500 years.

★ **St Mary's Church.** – **Monuments** to St Johns dominate the minute parish church, so
tc that, in the words of John Aubrey, the antiquary, it "exceeds all the churches of this countie". Eighteen figures are represented – recumbent in alabaster, kneeling or standing behind the original railings, beneath funeral helms, painted in a remarkable 17C triptych, or, in the case of Edward who died in the Civil War, standing between parted curtains in gilded armour.
The church is older than the monuments, dating from late 13-15C. Note the traces of mediaeval wall paintings, Jacobean pulpit, 18C altarpiece and wrought iron **communion rail** and the **Jacobean screen** with the royal arms borne by robust supporters.

★ MALMESBURY   Pop 2 581

Michelin map ▨▨▨ fold 29 – N29

The abbey outlined against the sky, crowns a spur. Below, at the centre of the town, is one of England's finest market crosses.

St Aldhelm (639-709). – The future saint and man who by his preaching, it is said, completed the conquest of Wessex, was a pupil at the school which was part of the religious community established in the town in 7C by the Irish teacher, Maidulf; uniquely for the time, he went on to Canterbury, so becoming the first English scholar to combine the learning of Ireland and Europe. In 676 he returned to Malmesbury as teacher, **abbot**, builder of churches in the town, at Bruton and Wareham, founder of monasteries at Frome, and Bradford-on-Avon, and counsellor to his kinsman, the West Saxon King, Ine (r 688-726). In 705, when the See of Sherborne was founded, Aldhelm was appointed the first bishop *(p 139)*. He is buried at Malmesbury. The town name is a combination-corruption of Maidulf and Aldhelm: Maelhelmsbury.
Other men associated with Malmesbury include Elmer, the **Flying Monk**, who launched himself from the old abbey tower in 1010 and "flew" 250yds before crashing but

(After Zodiaque photo)

The tympanum

remained convinced that it was only lack of a tail which had brought him down; **William of Malmesbury** (1095-1143), monk, abbey librarian and great early historian *(p 162)* and the philosopher, **Thomas Hobbes**, born in the town in 1588 (d 1679).

Three historic American families also have associations with the area: the **Washingtons** who in 17C lived in Garadon *(3m E)*; the **Penns** who originated in Minety *(6m NE)*; and **Abraham Lincoln's mother**, Nancy Hanks, who was a member of an old Malmesbury family.

★ The ABBEY *time: ¼ hour*

The present church, an amazing conjuncture of gaunt ruin and living architecture, was begun in 12C. At its zenith, in 14C, it extended 320ft from east to west, had a clerestory and vaulted roof, possessed a central crossing tower with a spire, also a west tower. It was surrounded by Benedictine conventual buildings.

In 1479 a fierce storm brought down the spire and tower, which in their fall destroyed the east end, transepts and crossing; one hundred years later the west tower fell, destroying three west bays of the nave. A majestic six bays remain.

Between these cataclysmic events there occured on 15 December 1539, the Dissolution of the monastery and its sale by Henry VIII for £1517 15*s* 2½*d* to a local clothier. He built a house, Abbey House, with stone from the monastic buildings and set up looms in the church, but in 1541 gave the abbey as a church to the parish.

Porch. – The unique feature of the abbey is the **porch,** a sunset of mid-12C Romanesque carving with trail and geometrical patterns on the eight orders, medallions of Biblical scenes (defaced), continuous banding and, in the **tympanum,** two angels supporting a mandorla with Christ in Glory at the centre – the figures are elongated like those in the lunettes on either side above the blind arcading.

Interior. – The massive Norman pillars with scalloped capitals, support just-pointed arches and a **triforium** of great rounded bays, crisply collared with zig-zag carving. On the south side note the **watching loft** from where the abbot or a monk could follow the service beyond the chancel screen. The mediaeval stone screen at the end of the south aisle marks the chapel of St Aldhelm who was buried in an earlier abbey destroyed by fire in 1050; also buried in this earlier church (mediaeval tomb: *N aisle*) was **King Athelstan** (r 925-39), like his grandfather Alfred, a great admirer of Aldhelm. As you leave note the tombstone in the churchyard *(left of the path)* of Hannah Twynnoy, mauled to death by a tiger from a travelling circus in 1703.

★★ MARKET CROSS

The cross was built of local stone in 1490 when the town was known for its tanning and felt making, silk weaving, lace making, spinning and, of course its woollen weaving; it had a twice weekly market. More than a mere shelter, the cross rises 40ft high in a paeon of buttresses, crocketed pinnacles, castellations and flying arches to a spirelet, supreme pinnacle and cross. Note the carving and small, grinning masks everywhere – "a right faire costly peace of worke" as John Leland declared.

ADDITIONAL SIGHTS

St John's Bridge. – The bridge *(on A429)* got its name from the hospital built by the Order of St John of Jerusalem on the town outskirts in 13C. The hospital was Dissolved, the Templars banished; in 1694 the aged buildings were re-founded as almshouses. Through an archway is the former Old Courthouse.

Bell Hotel. – The hotel was built in 16C to replace the Dissolved monastery guesthouse using stone and timber from the conventual buildings.

High St. – The street and those behind it are lined with 16-19C terrace houses with stone tiled roofs, many of which were refaced in 18C with stone ashlar. The network of older streets and alleys is interconnected by a rare number of footbridges crossing tributaries of the Avon and Ingleburn Rivers which almost encircle the town.

★ **MARLBOROUGH** Pop 5 774

The town, strategically placed on the London-Bath road *(A4)*, has been known since 19C for its school and in earlier centuries was famous as a market town – it was named by John Aubrey as "one of the greatest markets for cheese in the West of England". The main street, parallel to the River Kennet, developed eastwards from a Saxon settlement (now The Green), to where the Normans, soon after the Conquest, took over a 60ft, prehistoric, mound as the site for a motte and bailey castle *(see below)*.

By the time the castle had fallen into ruin in 14C, Marlborough had developed into a market: the long street was filled weekly with downland sheep and cattle and stalls of wool, meat, fresh produce and cheese. Room was needed to herd the animals; the cottages of the period were small and insubstantial and they were pushed further and further back until the street attained the extraordinary width which even permitted open stalls, or shambles, to be pitched in a double line down the centre as they are still on market days.

The Civil War left scars, but they were nothing compared to the fire of 1653 when, it is recorded, "in the space of three of foure houres, there was burnt down to the ground about two hundred twentie foure dwelling Houses, besides many out-houses and stables, and most of the Household goods and Wares in the shops of many of the Inhabitants... The whole losse arising unto four score thousand pounds likewise there was burnt downe to the ground one of the Churches (St Mary's), and the Market House."

The Marlborough Downs. – The Downs which extend in a wide semi-circle north of the town, are traversed by the aeons-old **Ridgeway Path** *(p 199)*. The chalk slopes once grazed by the vast flocks of sheep, which make every town in Wiltshire a wool town in origin, to the west especially are now scattered with small towns and villages, and threaded by local roads running between high hedges; to the east, the land folds in a quilt of large arable fields outlined by straggling files of trees, hedges and ditches, and, on the skyline, stalwart clumps of dark green deciduous broad-leaves.

SIGHTS

The High St. – The wide High St leads from the Green at the far west end of the town to the College at the east end. It is not the architecture which makes the street attractive but the up and down rooflines, the individuality of the houses with their ground floor shopfronts, and at the west end "the pent houses", as Pepys called them when he stayed in the town in 1653, "supported on pillars which makes a good walk". In the same range are several shops which were "improved" in Georgian times by the insertion of first floor Venetian windows.

Town Hall. – The hall in brick and stone, overlooking the High St along its full length from the west end, was built to a Classical 17-18C design on a island site by late Victorian craftsmen.

St Mary's Church. – The church, standing amidst a network of small streets – Perrin's Lane, Patten Alley – at the west end of the High St, was rebuilt after the fire during the Commonwealth – hence the Puritanical austerity. The chancel is 19C.

The Green. – The Green, beyond the west end of the High St, was the site of the Saxon settlement; the nearby Silverless and Kingsbury Sts, are bordered by 17-19C houses of every variety: timber-framed, Classical 18C with pillared porches, ashlar-faced and weatherboarded and with windows from lattice to sash, oriel to Venetian.

Castle and Ball. – *High St, S side*. The inn, built in 17C, was refronted after the fire and turned into a coaching inn in 1745. The house next door, which was pantiled in 18C, was once an inn where Shakespeare is said to have played.

Sun Inn. – *SE end*. The inn and the modest brick range of which it is a part, is timber-framed and dates from the early 17C.

Sts Peter and Paul. – *E end*. The church on the green island site is, like St Mary's, Norman in origin with Perpendicular remodelling, but ferociously renewed in 19C.

tc **Marlborough College.** – The mound-site of the Norman castle *(see above)* was acquired in 1550 by Protector Somerset; in 17-18C, both his grandson and 6th Duke, built separate mansions in the grounds, 1½ million bricks being required before the second was completed in *c*1725.

In 1750 the house was let as a coaching inn, which reigned supreme until the advent of the railway, when it was sold to become a school. The College, at its foundation in 1843, numbered 200 boys; in the century and a half since, buildings have proliferated and Malburians increased in number to 900.

Marlborough White Horse. – Continue about 200yds along the Bath road (A4); look left across the field at the low escarpment *(p 183)*.

EXCURSIONS

★★ **Savernake Forest.** – *2m SE. Entrances off A346 Andover and A4 London rds; parking and picnic places; hearths for open fires – other wise NO FIRE; modestly equipped camping sites (c/o Forestry Commission).*

Savernake was a royal forest, hunted by Norman and Tudor kings alike, its woodland yielding boar and deer. In 18C Capability Brown replanted the 4 000 acres, which it now comprises, with oak, ash, larch and thousands upon thousands of beech trees. Crossing the forest in a NW-SE line, passing halfway along its 3-mile course through the compass point intersection known as the Eight Walks, is the **Grand Avenue ★★★**, palisaded with the superb grey-green trunks of 130ft beeches, dappling the light with tender green, autumn gold and russet leaves...

Round tour. – *14 miles; leave Marlborough S by A346, bear left on to A338.*

★ **Wilton Windmill.** – The mill (visible from A338 beyond East Grafton), was built in 1821
tc on top of the down behind the small village of Wilton, grouped around its
duckpond.

The sweeps, two rigged with canvas sails, two with louvres, turn when corn is being
ground, but cannot be allowed to operate when visitors are in the mill because there
is insufficient room in the cap. What you do see when you climb up and into the
cap, is the grinding machinery *(p 157)* and how the fantail, which never stops whirring,
turns the sweeps into the wind.

Great Bedwyn. – Pop 974. The once large village contains an unusual museum and an
old church. The first, a mason's yard, is a surprising outdoor display of old statuary
and tombstones, the second, a flint church with a square tower dating from the late
12C is built in transitional Norman-EE style.

Inside the church are dogtooth decorated arcades on round columns with deeply
undercut, all different capitals, corbels carved with crowned heads and Seymour
memorials: the tomb of Sir John (d 1536), father of Edward Seymour (Protector
Somerset) and of Jane Seymour, a brass to John Seymour (d 1510) and a bust and
gay cherubs on the tomb of 17C duchess.

★ **Crofton Beam Engines.** – The pumps were installed near the highest point along 81mile
tc Kennet and Avon Canal *(p 40)* to supply water from underground sources to the locks
descending in either direction. There are two engines, one being 1812 **Boulton and
Watt** with 42in piston and cast iron beam which is the oldest beam engine regularly
in steam in the world.

Rejoin the A346 to Marlborough.

Pewsey. – Pop 2 579. *7m S on A3455.*

Pewsey, whose chief feature since 1911 has been a statue of King Alfred, gives its
name to the **Vale of Pewsey★**, a beautiful stretch of country between Salisbury Plain
and the Marlborough Downs. On the town outskirts is the Pewsey White Horse *(p 184)*.

★★ The RIDGEWAY PATH

Michelin map 403 folds 28 and 29 – O, P and Q 29

Length, course, conditions. – The modern Ridgeway Path extends 85 miles from
Overton Hill near Avebury via the Uffington White Horse *(p 183)* to the Ivinghoe
Beacon near Tring; it passes through five counties, Wiltshire, Berkshire, Oxfordshire,
Buckinghamshire and Herfordshire, combining as it does the prehistoric ridgeway
path across the chalk downs west of the Thames with the Roman, Lower Icknield
Way beyond the river crossing at Streatley. The modern path, opened in 1973, is
waymarked by Countryside Commission acorns *(p 200)*.

*The west section is suitable for walking, riding and bicycling; no part may by
motorcycled or driven along. There are car parks at intersections with main
roads.*

The going is straightforward; the grass and earth track, which occasionally rises to
900ft, is generally wide, passing along downland crests, beside fields, through woods
and coppices. It is mostly out in the open, affording wide **views** across the downs
– beware the ruts in the path and remember that chalk is muddy and slippery after
heavy rain.

If you intend to walk a considerable distance or the full length, buy the 1: 50 000
(1¼ inch) Ordnance Survey maps: nos 173, 174, 175 and 165.

You will see as you walk, particularly over the chalk, **wild flowers** and **herbs, butterflies**
– chalk hill blues and many of the browns – and **birds** – particularly skylarks, and very
occasionally a kestrel or buzzard.

History. – Before the Uffington White Horse, Avebury or Stonehenge, before the sea
broke through the chalk in *c*7000 BC to form the English Channel and make Britain
an island, our prehistoric ancestors were walking the Ridgeway Path.

The **Palaeolithic** and **Mesolithic** peoples (600 000-2500 BC) were nomadic and able to
wander freely to and from the continent, to hunt the forests and scrub which covered
all but the chalk uplands and these, because they were less overgrown and offered
easier going, the nomads began very early to use as regular tracks. In time, the paths
penetrated across country following the line of chalk which extends in a swathe from
the Norfolk coast, through the Chilterns to the North Wessex and Hampshire Downs
where tracks along the North and South Downs also converged. Finally, all led down
to the Dorset coast and the sea.

In the next, **Neolithic period** (2500-1900 BC), by which time the Channel was in being,
the huntsmen and herdsmen began to settle, grazing the downlands with sheep and
scratching the soil to grow grain. They made pottery and wove cloth; they buried
their dead in long barrows and, as they began to come together in tribes, constructed
the prehistoric monuments in the Avebury area (Windmill Hill Camp, *p 187*). Finally
they traded, bartering with early, itinerant traders who came along the tracks with
fine axe and arrowheads from Cornwall, Cumbria and Wales.

The **Bronze Age** (1900-450 BC), saw the invasion of the east coast and of Dorset by
Beaker Folk, who used the chalk upland tracks to penetrate far inland. They fashioned
metals for their own use – copper tin, bronze and gold (from Cornwall and Ireland),
exported bronze tools and weapons and obtained in exchange, the pottery and
weapons from Brittany, Holland, the Mediterranean and central Europe, discovered
by modern archaeologists in their graves. The constant traffic of traders and itinerant
smiths, who cast tools and weapons and, resmelting the metal, exchanged new for
old, meant that by 1700 BC the Ridgeway and Icknield Way had become regular trade
routes.

The RIDGEWAY PATH ★★

The Beaker Folk were overcome by the **Urn People,** invading warriors from Brittany (1700 BC) who had a sophisticated taste for luxuries which were brought by new traders along the old upland routes: gold from Ireland, jet from Yorkshire, amber from the Baltic, blue pottery beads from Egypt. They got their name from their practice of burying the cremated ashes of their dead in urns in the round barrows which may still be seen on the Wiltshire Downs.

The first wave of **Celts** came over in 8C BC: their weapons were still of bronze although their agriculture was well advanced – their small rectangular field cultivation is even now visible from the air. In turn they fell before a second wave of Celts: 5C BC men of the **Iron Age.** As invasion followed invasion, Celts already established defended themselves in the hillforts to be seen everywhere in the region.

The **animals** of the early herdsmen – cattle, sheep, horses, hogs – were leaf, tree bark and scrub eaters; the forests became so reduced that the nature of the countryside was changed for ever; the animals became herbivores. Man, however, had reached the **Iron Age:** not only weapons but tools for clearing scrub and forest had become keener and agricultural implements had begun to evolve.

With the **Romans** began settlement of the valleys and lowlands with paths and even made-up roads linking the towns. The Ridgeway was abandoned except by drovers who, until the advent of rail and road transport, continued to travel the tracks with their cattle and sheep, heading for London.

AVEBURY to the WILTSHIRE BORDER – *17m*

The track, by its nature, does not progress from sight to sight, but skirts them by a mile or two.

★ **Avebury. –** *P 186.*

White Horse. – *Hackpen Hill. Ridgeway-Marlborough-Wootton Bassett road crossing.* You come out at 892ft on the horse and cannot therefore "see" it, though you can examine it from close to; the commanding **view** ★ includes Windmill Hill *(p 187).*

Barbury Castle. – The Iron Age hillfort crowning the down, is a triple embanked earthwork enclosing 11 ½ acres, with openings to west and east through which the modern path passes. The castle is named after an Anglo-Saxon chief, Bara, who fought a battle in 566 on the slopes to the north.

Liddington Castle. – Iron Age hillfort.

Fox Hill and Charlbury Hill. – The hills are marked respectively by a radio tower and an orange-flashing, aircraft beacon.

The acorn sign which waymarks the Ridgeway Path.

★★★ **SALISBURY**

Pop 100 946

Michelin map **403** fold 28 – 030
See town plan in the current Michelin Red Guide Great Britain and Ireland

The **cathedral,** which is so spectacularly beautiful with its great **spire,** is a building planned and executed in a single style; the town, equally, was planned and did not just grow – such order was the result of both town and church having been brought specifically to the site in 13C.

The earlier city of **Old Sarum** *(p 203)* was two miles away, an Iron Age hillfort, a Saxon, Roman and finally, a Norman strongpoint where, in the outer bailey, two successive cathedrals were built: the first by Bishop, later **St Osmund,** nephew of the Conqueror, which, five days after its consecration, was struck by lightning and largely destroyed, the second a much larger, richer building, designed by **Bishop Roger.** The bishop also converted the existing keep into an episcopal castle-palace which, on his fall from power in 1139, was garrisoned by the king's men. His immediate successor, Bishop Joscelin, built a new episcopal palace beside the cathedral but friction between the king's garrison and the clergy, want of water, the bleakness of the hilltop, the lack of fear of attack, finally combined in 13C to make the citizens and clergy of Old Sarum seek pastures new and undertake the construction of a third Cathedral Church to the Blessed Virgin.

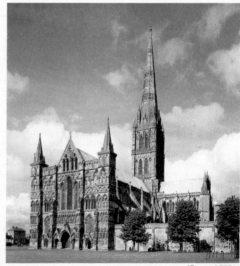

(Everts / ZEFA)

Salisbury Cathedral

★★★ The CATHEDRAL

Salisbury epitomises for most of us the Early English style at its best, Gothic, in its purest, most mediaevally ascetic, form. It is unique among England's older cathedrals in being in a single style, in possessing the tallest spire, the slimmest Purbeck marble column shafts... none of which would be of interest if the whole was not a perennial triumph.

It was built in **two phases:** foundation stone to consecration and completion of the west screen, 1220-58-65, heightening of the tower and construction of the spire, 1334-80; the materials used were silver-grey limestone from Chilmark, 12 miles away, Purbeck marble, cement (the vaulting is painted, cast concrete), lead for the roofs and timber – forests of wood were used as scaffolding, shuttering and supports for the spire.

Exterior

West Screen. – As you approach look up at the west screen, rising from the gabled portals through lines of statue-filled niches, lancet windows and arcading to the pointed gable and corner towers with their miniature angel pinnacles and ribbed spires.

Tower. – Notice how the upper stages of the tower of a century later than the base are complemented by the proportions of the lancets, just two friezes of crested decoration and, at the foot of the spire, how corner pinnacles and subpinnacles rise like fountains but fall just short of the first of the three carved bands encircling the spire itself.

The Spire. – The summit stands 404ft above the ground, the spire itself, mounted upon the heightened tower and with stone walls 2ft thick at the base, comprises nearly half the total height being 180ft tall. *See also below: The Crossing.*

Floodlighting. – The Cathedral is floodlit nightly in summer.

Interior ¾ *hour excluding the tower ascent*

tc The west screen, outside, is effective through overall decoration; the interior exemplifies the beauty of line alone, all the mediaeval colour – black, red, gold – having been removed.

Nave. – Walk up the nave – 229½ft out of a total length of 449ft, beneath 84ft vault. The *piers* of Purbeck marble, quatrefoils of grey, unpolished stone, canted by polished black shafts, are caught by slim, black, moulded capitals from which spring the pointed arches of the arcades, the galleries with their clusters of black columnettes and the tall lancets of the clerestories.

Between the arcade pillars, tomb chests with recumbent figures recall the great of Old Sarum, Salisbury and the West Country: on the south side, **Bishops Roger** (d 1139) and **Joscelin** (d 1184), the shrine of **St Osmund** (d 1099) and, the chain-mailed, **William Longespée** (d 1226), half-brother of King John, husband of Ela, the founder of Lacock Abbey *(p 193)*; opposite are Longespée the Younger (d 1250), warrior and crusader, Montacute (d 1390) and Hungerford (d 1449).

The Crossing. – Marking the crossing are **giant piers** of clustered black marble columns, intended to support the original low tower but, since 14C, required to bear the extra 6 500 tons of the heightened tower and spire. Re-inforcing internal and external buttresses and, since 15C, massive tie-beam arches across the transepts and a Decorated stone vault over the crossing, have relieved the strain in part but the piers have buckled by a clearly noticeable 3½in.

Pavement octagon. – At the centre of the crossing pavement an octagon reflects the outline of the spire 45ft below its apex; in 1668, Sir Christopher Wren, when surveying the cathedral, dropped a plumbline from the **spire point** (brass plate) which shows that it has settled with a declination of 29½ins to the southwest.

Tower ascent. – The tough climb is by way of mostly spiral staircases, to the triforium; across the west end of the nave; along the inside of the nave roof and up the tower to the base only of the spire (224ft) – views of the Close and Old Sarum.

North Transept. – Note the statue to Sir Richard Colt Hoare *(p 206)* and 13C cope chest.

South Transept. – The Mother's Union Chapel has an altar-frontal and hangings made from material from the 1953 Coronation.

South Chancel Aisle. – The coloured tomb is of Sir Richard Mompesson (d 1627) and his wife, ancestors of the builder of the house in the Close *(p 202)*; the window behind them is by Burne-Jones.

Note the inverted, 14C scissor arches in the sub-transepts.

Chancel. – On either side of the choir are **chantry chapels**, monumental tombs and the ledger stone or plain lid of the coffin of **St Osmund** – *(SE corner)*.

The Trinity Chapel. – The **blue window**, *Prisoners of Conscience*, glazed in 1980, is by a stained glass maker from Chartres, Gabriel Loire, an artist working in the mediaeval and modern tradition. Turn to look, by contrast, at the great **west window**, which contains six mediaeval shields (once in the chapter house) and 15-16C figures. (The other glass is almost all monotone or grisaille.)

Most beautiful of all in the Chapel are the slimmest of slim, black Purbeck **marble shafts** rising as ringed pilasters, columns and clustered piers, to the groined vaulting.

CLOISTERS and CHAPTER HOUSE

Work began on building the chapter house and the cloisters in *c*1263 making the latter the earliest and, at 181ft, among the longest in any English cathedral; both are in Decorated Gothic style.

Chapter House. – The octagonal chamber, 58ft across, rises from a single central column surrounded by eight, ringed, Purbeck shafts which ascend from the foliated capital as ribs to ceiling bosses before dropping to clusters of slim columns which frame the eight giant windows. Below these a frieze of stories from the Old Testament (restored in 19C) fills the spandrels between the niches which circumscribe the canon's seats.

★ The CLOSE

The Close, spacious and mellow with the ancient stone and terracotta bricks of 16-18C houses, was enclosed in 1330s against the "riotous citizenry". The walls are of stone from the disused cathedral and castle of Old Sarum.

A secondary close in the northwest corner is known as the **Choristers' Close.**

There are four openings in the Close walls:

North or High St Gate. – The gate with a statue of Edward VII opens from Choristers' Close into the town by way of an alley bordered by old houses and the **Matrons' College,** built in 1682 as almshouses for canons' widows;

Harnham or South Gate. – The distant, south gate leads to the Dissolved De Vaux College and St Nicholas Hospital, the latter the source of Trollope's *The Warden;*

St Ann's and Bishop's Gates. – The two gates in the east wall *(opening onto St John's and Exeter Sts)* abut 18C Malmesbury House and the Old Bishop's Palace, an island building begun in *c*1220, now the Cathedral School.

A *Walking Madonna,* a bronze by **Elizabeth Frink** (1981) strides across the grass on the cathedral's north side.

Three houses in the Close, of interest in themselves, present rare collections with great attraction.

★★ **Mompesson House.** – Through 18C wrought iron gateway and the door with its *tc* cartouche bearing the initials of Sir Charles Mompesson, builder of the two-storey house in 1701, is a well furnished interior set against high quality plasterwork. There is also a unique collection of English drinking glasses.

The Staircase. – The staircase, inserted in 1740s beyond a wide arch at the back of the marble paved hall, is the house's principal architectural feature. Of oak, it rises by shallow flights with three crisply turned bannisters to each tread, a perfect foil to the generous outpouring of **Baroque plasterwork** swags, scrolls and cartouches which completely cover the walls and ceiling.

There is further notable plasterwork in the Dining Room, the Green Room *(upstairs)* where there is an eagle with spread wings, and the Drawing Room.

English drinking glasses. – The collection, numbering 370 different types of glass is displayed in period cabinets in the Dining and Little Drawing Rooms. The early examples of 1700-45 are characterised by thick glass and knobbed stems, the later glasses – after an excise tax of 1745 placed a levy on glass by weight – by lighter bowls and slender stems. Decoration as well as shape took all forms including air and opaque twist stems, enamelling and engraving, which was often commemorative or had a hidden or symbolic meaning as in Jacobite toasting glasses.

★★ **Military Museum.** – *W side of the Close.* The museum of the Duke of Edinburgh's *tc* Royal Regiment, formed in 1959 by the amalgamation of the Royal Berkshire and Wiltshire Regiments, is in the large flint and brick house built as the bishop's document and storehouse in 1254 from which time, although altered in 15C and again when it became a house, it has been known as **The Wardrobe.**

Against the lime-yellow, *papier maché* wall decoration in the hall, in the decorated 18C reception rooms and in the ancient cellar, epic moments in the regiments' histories are illustrated through encapsulated displays of a soldier's combat dress, his hat, the weapons of the day, a despatch, an object to localise the action, an enemy weapon or bit of uniform... A world map names campaigns by means of medals... a medal room displays the soldiers' valour... regimental silver, the overseas postings: William and Mary tankards (1691), snuffboxes, chased Indian silver claret jugs (1875) and centrepieces, including a very long and scaly Chinese dragon.

★★ **Salisbury and South Wiltshire Museum.** – *W side of the Close.* The mediaeval house *tc* of stone to which brick additions have been made throughout the centuries, has been known ever since James I lodged in it on a visit to the city, as **The King's House.**

The museum contains a large Stonehenge collection. In addition there are a model of Old Sarum and carved figures and corbels from 12C cathedral, a gallery on life in the city from the Middle Ages to 19C with period artefacts including the giant, a small but interesting number of paintings, a collection of English china enlivened by Bow and Chelsea figures and a great gathering of tea-pots.

ADDITIONAL SIGHTS

Mediaeval streets. – Between the cathedral and 19C **Market Sq** to the north, there remains a network of mediaeval streets and cut-throughs, lined by half-timbered houses with high oversailing upper floors and tall gables, dating from 14-17C with a few later insertions – the alley names, Fish Row, Butcher Row, Silver St, Blue Boar Row, Ox Row, Oatmeal Row, indicate the shops and stalls which once flourished along their length. At the centre in a small treed square is 15C hexagonal **Poultry Cross,** decorated with buttresses, pinnacles and a spirelet.

★ **Sarum St Thomas Church.** – *NE end of the High St, overlooking St Thomas Sq and the mediaeval streets west of Market Sq.* The low, castellated, square tower of 1390 and the Perpendicular church are a rebuilding on the site of a wooden chapel of ease erected in *c*1219 to provide a place of worship for the cathedral craftsmen.

Chancel Arch and Chancel. – The arch is the setting for a *Doom Painting* (*c*1475) with, at the apex, Christ in Majesty in the New Jerusalem – 15C Salisbury? The choir, of 1470 ("modernised" in 19C) has angel musician roof supports, the names and marks of contributing merchants on the south pillars and a brass to John Webbe, his wife and six children, 16C wool merchant and mayor.

Lady Chapel. – The chapel, built by a wool merchant, master of the Tailors' Guild and mayor, is decorated with very small 15C frescoes and, since 1725, by splendid wrought iron **railings** and finely carved **woodwork**.

South nave wall. – Note the carved oak **panel** of 1671, "his own worke", by Humphrey Backham, the painted **royal arms** of Queen Elizabeth with the Welsh dragon supporter which preceded the Scots unicorn.

EXCURSIONS

★ **Old Sarum.** – *2m N on A345 (W side – signposted; car park through East Gate).*
tc Standing on the rubble walls of the Norman inner bailey, one scans the Salisbury Plain as did the guards of old. Two miles away to the south is the cathedral spire. From the walls, which are those of Bishop Roger's 12C castle in the inner bailey – the first castle-keep on the site – can also be seen in the foreground, in the north-west corner of the outer bailey, the footings of Bishop St Osmund's **11C cathedral** and, superimposed, Bishop Roger's larger, **12C church**. Models in Salisbury Museum.

Salisbury Plain. – The Plain, some 10 × 20 miles across, extends from the Vale of Pewsey in the north to the Wylye Valley in the south. Although known as a plain it is, in fact, gently undulating, clay-chalk downland with many of its knolls marked by prehistoric monuments – burial barrows, hillforts and Stonehenge *(p 204)*.
Prehistoric forts were succeeded by defended towns such as Old Sarum and Wilton and, eventually, by peaceful settlement. Today the Plain remains an agricultural area of open pasture and arable farms despite the roads crossing it to converge on Salisbury, despite the army, which arrived in 19C and which, besides charging about in tanks **(road warning panels)**, is said to fire some 230 000 shells and bombs annually on designated ranges, and despite the RAF, which arrived this century.

Wylye Valley. – *21m by A30 W and A36 N.*
The road follows the course upriver of the Wylye, passing through Wilton *(p 210)* before turning to skirt the southern edge of Salisbury Plain. Attractive villages, usually comprising a church, one "big" house of 17 or 18C, two or three lesser houses and several cottages, nearly all stone-built, mark the route every few miles.

Stapleford. – Pop 260. The village is notable for its castle earthworks and a **church** with a square north tower, pinnacled, demi-pinnacled and balustraded which makes it a landmark. Inside, the pillared arcade and font are both Norman.

Steeple Langford. – Pop 526. The village is named after the small lead-covered **broach spire**, crowning its EE church.

Australian War Graves Cemetery. – *1m before Codford St Mary (right), signposted footpaths.* The cemetery is distinguished by 100ft high, chalk figure of a crown and scroll.

Heytesbury. – Pop 632. Note 17C style **almshouses** of brick with a pedimented centre and lantern, the Hospital of St John and St Katherine *(left side of the road)*.

Warminster. – *P 208.*

★ **Wardour Castle.** – *10m W by A30 and by-road. P 207.*
The **Fovant** badges can be seen carved into the southern chalk hillside *(p 184)*.

tc **Newhouse, Redlynch.** – *9m S by A338 and B3080.*
The three-storeyed, Jacobean house of *c*1619, built of red brick to a Y or "Trinity" **plan**, has pitched roofs and so gables at the end of each wing and, in addition, three gables at the front. In 18C the house was enlarged by flat-roofed, single-storey extensions to the two front wings.
In 17C it was bought by the Eyres in whose family it has remained ever since; in 19C a daughter of the house married Horatio Nelson's nephew, from which there are numerous **Nelson relics** and Horatia's cradle to be seen inside.

★ SHELDON MANOR

Michelin map ███ fold 28 – N29 – 1½m W of Chippenham

tc The manor's stone exterior with its several additions was complete by the late 17C. The oldest parts of the house are the **Plantagenet porch** of 1282 and the massive wall behind it. Building phases in *c*1431 and 1659 added new fronts, the **detached chapel**, and introduced Tudor **fireplaces**, linenfold **panelling**, the Jacobean **staircase**...
Inside, among splendid 16-17C **furniture**, massive in size, translucent with polishing, are refectory tables, 17C chests, a four-poster bed with 17C embroidered cover, **17C embroidery** of a *Tree of Life* with an elephant in the corner, and 15C plank chest in the Priest's Room which has **13C roof**.
In addition there are small collections of Nailsea glass *(p 40)*, Eltonware *(p 40)* and William de Morgan ceramics, a Breughel in the dining room, 19C sporting prints, cartoons and family mementoes from far and wide – it is a house full of stories.
Outside, high yew hedges enclose a pond garden, a flower garden, an orchard and a **garden** filled with species old fashioned and climbing roses.

★ STEEPLE ASHTON
Pop 2 076

Michelin map **403** fold 27 – N30 – 7m E of Trowbridge

Steeple Ashton gives the lie to the saying that lightning never strikes twice in the same place: the church possessed a "Famous and Lofty Steeple, Containing a height above the Tower 93 Foot" – it was breached on 25 July 1670 and had almost been rebuilt when "another terrible Storm of Thunder and Lightning happened October 15 the same year, which threw (it) down'. The church, but not the steeple, was restored, the parish, by this date, being both less wealthy and less numerous.

A local church had been in existence since 1252 and a weekly market and annual fair established since 1266. In the two centuries which followed, wool merchants and clothiers prospered, work people were attracted to the village and many of the houses, forges and inns surrounding the green and lining the main street were built. During what turned out to be the village's high noon, two clothiers and their wives added new north and south aisles to the church, the rest of the parish a new nave and the illfated steeple.

Nemesis occurred in 16-17C with a series of fires which damaged and destroyed many houses and the invention of fulling, a process in the manufacture of woollen cloth which requires the running water which the village lacks. The people turned to agriculture and, in 19C, emigrated in considerable numbers to America, Australia and New Zealand.

★ **The Green.** – The **market cross** dates from 1714, the octagonal stone lockup or **blind house** with a domed roof and no windows, from 1773.

Houses on the Green and in adjoining streets. – The two black and white half-timbered houses, one known as the **Old Wool Market,** are 16 and 17C; the timber-framed house with brick herringbone infilling on the upper floor, variously known as the Old Merchant's Hall and **Judge Jeffreys' House,** is 16C; **Ashton House** is early 16C with additions, extensions and a 1724 refronting; The Longs Arms, 17C. Blackburn Farmhouse *(by the telephone box)* was begun *c*1500; the cottage with three big brick chimneys, at the end of the High St, is built on cruck beams *(p 193)*; **The Sanctuary,** off Dark Lane, according to the records, had an extension built on in 1500...

The Church. – No steeple but a grin of gargoyles now decorates St Mary's Perpendicular exterior. Inside, it is the **roofs** which are chiefly of interest: the nave, even before the steeple fell upon it (possibly because an earlier stone roof had cracked), is covered with a lofty fan vault of oak and plaster; the aisles have intricate, lierne vaulting in stone, the ribs descending to canopied niches supported on boldly carved half-figures. The chancel was added when the building was restored in 19C.

★★★ STONEHENGE

Michelin map **403** fold 28 – O30

tc Stonehenge is one of the world's classic sights – and classic enigmas!
Perfectly oriented so that on midsummer's day the sun, rising in its most northerly position, appears exactly over the Heel Stone to anyone standing at the centre, Stonehenge is 4 000 years old, dating from *c*2800-1550 BC (although some now put it 800-1000 years earlier). It is, therefore, several centuries later than the Great Pyramid in Egypt, contemporary with the Minoan culture in Crete, a millenium earlier than the first Great Wall of China, 2 000 years earlier than the Aztec constructions (and carved stone calendars) of Mexico and 3 500 years older than the figures on Easter Island.

The Druids, a Celtic priesthood, are a "modern" appendage, they arrived from Europe only in 250 BC.

(F Gohier / Explorer)

Stonehenge – The trilithons

The Stones. – There are two types of stone at Stonehenge: **bluestones** from the Preseli Mountains and the shores of Milford Haven in south Wales, and **sarsens** from the Marlborough Downs, 20 miles away.

The bluestones, so-called from their colour when first cleaved and weighing up to 4 tons each, were transported, it is believed, along the South Wales coast to the Bristol Avon, along the Frome, overland to the Wylye and Salisbury Avon and, finally, overland from West Amesbury to the site – a total distance of 240 miles on log rollers, sledges, rafts and lashed alongside small boats. Some, at least, were brought to Wiltshire even before construction began on Stonehenge, a large one having been discovered in a long barrow of *c*3000 BC near Warminster. The sarsens weigh up to 50 tons each; the journey was shorter but partly uphill. Motive power was human muscle.

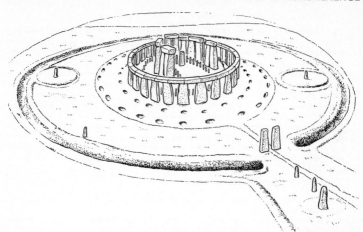

(With the permission of the Controller, HMSO)

Stonehenge when complete

The stones, blue and sarsen, were shaped on arrival with football-sized sarsen hammers: the **standing stones** were tapered at one end and tenoned at the top to secure the curving, morticed **lintels** which were linked to each other by tongues and grooves. To position the stones, holes were dug (with red deer antler picks and cattle shoulderblade spades) into which the stones were levered until they toppled upright and could be made fast with rammed stones and earth. The trilithon lintels were next positioned at the base and gradually levered up on ever rising log platforms.

The period. – Stonehenge was built in **four phases** between 2800 and 1550 BC, when its purpose in the life of the people of Wessex, of Britain entirely and probably nearby areas of Western Europe, must have been self-evident.

When work began the area was inhabited by nomadic hunters and their families and by early farming settlers who had crossed the Channel and North Sea in skin boats. By 2000 BC the Beaker people who had spread into Wessex along the chalk upland tracks *(p 199)*, had grown into a community of perhaps 12-15000 people, ruled by the powerful cattle-barons of the Salisbury Plain who also controlled the metal industry. There was a growing priesthood, who at peak periods in the construction of Stonehenge would call on the population to provide as many as 600 men at one time to pull the heaviest sarsen stones up the south slope of the Vale of Pewsey or 200 to erect a sarsen upright...

The building design. – In the **first phase**, *c*2800 BC, a ditch, an inner, chalk rubble bank, 6ft high, and a ring of holes, known after 17C antiquary, as the Aubrey Holes, were dug to enclose an area 1½ acres in extent, 300ft in diameter. To the northeast the ditch and bank were cut to afford an entrance marked inside by two upright stones and, outside *(near the road)*, by the **Heel Stone** (and a timber gateway). Inside the enclosure, four **Station Sarsens** were set up at the cardinal points of the compass.

In the **second phase**, in *c*2100 BC, a double ring of bluestones began to be set up at the centre and the **Avenue** was begun towards the Avon at West Amesbury.

In *c*2000 BC, the **third phase**, the structure was transformed: the incomplete bluestone rings were replaced by a circle of tall sarsen trilithons, the lintels forming an upraised stone hoop; inside, five, separate, giant trilithons rose in a horseshoe opening towards the Heel Stone. The entrance was marked by new uprights, one of which, the Slaughter Stone, now fallen, remains (names, now irrelevant, were given to many stones in 18C); the bluestones were re-introduced to form an inner horseshoe. In the **final phase**, in *c*1550 BC, Stonehenge appeared, it is believed, as illustrated.

Gradually the population and prosperity declined; Stonehenge, in use in 1100 BC, fell into ruin as stones tumbled and were removed. While it is certain that the axis of the sarsen stones points to where an observer at the centre would see the sunrise on midsummer's day, other original sightlines to the horizon have been largely destroyed; lines joining the Station Stones could have marked the most northerly and southerly points on the horizon of sun and moon settings, making the theory tenable that Stonehenge could have been constructed as an observatory by a people who had a considerable knowledge of astronomy but...

EXCURSION

★ **Heale House.** – *6m S. Turn left off A303 on to A360 then left into the secondary,*
tc *Woodford Valley Rd; Heale House is between Middle and Upper Woodford.*

The 17C house of old rose brick with stone dressings, tall windows, pediments and a pitched roof, where Charles II sheltered after the Battle of Worcester in 1651, stands in a wooded valley at the end of a long avenue of poplars.

The garden of eight acres, secluded by clipped yew hedges, opens onto the River Avon; it is scented by a border-hedge of musk and other sweet smelling, old-fashioned roses and coloured by a long, wide herbaceous border, rich in everything you can name. A walled garden, part flowers, part vegetables, is quartered by a pergola of pleached apple trees; a water garden, planted with magnolia, a cherry tree, an acer, surrounds a Japanese tea-house approached over a red painted bridge. After the mysteries of prehistory, the quintessence of civilisation.

The garden is an example of **18C "designed" English garden** at its supreme best. In early spring the trees in bud present infinite shades of tender green, summer enriches the tones until in autumn the leaves turn to gold, scarlet, russet, brown, before baring the brown-black branches to winter.

Daffodils, bluebells, rhododendrons and azaleas, afford brilliant background colour. The creator and first architect of these "pleasure grounds", which occupy some 400 acres, was **Henry Hoare II** (1705-85).

Henry Hoare I (1677-1725), son of the founder of Hoare's Bank (*c*1673) in the City of London, acquired the property in 1717 and built a new house on the site, designed by **Colen Campbell**, pioneer of English Palladianism. The house of 1721 comprised the present centre wing only, the flanking pavilions containing the library and picture gallery being added by Henry Hoare II's heir, **Sir Richard Colt Hoare** (1758-1838), antiquary, county historian and, like his grandfather, a traveller and collector.

tc The GARDENS *illustration p 25*

The short path, at the water's edge, is 1 ¼ miles easy going with benches at several vantage points.

Henry Hoare II was influenced in his garden design by the landscapes he saw on his travels and even more by the paintings of Claude and Nicholas and Gaspard Poussin in which nature is presented in luminous shades and focal points are provided by Classical buildings. In the same way as one viewed a picture, therefore, and in contrast to the preceding fashion of overlooking a formal, parterre garden from the house, the grounds were laid out to be viewed from specific vantage points.

Hoare first formed the great triangular **lake**; then, as he began his plantings of deciduous trees and conifers, "ranged in large masses as the shades in a painting", he started, with his architect, Henry Flitcroft, to build the Classical style **focal points** which, if you circle the lake in an anti-clockwise direction, you may pinpoint from across the water as the Temple of Flora, the Grotto, the Old Watch Cottage, the Pantheon – originally known as the Temple of Hercules for which the statue was carved by Rysbrack after his earlier terracotta figurine in the Picture Gallery.

In 1765, Hoare was given the **Bristol Cross** *(p 34)*, which enabled him to create a vista which was entirely English, of the lake, the Turf Bridge, the Cross and, in the background, Stourton church and village.

Colt Hoare laid the continuous paths, added new trees to increase the range of colour and introduced the first rhododendron in 1791.

tc The HOUSE *time: ¾ hour*

The house suffered a grim sale of much of its contents in 1883 and a fire in 1902 which destroyed the early 18C interiors although nearly all the contents of the ground floor staterooms were saved.

Hall. – In the cube plan entrance hall, are 18C **console tables** with fox supports, wheelback chairs, a gilded bronze **bust of Charles I** by Le Sueur, also **portraits** of Sir Richard Hoare, founder of the bank, Henry Hoare I holding plans of the house, Henry Hoare II (figure by Michael Dahl, horse by Wootton) and Colt Hoare and his son.

Library. – The long gallery with a barrel vault, contains fine pieces of furniture made by **Thomas Chippendale the Younger**, notably the mahogany library table for which he was paid £115. The two busts of Milton are by **Rysbrack**, the pen and wash drawings of Venice by **Canaletto**. Note the carved wood chimneypiece and plaster relief of the Apochryphal story of Tobit.

Music Room. – The **square piano** of 1784 is by **Ganer** and the mahogany **card-table** with lion legs and a bacchic frieze of 1740 by **William Linnell**.

Little Dining Room. – The shell back **chairs** are of 1740. 17C **silver-gilt centrepiece**, which was made in Germany, incorporates the double-headed eagle of the Habsburgs, adopted by the Hoares as their bank emblem.

Staircase Hall. – The two Rococo gilt **pier-glasses** are by **John Linnell** (1753).

Cabinet Room. – The mid-17C **cabinet** of ebony and gilt bronze with stone inlay, is Florentine, 18C blue-john vase from Derbyshire.

Picture Gallery. – On the walls hang the Claude and Poussin **landscapes** which inspired Henry Hoare II in his garden design, also early Italian paintings. Note especially the **Chippendale furniture**, 18C **satinwood commode**, a beautiful oval, inlaid, **rent-table** and the **Rysbrack** Hercules figurine which served as the model for the sculpture in the Pantheon in the garden.

SWINDON   Pop 91 136

Swindon was the Mecca of the Great Western Railway from 1831, when it was chosen as the line's main junction and site for its locomotive and carriage workshops, until 1948 brought about the demise of individual lines under nationalisation.

Old Swindon, in the early 19C, was a typical, hilltop market town of some 1 700 souls; by the end of the century, New Swindon, the railway town below, numbered nearly 40 000 of who 4 000 were directly employed by the GWR and most of the rest in growing and selling food, providing houses and lodgings... Today the town, still prosperous, is ringed by light industry estates, the centre stacked tall with 20C office blocks.

SIGHTS

★ **Great Western Railway Museum.** – *Farringdon Rd.* The museum is in the onetime
tc "model lodging house", built by the company for its workers who came from all parts
of England, particularly the North, Wales and Ireland. The house was not popular and
was remodelled as a Wesleyan Chapel – an appearance it maintains outside. Inside
it has been rebuilt and sparingly decorated with Victorian iron station furniture, as
a suitable hall of fame.

There stand a full size replica of the **North Star** (which hauled the first GW passenger
train from Paddington to Maidenhead), the original **Lode Star**, a "Dean Goods", the 1903,
City of Truro and an 0-6-0 1947 tank engine. Carriage doorlocks, signals, working
models, the prized gold disc railway pass, silver table centres and coffee urns modelled
on famous locomotives, rattles, truncheons, lights, headboards... give some indication
of the array of equipment needed to run the line which, in its heyday, extended over
9 000 miles of track between London, Bristol, Penzance, Fishguard and Liverpool,
maintained 3 600 locomotives, 9 000 passenger coaches, 82 000 freight wagons
and employed more than 100 000 men.

Lining the corridor walls are posters, commands for royal trains and, in one gallery,
Brunel's signed drawings for the Clifton Suspension Bridge competition after which
he was appointed, in his own words "Engineer to the finest work in England" *(p 38)*.

★ **The Railway Village Museum.** – *34 Farringdon Rd.* To house its workers the company
tc built not only the lodging house but also 300 one, two, three-up and three-down
houses. The building material used was the limestone excavated from the nearby
3 212yd long Box Tunnel (1837-41).

In 1969-80 the cottages were cleaned to reveal beneath soot and grime the original
silver limestone; all were modernised save one, **no 34,** a three bedroomed house which
was left with gas and oil lighting, a range, washing dolly, copper, mangle, brown
glazed sink and tin bath in the kitchen and a flowered outside lavatory. It is furnished
in 1880s style in the bedrooms, front parlour and dining room – note the bowler on
the peg in the hall: the unmistakeable mark of a foreman's rank !

Civic Centre and Brunel Shopping Centre. – The **Civic Centre,** with law courts,
administrative offices, the Wyvern Theatre, The College and monolithic commercial
buildings, constructed of diverse materials from black brick to white marble and all
of late 1950s-1980s vintage, remains strangely inchoate. The **Brunel,** of the mid-1970s,
adjoining an earlier, shopping centre, is, by comparison, closely knit, the overhead
arching above the mosaic pavement and the peripheral arcading, all airily reminiscent
of the iron-work and glass of the great 19C railway termini. In one avenue stands
a larger than life statue of Brunel.

tc **Museum and Art Gallery.** – *Bath Rd.* The museum, in 19C house in Swindon Old
Town, has a large and rare collection of **Prattware** – the mid-late 19C pot-lids decorated
with coloured landscapes, portraits, rural and dramatic scenes to attract Victorian
housewives into buying, possibly in inordinate quantities to complete a set of lids,
commodities such as fish and meat pastes, pommades and cream. So popular were
the decorations that they were later applied to table china. A modern gallery displays
a growing collection of paintings and ceramics by 20C artists.

tc **Richard Jefferies Museum.** – *Malborough Rd, Coate. A345 before the roundabout,
opposite a large garage and hotel.* In the farmhouse in which Jefferies, naturalist and
writer was born in 1848, are early editions of his works and personal mementoes
also writings of Alfred Williams, the Hammerman or Railway Poet.

EXCURSION

Lydiard Park. – *5m W off A420. P 196.*

TROWBRIDGE   Pop 23 123

Michelin map **403** fold 27 – N30

Trowbridge, long established as a major wool and cloth town, became the county
town only when 1888 Local Government Act required councillors to be elected and
it was found that Trowbridge, being on the railway, was accessible and convenient.
Since the decline of the cloth trade it has turned to brewing and the manufacture
of dairy products, bacon, pies, sausages and yogurt, in some cases, in the old mills.
Witness of the earlier prosperity remains in the multitude of 19C non-conformist
chapels and schools, the workers' terraced houses and Georgian houses.

★ WARDOUR CASTLE

Michelin map **403** fold 28 – N30

tc The castle stands on a spur, sheltered on three sides by wooded hills looking out
west across a lake, known as the Fish Pond. In May-June the lawns, where once the
inner bailey was, are vividly outlined by rhododendrons.

The tower house, rock-like in its mass, hexagonal in form with corbel turrets marking
the angles and a front advanced squarely as twin bastions to guard the entrance,
has been falling into romantic ruin since the Civil War – its heroic hour.

The castle, a royal manor in King Alfred's reign, a Benedictine property from Domesday
to the Dissolution, was purchased in 1547 by Sir Thomas Arundell.

In the Civil War, the castle's defences were put to the test: the Arundells were Royalists
and in 1643, when Lord Arundell was at Oxford with the king, a Parliamentary force
of 1300 men laid siege to the castle which had a garrison of 25. On its surrender

the house was looted, the contents sold, the park plundered. In 1644 the 3rd Lord Arundell besieged the place in his turn and again, after mining had wreaked further damage, the garrison surrendered.

In 1769-77 the then Lord Arundell commissioned the architect James Paine to build what turned out to be the largest Georgian mansion in the country. The stone house.

tc **New Wardour Castle** (now a girls' boarding school), has a circular, marble floored hall, from which twin cantilevered **staircases** rise round the walls to a gallery ringed by Corinthian columns.

The CASTLE

The ruins are those of 15-16C fortified tower house, built with accommodation for domestic living and lavish entertainment.

The house was constructed around a hexagonal courtyard. The Great Hall above the gateway, was adjoined on one side by the chapel, solar and lord's chambers and on the other by the screens passage, service rooms and kitchens. The remaining rooms were guests' lodgings which were approached by spiral staircases built into the walls.

Walk through 16C Renaissance entrance, decorated with the Arundell arms and a bust of Christ in a niche. Just inside the courtyard *(left)* are the stairs to the Great Hall, framed by a **Grand Entrance**, lion decorated, Tuscan pillared and with a contrasting, plain entablature.

WESTBURY   Pop 7 280

Michelin map ⓘ fold 27 – N30

The small town, its 18-20C shop and house lined main street loud with traffic, has an old **market square** at one end, quiet but lively, overlooked by a Tuscan pillared 19C town hall, a few houses, a few shops, three inns – one now Georgian, said to date back as an inn to 14C. Nearby in its churchyard, surrounded by **Georgian houses** of every degree, is 19C renewed Perpendicular Church of All Saints with a rare, oblong crossing tower, a lierne vaulted porch and battlements cresting the nave and aisles.

EXCURSIONS

Bratton Castle. – *3½m S off B3098.*

White Horse. – *P 183.*

Bratton Castle. – A side road leads up to Bratton Castle and the horse's back and head (the view of the horse is too distorted to be comprehensible).

Bratton Castle, an Iron Age hillfort, with earth mound ramparts enclosing some 25 acres, commands **views★★** from its 300ft down, far across Salisbury Plain, northeast to the Marlborough Downs, across the Vale of Pewsey, southeast along the Wylye Valley and south and west to the hills of Dorset and Somerset.

Edington. – *4m NE on B3098. P 192.*

Warminster. – *Pop 15 089. 8½m S on A350.*

The former wool and cloth town straddles the main road, now thundrous with lorries which, however, cannot be heard in the galleried courtyards and inner rooms of the several Elizabethan and Georgian hostelries. Off the street, the tributary roads, with end-on views of the countryside, are marked by small Classical 18C houses.

The small church of **St Lawrence** in the High St was founded as a chapel of ease in the early 13C and from 15C housed the town bell which rang the daily curfew at 4am and sounded feast and holy days. Closed by Edward VI, it was bought back by the townspeople for £38. 6*s* 8*d* in 1675 and committed, uniquely, to the temporal care of local foeffees or trustees. In the chapel only the base of the tower is mediaeval.

tc **Chalcot House.** – *2m SW of Westbury, right, off A3098.* The small 17C Palladian manor of brick with stone dressings, pedimented windows, a parapet and decorated panels and an urn-filled niche on its garden front, was given a grandiose Victorian porch in 19C.

The rooms inside serve as the well appointed setting for the owner's interests in the Boer War, Indian raj, Victorian memorabilia – each of 9 bedrooms has a different theme – modern and traditional embroidery and, most conspicuously, a collection of modern painting.

★ WESTWOOD MANOR

Michelin map ⓘ fold 27 – M29 and 30 – 1½m SW of Bradford-on-Avon

tc It is the **ensemble** which counts in this small, two-storey house which has been continuously occupied and altered since construction began in *c*1400.

Among the tenants of the manor, owned by Winchester Cathedral from Saxon times to the mid-19C, were Thomas Horton, the clothier from Bradford-on-Avon, who benefitted the adjoining Perpendicular church by building the splendid **west tower**, crowned with a dome – note the initials TH in the door spandrels.

Major alterations were made to the house in the first half of 17C: the **porch** and **staircase turret** were added, the Great Hall was divided horizontally to create the **Great Parlour** above, **panelling**, including the frieze of landscape scenes, was installed in the Panelled Room and the Biblical or symbolic **plaster overmantels** (geese hanging a fox, a rose and thistle growing from the same stem) set into the Panelled, Oriel, Dining and King's Rooms. By 19-20C neglect had almost brought the house to ruin, before it was bought by a new owner who restored it to mellow life and collected for it the 1537 **Italian virginal**, late 17-18C **spinet**, 17C English furniture and worked needlework covers for the chairs.

★★★ WILTON HOUSE

Michelin map 403 fold 28 – O30

tc William Herbert, the quickwitted favourite of Henry VIII, received from his sovereign – to whom he was related – the property of the Dissolved Wilton Benedictine Convent in 1544. Within ten years he had been created Lord Herbert of Cardiff and Earl of Pembroke and had constructed a house on the old convent site worthy of receiving the new king, Edward VI.

The idiosyncratic contributions of successive generations can still be clearly distinguished as they meld into the whole: 2nd Earl married "the greatest patronesse of wit and learning of any lady of her time", the sister of **Sir Philip Sidney** who, while staying at Wilton, composed his poem *Arcadia* – pictures in the Cube Room; 4th Earl, munificent patron, in 1647, when all but the east front and most of the contents had been destroyed in a fire, commissioned **Inigo Jones** to design the house anew and incorporate within the plan a stateroom in which to hang his collection of royal and family portraits by **Van Dyck**; 8th Earl, founder of the Carpet Factory *(p 210)*, traveller, connoisseur, collector, notably of the Wilton Diptych (since 1929 in the National Gallery, London), appointed agents to find new pictures, and marbles to replace those sold to pay the debts of the spendthrift 7th Earl; 9th Earl, soldier, architect and friend of Lord Burlington and William Kent, built the **Palladian Bridge** and redesigned the **garden**; 10th Earl, also a soldier and an authority on equitation, commissioned the **equestrian portraits** and 55 **Spanish Riding School gouaches** which hang in the two smoking rooms; 11th Earl employed

(BTA)

The Palladian Bridge

James Wyatt in 1801 to recast the house, demolish the old great hall, rebuild two fronts and build the two-tier Gothic cloister in the original inner court to provide galleries for statuary and historic mementoes such as Napoleon's despatch box, a lock of Queen Elizabeth's hair, verses by Sir Philip Sidney in his own hand...

TOUR *1 hour*

Cloisters. – The cloisters are a remodelling of the former inner courtyard.

State Apartments. – The suite of apartments by **Inigo Jones**, are characterised by a Classical wealth of enrichment, including giant Italian ceiling paintings, marble chimney-pieces, superbly carved cornices, covings, doorways, overmantels, columns, escutcheons at the centre of broken pediments, great carved drops... all picked out in gold leaf. In such surroundings, the **furniture** ranges from the solid mass of marble and gilt tables and red velvet and gilt sofas by William Kent to pieces by the younger Chippendale, 18C French commodes and Boulle-style tortoise-shell brass tables.

Cube Room. – The 30 × 30 × 30ft room is decorated in white and gold, the ornament delicate in keeping with the size of the room. The generations of portraits include Henriette de Querouaille, sister of Charles II's mistress and wife of 7th Earl by Lely, and a portrait of *Van Dyck* by Charles Jervas.

Double Cube Room. – The gallery of 60 × 30 × 30ft was especially designed by Inigo Jones as the sumptuously rich gold and white setting for 4th Earl's unique collection of splendid **Van Dyck** portraits of the Herbert family and of Charles I, his Queen and their children.

Great Ante-Room. – The seascapes are by **Van der Velde,** the **Rembrandt** portrait is of his mother reading (*c*1629).

Colonnade Room. – The family portraits are almost all by **Joshua Reynolds.**

Corner Room. – A **Titian** portrait and religious and landscape paintings by **Andrea del Sarto** and **Rubens** adorn the walls; the portrait over the fireplace is of Prince Rupert by von Horthorst.

Little Ante-Room. – Among the pictures are a **Lucas van Leyden** and a **Mabuse** – note the view from the window.

Smoking Rooms. – Besides the oil equestrian portraits and the Spanish Riding School gouaches *(see above)*, note the typical Inigo Jones moulded detail in cornices, doorways and chimneypieces and the beautiful **furniture** including a late 17C walnut table, a mirror and stands with ivory marquetry, the Chippendale Spanish mahogany bookcases and music cabinet (*c*1750), the walnut and leather Regency chairs.

Hall. – The 19C Gothic hall includes portrait busts of **Sidney Herbert** and **Florence Nightingale** (Lord Herbert of Lea was Secretary of State for War in 1852 when Florence Nightingale went to the Crimea).

East, Garden Front. – The front is still reminiscent of the original Tudor mansion with angle pavilions and a central door beneath tall oriel windows. *Illustration p 12.*

WILTON HOUSE★★★

WILTON VILLAGE Pop 4 019

Wilton became the local fortified capital in 7-8C in the reign of Ine, King of Wessex, when "hundreds" were being grouped into "shires" which then, in many cases, took the name of their appointed centres – thus Wiltshire. In 9C Alfred founded a Benedictine convent in the town; in 1033 Wilton was sacked by invading Danes and hardly had it recovered before it was decimated by the Black Death. Finally, although nominally it remained the county town, it was outstripped by Salisbury.

Market Place. – At the centre trees shade the ruined Perpendicular arcade and west window of the originally **Saxon church.** The Cross nearby, is a composite of artefacts from an early Crucifixion to 18C urn.

West St. –The wide Cotswold-style shopping street of 17C houses with later shopfronts is distinguished by the **Basilica of St Mary and St Nicholas,** a mid-19C feat of Italianate Romanesque by Thomas Wyatt, complete with 110ft high campanile and ornately decorated, gabled, west front.

★ **Royal Wilton Carpet Factory.** – *King St.* Carpet weaving began as a cottage industry *tc* but by 17C had declined to so poor a standard that the much-travelled 8th Earl of Pembroke arranged for two skilled French Huguenot weavers, who were banned from leaving France on pain of death, to be smuggled over in wine barrels to set up a carpet factory. This succeeded so well that in 1699 it was granted "royal" status by William III. Two rivers, the Wylye and the Nader, flow through the mill which comprises buildings of 17-20C.

Tour. – *¾ hour.* Visitors see old carpet making crafts on original machinery, samples of carpets woven in the last 300 years and modern Wilton and Axminster looms at work.

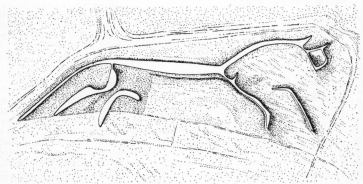

After illustrations in White Horses and other Hill Figures by Morris Marples (Alan Sutton, 1981)

The Uffington Horse

Index

Names of places, houses, streets are in roman type : Avon, Tamar, Lanyon Quoit, Cheddar, Dartmoor, the Pump Room, Industrial Museum, Longleat, Up-a-long...

People, historical events, subjects are in italics : *Drake, Sir Francis, Sedgemoor, Battle of, mermaids, glass, industrial archaeology, military museums...*

Where there are several page references the most important is in bold type : Adam, Robert **112**, 113, 135. Only exceptional works by the great painters (Van Dyck, Gainsborough, Stubbs, Reynolds), works by two local painters (Opie, Danby) and major cabinet-makers (Chippendale) have been indexed.

The Thomas Hardy pages (pp 121-4) have not been indexed.

215

(After Murray King, St Ives / Penwith Council photo)

Celtic Cross – Sancreed

Times and charges for admission

Times and charges for admission are liable to alteration without prior notice. The prices quoted apply to individual adults; where a property belongs to the National Trust, the letters NT appear after the charge. Many places offer reduced rates for children and OAPs.

Groups should apply in advance in writing or at least phone ahead – some houses and museums are small and have limited space and facilities, limited parking space etc. Many places have special days for groups; many offer special rates for advance bookings.

Several gardens raise plants for sale in adjoining plant centres; houses have restaurants providing light refreshments, often home-made and delicious.

The times quoted are those of opening and closure; heritage, ruined and small sights are liable to closure at midday. Most places do not admit visitors in the last hour or half hour – arrive, therefore, with plenty of time to spare.

a

ABBOTSBURY

Swannery. – Daily, mid-May to mid-September, 9.30am-4.30pm; ☎030587 242 (evenings). 80p.

Sub-Tropical Gardens. – Daily, mid-March to mid-October, 10am-4.30pm; ☎ 030587 397. £1.

St Catherine's Chapel. – 15 March to 15 October, Monday-Saturday, 9.30am (Sunday 2pm)-6.30pm (winter 4pm); ☎ Bristol (0272) 734472. Nominal charge.

A LA RONDE

House. – Daily, April to late October, 10am-6pm, Sunday 2-7pm; ☎ Exmouth (0395) 265514. £1.20.

ANTONY HOUSE

House. – April to late October, Tuesday-Thursday, holiday Mondays, 2-6pm; ☎ Plymouth (0752) 812191. £1.80, NT.

APPLEDORE

North Devon Maritime Museum. – Daily, Easter to late September, 2.30-5.30pm also Tuesday and Friday mornings, 11am-1pm; ☎ Bideford (02372) 6042. 50p.

ARLINGTON COURT

House. – April to late October, Sunday-Friday and holiday weekend Saturdays, 11am-6pm; ☎ Shirwell (027182) 296. £2.30 inclusive ticket, NT.

Garden and park. – Daily, summer 11am-6pm; winter daylight hours; £1.30 including Carriage Collection, NT.

ASHLEY

Countryside Collection. – Easter to October, Monday, Wednesday, Saturday, Sunday and holiday Mondays; August, Friday-Wednesday; 10am-6pm; ☎ Ashreigney (07693) 226. 80p.

ATHELHAMPTON

House. – Easter to October, Wednesday, Thursday, Sunday, holiday Mondays (August also Tuesday, Friday), 2-6pm; ☎ Puddletown (030584) 363. House £1; garden £1.

AVEBURY

Alexander Keiller Museum. – Daily, 15 March to 15 October, 9.30am (Sundays in March and October 2pm) -6.30pm; winter 9.30am (Sunday 2pm)-4pm; ☎ 06723 250. 40p.

Manor. – Daily, April to October, 11.30am (Sunday 1.30pm)-6.30pm; winter, weekends 1.30-5pm; ☎ 06732 203. £1.40.

Museum of Folk Life. – Daily, late March to late October, 10am (Sundays, holidays, 10.30am)-5.30pm; winter weekends, 2-4pm; ☎ 06273 33. 70p.

AXBRIDGE

King John's Hunting Lodge. – Daily, April to late September, 2-5pm. ☎ 0934 732012.

AXMINSTER

Carpet Factory. – All year, Monday-Friday, 9am-12.30pm, 1.30-5pm; closed last weeks in May, July and public holidays; ☎ 0297 32244.

b

BADMINTON

House. – Enquire locally for days and times open to the public; ℡ Chipping Sodbury (045421) 202 or 221.

BARFORD

The Park. – May to September, Wednesday, Thursday, holiday weekends, 2-6pm; ℡ Spaxton (027867) 269. £1.

BARNSTAPLE

Guildhall. – All year, Monday-Friday, by *appointment only;* ℡ 0271 73311
Craft Market. – Monday-Saturday, 10am-5pm.
North Devon Athenaeum. – All year, Monday-Saturday, 10am-1pm, Monday, Wednesday, Thursday, Friday also 2.15-5 pm; closed all public holidays; ℡ 0271 42174

BARRINGTON COURT

The Court. – Late April to late September, Wednesdays, 2-5pm. 50p, NT.
Garden. – Late April to late September, Sunday-Wednesday, 2-5.30pm; ℡ Ilminster (04605) 2242. £1, NT.

BATH

Pump Room. – Daily, all year, 9am-6pm (5pm November to March); closed 25, 26 December; ℡ 0225 62831. Free.
Roman Baths. – Daily, all year, 9am-6pm (7pm July, August, 5pm November to March); closed 25, 26 December; ℡ 0225 61111 (ext 327) £1.40.
Burrow's Toy Museum. – Daily, all year, 10am-5.30pm; closed 25, 26 December; ℡ 0225 61819. 80p.
Royal Photographic Society. – All year, Monday-Saturday, also Sundays during school summer holidays 10am-5.30pm (Sundays 11am-4.45pm); ℡ 0225 62841. £1.
Assembly Rooms. – Daily, all year, 9.30am (Sunday 10am)-6pm; winter 10am (Sunday 11am)-5pm; ℡ 0225 61111 (ext 327). £1.10 inclusive ticket with Costume Museum (£1.20, July August).
Museum of Costume. – As Assembly Rooms, see above.
Camden Works Museum. – Daily, all year, 2-5pm; closed winter Fridays, 24-26 December; ℡ 0225 318348. £1.
Carriage Museum. – Daily, all year, 9.30am-5pm; closed 25 December; ℡ 0225 25115. 80p.
No 1, Royal Crescent. – March to late October, Monday-Saturday, 11am-5pm (Sundays, holiday Mondays, 2-5pm); ℡ 0225 28126. £1.
Victoria Art Gallery. – All year, Monday-Saturday, 10am-6pm (Saturday 5pm); ℡ 0225 61111 (ext 418).
Postal Museum. – Daily, all year, 11am (Sunday 2pm)-5pm; ℡ 0225 60333. 50p.
Holburne of Menstrie Museum. – Daily, February to December, 11am-5pm (Sunday 2.30-6pm); closed 25, 26 December; ℡ 0225 66669. 70p.
Herschel House. – March to October, Wednesday, Saturday, 2-5pm; winter, Sunday only 2-5pm; ℡ 0225 336228. 50p.
Museum of Bookbinding. – All year, Monday-Friday, 9am-1pm, 2.15-5.30pm; closed all public holidays; ℡ 0225 660000. 75p.
Railway Display Museum. – All year, Tuesday-Saturday, 10.30am-12.45pm, 2-4pm; ℡ 0225 66867. 35p.
Beckford Tower. – April to late October, weekends 2-5pm; ℡ 0225 336228. 30p.
Prior Park. – Chapel and grounds open in daylight hours.

BEDRUTHAN

Steps. – Cliff staircase: April to late October, 10.30am-6pm; ℡ St Mawgan (06374) 563.

BICKLEIGH

Mill Craft Centre. – Daily, all year, April-December, 10am-6pm; January-March, 2-5pm; ℡ 08845 419. £2. (winter £1.50).
Castle. – June to mid-October, Sunday-Friday, also Easter week and Sundays and holiday Mondays in May, 2-5pm; ℡ 08845 363. £1.50.

BICTON

Gardens. – Daily, April-October, 10am-6pm; winter daylight hours; ℡ Budleigh Salterton (0395) 68465. £1.95.

BIDEFORD

Burton Art Gallery. – All year, Monday-Friday, 10am-1pm, 2-5pm, Saturday 10am-1pm; ℡ 02372 6711 (ext 275).

BLAISE

Castle House Museum. – All year, Monday-Wednesday, Saturday, Sunday, 10am-1pm, 2-5pm; ℡ Bristol (0272) 506789.

BLANDFORD

Royal Signals Museum. – All year, Monday-Friday, 9am-4.30pm; closed all public holidays; ℡ 0258 52581 (ext 248).

BOURNEMOUTH

Rothesay Museum. – All year, Monday-Saturday, 10.30am-5.30pm; closed 25, 26 December, Good Friday; ℡ 0202 21009. 35p.

Russell-Cotes Art Gallery and Museum. – All year, Monday-Saturday, 10.30am-5.30pm, Sunday (April to November) 3-5.30pm; ℡ as above. 50p; June to September Sundays, 75p.

Shelley Museum. – June to September, Monday-Saturday, winter Thursday-Saturday, 10.30am-5pm; ℡ as above. 20p.

BOVEY TRACEY

Parke. – Daily, April to late October, 10am-6pm; ℡ 0626 833909. £1.20 NT.

BOVINGTON

Tank Museum. – Daily, all year, 10am-5pm; closed at Christmas and New Year; ℡ Bindon Abbey (0929) 462721 (ext 463). £1.10.

BOWOOD HOUSE

House. – July, August daily; April, May, June, September, Tuesday-Sunday and holiday Mondays, 11am-6pm; ℡ Calne (0249) 812102. £1.20.

BRADFORD-ON-AVON

Bridge. – Chapel key at Tourist Information Office, 1 Church St. ℡ 02216 2224.

BRIDGWATER

Admiral Blake Museum. – All year, Tuesday, 11am-4pm, Wednesday -8pm, Friday -4pm, Saturday, Sunday -5pm; closed 25, 26 December, Good Friday, New Year and May Day holidays; ℡ 0278 56127.

BRIDPORT

Museum. – June to September, Monday-Wednesday, Friday, 10.30am-1pm, 2.30-4pm, also Thursday afternoons, Saturday mornings; winter, mornings only; ℡ 0308 22116. 20p.

BRISTOL

Lord Mayor's Chapel. – All year, Monday-Friday, 10am-12 noon, 2-4pm; closed all public holidays; ℡ 0272 26031.

Harvey's Wine Museum. – All year, Fridays 10am-5pm; Monday-Thursday guided tours by appointment only; closed public holidays; ℡ 0272 277661. 50p. *Persons under 16 years not admitted.*

Georgian House. – All year, Monday-Saturday, 10am-1pm, 2-5pm; closed 25, 26 December, New Year, May Day holidays and Good Friday; ℡ 0272 299771 (ext 237).

Cabot Tower. – Daily all year, except 25 December, 9am approximately to dusk; ℡ 0272 26031 (ext 509). 10p *(coin operated turnstile).*

City Museum and Art Gallery. – All year, Monday-Saturday 10am-5pm; closed Sundays, all public holidays and Tuesdays after holiday Mondays; ℡ 0272 299771.

Bristol University. – Entrance hall below tower; ℡ 0272 24161 (ext 410).

Red Lodge. – All year, Monday-Saturday, 10am-1pm, 2-5pm; closed 25, 26 December, New Year, May Day and holiday Mondays, also Good Friday and Tuesday following spring holiday Monday; ℡ 0272 299771 (ext 236).

St Nicolas Church Museum. – All year, Monday-Saturday, 10am-5pm; closed 25, 26 December, New Year, May Day and holiday Mondays also Good Friday and Tuesday following spring holiday Monday; ℡ 0272 299771 (ext 243).

John Wesley's New Room. – All year, Monday, Tuesday, Thursday-Saturday, 10am-4pm; closed all public holidays; ℡ 0272 24740.

Quakers' Friars. – All year, Monday-Friday, 1-4.30pm, Saturday 9.30am-12.30pm; closed all public holidays; ℡ 0272 26031 (ext 671).

SS Great Britain. – Daily, all year, 10am-6pm (late October to March, GMT, 5pm); closed 25, 26 December; ℡ 0272 20680. £1.

Industrial Museum. – All year, Saturday-Wednesday, 10am-1pm, 2-5pm; closed 25, 26 December, New Year holiday, Good Friday; ℡ 0272 299771 (ext 299).

National Lifeboat Museum. – Easter Monday to late September, Saturday – Thursday, 10.30am-4.30pm; ℡ 0272 213389. 30p.

Arnolfini. – 2 January-24 December, Tuesday-Saturday, 11am-8pm, Sunday, 2-7pm; ℡ 0272 299191.

Zoo. – Daily, all year, 9am (Sunday, 10am)-6pm (September-May, 5pm); ℡ 0272 738951. £2.40.

BROWNSEA ISLAND

Access by boat from Poole (the Quay) or Sandbanks : daily services April to late September, 10am-8pm or dusk – enquire time of last boat. No dogs. Landing fee 70p.
Nature reserve: daily guided tour (Dorset Nauralists' Trust) 2.30pm. Nominal charge.

BRYMPTON d'EVERCY

House. – May to September, Saturday-Wednesday and Easter, 2-6pm; ℡ West Coker (093586) 2528. £2.80.

BUCKFASTLEIGH

Dart Valley Railway Centre. – Easter, then May-September, daily 10am-5.30pm; ℡ 0365 43536. 50p.

BUCKLAND ABBEY

The Abbey. – Daily, Easter to September, 11am (Sunday, 2pm)-6pm; October to Easter, Wednesday, Saturday, Sunday, 2-5pm; closed 25 December, Good Friday; ℡ Plymouth (0752) 668000 (ext 4383). £1.30, NT.

C

CADHAY

House. – July, August, Tuesday-Thursday and spring and summer holiday Sundays and Mondays, 2-6pm; ℡ Ottery-St-Mary (040481) 2432. £1.

CAMBORNE and REDRUTH

Cornish Pumping Engines. – Daily, April to late October, 11am-6pm or sunset if earlier. 80p, NT.

CAMELFORD

North Cornwall Museum of Rural Life. – April to late September, Monday-Saturday, 10,30am-5pm; ℡ 0840 213242. 50p.

CARN EUNY

Prehistoric village. – Daily, 15 March to 16 October, 9.30am (Sunday 2pm)-6.30pm; winter, 4pm; closed 24-26 December, New Year holiday; ℡ Bristol (0272) 734472. Nominal charge.

CARTHEW

Wheal Martyn Museum. – Daily, April to late October, 10am-5pm; ℡ St Austell (0726) 850362. £1.40.

CASTLE DROGO

The Castle. – Daily, April to late October, 11am-6pm; ℡ Chagford (06473) 3306. £2 inclusive ticket, NT.

Garden and grounds. – £1, NT. Croquet lawn: to hire equipment book 24 hours in advance.

CHAMBERCOMBE

The Manor. – Easter to late September, Sunday-Friday, 10.30am-5pm; ℡ Ilfracombe (0271) 62624. £1.

CHARMINSTER

Wolfeton House. – May to September, Sunday, Tuesday, Thursday, holiday Mondays, August, Sunday-Friday, 2-6pm.; ℡ Dorchester (0305) 63500. £1.50.

The CHEDDAR GORGE

Jacob's Ladder. – Daily, Easter to mid-October, 10am-6pm; ℡ 0934 742343. 25p.

Gough's Cave. – Daily, all year, Easter to mid-October, 10am-6pm; winter 11am-5pm; closed 25 December; ℡ as above. £1.30

Cox's Cave. – As Gough's Cave. 80p.

Fantasy Grotto. – Daily, Easter to mid-October, 10am-6pm; ℡ as above. 40p.

Museum. – Daily, Easter to mid-October, 10am-6pm; ℡ as above. 25p.

Adventure Caving. – All year (not Christmas); 4 trips daily, 9.30am, 11.30am, 2pm, 4pm. each 1-1½ hours duration; maximum of 10 persons over 12 years and fit. Wear old clothes and sensible footwear (wellingtons); arrive 30-15 minutes before start of trip. Book well in advance; ℡ 0934 742343. £2.30

Chewton Cheese Dairy. – Daily, all year : two cheese makings, 9am, 12.30pm; ℡ Chewton Mendip (076121) 666. 50p.

CHIPPENHAM

Yelde Hall. – Mid-March to late October, Monday-Saturday, 10am-12.30pm, 2-4.30pm; closed holiday Mondays; ℡ Corsham (0249) 653145.

CHRISTCHURCH

Red House Museum. – All year, Tuesday-Saturday, 10am-1pm, 2-5pm, Sunday 2-5pm; closed 24-26 December and all public holidays; ☎ 0202 482860. 40p.

CHYSAUSTER

Prehistoric village. – Daily, 15 March to 15 October 9.30am (Sunday 2pm)-6.30pm; winter, 4pm; closed 24-26 December, New Year holiday; ☎ Bristol (0272) 734472. Nominal charge.

CLAPTON COURT

Gardens. – All year, Monday-Friday, 10am-5pm, Sunday 2-5pm also Easter and all Saturdays in May, 2-5pm; ☎ Crewkerne (0460) 73220. £1. (House not open.)

CLAVERTON

American Museum. – April to October, Tuesday-Sunday, 2-5pm; holiday Mondays and preceding weekends, 11am-5pm; ☎ Bath (0225) 60503. £2.

Pump. – Late April to late October, every Sunday 10.30am-2pm; in steam, holiday weekend Sundays, Mondays and last weekend of each month : Sundays 10.30am-2pm, Mondays, 12.30-6pm; ☎ Bristol (0272) 711038. 20p.

CLEEVE ABBEY

The Abbey. – Daily, 15 March to 15 October, 9.30am (Sunday, 2pm)-6.30pm; winter, 4pm; closed 24-26 December, New Year holiday; ☎ Bristol (0272) 734472. Nominal charge.

CLEVEDON COURT

The Court. – April to late September, Wednesday, Thursday, Sunday and holiday Mondays, 2.30-5.30pm. £1.30, NT.

CLOUDS HILL

The Cottage. – April to late September, Wednesday-Friday, Sunday, Good Friday, holiday Mondays, 2-5pm; October to March, Sunday 1-4pm. £1, NT.

COMBE MARTIN

Motorcycle Collection. – Daily, late May to mid-September, 10am-6pm; ☎ 027188 2346. 50p.

COMBE SYDENHAM HALL

The Hall. – July, August, Monday-Friday; June, September, Tuesday, Wednesday, Friday, 1-5pm; ☎ Watchet (09846) 284, £1.60 inclusive ticket; park only £1.20.

COMPTON ACRES

Gardens. – Daily, April to October, 10.30am-6.30pm; ☎ Bournemouth (0202) 708036. £1.20 (House not open.)

COMPTON CASTLE

The Castle. – April to late October, Monday, Wednesday, Thursday, 10am-12 noon, 2-5pm; ☎ Kingskerswell (08047) 2112. £1, NT.

CORFE CASTLE

The ruins. – Daily, March to late October, 10am-6pm or sunset if earlier; winter, weekends only, 2-4pm weather permitting; ☎ 0920 480442. 80p, NT.

CORSHAM COURT

The Court. – 15 January to 15 December, Tuesday-Thursday, Saturday, Sunday, 2-6pm (4pm, 15 January to 30 May, October to 15 December); ☎ 0249 712214. £1.50.

COTEHELE

The House. – Daily, April to late October, 11am-6pm; ☎ Liskeard (0579) 50434; £2.30 inclusive ticket, NT.

Garden and Mill. – All year, daylight hours; £1, NT.

CRANBORNE MANOR

Gardens. – April to October, first full weekend in each month and holiday Mondays; Saturdays, holiday Mondays 9am (Sundays 2pm)-5pm; ☎ 07254 248; £1. (House not open.)

CRANMORE

East Somerset Railway. – Daily, April to October, weekends in March, November, 10am-5.30pm; trains run at weekends and on Wednesdays in July, August; ☎ 074988 417. £1.40 including train ride; 80p depot only.

CRICKET ST THOMAS

Wildlife Park. – Daily, all year 10am-6pm (dusk in winter); dogs on leads only; ☎ Winsham (0460) 30396. £2.20. (House not open.)

CULDROSE

Cornwall Aero Park and Flambards Village. – Daily, Easter to late October, 10am-5.30pm; ☎ Helston (03265) 4549; £1.95.

DARTINGTON

Cider Press Centre. – All year, Monday-Saturday, also Sundays in August and December, 9.30am-5.30pm; ℡ Totnes (0803) 864171.

DARTMOUTH

Newcomen Engine. – All year, Monday-Saturday, 11am-5pm; machinery working, Easter to October; ℡ 08043 2923. 30p.

No 6, The Butterwalk : local museum. – April to October, Monday-Saturday, 11am-5pm; winter 2.15-4pm; ℡ 08043 2923. 30p.

The Castle. – Daily 15 March to 15 October, 9.30am (Sunday 2pm)-6.30pm; winter 4pm; closed 24-26 December, New Year holiday; ℡ Bristol (0272) 734472. Nominal charge.

River Dart Boat Trips. – Embarkation point : South Embankment; trips 1-1½ hours.

Dartmouth-Torbay Railway. – See Torbay, p 230.

DELABOLE

Quarry. – Daily, April to late September, 10am-5pm; ℡ Camelford (0840) 212242. 25p.

DEVIZES

Museum. – Open all year, Tuesday-Saturday, 11am-1pm, 2-5pm (winter 4pm); closed public holidays; ℡ 0380 2765. 50p – free entry on Thursdays.

DORCHESTER

Old Shire Hall. – All year, Monday-Friday, 9am-1pm, 2-4.30pm; closed all public holidays; ℡ 0305 65211.

Dorset County Museum. – All year, Monday-Saturday, 10am-5pm (closed Saturday 1-2pm); open Easter and summer holiday Mondays; closed 24-26 December, New Year holiday, Good Friday; ℡ 0305 62735. 50p.

Dorset Military Museum. – All year, Monday-Saturday, 9am-5pm (October-June, Saturdays 9am-12.30pm only); ℡ 0305 64066. 40p.

DOWNSIDE ABBEY

The Abbey. – All year daily, 6.30am-8pm; ℡ Stratton-on-the-Fosse (0761) 232205.

DUNSTER

The Castle. – Saturday-Wednesday, April to late September, 11am-5pm, October 12 noon-5pm; ℡ 064382 314. £2 inclusive ticket, NT; park £1, NT.

Water Mill. – Daily, July, August, 11am-5pm; April, May, June, September, Saturday-Wednesday, 11am-5pm, October, 12 noon-4pm; ℡ 064382 759. 60p.

Molly Hardwick Doll Collection. – May to September, Sunday-Friday and Easter weekend, 10.30am-4.30pm. 10p.

DUNSTONE

Devon Shire Horse Farm Centre. – Daily all year, 10am-5pm; closed Christmas; ℡ Plymouth (0752) 880268. £1.50.

DYRHAM PARK

House. – June to September, Saturday-Thursday, 2-6pm; April, May, October, Saturday-Wednesday, 2-6pm or dusk if earlier; ℡ Abson (027582) 2501. £2 inclusive ticket, NT.

Park. – Daily, all year, noon-6pm or dusk if earlier. 50p, NT.

e

EAST LAMBROOK

The Manor. – March to late November, Thursday 2-5pm; guided tours; ℡ South Petherton (0460) 40328. 50p.

Garden. – All year, daily, 9am-5pm. 30p.

EXETER

Maritime Museum. – Daily all year, 10am-6pm (5pm in winter); closed 25, 26 December; ℡ 0392 58075. £2.

Royal Albert Memorial Museum. – All year, Tuesday-Saturday, 10am-5.30pm; closed public holidays; ℡ 0392 56724. 60p.

Guildhall. – All year, Monday-Saturday, 10am-5.15pm; closed all public holidays; ℡ 0392 72979.

Rougemont House Museum. – All year, Tuesday-Saturday, 10am-1pm, 2-5pm; ℡ 0392 56724. 40p.

St Nicholas Priory. – All year, Tuesday-Saturday, 10am-12.30pm, 2-5.30pm; closed 25, 26 December, Good Friday, all holiday Mondays; ℡ 0392 72434. 40p.

Tuckers' Hall. – June to September, Tuesday, Thursday, Friday, 10.30am-12.30pm; winter, Friday only; closed all public holidays; ℡ 0392 36244.

Underground Passages. – All year, Tuesday-Saturday, 2-4.40pm; closed public holidays; ℡ 0392 56724. 40p.

f

FALMOUTH

Pendennis Castle. – Daily, 15 March to 15 October 9.30am (Sunday 2pm)-6.30pm; winter 4pm; closed 24-26 December and New Year holiday; ☎ Bristol (0272) 734472. Nominal charge.

FARLEIGH HUNGERFORD

The Castle. – Daily, 15 March to 15 October, 9.30am (Sunday 2pm)-6.30pm; winter 4pm; closed 24-26 December and New Year holiday; ☎ Bristol (0272) 734472. 40p.

FARWAY

Countryside Park. – Good Friday to late September, Sunday-Friday, 10am-6pm; ☎ 040487 224 or 367. £1.25.

FORDE ABBEY

The House. – May to September, Sunday, Wednesday and holiday Mondays, 2-6pm; ☎ Chard (0460) 20231. £1.75.

FOWEY

Noah's Ark. – All year, Monday-Friday, 10am-1pm, 2-4pm (Wednesday, 10am-1pm only); closed Christmas, Good Friday, some holiday Mondays; ☎ 072683 3304. 50p.

g

GAULDEN MANOR

The Manor. – Easter and holiday Monday weekends; May to September, Sundays and Thursdays; July, also Wednesdays; 2-6pm; guided tours; ☎ Lydeard St Lawrence (09847) 213. £1.40.

GEEVOR

Tin Mine. – April to late October, Monday-Friday, 10am-4pm. Treatment plant closed holiday Mondays; ☎ Penzance (0736) 788662. £1.40.

GLASTONBURY

The Abbey. – Daily all year: June to August, 9am-7.30pm. Other months 9.30am-7pm, May, September; 6pm, March, April, October; 5.30pm, February; 5pm, January, November; 4.30pm, December. Closed 25 December; ☎ 0458 32267. 60p.

The Tribunal. – Daily, 15 March to 15 October, 9.30am-1pm, 2pm (Sunday, 2pm)-6.30pm; winter 4pm; closed 24-26 December, New Year holiday; ☎ Bristol (0272) 734472. 40p.

Somerset Rural Life Museum. – Daily all year, Monday-Saturday, 10am-5pm, Sunday, 2-6.30pm (November to March, 2.30-5pm), closed 25, 26 December, Good Friday; ☎ 0458 32903. 50p.

Chalice Well. – Daily, Easter to late October, 10am-6pm; November to Easter, 1-3pm; ☎ 0458 31154. 30p.

GLENDURGAN GARDEN

The Garden. – March to late October, Monday, Wednesday, Friday, 10.30am-4.30pm; closed Good Friday. £1, NT. (House not open.)

GREAT BEDWYN

Crofton Beam Engines. – April to late October, Sunday 10am-1pm, 2-5pm. For weekends in steam ☎ Goring (0491) 874072 or Marlborough (0672) 810575. £1.

Canal trips. – ☎ Swindon (0793) 872375.

GREAT CHALFIELD

The Manor. – April to late October, Monday-Wednesday, 12 noon-1pm, 2-5pm; guided tours – only morning tour, 12.15pm; closed all public holidays. £1.30, NT.

GREAT TORRINGTON

Dartington Glass. – All year, Monday-Friday, 9.30am-3.30pm; guided tours; closed weekends and public holidays; ☎ 08052 3797. 75p.

GWEEK

Seal Sanctuary. – Daily, all year, 9.30am-6.30pm or dusk if earlier; feeding times 11am, 4pm; closed Christmas; ☎ Mawgan (032622) 361. £1.50.

h

HATCH COURT

The Court. – July to mid-September, Thursday, 2.30-5.30pm; ☎ Hatch Beauchamp (0823) 480208. £1.

HAYLE

Paradise Park. – Daily, all year, 10am-7pm (6pm May, 5pm April, 4pm October to March); ☎ Penzance (0736) 753365. £2.

HELSTON

Folk Museum. – All year, Monday, Tuesday, Thursday-Saturday, 10.30am-12.30pm, 2-4.30pm; Wednesday 10am-12 noon; closed all public holidays; ☎ 03265 61672.

HIGHER BOCKHAMPTON

Hardy's Cottage. – Garden : daily, April to late October, 11am-6pm or sunset if earlier; closed Tuesday morning.
House: by *appointment only* with tenant; ☎ Bourton (0747) 840224. £1, NT.

HIGH HAM

Windmill. – Easter Sunday to late September, Sundays and holiday Mondays, 2-5.30pm; ☎ Langport (0458) 250818. 50p, NT.

HONITON

All Hallows Museum. – Mid-May to late September, Monday-Saturday, 10am-5pm. 25p.

HORTON COURT

The Court, Hall, Garden. – April to late October, Wednesday, Saturday, 2-6pm or sunset if earlier. 50p, NT. (House interior not open.)

i

ILFRACOMBE

St Nicolas Chapel. – Daily, early May to mid-October, 9.30am-5.30pm; June to August also 7pm-dusk; ☎ 0271 62857.
Tunnels Beach. – Daily, May to late September, 9am-dusk; ☎ 0271 64559. 25p.

INSTOW

Tapely Park. – Gardens, Easter to October, Tuesday-Sunday 10am-6pm; winter, daylight hours; ☎ 0271 860528. 80p.
House : in summer, guided tours, 12 noon, 2.30pm, when numbers sufficient. £1.

k

KILLERTON

The House. – Daily, April to late October, 11am-6pm; ☎ Exeter (0392) 881345. £2 inclusive ticket, NT.
Garden. – Daily, all year, daylight hours. £1.30, NT.

KINGSBRIDGE

Cookworthy Museum. – Easter to late September, Monday-Saturday, 10am-5pm; October, 10.30am-4.30pm; ☎ 0548 3235. 50p.
Boat trip to Salcombe. – Average 4 trips daily each way; ☎ 0548 3607 or 3525. 90p.

KINGSTON LACY

National Trust. Enquire locally as to opening times; ☎ Bourton (0747) 840224.

KNIGHTSHAYES COURT

The Court. – Daily, April to late October, 1.30-6pm; ☎ Tiverton (0884) 254665. £2 inclusive ticket, NT.
Garden and grounds. – April to late October, 11.30am-6pm. £1.30, NT.

I

LACOCK

Fox Talbot Museum. – Daily, March to late October, 11am-5pm; closed Good Friday; ℡ 024973 459. 80p, NT.

The Abbey. – April to late October, Wednesday-Monday, 2-6pm; closed Good Friday; ℡ 024973 227. £1.50, NT.

LAMANVA

Military Vehicle Museum. – Daily, Easter to September, 10am-5.30pm;℡ Helston (0326) 72446. £1.

LANHYDROCK

The House. – Daily, April to late October, 11am-6pm; ℡ Bodmin (0208) 4287; £2.30 inclusive ticket, NT.

Garden. – As above plus daylight hours November to March. £1, NT.

LAUNCESTON

The Castle. – Daily, 15 March to 15 October, 9.30am (Sunday 2pm)-6.30pm; winter 4pm; closed 24-26 December, New Year Holiday; ℡ Bristol (0272) 734472. Nominal charge.

South Gate. – April to December, Monday-Saturday, 10am-3pm; ℡ 0566 3121.

Local History Museum. – April to late September, Monday-Friday, 10.30am-12 noon, 2.30-4.30pm; ℡ 0566 2833.

LISKEARD

Merlin Glass. – Weekdays 10am-5pm.

LITTLECOTE

The House. – July to late September, Monday-Friday 2-5pm, weekends, holiday Mondays, 2-6pm; ℡ Hungerford (0488) 82170. £1. 50.

Mosaic Pavement. – April to September, weekdays 10am-5pm, weekends, holiday Mondays 6PM. £1.

Frontier City. – July, August, Monday, Wednesday, Thursday, Friday, 12 noon-5pm, Saturday. Sunday, holiday Mondays, 6pm; April, May, June, September, Saturday, Sunday, holiday Mondays only, 12 noon-6pm; £1.50.

LONGLEAT

The House. – Daily, all year, 10am-5pm (4pm October to Easter); closed only 25 December; ℡ Maiden Bradley (09853) 551. £1.80.

Safari Park. – Daily, mid-March to late October, 10am-6pm or sunset if earlier; ℡ Maiden Bradley (09853) 328. £2.30 per person by car, £2.50 by safari bus.

Narrow Gauge Railway. – 65p.

Safari Boats. – 70p.

Maze. – 30p (30-60 minutes).

Victorian Kitchens. – 80p.

19C Dolls' Houses. – 20p.

Coarse Fishing (16 June-15 March). – Permits from water bailiff at lakeside; £2 per day.

LOOE

Monkey Sanctuary. – Two weeks at Easter then early May to late September, Sunday-Friday, 10.30am-5.30pm; ℡ 05036 2532. £1.85.

LYDFORD

The Gorge. – Daily, April to late October, 10.30am-6pm; winter, Waterfall entrance only open and path to Waterfall, 10.30am-6pm. £1, NT.

LYDIARD PARK

House. – All year, Monday-Saturday, 10am-1pm, 2-5.30pm, Sunday 2-5.30pm; closed 25, 26 December, Good Friday; ℡ Swindon (0793) 770401. 50p.

Church. – Key in house.

LYME REGIS

Museum. – Daily, April to late October, Monday-Saturday, 10.30am-1.30pm, 2.30-5pm, Sunday 2.30-5pm; ℡ 02974 3370. 30p.

LYNTON and LYNMOUTH

Cliff Railway. – Daily mid-March to 26 December, 8am-7pm. 13p.

LYTES CARY

The House. – March to late October, Wednesday, Saturday 2-6pm. £1.30, NT.

m

MAIDEN CASTLE

The earthworks. – Daily, 15 March to 15 October, 9.30am (Sunday 2pm)-6.30pm; winter 4pm; closed 24-26 December, New Year holiday; ☏ Bristol (0272) 734472. Nominal charge.

MARLBOROUGH

College. – Chapel only: daylight hours (until 7pm); apply at porter's lodge.

MIDELNEY

The Manor. – Early June to mid-September, Wednesdays, holiday Mondays, 2-5.30pm; ☏ Langport (0458) 251299. £1.

MILTON ABBAS

The Abbey. – Daily throughout the year.
The House. – Daily, Easter and summer school holidays, 10am-7.30pm. 50p.

MONTACUTE

The House. – April to late October, Wednesday-Monday, 12.30-6pm or sunset if earlier; ☏ Martock (0935) 823289. £2 inclusive ticket, NT.
Garden and park. – All year, Wednesday-Monday 12.30-6pm or dusk if earlier. June to September, 80p; October to May, 40p, NT.

MORWELLHAM

The site. – Daily, March to late October, 10am-6pm; dusk in winter – last admissions : summer 4.30pm, winter 2.30pm; closed 25 December; ☏ Tavistock (0822) 832766. £2.70.

MOUNT EDGCUMBE

The House and Higher Gardens. – May to late September, Monday, Tuesday, 2-6pm; ☏ Plymouth (0752) 822236. 80p.
Lower Gardens. – Daily, all year until dusk.

MUCHELNEY

The Abbey. – Daily, 15 March to 15 October, 9.30am (Sunday 2pm)-6.30pm; closed in winter; ☏ Bristol (0272) 734472. Nominal charge.
Pottery. – All year, Monday-Friday, 9am-1pm, 2-6pm, Saturday 9am-1pm; ☏ Langport (0458) 250324.

n

NETHER STOWEY

Coleridge Cottage. – April to late September, Tuesday-Thursday, Sunday, 2-5pm; ☏ 0278 732663. 50p, NT.

NUNNEY

The Castle. – Daily, 15 March to 15 October, 9.30am (Sunday, 2pm)-6.30pm; winter 4pm; closed 24-26 December, New Year holiday; ☏ Bristol (0272) 734472. Nominal charge.

o

OAKHILL

The Manor. – Daily, Easter to early November; 12 noon-6pm; ☏ 0749 840210. £2.40.

OKEHAMPTON

Museum of Dartmoor Life. – April to late October, Monday-Saturday, 10.30am-4.30pm; ☏ 0837 3020 50p.
The Castle. – Daily, 15 March-15 October, 9.30am (Sunday 2pm)-6.30pm; winter 4pm; closed 24-26 December, New Year holiday; ☏ Bristol (0272) 734472. Nominal charge.

OLD SARUM

Castle ruins. – Daily, 15 March-15 October 9.30am (Sunday 2pm)-6.30pm; winter 4pm; closed 24-26 December, New Year holiday; ☏ Bristol (0272) 734472. 40p.

OTTERTON

The Mill. – Daily, Easter to late October, 10.30am-5.30pm; winter 2-5pm; closed Christmas. 90p (winter 40p).

OVER COMPTON

Worldwide Butterflies. – Daily, April to October, 10am-5pm; ☏ Sherborne (0935) 74608. £2.15.

p

PAIGNTON

Zoo. – Daily, all year, 10am-5pm (4pm September to Easter); ☏ 0803 557479. £2.30.

Oldway Mansion and Gardens. – All year, Monday-Saturday, 9am (Sundays, May to September, 2pm)-5pm; closed winter public holidays; ☏ 0803 26244 (ext 286).

Kirkham House. – Daily, 15 March to 15 October, 9.30am (Sunday, 2pm)-6.30pm; winter, 4pm; closed 24-26 December, New Year holiday; ☏ Bristol (0272) 734472. Nominal charge.

PARNHAM HOUSE

The House. – April to October, Sunday, Wednesday and public holidays, 10am-5pm; ☏ Beaminster (0308) 862204. £1.75.

PENCARROW

The House. – Easter to late September, Sunday, Tuesday-Friday and holiday Mondays 11am (April, May, September, 1.30pm)-5pm; ☏ St Mabyn (020884) 369. £1.60 inclusive ticket; garden only, 80p.

PENZANCE

Local Museum. – All year, Monday-Saturday and holiday Mondays, 10.30am-4.30pm (Saturday to 12.30pm); ☏ 0736 36125.

Museum of Nautical Art. – April to October, Monday-Saturday, 10am-5pm (also possibly 7-9pm at peak holiday period); ☏ 0736 3324. 80p.

PLYMOUTH

Drake's Island. – Ferry service from Mayflower Steps: Saturday of spring holiday weekend to 3rd Sunday September, 10am hourly to 4pm; ☏ 0752 668000. £1.40 rtn + 10p landing fee.

Smeaton's Tower. – Daily, Easter to September, 10.30am-sunset; ☏ 0752 264840. 15p.

Civic Centre. – All year, Monday-Friday, 9am-5pm (Friday 4.30pm);
Roof-Deck: April to late September, Monday-Friday, 10am-4pm. 15p.
Tourist Information Centre : Monday-Saturday, 9am-5pm (Friday 4.30pm; holiday Mondays 10am-4pm; winter Saturdays, 9am-12.30pm); ☏ 0752 668000.

Council House. – All year, Monday-Friday, 10am-12noon, 2-4pm; closed all public holidays; ☏ as above.

Guildhall. – All year, Monday-Friday, 10am-4pm; closed all public holidays; ☏ as above.

Prysten House. – April to October, Monday-Saturday, 10am-4pm; ☏ 0752 661414. 40p.

The Merchant's House. – All year, Monday-Saturday, 10am-6pm (Saturday 5pm) also Sundays Easter to late September, 2-5pm; ☏ 0752 668000 (ext 4383). 25p.

Royal Citadel. – Daily, May to September; guided tours only; at 2, 3, 4 5pm; ☏ 0752 660582. Free. (Book guides in advance (fee) for parties.)

Elizabethan House. – All year, Monday-Friday 10am-1pm, 2.15-6pm (4.30pm, October to Easter), Saturday 5pm, Sunday (summer only) 2-5pm; ☏ 0752 668000 (ext 4383). 25p.

Coates Gin Distillery. – Enquire locally as to times; ☏ 0752 665292.

City Museum. – All year, Monday-Saturday, 10am-6pm (Saturday 5pm); closed 25, 26 December, New Year holiday, Good Friday; ☏ 0752 668000 (ext 4383).

Aquarium. – All year, Monday-Saturday, 10am-6pm; closed 25, 26 December, New Year holiday, Good Friday; ☏ 0752 21761. 50p.

POOLE

Poole Pottery. – All year, Monday-Friday, 10.15am-3.45pm – guided tours (last tour Friday, 11.30am); closed all public holidays; ☏ 0202 672 866. £1.55.

RNLI Museum. – All year, Monday-Friday, 9.30-4.30pm; closed weekends and public holidays; ☏ 0202 671133 (ext 239).

Maritime Museum. – All year, Monday-Saturday, 10am-5pm, Sunday 2-5pm; closed 25, 26 December, Good Friday; ☏ 0202 675151 (ext 3551). 35p.

Scalpen's Court. – As above. 35p.

Guildhall Museum. – As above. 35p.

PORTLAND

Museum. – May to September, Monday-Saturday, 10am-5.30pm Sunday 11am-5pm; winter Tuesday-Saturday, 10am-1pm. 2-5pm; closed 24-26 December, Good Friday; ☏ 0305 821804. 40p.

The Castle. – Daily, 15 March to 15 October, 9.30am (Sunday 2pm)-6.30pm; winter 4pm; closed 24-26 December, Good Friday; ☏ Bristol (0272) 734472. Nominal charge.

POUNDISFORD

The Park. – Easter Sunday to mid-September, Sunday, Thursday, holiday Mondays, 2-6pm; ☏ Blagdon Hill (082342) 244. £1.25.

PROBUS

County Demonstration Garden. – All year, Monday-Friday, 10am-5pm (4.30pm, October to April), also Sundays, May to September 2-6pm; ☏ Truro (0872) 74282. 50p.

PURSE CAUNDLE

House. – Enquire locally for days and times open to the public.

r

REDLYNCH

Newhouse. – Saturdays, Sundays, June, July, August, also Easter, spring and summer holiday Mondays, 2-6pm; ☏ Downton (0725) 20055. £1.

REDRUTH

Tolgus Tin Streaming. – Daily, Easter to late October, 10am-6pm, guided tours; ☏ 0209 215171. £1.50.

RESTORMEL

Castle. – Daily, 15 March to 15 October, 9.30am (Sunday 2pm)-6.30pm; winter 4pm; closed 24-26 December, New Year holiday; ☏ Bristol (0272) 734472. Nominal charge.

RODE

Tropical Bird Gardens. – Daily, all year, 10.30am-7pm or sunset if earlier; ☏ Frome (0373) 830326. £1.65.

s

ST IVES

Barbara Hepworth Museum. – All year, Monday-Saturday, 10am-6.30pm (5.30pm, April, June, September; 4.30pm October-March) also Sundays, July, August, 2-6pm; ☏ 0736 796226. 50p.

Barnes Museum of Cinematography. – Daily, Easter to late September, 11.30am-1pm, 2.30-4.30pm. 40p.

St Ives Museum. – Daily, mid-May to early October, 10am-5pm; ☏0736 795575. 20p.

ST KEYNE

Paul Corin Musical Collection. – Daily, Easter to late September, 10.30am-1pm, 2.30-5pm; ☏ Liskeard (0579) 43108. £1.

ST MAWES

Castle. – Daily, 15 March to 15 October, 9.30am (Sunday 2pm)-6.30pm; winter 4pm; closed 24-26 December, New Year holiday; ☏ Bristol (0272) 734472. Nominal charge.

ST MICHAEL'S MOUNT

The Mount. – June to late October, Monday-Friday, 10.30am-5.45pm; April, May, Monday, Wednesday, Friday, 10.30am-5.45pm; November to March, Monday, Wednesday, Friday guided tours only, at 11am, 12 noon, 2 and 4pm – weather and tide permitting (no regular ferry service in winter); ☏ Penzance (0736) 710507. £2, NT; ferry, 40p.

SALCOMBE

Ferries to Kingsbridge: see Kingsbridge p 224.

SALCOMBE REGIS

Donkey Sanctuary. – Daily, all year, 9am-5pm.

Slade Centre. – All year; Sunday all day; Saturday after 12 noon, Monday-Friday before 10am and after 3pm; ☏ Sidmouth (03955) 6592.

SALISBURY

Cathedral. – Daily, all year, 50p; Chapter House exhibition, 20p; Tower tours, 50p.

Mompesson House. – April to late October, Saturday-Wednesday, 12.30-6pm or sunset if earlier; closed Good Friday; ℡ 0722 335659. £1, NT.

Military Museum. – All year, Monday-Friday, 10am-5pm; April-October, Sunday also, 10am-5pm; closed Christmas, New Year holidays. 60p.

Salisbury and South Wiltshire Museum. – 3 January to 23 December, Monday-Saturday, 10am-5pm (4pm October to March), Sundays also in July, August, 2-5pm; ℡ 0722 332151. £1.

SALTRAM

The House. – April to late October, Tuesday-Sunday and holiday Mondays, 12.30-6pm; ℡ Plymouth (0752) 336546. £2.30, NT.

SANDFORD ORCAS

Manor House. – May to September, Sundays 2-6pm, Mondays (including Easter and holiday Mondays) 10am-6pm; guided tours; ℡ Corton Denham (096322) 206. £1.

SHAFTESBURY

Local History Museum. – Daily Easter Saturday to late September, 11am (Sunday 2.30pm)-5pm; ℡ 0747 2157 or 3426. 25p.

The Abbey. – Daily, Good Friday to mid-October, 10am-6.30pm; ℡ 0747 2910. 25p.

SHARPITOR

Overbecks Museum. – Museum : daily, April to late October, 11am-1pm, 2-6pm; £1.10 inclusive ticket.
Garden : daily all year; 80p.

SHELDON MANOR

The Manor. – April to October, Thursday, Sunday, holiday Mondays, 2-6pm (garden open 12.30pm); ℡ Chippenham (0249) 653120. £1.25.

SHEPTON MALLET

Museum. – All year, Monday-Friday, 2-4.30pm, Saturday, 10am-4pm; ℡ Taunton (0823) 55507.

SHERBORNE

Castle. – Easter Saturday to late September, Thursday, Saturday, Sunday, holiday Mondays, 2-6pm; ℡ 0935 813182. £2.

Old Castle. – Daily 15 March to 15 October, 9.30am (Sunday, 2pm)-6.30pm; winter 4pm; closed 24-26 December, New Year holiday; ℡ Bristol (0272) 734472. Nominal charge.

School. – Open by *appointment only* in school holidays. ℡ 0935 812249.

Museum. – All year, Tuesday-Saturday, 10.30am-12.30pm (November to March to 12 noon), 3-4.30pm; also Sundays, April to October, 3-5pm; ℡ 0935 812252. 25p.

SMEDMORE

The House. – Wednesdays from 1st in June to 2nd in September, also last Sunday in August, 2.15-5.30pm; ℡ Corfe Castle (0929) 480717. £1.10.

SOUTH MOLTON

Quince Honey Farm. – Daily, Easter to September, 8am-6pm, October to Easter, 9am-5pm ; ℡ 07695 2401. £1.

SPARKWELL

Dartmoor Wildlife Park. – Daily all year, 10am-dusk; Cornwood (095539) 209. £1.90.

STANTON DREW

Stone Circles. – All year, Monday-Saturday, daylight hours. Nominal charge.

STICKLEPATH

Finch Foundry. – Daily, all year, 11am-5.30pm (dusk in winter); closed 25, 26 December; ℡ 083784 286. £1.

STONEHENGE

The Stones. – Daily, 15 March to 15 October, 9.30am (including Sunday)-6.30pm; winter 4pm; closed 24-26 December, New Year holiday; ℡ Bristol (0272) 734472. 80p.

STOURHEAD

The Gardens. – Daily, all year, 8am-7pm or sunset if earlier. £1.20 (December to late February, 60p), NT.

The House. – May to September, Saturday-Thursday, 2-6pm; April, October, Monday, Wednesday, Saturday, Sunday, 2-6pm or sunset if earlier. £1.60, NT.

STREET

The Shoe Museum. – Easter Monday to late October, Monday-Saturday, 10am-4.45pm; ℗ 0458 43131.

STUDLAND

Shell Bay. – Ferry. Daily all year, 7am-11pm at 30 or 20 minute intervals; ℗ 092944 203. Passengers 10p; cars 55p.

SWINDON

GWR Museum. – Daily, all year, 10am (Sunday, 2pm)-5pm; closed 25, 26 December, Good Friday; ℗ 0793 26161 (ext 3131). 70p.

Railway Village Museum. – Daily, all year, 10am-1pm, 2-5pm (Sunday 2-5pm); closed 25, 26 December, Good Friday; ℗ 0793 26161 (ext 3136). 30p.

Museum and Art Gallery. – Daily all year, 10am-6pm (Sunday 2-5pm); closed 25-26 December, Good Friday; ℗ 0793 26161 (ext 3129).

Richard Jeffries Museum – All year, Wednesday, Saturday, Sunday, 2-5pm; closed 25 26 December; ℗ 0793 26161 (ext 3130).

t

TAUNTON

Castle Museum. – All year, Monday-Friday and some Saturdays in summer; 10am-5pm ℗ 0823 55507. 40p.

British Telecom Museum. – All year, Saturdays 1.30-5pm; ℗ 0823 73391.

THORNBURY

Devon Museum of Mechanical Music. – Daily, Good Friday to late September, 10am 12 noon, 2-5pm; ℗ Milton Damerel (040926) 378. £1.

TINTAGEL

Arthur's Castle. – Daily, 15 March to 15 October, 9.30am (Sunday, 2pm)-6.30pm; winter 4pm; closed 24-26 December, New Year holiday; ℗ Bristol (0272) 734472. Nominal charge.

Old Post Office. – Daily, April to late October, 11am-6pm. 80p, NT.

TINTINHULL HOUSE.

Garden only. – April to late September, Wednesday, Thursday, Saturday, holiday Mondays 2-6pm. £1.30, NT. (House not open.)

TIVERTON

Castle. – Easter, then late May to mid-September, Sunday-Thursday, 2.30-5.30pm ℗ 0884 253200. £1.30.

Museum. – 2 January to 23 December, Monday-Saturday, 10.30am-4.30pm; closed all public holidays; ℗ 0884 256295.

TOLPUDDLE

TUC Museum. – Daily, all year, in daylight hours.

TORBAY

Torbay and Dartmouth Railway. – Easter, then Sundays and holiday Mondays, also Wednesdays in May; daily from spring holiday Monday to late September. First train departure 10am then 2 hourly; late July-August, extra trains; ℗ 0803 555872.

Torbay Trains, Aircraft Museum. – Daily, April to late October, 10am-6pm; ℗ 080 553540. £2.

TORQUAY

Kent's Cavern. – Daily, all year, 10am-6pm; 9pm mid-June to mid-September (Saturday 6pm); 5pm mid-September to Easter; closed only 25 December; ℗ 0803 24059. £1

Torre Abbey. – Daily, Easter to late October, 10am-4pm; ℗ 0803 27428. Nominal charge

TOTNES

Motor Museum. – Daily, all year, 10am-5pm; closed 25 December, New Year holiday ℗ 0803 862777. £1.

Elizabethan House. – April to late October and 2 weeks at Christmas (not 25, 26 December) Monday-Saturday, 10.30am-5.30pm or dusk in winter; ℗ 0803 863821. 25p.

Devonshire Collection of Period Costume. – Spring holiday Monday to late September Monday-Friday, 11am-5pm, Sundays and holiday Mondays 2-5pm. 40p.

The Castle. – Daily, 15 March to 15 October, 9.30am (Sunday, 2pm)-6.30pm; winter 4pm closed 24-26 December, New Year holiday; ℗ Bristol (0272) 734472. Nominal charge

TRELISSICK

The Garden. – Daily, March to late October, 11am (Sunday, 1pm)-6pm or dusk if earlier; ℡ Devoran (0872) 862090. £1.40, NT. (House not open.)

TRENGWAINTON

The Garden. – March to late October, Wednesday-Saturday and holiday Mondays, 11am-6pm; ℡ Penzance (0736) 66869. £1, NT. (House not open.)

TRERICE

The House. – Daily, April to October, 11am-6pm; ℡ Newquay (06373) 5404. £1.80, NT.

TRESCO

Abbey Gardens. – Daily, all year, 10am-4pm; ℡ Scillonia (0720) 22849. £1.75.

TREWITHEN

Garden. – March to September, Monday-Saturday, 2-4.30pm. March-June, 90p; July-September, 80p.
The House. – April to July, Monday, Tuesday, 2-4.30pm; ℡ St Austell (0726) 882418. £1.70 inclusive ticket.

TRURO

Cornwall County Museum. – All year, Monday-Saturday, 9am-5pm; closed all public holidays; ℡ 0872 72205.

U

UFFCULME

Coldharbour Mill. – Daily, May to August, 11am-5pm; March, April, September, October, Monday-Friday, 11am-5pm, Sunday 2-5pm; November to February, Wednesday-Friday and Sunday, 2-5pm; ℡ Craddock (0884) 40960. £1.50.

W

WARDOUR CASTLE

The Old Castle. – Daily, April to September, 9.30am-6.30pm; ℡ Bristol (0272) 734472. Nominal charge.
New Wardour Castle. – School summer holidays, Monday, Wednesday, Friday, Saturday, 2.30-6pm; ℡ Shaftesbury (0747) 870464. 80p.

WAREHAM

Local History Museum. – Easter to late September, Monday-Saturday, 10am-1pm, 2-5pm.
Blue Pool. – Easter to late October, Sunday-Friday, 10am-4.30pm; ℡ 09295 51408. 70p.

WELLS

Bishop's Palace. – Easter Saturday, Sunday, Monday; thereafter Thursdays, Sundays and holiday Mondays to late October and daily in August, 2-6pm; ℡ 0749 78691. 80p.

WENDRON

Poldark Mine. – Daily, Easter to late October, 10am-6pm (June to August 10pm); ℡ Helston (03265) 3137. £2.

WESTBURY

Chalcot House. – Daily, July-August, 2-6pm; ℡ Chapmansdale (037388) 466. £1.

WESTWOOD

The Manor. – April to September, Sunday, Monday, Wednesday, 2-6pm; ℡ Bradford-on-Avon (02216) 3374. £1.30, NT.

WILTON (Wiltshire)

The House. – The week before Easter to mid-October, Tuesday-Saturday and holiday Mondays, 11am-6pm; Sunday, 1-6pm; guided tours; ℡ Salisbury (0722) 743115. £2.
Royal Wilton Carpet Factory. – All year, Monday-Friday, 10am-4pm; guided tours; closed all public holidays; ℡ Salisbury (0722) 742733. £1.20.

WILTON (Wiltshire)

Windmill. – Easter to late September, Sundays and holiday Mondays; guided tours; ℡ Marlborough (0672) 870268. 40p.

WIMBORNE MINSTER

Priest's House. – Easter to late September, Monday-Saturday, 10.30am-12.30pm, 2-4.30pm; 0202 882533. 20p.

WOODFORD

Heale House. – Garden: Good Friday to late September, Monday-Saturday and first Sunday in the month, 10am-5pm; Middle Woodford (072273) 207. 70p. (House not open.)

WOOKEY HOLE

The Hole. – Daily, all year; summer (BST), 9.30am-5.30pm; winter (GMT) 10.30am-4.30pm; closed only the week before and Christmas Day; Wells (0749) 72243. £2.55.

Y

YEALMPTON

Kitley Caves. – Daily, spring holiday weekend to late September, 10am-5.30pm; Plymouth (0752) 880202. £1.

YELVERTON

Paperweight Centre. – Week before Easter to late October, Monday-Saturday, 10am-5pm; 0822 854250.

YEOVIL

Museum. – All year, Monday-Wednesday, Friday, Saturday, 9.30am-1pm, 2-5pm; 0935 75171 (ext 302).

YEOVILTON

Fleet Air Arm Museum. – Daily, all year, 10am-5.30pm (November to February, dusk); closed 24, 25 December; Ilchester (0935) 840565. £1.70.

Z

ZENNOR

Museum. – Daily, Easter to late October, 10am-sunset; Penzance (0736) 796945. 50p.

MANUFACTURE FRANÇAISE DES PNEUMATIQUES MICHELIN

Société en commandite par actions au capital de 700 000 000 de francs

Place des Carmes-Déchaux – 63 Clermont-Ferrand (France)

R.C.S. Clermont-Fd B 855 200 507

© Michelin et Cie, Propriétaires-Éditeurs 1984

Dépôt légal 1.85 – ISBN 2.06.015.621-1 – ISSN 0293-9436

Printed in France – 9.84.50

Photocomposition et impression : MAURY Imprimeur S.A., Malesherbes, n° A 84/14305